Cultural Values in Strategy and Organization

A volume in
Research in Strategy Science
T. K. Das, *Series Editor*

RESEARCH IN STRATEGY SCIENCE

T. K. Das, *Series Editor*

Published

Time Issues in Strategy and Organization (2019)
Edited by T. K. Das

Cultural Values in Strategy and Organization (2021)
Edited by T. K. Das

In Development

Managerial Practice Issues in Strategy and Organization

Cultural Values in Strategy and Organization

edited by

T. K. Das
City University of New York

IAP

INFORMATION AGE PUBLISHING, INC.
Charlotte, NC • www.infoagepub.com

Library of Congress Cataloging-in-Publication Data

A CIP record for this book is available from the Library of Congress
http://www.loc.gov

ISBN: 978-1-64802-512-9 (Paperback)
978-1-64802-513-6 (Hardcover)
978-1-64802-514-3 (E-Book)

Printed in the United States of America

Cultural Values in Strategy and Organization

edited by

T. K. Das

City University of New York

INFORMATION AGE PUBLISHING, INC.
Charlotte, NC • www.infoagepub.com

Library of Congress Cataloging-in-Publication Data

A CIP record for this book is available from the Library of Congress
http://www.loc.gov

ISBN: 978-1-64802-512-9 (Paperback)
978-1-64802-513-6 (Hardcover)
978-1-64802-514-3 (E-Book)

Printed in the United States of America

CONTENTS

ABOUT THE BOOK SERIES

The field of strategy science has grown in both the diversity of issues it addresses and the increasingly interdisciplinary approaches it adopts in understanding the nature and significance of problems that are continuously emerging in the world of human endeavor. These newer kinds of challenges and opportunities arise in all forms of organizations, encompassing private and public enterprises, and with strategies that experiment with breaking the traditional molds and contours. The field of strategy science is also, perhaps inevitably, being impacted by the proliferation of hybrid organizations such as strategic alliances, the upsurge of approaches that go beyond the customary emphasis on competitiveness and profit making, and the intermixing of time-honored categories of activities such as business, industry, commerce, trade, government, the professions, and so on. The blurring of the boundaries between various areas and types of human activities points to a need for academic research to address the consequential developments in strategic issues. Hence, research and thinking about the nature of issues to be tackled by strategy science should also cultivate requisite variety in issues recognized for research inquiry, including the conceptual foundations of strategy and strategy making, and the examination of the critical roles of strategy makers, strategic thinking, time and temporalities, business and other goal choices, diversity in organizing modes for strategy implementation, and the complexities of managing strategy, to name a few. This book series on *Research in Strategy Science* aims to provide an outlet for ideas and issues that publications in the field do not provide, either expressly or adequately, especially as regards the comprehensive coverage deserved by

Cultural Values in Strategy and Organization, pages vii–viii

certain emerging areas of interest. The topics of the volumes in the series will keep in view this objective to expand the research areas and theoretical approaches routinely found in strategy science, the better to permit expanded and expansive treatments of promising issues that may not sufficiently align with the usual research coverage of publications in the field.

—T. K. Das
City University of New York
Series Editor
Research in Strategy Science

CHAPTER 1

ECOLOGICAL ORGANIZING

Implications of Evolving Cultural Values for Organization and Strategy

Peter J. Robertson
Joseph W. Harder

ABSTRACT

The primary claim of this chapter is that organizations are evolving from a bureaucratic form grounded in the mechanistic thinking of the Industrial Era into a new organizational form we call "ecological organizing" that is informed by a new ecological paradigm emerging as society transitions into the Information Age. After introducing the framework of cultural values underlying our analysis, we begin by identifying four core values incorporated into the bureaucratic model and summarizing key criticisms of this organizational form. Next we explain how organizations began changing in response to these criticisms, initially through the organization development movement and then more substantially as growing environmental turbulence demanded more organic organizations. We then introduce some of the foundational ideas of the new paradigm and indicate how they are influencing thinking about and practices in organizations. This leads to the discussion of ecological organizing, where we first address the notion of living organizations and

Cultural Values in Strategy and Organization, pages 1–64

then describe the four primary features of our model: holarchical structure, synergistic relationships, shared purpose, and conscious development. This is followed by a consideration of strategic management in this context, in particular the recent emphases on the adaptive capacity of organizations and their ability to function effectively in the context of organizational ecosystems. The chapter concludes with further thoughts about the paradigm shift in progress and its role in the conscious evolution of society.

INTRODUCTION

Most large, complex organizations in the world today are designed and managed according to a set of principles that were established more than a century ago. Known as the bureaucratic model of organization, these principles specified normative features of organization and management that were intended to enable organizations to function effectively by insuring the efficiency, predictability, and stability of organizational activity. As the industrialization of society increased the size, scale, and scope of both private and public organizations, these organizing principles diffused widely such that, by the late 20th century, the bureaucratic model was institutionalized as the dominant organizational form (Zucker, 1983).

The argument put forth below is that organizations are evolving into a new and different organizational form we call ecological organizing. The bureaucratic model was designed in and for the Industrial Era, reflecting a root metaphor of an organization as a machine. With the world now transitioning into the Information Age, we believe that the bureaucratic model is on its way to obsolescence and a new organizational template is needed. And in contrast to the mechanistic foundations of bureaucracy, we think it wiser to ground this new model in an ecological perspective regarding how living systems function. We argue that viewing organizations as living systems and implementing management philosophies and practices consistent with that perspective will enable organizations to achieve the adaptability and agility needed to survive and thrive in a globally connected world.

The broader thesis of this chapter is that, by understanding organizations as living systems, it is possible to see patterns of evolution in how they have been designed and managed, in response to changing environmental circumstances over time. Until recently, this evolution has been reflected primarily in incremental modifications to the bureaucratic form, in an effort to make them more organic, rather than a transition to a new and different form. But with interest growing in the idea of organizations as living systems, we propose that organizations are indeed in the midst of a transformational process that is leading to a new, organic, ecological approach to organizing that is more appropriate for life in the Information Age. Whereas bureaucracies reflect a core set of values underlying Western culture, ecological organizing is based on an emerging worldview that supports a new set of values and beliefs regarding the design and management of complex organizations. Since this new paradigm is emerging globally, reflecting core human values not specific to any single culture, we believe that ecological organizing provides a generalizable model that is compatible with and conducive to the conscious evolution of global society.

The chapter is organized as follows. We start with a brief explanation of our perspective on cultural values and their relevance to our thesis regarding the emergence of a new organizational form. This is followed by a discussion of the bureaucratic form of organization, first identifying four core values incorporated into this model and then summarizing some of the key criticisms of bureaucracy. Next we describe how organizations began changing in response to these criticisms, initially through the efforts of those in the Organization Development movement and then more substantially as growing environmental turbulence demanded that organizations become more organic. We then turn attention to the new emerging paradigm, explaining some of its foundational ideas and indicating how these ideas are influencing thinking about and practices in organizations. This leads to the discussion of ecological organizing, where we first address the notion of living organizations and then discuss the four primary features of our model: holarchical structure, synergistic relationships, shared purpose, and conscious development. This is followed by a consideration of strategic management in this context, in particular the recent emphases on the adaptive capacity of organizations and their ability to function effectively in the context of organizational ecosystems. The chapter concludes with further thoughts about the paradigm shift in progress and its role in the conscious evolution of society.

EVOLVING CULTURAL VALUES

Our thinking about the nature of cultural values reflects the framework developed by Schein (1985), who argued that an organizational culture should be understood as comprising three interrelated levels. The deepest level is the set of assumptions or taken-for-granted beliefs about "the way things are" that define a dominant reality (Culbert & McDonough, 1985) that is generally accepted as the basis for action in that culture. While these assumptions are often tacit, the next level consists of core values that are more explicit, and that are not just espoused but actually influence organizational decisions and activities. The third, most surface level includes the various cultural artifacts through which the underlying values and beliefs are expressed or manifested. The symbolic meanings embedded in these artifacts serve to reinforce organizational beliefs (Hatch, 1993) and thus help to maintain the stability of the culture.

Adapting this framework to a broader society, we view culture as defined in terms of three equivalent levels: an underlying worldview that incorporates starting assumptions about the nature of reality; institutional arrangements that reflect and reinforce core societal values; and the practices and patterns that characterize individual and collective behavior and its artifactual outputs. When a society undergoes a cultural transformation, change in all three levels is inherent to the process. This can be seen in the shift from the pre-modern, agrarian culture that dominated the planet from the beginning of civilization, to the modern, industrial culture that has been diffusing around the world over the last two centuries. Rooted in ideas from the Renaissance and the Enlightenment, the "scientific revolution" gave rise to a new worldview that has enabled humans to harness the elements and forces of nature to such an extent that we have shifted the planet into the "anthropocene," a new human-dominated geological epoch (Lewis & Maslin, 2015). The emergence of modern culture also spawned new institutional arrangements—political, economic, and organizational—that have come to dominate global society. The patterns of behavior generated in this culture have resulted in significant improvements in the quality of life for most of humanity, but are also having deleterious consequences on the natural environment that threaten our present and future well-being.

The starting premise of our analysis below is that the transition from an industrial society into a digitized, information-based world, and the shift into the anthropocene, entails the emergence of a new worldview along with new institutional arrangements that are more congruent with contemporary beliefs and ideals. The cultural values of global society are evolving (Ray & Anderson, 2000), becoming more consistent with the humanistic ideals of mutual respect, justice, inclusion, collaboration, and self-actualization. As a result, there are growing expectations for these values to be reflected in contemporary institutions, such that leaders of these systems are increasingly obliged to implement compatible changes in institutional structures and processes.

At the same time, the pace of technological change and level of global interdependence are greater than ever, generating pressure on existing institutions to adapt to new demands and capabilities. Our particular focus is on organizations, and the widely recognized need for them to become much more adaptable in order to survive and effectively achieve their purposes (Reeves & Deimler, 2011). Since bureaucracy is a product of an older worldview and cultural values, it is reasonable to anticipate that the evolution of cultural values and assumptions will elicit congruent changes in the institutional arrangements through which we organize purposive collective action. We believe that an ecological perspective on organizing—ecological organizing—is more congruent with the emergent worldview and evolving cultural values, and more conducive to organizational adaptability, agility, and achievement in the complex, dynamic conditions of 21st century global society.

MECHANISTIC BUREAUCRACY

Core Values

The cultural transformation of Western Europe and North America known as the Industrial Revolution precipitated a shift in society from rural and agrarian-based to urban and manufacturing-based. With improved transportation systems enabling greater movement of people and goods across larger distances, new organizational and management approaches were needed to deal with the larger scale and faster speed of business and government activity. Max Weber (1947 tr.) articulated the features of the bureaucratic form of organization that he viewed as an appropriate template for organizational design given the emerging conditions of industrial society. These features can be summarized as a formal hierarchy of authority; job specialization and fixed division of labor; use of formal rules and regulations; impersonal treatment of employees; employment based on technical qualifications and competence; and employment viewed as a career, with protection against arbitrary dismissal. We believe that the development and diffusion of the bureaucratic model reflect four core value themes that came to dominate modern, industrial society, namely, hierarchy, rationality, science, and individualism (Robertson, 1999). We discuss each of these briefly below.

The dominant feature of a bureaucratic organization is a relatively rigid hierarchy of authority that dictates patterns of communication and decision making. The notion that a large organization must be arranged in a hierarchy is one of the most pervasive and deep-seated beliefs people have about the requirements for organizational effectiveness. At a time when there were relatively few educated workers, a hierarchy in which the capable few managed and monitored the activities of the rest was logical and practical if not necessary. That said, a hierarchical structure can also be seen as a manifestation of the mechanistic worldview that was diffusing throughout society as industrialization proceeded (Freudenthal, 1986). Beginning with Sir Isaac Newton's description of the universe as a "clockwork" operating according to a set of natural laws (Newton, 2009), scientific investigation of these laws and their effects resulted in dramatic advances in technological capabilities that provided great benefits to society. The new machines being created required some understanding of the laws of physics as well as the cause-and-effect relationships among the machines' various components. The goal was to produce machines that operated reliably and could be easily controlled by the operator. Since business and government organizations were, like machines, tools created by people to accomplish certain tasks and/or serve particular purposes, it is not surprising that Weber's organizational design included hierarchy and rules as mechanisms to insure control and reliability.

The Industrial Era has been referred to as "the age of reason" since a key cultural change in post-Enlightenment society was a de-emphasis of "faith" as an arbiter of truth and a focus instead on empirical evidence and logical deduction to determine what was true or false. This cultural emphasis on reason found expression in the bureaucratic model as a primary focus on organizational rationality (Scott, 1981). Reflecting mechanistic thinking, Weber (1947 tr.) and other classical administrative theorists (Fayol, 1949; Gulick & Urwick, 1937) aimed to specify a set of principles of administration that would help to ensure that organizations accomplished their objectives efficiently and effectively. Their concern was not only with business firms but with government organizations as well, where the challenge was to make sure that public bureaucracies faithfully implemented policies determined by relevant legislative bodies. Proponents of the Progressive movement, led by President Woodrow Wilson, aimed to "rationalize" the federal bureaucracy by implementing bureaucratic approaches to organization and management.

The importance and value of science to the societal improvements generated by industrialization led naturally to the conclusion that the scientific method could and should be used to improve organizational functioning. Accordingly, Frederick Taylor initiated the scientific management movement by utilizing "time and motion studies" to determine the most efficient methods for workers to perform their jobs (Taylor, 1911). Again reflecting a mechanistic mindset, maximizing efficiency became a primary organizational objective, and management systems were designed to maintain and increase employee productivity. Henry Ford's development of the assembly line capitalized on the bureaucratic notion of job specialization to radically improve overall efficiency and productivity. Ultimately, the success of these rational, efficient bureaucracies left little doubt about the superiority of this approach to organization and management over those that had been prevalent prior to industrialization, such as apprenticeships and guilds.

The fourth core value reflected in the bureaucratic model is individualism, the liberal belief in the importance and worth of the individual. Whereas people for centuries had been subjects to sovereign kings and popes, enlightened societies recognized the right of individuals to shape their own destinies. Economic and political theory provided support for the supposition that people should be free to pursue their economic interests and should be involved in deciding how they are governed. This heightened attention to the value of the individual is demonstrated in bureaucracies in a number of ways. Fundamentally, individuals are the primary unit of analysis in a bureaucracy—organizational activity is divided into sets of tasks carried out by individual employees. Impersonal treatment and application of rules is intended to promote equality among individuals by eliminating favoritism and other biases. Reward systems are typically designed to measure individual performance and compensate individuals accordingly, and the hierarchical structure provides a mechanism through which individuals can strive to enhance their position in the organization, and thus in society, via promotion. However, given the underlying mechanistic orientation, bureaucracies also tend to treat individuals like "cogs in the machine," standardized components that are replaceable whenever they no longer function well enough.

Key Criticisms

The principles of bureaucracy gained prominence in the context of a society in the midst of a process of industrialization, with bureaucratic structures and processes providing significant improvements in the management of the growing number of large, complex organizations. Of course, early organizational studies indicated that bureaucracies didn't function quite as rationally as suggested by theory, and that human behavior and interactions demonstrated "natural" (Scott, 1981) patterns and tendencies not accounted for by administrative theorists. Based on his experiences as an executive, Barnard (1938) acknowledged the importance of the "informal organization" in helping to secure the cooperation necessary for an organization to achieve its objectives. The Hawthorne studies (Roethlisberger & Dixon, 1939) provided evidence that social dynamics in the workplace affect individual attitudes and behavior; for example, employee motivation and performance were influenced by such factors as supervisory style, group social norms, and workplace morale. Recognizing the importance of human behavioral dynamics, Simon (1946) provided a compelling critique of the "proverbs of administration" that had become readily accepted as management truths. Other analyses (March & Simon, 1958) explained how natural reactions to bureaucratic properties could result in unanticipated, unintended, and undesirable outcomes.

While the features of bureaucracy may have been appropriate and advantageous at the beginning of the 20th century, technological advances, societal improvements, and a better educated workforce generated a growing discrepancy between bureaucratic and contemporary human values. In light of growing awareness that human feelings, attitudes, and behavioral tendencies should be taken into account in thinking about how best to design and manage organizations, organization and management theorists began to focus more attention on the undesirable consequences of mechanistic bureaucratic arrangements. In particular, their critiques of bureaucracy helped to clarify how the four core values discussed above—hierarchy, rationality, science, and individualism—resulted in organizational dynamics that were dysfunctional not only for the people working in these organizations but for the organizations as well. These criticisms can be summarized as follows.

The hierarchy in mechanistic bureaucracies is a tall pyramid with many layers of management, creating a significant gap between the top and the bottom of the organization. Information going up and down the chain of command is readily distorted along the way, and decisions along this chain are often slow and ineffective. The discrepancies in power, status, and wealth across hierarchical levels generate internal competition for promotions that can undermine cooperation and effective task performance. Moreover, these discrepancies seem incompatible with a contemporary emphasis on equality, just as the autocratic nature of a bureaucracy seems incompatible with the ideals of democracy. More layers of hierarchy usually produce more rules and regulations that constrain employee behavior and make it difficult to get things done, that is, the "red tape" that renders bureaucracies inefficient and inflexible. With too much hierarchy and too many rules, employees too often feel micromanaged and overcontrolled, resulting in frustration, demotivation, anomie, and even learned helplessness. By institutionalizing a distinction between those who plan the work (management) and those who do the work (labor), bureaucratic organizations exclude employees from relevant decision processes, who then in response typically display a tendency to resist change.

An emphasis on rationality in mechanistic bureaucracies is manifested as a preoccupation with stability, efficiency, and control. Standard operating procedures are used along with rules and regulations to specify required and prohibited behavior, and organizational logic then dictates that rational behavior is defined in terms of obedience (Denhardt, 1984). More generally, rational/technical demands are given a higher priority than human/social needs, with employees expected to adapt to any new technologies adopted to improve productivity. Organizational decision processes are also supposed to be rational in the sense that they aim to identify the alternative course of action that will most effectively help accomplish the decision maker's objective. Even taking into account the limitations imposed by bounded rationality (Simon, 1957), organizational decisions do not in fact usually follow a rational process (Nutt, 1984), and they are often based on limited information since many people with relevant input are not included in the process. Given the emphasis on reliability and efficiency, rational decision making is also biased against creativity and innovation in favor of the tried and true. Finally, with rationality narrowly defined as the pursuit of self-interest, conflict is common among bureaucratic actors who are more focused on accomplishing their own objectives than on cooperating with others.

Belief in the value of science, and scientific approaches to management, shape bureaucracies in important but subtle ways. Given the scientific emphasis on empirical evidence, rational decision making is thought to require data collection and analysis in order to provide support and justification for preferring one course of action to another. Given a preference for objective data and analysis, more subjective factors like people's feelings and values are discounted in, if not entirely omitted from, organizational decision processes, helping to maintain bureaucratic impersonality. More generally, this bias toward an objective, impersonal way of operating serves to maintain a materialistic mindset in mechanistic organizations. For example, reward systems rely primarily on a range of extrinsic rewards while largely ignoring the possibility of generating more intrinsic rewards for employees. A deeper criticism is that impersonal, materialistic bureaucracies essentially ignore the inner lives of their employees and provide little meaning or purpose to engage people at work.

The individualistic design of bureaucracies exacerbates some of the above concerns. Mechanistic organizations have specialized jobs, organized into specialized units, and these narrow job descriptions add another layer of control by specifying which activities are and are not within a particular employee's purview. Moreover, most jobs in bureaucratic organizations are tedious and boring with little discretion or potential for self-determination, conditions which naturally breed passivity, indifference, and detachment. Coupled with all the inequality, micromanagement, rules and regulations, and standard operating procedures, employees easily develop negative attitudes and respond by looking out first and foremost for their own interests. Such behavior, reinforced by reward systems that aim to benefit those individuals who outperform their co-workers, results in overly competitive work environments in which cooperation among individuals, groups, and subunits can be difficult to achieve. Ironically, collaboration—co-laboring, or working together—becomes a challenge in organizations ostensibly designed to enable just that.

In short, much of the criticism of mechanistic bureaucracies reflected growing awareness that their design principles and management practices did not adequately take the full range of human needs (Maslow, 1954) into account. In particular, management theorists (e.g., Herzberg, 1966) criticized bureaucratic organizations for focusing primarily on employees' lower order needs (e.g., safety and security) while largely ignoring their higher order needs (e.g., self-esteem and self-actualization). They argued that bureaucratic features create conditions that actually undermine people's self-esteem and their opportunities for growth and development (Argyris, 1957). McGregor (1960) argued that the cause of this problem was rooted in managers' underlying belief systems, distinguishing between Theory X and Theory Y beliefs. Theory X assumes that people are naturally lazy, unmotivated, self-centered, and resistant to change, whereas Theory Y posits that people have motivation, potential for development, capacity for assuming responsibility, and readiness to direct their behavior toward organizational goals. Historically, most bureaucratic organizations have operated according to Theory X assumptions, the natural consequence of which is that too many workers become demotivated and alienated, resulting in behavioral tendencies that simply reinforce for managers their starting assumptions.

A primary effect of these behavioral dynamics is that bureaucratic organizations tend to be rigid, cumbersome, inefficient, and less effective than they could be. Burns and Stalker (1961) concluded that mechanistic features are not inherently problematic, as long as an organization is operating in an environment that is relatively stable. But they argued that, in more dynamic or turbulent environments (Emery & Trist, 1965), organizations need to be more organic in order to be more innovative and adaptive. Coupled with growing interest in creating more humanistic organizations that are better for their people, these criticisms of the bureaucratic model stimulated efforts to implement significant changes in how organizations function. The premise was that, by developing organizations in which people are engaged in their work and involved in decision making with opportunities for growth, those organizations will perform more effectively. With various social movements in the 1960s challenging many traditional Western values, the goal was to help create more organic organizations that could adapt more effectively to these changing circumstances.

CHANGING ORGANIZATIONS

Organization Development

In response to growing recognition of these bureaucratic dysfunctions, management scholars and practitioners became interested in applying behavioral science knowledge to improve organizational functioning (e.g., Bennis, 1965). Their efforts gave rise to the field of Organization Development (OD), which focused on generating theoretical insights and practical approaches to support the implementation of planned organizational change (Argyris, 1970; Beckhard, 1969; Bennis, 1969; French & Bell, 1973). The OD approach to change was explicitly oriented towards improving organizational effectiveness by changing bureaucratic structures and processes so as to align them better with contemporary human values

(Tannenbaum & Davis, 1969). In particular, OD was based on the core underlying values of trust and respect, open communication, authentic interpersonal relationships, participation in decision making, and collaboration and cooperation.

OD change "interventions" primarily addressed two broad categories of organizational issues (Friedlander & Brown, 1974). Human-processual interventions aimed to improve the quality of interactions among people who work together to accomplish organizational objectives. Key approaches in this category included efforts to improve managerial style and competence (Blake & Mouton, 1966), build better teams (Dyer, 1977), enhance the quality of group dynamics (Schein, 1969), and provide mechanisms for resolving conflict (Walton, 1969). In contrast, techno-structural interventions sought to change the technological and structural arrangements in organizations that determine how work is accomplished. A primary objective of these approaches was to give workers more input into, if not control over, the decisions regarding how best to organize and carry out their work. Job enrichment efforts tried to redesign jobs to make them more interesting and thus motivating (Hackman, Oldham, Janson, & Purdy, 1975). The socio-technical systems approach (Cummings & Srivastva, 1977; Taylor, 1975) reorganized work by combining individual jobs into autonomous work groups that were responsible for making decisions about how best to accomplish their objectives. These OD interventions aimed to humanize bureaucratic organizations by decentralizing authority, removing unnecessary rules and red tape, and establishing mechanisms for improving coordination among different groups and subunits.

Despite the implementation of OD change programs in numerous private and public organizations, and the many beneficial results generated by these changes, it is fair to say that most of this planned change was incremental in nature and did not produce any widespread or significant revision of the underlying bureaucratic organizational form. OD change efforts were frequently resisted, especially by leaders, managers, and employees who remained committed to bureaucratic values, structures, and processes. Their efficacy was also limited by the underlying OD conceptualization of planned change as a process of shifting an organization from one stable state to another. As the social unrest of the 1960s and economic upheavals of the 1970s generated more turbulent environments for most industries and organizations, it became increasingly clear that change was no longer a temporary phase between periods of stability. Instead, change was becoming a constant requirement in a world characterized by increasing dynamism. There was growing awareness that traditional bureaucracies oriented towards stability and biased against change are problematic in this context, and long, slow, incremental OD change processes lost some of their utility in light of the pressing need for faster and more fundamental organizational transformation.

Becoming Organic

By the early 1980s, organization and management theorists began to pay more explicit attention to the role that values play in organizational functioning. This was stimulated in part by research on Japanese approaches to organization and management (Ouchi, 1981; Pascale & Athos, 1981), which argued that the success of Japanese firms (especially compared to many of their American counterparts) was based to a considerable extent on fundamental differences in the nature of the interactions and expectations between managers and their employees. But the primary trigger of widespread interest in the role of organizational values was the research by Peters and Waterman (1982) on excellent American organizations. They attributed the success of the high-performing firms they studied to eight key features reflecting a set of core values and practices that enabled these organizations to function quite differently than traditional bureaucratic organizations. The inevitable conclusion from this research was that traditional bureaucratic values were undermining organizational performance. The obvious implication was that leaders who wanted to achieve success needed to initiate a process of transformational change aimed at de-bureaucratizing their organizations.

Subsequent efforts to transform bureaucratic organizations into more organic, adaptable forms reflect four broad themes, each of which addresses one of the core bureaucratic values discussed above. First, there was broad recognition of the need to change organizational cultures to address human-oriented values more directly and fully, rather than emphasizing only technical and financial criteria and indicators of effectiveness. Second, there was a concerted effort to mitigate the detrimental effects of hierarchy by flattening structures, decentralizing decision making, and empowering employees through increased participation and involvement. Third, organizations started to make greater use of groups and teams as structural components, as a response to the individualistic nature of bureaucracy and the difficulty of ensuring requisite collaboration. Fourth, to overcome the bureaucratic bias towards stability and predictability derived from an emphasis on rationality, organizations tried to enhance their capacity to learn and thus to innovate and adapt more readily. Below, we provide brief elaboration of each of these approaches to creating more organic organizations.

A focus on changing organizational cultures stemmed directly from the premise that adherence to traditional bureaucratic values was a primary source of organizational problems; and a change in organizational values demanded a change in organizational culture. Organizational cultural values are expressed through various artifacts (Schein, 1985), such as organizational stories and heroes, rituals and ceremonies, and language and symbols (Deal & Kennedy, 1982; Trice & Beyer, 1984). Thus, culture can be shaped by strategically utilizing artifacts to consistently communicate core values and vision, and paying close attention to the symbolic messages being sent through organizational and managerial decisions and actions (Pfeffer, 1980). Ultimately, however, transformation of an organization's culture requires not just a change in artifacts and espoused values but also a revision of its tacit assumptions about the nature of reality (Schein, 1985).

This idea that the foundations of a culture are to be found in shared beliefs about "the way things are" reflects the notion that organizations are "socially constructed realities" (Berger & Luckmann, 1966; Culbert & McDonough, 1985) with people and organizations engaged in an ongoing process of sensemaking and enactment (Weick, 1979). Thus, an important role for those leading efforts to change an organization's culture is the "management of meaning" (Smircich & Morgan, 1982) by shaping how participants interpret events and circumstances. This cultural perspective further suggests that organizations are not objective realities that can be analyzed using traditional positivist scientific methods. Instead, they are intersubjective phenomena that can best be investigated using more qualitative approaches that aim to apprehend how people make sense of their situations through their interactions and communications (Louis, 1983). The culture perspective thus challenged bureaucracy's scientific emphasis on objectivity by stressing the need to acknowledge, analyze, and manage the intersubjective, symbolic aspects of organizations.

To change their cultures, organizations began taking steps to reduce the negative effects of their hierarchical structures. In many cases this involved removing layers of management in order to flatten the hierarchy, so as to reduce both administrative expenses and bureaucratic inefficiencies. It has also been reflected in efforts to decentralize decision making, which is all but necessary when there is a reduction in managerial layers. Interest in decentralization also gave new momentum to old ideas about the value of participative management (Collins, 1997; Dachler & Wilpert, 1978; McLagan & Nel, 1997), with numerous approaches available for getting more people involved in more organizational decisions (Cotton, 1993; Miller & Monge, 1986). Management theorists advocated the goal of becoming a "high-involvement organization" (Lawler, 1992), if not democratizing organizations more generally (Ackoff, 1994; Elden, 1985; Halal, 1996; Rothschild & Russell, 1986).

Likewise, there has been growing interest in the issue of employee empowerment (Quinn & Spreitzer, 1997), with organizations trying to overcome decades of bureaucratic disempowerment by giving employees the motivation, skills, and opportunities to engage more fully in work-related decisions. Management literature has identified new roles for leaders and managers in these participative systems, including many that reflect a more egalitarian perspective, such as leaders as stewards and servants (Block, 1993; Greenleaf, 1977), and managers as coaches, developers, and facilitators (Bradford & Cohen, 1984; Evered & Selman, 1989; Orth, Wilkinson, & Benfari, 1987; Waldroop & Butler, 1996). In short, a notable shift away from hierarchy and towards participation has been apparent in the organizational landscape.

Complementing their efforts to become more participative, organizations also started using groups and teams more extensively to accomplish important tasks that require input from multiple people and/or subunits. While bureaucracies have always organized workers into groups to accomplish relevant tasks under the direction of a supervisor or manager, the use of groups for other kinds of problem-solving purposes began more recently. As early examples, quality of work life initiatives (Davis, 1977) and the use of quality circles (Gibson, 1982) entailed groups of front-line employees working together to identify issues that needed to be addressed to improve the organization's products, services, processes, and/or work environment.

With life and work becoming more complex, that is, with more interdependencies among more organizational components, teams started proliferating in a variety of forms and for a variety of purposes (Cohen, 1993; Lipnack & Stamps, 1994). Some organizations started adopting team-based structures (Koehler & Pankowski, 1996; Mohrman, Cohen, & Mohrman, 1995; Shonk, 1992), in which groups and not individuals are the primary locus of task responsibility. This also led to renewed interest in the use of self-managing work teams (Cohen, Ledford, & Spreitzer, 1996; Manz & Sims, 1993; Purser & Cabana, 1998), reflecting awareness that teams work best when all members share a sense of responsibility for how the group performs (Bradford & Cohen, 1984). Finally, efforts were made to "reengineer" organizations (Hammer & Champy, 1983; Linden, 1994; Teng, Grover, & Fiedler, 1994) by redesigning processes and realigning structures to eliminate unnecessary inefficiencies and ensure necessary coordination. Together, these changes can be seen as a shift away from the individualistic foundations of bureaucracy so as to enable more and better collaboration among organizational members.

With more people working together to address key concerns, organizations began taking steps to improve their capacity to learn from all this involvement and interaction. Interest in organizational learning stemmed in part from organization theorists' concerns with how organizations acquire and utilize information to make decisions (Huber, 1991; Levitt & March, 1988). It also grew out of organizational efforts to develop the capacity for "continuous improvement" advocated in the total quality management movement (Cohen & Brand, 1993; Deming, 1986; Jablonski, 1992; Schmidt & Finnigan, 1992).

Senge (1990) helped to popularize the notion of a learning organization, which is good not only at sensing its environment, making effective decisions, and addressing apparent problems, but also creating new knowledge (Nonaka, 1994). Learning organizations work to overcome the bureaucratic bias towards standardization and exploitation in an effort to induce more experimentation and exploration. They also aim to enable better double-loop learning (Argyris, 1977), in which decision parameters such as starting assumptions, core values, and extant goals are reconsidered in light of new knowledge and circumstances. This focus on improved learning thus reflects a shift away from a dominant emphasis on rationality and efficiency to a growing appreciation for the creativity and innovation required for organizations to be flexible and adaptable.

It is worth noting that interest in changing organizations to be more adaptive and responsive was not limited to the private sector, as there was a growing call for the de-bureaucratization of government organizations as well (Barzelay, 1992). For example, Osborne and Gaebler (1992) advocated for "reinventing government," suggesting 10 principles to guide the management of public agencies. These included similar themes as could be found in the private sector: Government needed to be more mission-driven and less rules-oriented; more catalytic, that is, "steering rather than rowing"; more customer-driven and results-oriented; with decentralized hierarchies and more participation and teamwork. The Clinton administration initiated the National Performance Review (Gore, 1993) in an effort to reform the culture of federal government organizations by making them less rigid and more flexible (Ingraham, Thompson, & Sanders, 1997; Kamensky, 1996), and similar reform efforts took place in state (Brudney, Hebert, & Wright, 1999) and local (Moon & deLeon, 2001) governments as well. Public management theorists designated these and related reforms as the "new public management" (Ferlie, Ashburner, Fitzgerald, & Pettigrew, 1996; Hood, 1991; Lane, 2000; Lynn, 1998) to distinguish these contemporary ideas and practices from traditional public administration grounded in the principles of bureaucracy. While the changes actually implemented were often more incremental than transformational, the expectation that public organizations should be more effective and responsive was quite clear.

As the 20th century drew to a close, environmental pressures were stimulating organizational changes in both the public and private sectors, with the goal of removing bureaucratic constraints that preclude adequate adaptability and impede effective performance. The sense that substantial change was possible had been heightened considerably by recent advances in information technology, in particular, the development and diffusion of personal computing and the internet. The new information, analysis, and communication capabilities provided by these tools were readily seen as transformative (Cleveland, 1985; Drucker, 1988; Grossman, 1995), by undermining the foundations of bureaucratic organization and enabling more participation, collaboration, and innovation. Indeed, it was becoming increasingly clear that Western civilization was transitioning into a post-industrial period, with information or intellectual capital (Stewart, 1997) as the most critical asset. The Information Age was bringing a new economy with new rules (Kelly, 1998; Raymond, 1999), hinting even at the possibility of a new paradigm for a new age. In the next section, we consider some of the foundations of this new paradigm and their relevance for organizations.

NEW PARADIGM

Foundational Ideas

The mechanistic worldview of the Industrial Era is grounded in classical physics with its various laws of nature that determine patterns of cause and effect in the physical world. In contrast, it is often suggested that quantum physics, with its different understanding of the nature of reality, provides the starting foundation for a new paradigm that incorporates a broader range of contemporary knowledge about life and the universe. For example, whereas matter and energy were thought to be distinct phenomena in classical physics, quantum theorists determined that, at the atomic level, all matter *is* energy; subatomic phenomena simultaneously have properties of both particles and waves. Another key finding from quantum physics is that, at the subatomic level of reality, the entire universe exists as one single entity, with its myriad elements and objects simply material manifestations of this underlying "quantum field" (Bohm, 1980; McTaggart, 2002). Whereas the classical, mechanistic perspective views all objects as separate from each other and from the world around them, a quantum perspective acknowledges that everything is connected at a deeper energetic level (Laszlo, 2003). Thus, while the scientific method has primarily been applied in a reductionist approach to analyzing systems by better understanding their parts, a quantum perspective results in a more holistic focus on how parts interact to create a system.

The holistic study of systems dynamics led to the development of chaos theory (Gleick, 1987; Parker, 1996; Prigogine & Stengers, 1984) and, in turn, to the interdisciplinary investigation of complex adaptive systems (Lewin, 1992; Waldrop, 1992). Chaotic systems are indeterminate in that their performance varies considerably and cannot be predicted given a set of starting conditions, although this variability is constrained by an "attractor" that limits performance to a certain range. In other words, while the dynamic activity of a chaotic system can appear to be random, underlying this chaos there is also some order or pattern that helps define the nature of the system (Strogatz, 2003). Complex systems are those in which numerous system components interact in various ways to produce system-level outcomes. Interdependencies among components include nonlinear relationships and feedback loops that preclude precise prediction about the consequences of any changes in system components or their interactions. Thus, complex systems cannot be controlled in the same way that mechanistic systems can be. Their complexity makes it difficult to design in all the necessary interactions, and any steps taken to influence system performance can easily lead to unintended consequences. Instead, like the universe as a whole (Jantsch, 1980), complex systems are self-organizing (Kauffman, 1995) in that environmental changes trigger system dynamics reflected in interactions among components that generate systemic features. These features are thus emergent, in that they are not found in any of the components but rather emerge out of the interactions among the components, reflecting the more general process by which life has evolved on the planet (Morowitz, 2002). Complex systems are also susceptible to periodic transformations, especially when environmental turbulence creates more disequilibrium than the system can handle. Under those circumstances, if the system doesn't collapse and fail, it can undergo a spontaneous reconfiguration of components and their relationships that enable the system to handle the growing environmental complexity.

All living organisms are complex systems as well as elements in a larger complex system, that is, an ecology. Ecologies clearly display the above features: They have emergent, systemic qualities that are not found in any of the inhabitant organisms; there is no central control yet they display considerable order and stability; and they can transform or collapse in response to significant changes in the broader environment. They are autopoietic, dissipative structures (Capra, 1996), which means that they are able to maintain themselves in a state of dynamic equilibrium (i.e., homeostasis) while also being able to undergo qualitative changes to adapt to environmental disruptions. In fact, this pattern of "punctuated equilibrium"—long periods of relative stability punctuated by short periods of significant transformation—appears to be inherent in the process of evolution of life on this planet (Gould, 2002). Thus, these properties are applicable to ecosystems at all levels of scale, with Gaia theory (Lovelock, 1988) even suggesting that the entire planet can be thought of as a single, unitary complex ecosystem.

The formal study of ecology reflects an effort to apply a holistic, systemic perspective to the study of nature (Ulanowicz, 1997), in contrast to the more common reductionist analyses that do not yield a very good understanding of the dynamics of ecological systems. Ironically, Indigenous cultures have accumulated a wealth of ecological knowledge and wisdom across hundreds of generations (Booth & Jacobs, 1990; McGaa, 2004), yet the "younger" Western culture has tended to discount and ignore the value of these "older" cultures' beliefs and practices (Hartmann, 1998). But with environmental concerns becoming more apparent, the idea of living in ways more compatible with nature has gained currency. Advocates of green psychology (Metzner, 1999) and ecological consciousness (O'Sullivan & Taylor, 2004; Uhl, 2004) have articulated new beliefs, values, and practices derived from an ecological perspective, contrasting them with their mechanistic counterparts. Referring to this emergent organic worldview as the "new biology," Frenay (2006) described how these new ideas and insights are being applied to the development of systems at levels of scale ranging from nanoparticles to industrial ecology and democracy.

A significant manifestation of the emergent ecological worldview is the global emphasis on the notion of sustainable development. Initial interest in the issue of sustainability was triggered by the results of computer simulations which suggested that human society is operating in a way that ignores the existence of "the limits to growth" as defined by the carrying capacity of the planet's resources (Meadows, Meadows, Randers, & Behrens, 1972). Years later, the World Commission on Environment and Development (1987) published a report calling on the world's nations to pursue a path of sustainable development. The groundswell of support for the goal of a more sustainable society was obvious at the 1992 UN Conference on Environment and Development (i.e., the Rio Earth Summit), which was attended by about 40,000 people from 183 countries and produced the Agenda 21 declaration of goals and principles to guide development in the 21st century. It was also apparent in Seattle in 1999, when thousands of protestors disrupted the World Trade Organization meetings to demand a more humane and sustainable pattern of development than was being implemented through the neoliberal policies and practices that dominate the global trade regime. In 2015, the United Nations adopted the 2030 Agenda for Sustainable Development that specifies seventeen Sustainable Development Goals intended to guide countries' efforts to protect the natural environment, reduce inequality, and enable people to prosper.

A popular definition of sustainable development is development that meets the needs of the present without compromising the ability of future generations to meet their own needs (World Commission on Environment and Development, 1987). This conceptualization reflects a shift in thinking regarding the nature and role of economic activity in society, towards a new paradigm based on ecological thinking (Hansen & Christensen, 1995) and thus a different set of assumptions and values (Clark, 1995; Stead & Stead, 1994). In simple terms, sustainable development requires balanced attention to the "3 Es" of economy, environment, and equity, that is, by taking into account the impact of economic activity on interdependent social and natural systems (Hopwood, Unerman, & Fries, 2010). This includes the issue of intergenerational equity, and the goal of ensuring that future generations do not have to pay the price for the current generation's overconsumption and destruction of natural resources. Another important principle is captured in the slogan "think globally, act locally," which reflects awareness of global interdependence while encouraging change at the most viable scale of local activity. The precautionary principle holds that it is better to avoid taking actions that have a reasonable chance of resulting in significant negative effects on the public and/or the environment, with the burden of proof that it is not harmful falling on those proposing the action. All told, sustainable development provides a new social vision that can guide the necessary transition to a sustainable society (Olson, 1995), with the goal of developing people, the economy, and society while sustaining community, nature, and our life support system (Kates, Parris, & Leiserowitz, 2005).

Finally, there is an explicitly spiritual element to this burgeoning cultural transition, based on the fact that the "new science" provides some justification for a more spiritual perspective on the nature of reality (Capra, 1991; Lemkow, 1990; Wolf, 1996; Woodhouse, 1996). For example, both consciousness and the quantum field display holographic properties (Talbot, 1991), with evidence suggesting that the realms of mind and matter are more interconnected than previously understood (Laszlo, 2003; Lipton, 2005; Nadeau & Kafatos, 1999; Zohar, 1990). Philosophers and physicists alike have argued for a more holistic and integrated worldview that views the universe as imbued with spirit, with consciousness inherent in matter (de Quincey, 2002; Schwartz & Russek, 1999). Deep ecology (Naess, 1973), which views all life as having intrinsic value, is an inherently spiritual worldview (Capra, 1996).

From this spiritual perspective, the paradigm shift is seen as an awakening, with individuals around the world "waking up" through a process of personal transformation that is itself part of the broader cultural transformation underway (Elgin, 1993; Hartmann, 1998; Russell, 1998). The New Age movement of the 1990s had the appearances of a spiritual renaissance, with growing calls for the application of a more quantum, ecological, spiritual mindset to the consideration of how best to address contemporary societal concerns (Capra 2002; Lerner, 1996; McLaughlin & Davidson, 1994; Wilber, 2000; Williamson, 1997; Zohar & Marshall, 1994). Some visionaries have posited that this transformation reflects a shift in the collective consciousness of humanity (Harman, 1998), as part of our conscious evolution into the next phase of development of human civilization (Elgin, 1993; Hubbard, 1998; Korten, 2007; Laszlo, 2001). A common refrain in these discussions is that, just as the Industrial Revolution led to a transformation in the dominant institutions of society, the current transition into the Information Age will also require significant institutional reform. In particular, we argue that the mechanistic bureaucracy will eventually be replaced by a fundamentally different, much more organic organizational form that can function effectively in the complex, chaotic conditions of contemporary society.

Organizational Implications

Recognition of the need for organizations that transcend the limitations of bureaucracy had been growing for nearly half a century, and as society approached a "new millennium," there was no dearth of ideas about how organizations could and should function differently in order to survive if not thrive in the complex, uncertain world of a society undergoing a major transition. Labels for these new kinds of organizations include postmodern (Bergquist, 1993), new logic (Lawler, 1997), intelligent (Pinchot & Pinchot, 1994), inventive (Janov, 1994), flexible lateral (Galbraith, 1994), adaptive (Fulmer, 2000), self-designing (Mohrman & Cummings, 1989), self-managing (Purser & Cabana, 1998), bottom-up (Strebel, 2000), centerless (Pasternack & Viscio, 1998), boundaryless (Ashkenas, Ulrich, Jick, & Kerr, 1995), virtual (Davidow & Malone, 1993), chaordic (Hock, 1999), and the self-adapting, self-renewing, instant-action enterprise (Fradette & Michaud, 1995). It was clear that new forms of organization were needed for the 21st century (Ackoff 1999; Benveniste, 1994; Maynard & Mehrtens, 1993).

Creative thinking about new approaches for designing, leading, and managing organizations has also reflected the various new paradigm themes discussed above. Management theorists have considered the chaotic nature of organizational life and discussed ways of dealing with increasing chaos in organizations (Gregerson & Sailer, 1993; Guastello, 1995; Overman, 1996; Peters, 1987). The notion of organizations as complex systems has received even more attention, with efforts both to clarify the nature of this complexity and to discern its implications for effectively managing organizations (Comfort, 1994; Marion, 1999; Merry, 1995; Stacey, 1996). For example, researchers have found evidence of a punctuated equilibrium pattern in organizations and groups through which they undergo a spontaneous reorganization (Gersick, 1991; Tushman & Romanelli, 1985). Some theorists argued that the "new science" provides a foundation for new forms of organization and approaches for insuring their success (Sanders, 1998; Wheatley, 1992; Zohar, 1997). Others focused in particular on the requirements for effective leadership (Uhl-Bien, Marion, & McKelvey, 2007), for example, the need to be "ambidextrous" (Tushman & O'Reilly, 1996)—able to deal with paradoxes and address competing values (Handy, 1994; Lavine, 2014; Quinn, 1988). All in all, the idea that large organizations are indeed complex systems has been reasonably well established (Reeves, Levin, & Ueda, 2016).

The new paradigm emphasis on spirituality likewise has had a significant effect on thinking about organizations and management. It triggered considerable interest in the topic of spirituality in the workplace (Bowman, 2008; Giacalone & Jurkiewicz, 2002; Hawley, 1993; Marques, Dhiman, & King, 2007; Mitroff & Denton, 1999; Owen, 1987; Seybold-Clegg, 2007; Wagner-Marsh & Conley, 1999), along with advocacy of a more spiritual or soulful approach to leadership (Barrett, 1998; Bolman & Deal, 1995; Briskin, 1996; Conger & Associates, 1994; Fairholm, 1997; Fry, 2003; Marcic, 1997). Some have argued that organizational cultures grounded in spiritual values are better for people and thus for organizations (Marques et al., 2007; Milliman, Ferguson, Trickett, & Condemi, 1999), and others that a spiritual perspective can contribute to processes of organizational learning, development, and transformation (Egri & Frost, 1991; Howard, 2002). Empirical research has provided evidence of some of these benefits (Houghton, Neck, & Krishnakumar, 2016; Kolodinsky, Giacalone, & Jurkiewicz, 2008; Mitroff & Denton, 1999).

Growing awareness and acceptance of sustainable development as a societal agenda has a number of implications relevant to organizations (Gladwin, Kennelly, & Krause, 1995; Shrivastava, 1995). At a minimum, tighter environmental regulations imposed by government over the years have required firms to adapt their products and processes accordingly. More broadly, the notion of corporate social responsibility (Carroll, 1999; Waddock, 2009) has emerged as an important focus for top managers, with shareholders, the media, and various interest groups paying closer attention to the negative effects of organizational activities. With stakeholder theory (Donaldson & Preston, 1995; Freeman, 1984) expanding attention beyond just stockholders, there is a growing expectation that businesses should not just pursue profit but should tend to the "triple bottom line" (Elkington, 1997) and strive for a "balanced scorecard" (Kaplan & Norton, 1996) across a number of key outcomes. Evidence indicates that firms that put purpose before profit can outperform those focused solely on that narrow agenda (Collins & Porras, 1994; Orlitzky, Schmidt, & Rynes, 2003; Pfeffer, 1998; Van Beurden & Gössling, 2008). To pursue this agenda, social entrepreneurs have been creating "hybrid" organizations (Haigh & Hoffman, 2012) that are explicitly designed and managed to attend to social and/or environmental as well as financial goals.

Others have argued for more holistic reforms to help make the economy more compatible with the principles of sustainability and ecology more generally. The notions of "green corporations" (Bhat, 1996) and "green logic"

(Isaak, 1999) have been identified, along with numerous specific tactics, to help infuse sustainability thinking into an organization's culture (Eccles, Perkins, & Serafeim, 2012; Harris & Crane, 2002). Countering the notion that there is a tradeoff between profitability and protecting the environment, the four core principles of "natural capitalism" (Hawken, Lovins, & Lovins, 1999) enable firms to increase productivity and profitability by taking steps to reduce their negative environmental impact (Anderson, 1998) and contribute to environmental clean-up (McInerney & White, 1995). More generally, there have been numerous recommendations for greening the economy (Henderson, 2006; Jones, 2008; Meeker-Lowry, 1988) and otherwise making it work better for people and communities (Capra, 2002; Daly & Cobb, 1994; Henderson, 1996; Korten, 2015; Mander & Goldsmith, 1996; McKibben, 2007). Ecological economists have proposed revisions to the dominant neoclassical economics framework (Daly & Farley, 2004; Krishnan, Harris, & Goodwin, 1995), so as to acknowledge environmental constraints on the economy (Whiteman, Walker, & Perego, 2013) and to better measure the effects of the economy on the environment. This distinctly ecological orientation is reflected in efforts to develop tools to measure the "footprint" or environmental impact of economic activity (Barrett & Scott, 2001; Holland, 2003), and to utilize "green" or "full cost" accounting to incorporate more of an organization's negative externalities into its costs, prices, and profits (Bennett & James, 1998; Chouinard, Ellison, & Ridgeway, 2011; Epstein, 1996).

With new science providing the empirical foundation for a richer understanding of complex systems, ecological consciousness generating useful theoretical and practical innovations, global calls for fundamental institutional reform encouraging a path of sustainable development, and the insights and wisdom gained from appreciation of the relevance and value of human spirituality, the foundations of a new paradigm are in place. Building on existing efforts to change cultures, flatten hierarchies, improve collaboration, and enhance learning, organizations are increasingly taking steps to manage complexity, incorporate spirituality, act sustainably, and operate ecologically. While all of these changes can help organizations become more organic with greater capacity for adaptability, most organizational changes to date remain modifications of the bureaucratic model, still rooted in mechanistic thinking. In contrast, some theorists and practitioners are explicitly applying an organic or ecological metaphor to their thinking about organizational design and management. Next, we briefly review some of these ideas before articulating what we believe to be the key features of an ecological model of organizing.

ECOLOGICAL ORGANIZING

Living Organizations

An ecological perspective starts with the premise that organizations are living systems, with the same basic functions, structures, and processes as a plant or animal (Tracy, 1989). For example, organization activity takes place at multiple nested levels (e.g., individuals, groups, and the whole organization), growth and development are inherent processes, and the organization and its components require appropriate care and feeding. Nirenberg (1993) argued that "living organizations" are more like workplace communities, rooted in principles of democracy with a focus on relationship building and continuous improvement. De Geus (1997) also pointed out that the true nature of an organization is that of a community of humans rather than an economic machine. He proposed that "living companies" are focused more on survival and achieving long-term goals than on producing wealth for a small inner group, with the ability to learn key to their success. Cook (2000) posited that the new emerging corporation will have no resemblance to the old model but instead will be innately human, characterized by common values, mutual purpose, excess capacity, and creative action.

Miles, Snow, Mathews, Miles, and Coleman (1997) explained how organizations have been evolving away from hierarchy to a "cellular" form more appropriate for the knowledge age and the new era of innovation. Pointing out that 21st century organizations need internal flexibility to match the complexity of their environments, they describe a cellular form as a living, adaptive organization comprised of independent, self-organizing cells (e.g., self-managing teams or autonomous business units) that have entrepreneurial responsibility to contribute to the organization's improvement and growth. Cells can also collaborate with other interdependent cells to perform more complex functions or produce better outputs. Cellular organizations replace bureaucracy with jointly defined protocols that guide internal and external collaboration, with cells operating as member-owned profit centers to build psychological ownership. Since members require technical, collaborative, and governance skills, cellular organizations also require significant investment in human capability.

Also arguing that organizations are evolving away from the machine model, Wolfe (2011) characterized living organizations as complex, adaptable, living beings, with people analogous to their cells. However, he incorporated a more "quantum" perspective into this conceptualization by focusing on the interdependent fields of energy that shape organizational outcomes. In particular, these include the energy of doing at the level of activities, the energy of interactions at the level of relationships, and the energy of meaning and purpose at the level of context. Like all living systems, organizations create by transforming energy, and thus it is useful to understand how energy flows or is impeded in organizational processes. A living organization is a creative force that operates in harmony with its environment, growing and developing as it works to enhance the broader ecosystem(s). Rather than prioritizing profit above people, health, happiness, and the environment, living organizations focus on making a contribution to the broader system and reaping the rewards that naturally follow. Wolfe also brings a spiritual orientation to the concept of a living organization, noting that they are born, grow old, and die but also have goals, dreams, and a soulful purpose. They are able to achieve that purpose by tapping into the energy, passion, and love that people bring to the organization.

These themes are echoed by Bragdon (2016), who identified the key features of "companies that mimic life." He pointed out that society is gravitating toward a more holistic, ecocentric worldview rooted in the sciences of cognition, quantum theory, ecology, and system dynamics, and that companies with this mindset view the world as a self-regulating, complex, adaptive system whose defining property is life rather than as a mechanical system that works by a fixed set of laws. Bragdon argued that companies are inherently living systems, communities of people with shared goals who live and work at the intersection of biosphere and society. He concluded that, as living systems, their primary assets have to be living as well, meaning they place higher value on living assets (people and nature) than on nonliving capital assets, and invest energy in stewarding those assets. As "leaders of the emerging corporate renaissance," these companies adopt six lifelike properties: decentralized, self-organizing network structures; regenerative life strategies that increase evolutionary opportunities; frugal instincts that seek to optimize use of resources; openness to feedback that enables adaptive learning; symbiotic behaviors that link individual and systemic wellbeing; and consciousness of capabilities, interdependencies, and limits. Bragdon pointed out that the primary benefit of this mode of organization is its speed of learning and adaptation, which relies on heightened corporate consciousness. Thus, the more lifelike companies become, the more conscious they become, awakening the spiritual intelligence of employees and investing their work with meaning and purpose. The thinking capacity of these companies is greatly magnified, as a result of engaging the minds of all employees and benefitting from the inspired thinking of employees who seek to make the world a better place.

Reeves et al. (2016) asserted that companies are identical to a biological species in that both are complex adaptive systems comprised of nested systems, with emergent properties arising through local events and interactions, some tension between what is good for the parts and what is good for the whole system, and evolution through a cycle of interactions, emergence and feedback. They pointed out that businesses are disappearing faster than ever, because they are failing to adapt to the growing complexity of their environment resulting from greater diversity, faster technological innovation, and more interconnectedness. Arguing that adaptability is the new competitive advantage, Reeves and Deimler (2011) indicated that adaptable organizations require a flexible structure, the dispersal of decision rights, modular units that freely communicate and recombine according to the situation, weak or competing power structures, and a culture of constructive conflict and dissent. However, too many firms continue to rely on traditional structures and approaches to strategy designed for more stable circumstances, that is, focused on maximizing short-term performance rather than long-term robustness. Reeves et al. (2016) argued instead that organizations must contribute positively to their broader ecosystems while receiving enough benefits to justify their participation, warning that those which fail to create value for key stakeholders will eventually be marginalized.

Four Features

The idea that organizations can and should be thought of as organisms operating in ecosystems is clearly gaining currency, with considerable potential to provide useful insights for designing and managing adaptable organizations. As "multicephalous" systems, or systems with multiple brains, organizations constitute a collection of individuals acting in concert and using elaborate systems of shared meaning (Pondy & Mitroff, 1979). As such, they can also be thought of as conscious entities with the capacity to think, learn, decide, and act. Like human beings, organizations are intentional and purposive, with beliefs, values, morals, and ethics that influence the nature of organizational activity. As living, conscious beings, organizations can also be thought of as spiritual entities, with the capacity to develop their spirituality (Freer & Robertson, 2020). Below, we draw on these ideas as well as our previous efforts to articulate the features of living organizations (Harder & Robertson, 2007; Harder, Robertson, & Woodward, 2004; Robertson & Choi, 2010) to describe four key features of a new model of ecological organizing. In particular, we consider the holarchical structure, synergistic relationships, shared purpose, and conscious development that constitute the essential features of this new model of ecological organizing. This model is an extension of the process of organizational evolution that has been taking place for nearly a century, but constitutes a new organizational form distinct from the traditional machine bureaucracy.

Holarchical Structure

Ecological organizing is holarchical rather than hierarchical. A holarchy refers to a nested system comprised of "holons" (Koestler, 1967; Wilber, 1995)—something that is both a whole and part of a larger whole—in which smaller units are organized into larger units, which are organized into even larger units, and so on. Using the language of cellular organizing (Miles et al., 1997), organizational members as individuals or groups serve as cells with particular functions, and multicellular units collaborate to carry out more complex activities. Cells are thus both independent and interdependent, expected to strive for their own well-being while also contributing to the success of the larger units of which they are a part. Each cell has responsibility and authority over the tasks required to fulfill its function, and cells working together have joint responsibility and authority for their shared activities. All cells have authority over particular tasks, but no cell has authority over another cell. In this sense a holarchical, cellular form is uncentralized rather than decentralized—there is no center of power that determines who has what responsibility and authority. Like Robertson's (2015) model of holacracy, and as practiced successfully by large companies (Hamel, 2011; Semler, 1993), ecological organizing is a self-managing, "nobody-in-charge" (Cleveland, 2000) system with widely distributed leadership based on knowledge and expertise.

While its basic structure is a holarchy, ecological organizing does not rely on fixed structural arrangements that constrain patterns of interaction and activity, but instead is designed as a dynamic, self-organizing system that readily adapts to changing circumstances (Bragdon, 2016). Reflecting the dictum that form follows function, the composition of and relationships among the multicellular units in ecological organizing can be reconfigured as necessary so as to deploy requisite resources to the most urgent or critical tasks. However, these reconfigurations cannot be dictated but must be emergent among those involved and affected. Organizational capacity is largely a function of the functional differentiation of its cells, with greater diversity among cells and their interactions enabling more complex organizational activity and outcomes. Yet the effectiveness of a complex organization is also a function of the extent to which this diversity is integrated into a coherent unity. Organizational purpose and mission serve an integrating function, as does cellular commitment to core organizational principles and values, that is, mutually agreed standards on whatever is central to the system (Cleveland, 2000). The number of rules and regulations is minimized, as diversity in thought and action among cells is key to organizational creativity and vitality.

Decision making processes in ecological organizing reflect the core principles of democracy and subsidiarity (Ackoff, 1994; Halal, 1996; Melé, 2005; Nirenberg, 1993). Decision processes are democratic in the sense that people who are affected by a decision have a right to provide input into that decision. Cell or unit authority over an activity does not give it the right to act unilaterally, but instead there is an obligation to take into account the relevant information and perspectives of other interdependent parties. Subsidiarity means that decisions are made closest to where they will have an effect, by those who are most familiar with the relevant situation. Systemically, then, decision making in ecological organizing reflects an "inside out" (Robertson, 1999) rather than a top–down governance structure, meaning the decision process begins in small cellular systems and expands into ever-larger systems until it includes all cells and units needed to successfully implement the decision. Inside-out governance also includes decisions made by one or more cells or units that have responsibility and authority for particular systemic functions, such as developing organizational strategies and policies or making major budget allocations. These cells share the obligation to incorporate input and feedback from all relevant stakeholders, but then their decisions serve as parameters for or constraints on the activities of other cells in the system. Ultimately, ecological organizing is fundamentally egalitarian, with all cells as members/owners vested in successful organizational performance.

Synergistic Relationships

Whereas the bureaucratic model is organized around individual office holders, the primary focus in ecological organizing is the nature of the relationships among the cells. Organizational activity takes place through dynamic networks of interdependent cells, and the nature and quality of these relationships determine the system's capacity to perform effectively and produce intended results. Multiple types of relationships need to be managed in ecological organizing, including the interpersonal relationships among members, the intercellular and interunit relationships within the organization, and the external relationships with myriad entities in the broader ecosystems. Whereas natural ecosystems and even bureaucratic organizations typically entail a complex mix of parasitic, competitive, cooperative, and symbiotic relationships, ecological organizing precludes parasitism, constrains competition, and cultivates the kind of collaborative dynamics that can generate synergistic outcomes. All cells are expected to maintain positive relationships with other cells and units with whom they are interdependent, and to build new relationships that can further add systemic value. As an open, egalitarian network, ecological organizing has no hierarchical restrictions on who can interact with whom. It functions more like a community (de Geus, 1997; Nirenberg, 1993), bound together by shared beliefs, values, and practices as well as a common interest in collective well-being.

A key property of living systems is autopoiesis (Maturana & Varela, 1980; Zeleny, 1997), that is, the capacity to self-organize, self-manage, and self-regulate so as to maintain a dynamic equilibrium or homeostasis. This emergent capacity results from the patterns of interaction among system components, and depends heavily on the presence of deviation-amplifying and -reducing feedback loops that function to keep the system in a relative state of balance with variations constrained to a relatively small range of "normal" activity. A critical capacity in ecological organizing is a good understanding of these system dynamics (Senge, 1990), along with the proactive intentionality required to develop, modify, and/or eliminate relationships and interactions in ways that enhance system performance. In particular, all cells are expected to take the initiative both to acquire relevant information they need to fulfill their functions effectively, and to give relevant information to other cells that need it to fulfill their functions effectively. This open exchange of timely information makes possible a pattern of coordination and mutual adjustment among cells that enables the system to adapt quickly to real-time contingencies.

Relationships in ecological organizing are guided by the core principle of mutually beneficial reciprocity. The norm of reciprocity is nearly universal (Cohen & Bradford, 1989; Gouldner, 1960), and in organizations where a giving culture (Grant, 2014) is established and prosocial behavior (Brief & Motowidlo, 1986; Organ, 1988) is encouraged, cells readily establish positive, rewarding relationships with others while competitive, self-serving behavior becomes delegitimized as deviant. These systems are characterized by high levels of trust and social capital that facilitate the kind of collaborative, win–win problem-solving that can generate synergistic outcomes. These decision processes are based on open, inclusive dialogue (Bohm, 1996; Isaacs, 1999) and aim to reach consensus through identification of creative, integrative approaches that draw on diverse perspectives. Such methods can be used with large groups of people (Bryson & Anderson, 2000; Bunker & Alban, 1997), and thus provide a powerful tool for stimulating whole-system change (Weisbord & Janoff, 1995). High trust among organizational members also supports a level of openness and transparency with regards to information about cell, unit, and organizational performance as well as about the allocation of rewards (Dalio, 2017), with this transparency serving to induce greater alignment between the two. By increasing procedural and distributive justice, a greater sense of fairness among organizational members helps to maintain a positive, trusting, collaborative culture (Brockner, 1996; Folger & Konovsky, 1989; Korsgaard, Schweiger, & Sapienza, 1995; Moorman, 1991).

Shared Purpose

In ecological organizing, organizations are purposive entities that exist to add value by serving one or more functions that contribute to the health and well-being of the ecosystems of which they are an integral component (Wolfe, 2011). This replaces the mechanistic perspective that organizations are tools intended to serve the interests of those who provide the financial resources required for the organization to operate. In order to pursue these purposes, continued survival is a primary requirement (de Geus, 1997), which further suggests three important foci in ecological organizing. First, organizational activity needs to add sufficient value that stakeholders are willing to provide the resources needed to continue to function (Pfeffer & Salancik, 1978; Reeves et al., 2016). Synergistic relationships enable cells to generate surplus, that is, output that is more valuable than the input, which justifies this continued support. Second, organizations need to develop the capacity for resilience (Sutcliff & Vogus, 2003), which enables them to withstand systemic events that significantly disrupt normal activities. Resilience requires specific cognitive abilities, behavioral characteristics, and contextual conditions at the system level that are achieved through requisite cellular activities (Lengnick-Hall, Beck, & Lengnick-Hall, 2011), contributing to organizational "evolvability" (Kantur & İşeri-Say, 2012). Third, organizations need to operate sustainably (Epstein, 2008; McDonough & Braungart, 2002; Senge, Smith, Kruschwitz, Laur, & Schley, 2008), as reflected in their efforts to help maintain the long-term viability of the broader ecosystems in which they function. An emphasis on sustainability points to the value of slowing down organizational decision making processes in order to insure that choices made are congruent with this goal.

The purpose of ecological organizing is thus to enhance the quality of larger systems while maintaining the vitality of the smaller systems that comprise them. The specific ways that any cell, unit, organization, or business ecosystem intends to add value are reflected in its vision, mission, core values, and/or other expressions of what it aims to accomplish and how. This focal value proposition (Adner, 2017) serves as a system "attractor" both in the typical sense of attracting others who choose to contribute resources towards this purpose, and in the complex systems sense of serving to define and constrain the range of normal system activity. It explains why an organization exists, its raison d'être, giving meaning to the enterprise and tapping into the intrinsic motivations of its members (Pink, 2009; Sinek, 2009; Wolfe, 2011). This purpose is not necessarily fixed, but can evolve over time as life brings new needs and opportunities. Ecological organizing strives to be responsive to the changing circumstances, requirements, and preferences of relevant stakeholders, who contribute to the process through which an organization's purpose or mission is redefined. This collective definition of how it will serve the common good (Cook, 2000) helps to build a sense of shared accountability that supports members acting as good stewards of these living assets (Bragdon, 2016).

In the pursuit of purpose, ecological organizing is also committed to minimizing the amount of harm caused by organizational activity, as another key indicator of overall effectiveness (Keeley, 1984). These organizations also take responsibility for their negative externalities by internalizing these costs as much as possible (Chouinard et al., 2011). Instead of striving for greater efficiency in monetary terms, the goal in ecological organizing is to minimize the amount of waste generated by the production, distribution, and utilization of the organization's products and/or services. Business ecosystems can pursue this strategy through the use of closed-loop industrial ecologies (Ayres & Ayres, 2002; Socolow, Andrews, Berkhout, & Thomas, 1994) in which waste output from one organization constitutes a productive input for another organization, providing the basis for a circular economy (Lewandowski, 2016; Murray, Skene, & Haynes, 2017). It is also imperative in ecological organizing to refrain from harming the cells through which organizational activity takes place. Instead, cells should benefit from their participation in the system, not just in material terms but intellectually, emotionally, and even spiritually as well. This covenantal relationship (Graham, 1991)—in which cells contribute to the well-being of the organization in return for the organization contributing to the well-being of the cells—is reflected in an equitable distribution of the profits generated by their collective activity. In particular, most organizations require a mix of inputs to generate desired outputs, that is, natural, financial, technological, human, intellectual, and/or social capital, such that the returns on these investments in ecological organizing are distributed more fairly to those who provided them.

Conscious Development

Instead of focusing predominantly on growth as the primary development objective, ecological organizing is oriented towards evolving and developing more consciously (Bragdon, 2016). In natural systems, unrestrained growth is usually problematic, whether in the form of cancer cells inside a body or an invasive species taking over and destroying an ecosystem. Rather than simply wanting to become bigger, the goal in ecological organizing is to become better. Since better is defined in terms of adding more value to larger ecosystems and to society, conscious development relies heavily on input and feedback from stakeholders to determine how organizations and their cells can adapt and improve so as to fulfill their purposes and functions more effectively. Not just products and services but organizational processes are designed and redesigned to better meet the needs of those who use them (Brown & Wyatt, 2010; Martin, 2009), with a capacity for continuous improvement enabling ecological organizing to co-evolve with its environment. Experimentation is also encouraged, to stimulate the innovation needed to adapt and evolve successfully. In contrast to the order and predictability preferred in bureaucracies, ecological organizing operates at the "edge of chaos" (Pascale, 1999) where systemic stability is balanced with enough disorder and unpredictability to generate requisite creativity and novelty.

Performance assessment is also based on feedback and input from relevant others, especially those with whom a cell or unit is most interdependent. As with 360-degree performance evaluations (Antonioni, 1996; Lepsinger & Lucia, 1997; Tornow & London, 1998), the objective is to take into account all relevant perspectives regarding how well a cell or unit functioned and to provide constructive feedback regarding how it can perform better in the future. Cells and units also engage in regular reflection about their own work processes and outcomes, with failure to accomplish goals or meet standards recognized as a particularly useful learning opportunity (Argyris, 1991). While such assessments are used primarily for development purposes, the information gained through this process can also serve as input into decisions regarding salaries and other types of rewards and resources. Stakeholder involvement in this process enables a collective determination of an equitable distribution of rewards, which are based primarily on meritocratic criteria but tempered with a concern for equality and particular member needs. Cells and units establish explicit agreements with their stakeholders—relational psychological contracts (Rousseau, 1995)—regarding the particular activities and/or specific outcomes for which they are responsible as well as the kinds of rewards they can expect. Decisions regarding new hires, definition of job responsibilities, movement into new roles, and involuntary severance are also made collectively based on input from relevant others. All of these processes are guided by the underlying intent to enable system development by increasing conscious awareness of how cells and units can contribute more effectively to system success by improving their ability, capacity, and/or performance.

Growth in ecological organizing focuses primarily on the intellectual, emotional, and spiritual development of the system and its members. Physical growth can be limited to early life cycle stages, after which continued development is reflected in such features as better intellectual capital (Choo & Bontis, 2002; Horibe, 1999; Stewart, 1997), more emotional intelligence (Druskat & Wolff, 2001; Goleman, 1995), and greater spiritual maturity (Freer & Robertson, 2020). Systemic decision processes based on comprehensive input and feedback give ecological organizing a capacity for collective reflective consciousness that enables the double-loop learning (Argyris, 1977) needed to respond effectively to significant environmental perturbations, thereby increasing organizational resilience. Collective reflection and double-loop learning also contribute to the conscious development of the system and its cells, that is, the development of its consciousness from a lower to a higher level. In this way, ecological organizing answers the call for more conscious businesses and a more conscious form of capitalism (Aburdene, 2005; Benett, O'Reilly, Gobhai, & Welch, 2009; Benioff & Southwick, 2004; Mackey & Sisodia, 2013; Pavlovich & Corner, 2014; Strong, 2009; Taso & Laszlo, 2019).

Organizational Evolution

The apparent pattern of organizational evolution described above can be briefly summarized as follows. The core bureaucratic value of hierarchy was challenged for its many dysfunctional consequences, and organizations in response have been attempting to decentralize decision making and increase employee participation, involvement, engagement, and empowerment. Reflecting contemporary values of equality and democracy, and a better understanding of the structure of ecologies, ecological organizing incorporates an uncentralized holarchy as its basic structure. The core bureaucratic value of individualism resulted in work arrangements that impeded collaboration, so organizations have been increasing their use of groups, teams, and networks to accomplish key tasks. Reflecting the value of good connections in today's world, and greater insight into the dynamics of complexity, ecological organizing prioritizes the development and maintenance of synergistic relationships. The core bureaucratic value of science led to organizational indifference to employees' values and beliefs, with the culture movement pushing organizations to clarify their vision and values and to "manage meaning" proactively. Reflecting the value of a meaningful purpose as a source of inspiration and motivation, and more attention to the significance of spirituality, ecological organizing is oriented towards maximizing shared value created while minimizing harm caused. The core bureaucratic value of rationality played out as an overemphasis on efficiency, stability, and self-interested growth, so organizations have been trying to compensate by enhancing their learning capacity to support greater innovation. Reflecting the value of creativity, feedback, and reflection, and stronger commitment to the vision of a sustainable society, ecological organizing strives for conscious development that enables it to continuously grow better and wiser.

In light of this evolutionary process, we argue that ecological organizing represents both a logical next step given the direction in which these changes are already heading, as well as a qualitative break from the bureaucratic model of organization. Likewise, we believe that, as a new organizational model, ecological organizing is both idealistic and realistic. It is idealistic in the sense that it describes a type of organization that is very different from the way most organizations are today, with considerable inertia serving to maintain the dominance of the bureaucratic form. But it is realistic in the sense that the viability of all four features of ecological organizing has been demonstrated by organizations that have already incorporated them successfully. Our purpose here has been to integrate these disparate themes and trends into a single framework, and to clarify the normative foundations that help to explain and justify a transition from organizations based on the bureaucratic model to those adhering to the principles of ecological organizing.

Three holistic approaches to organizational design and management currently in use best reflect the principles of ecological organizing, and might be thought of as practical operationalizations of the conceptual and normative ideals specified in the ecological organizing model. The first is the "agile" methodologies that originally grew out of the need to speed up the software development process and are now being adopted in organizations more broadly (Denning, 2018; Holbeche, 2015; LeMay, 2018; Mergel, Gong, & Bertot, 2018). Seen as a radical alternative to command-and-control style management (Rigby, Sutherland, & Takeuchi, 2016), and an unstoppable business revolution (Denning, 2018), agile organizes employees into self-managed, customer-focused interdisciplinary teams. These teams include initiative owners who are responsible for delivering value to customers, and process facilitators who protect a team from distractions and help it put its collective intelligence to work (Rigby et al., 2016). Agile teams rely on an incremental and iterative test-and-learn approach, often using design thinking or crowdsourcing to identify promising opportunities for innovation. Evidence indicates that agile offers a number of benefits, including increasing team productivity and employee satisfaction, minimizing waste in time and resources, improving customer engagement and satisfaction, broadening organizational experience and building trust and respect (Rigby et al., 2016). The net effect is an organization that is better able to read changing conditions and priorities, develop adaptive solutions, and thereby respond more nimbly to constantly changing needs.

A second ecological approach to organization is "holacracy," a term coined to mean governance of and by the organizational holarchy (Robertson, 2015). Holacracy itself was developed through an iterative, trial-and-error process that, like in agile, is seen as fundamental to the goal of becoming more innovative and adaptive. It represents a new "organizational operating system" (Robertson, 2015), defined by a set of core rules regarding foundational aspects of the way the organization functions that are distinctly different from those of a conventionally governed organization. Four key elements of a holacracy are: a constitution that sets out the rules of the game and redistributes authority; a new way to structure an organization and define people's roles and spheres of authority within it; a unique decision making process for updating those rules and authorities; and a meeting process for keeping teams in sync and getting work done together. The aim is an organization with systemic capacity to dynamically update workflows, expectations, and even organization structure in light of the tensions that arise while getting the work done, without causing harm elsewhere in the process (Robertson, 2015). This capacity in turn can catalyze a much deeper transformation by unleashing the power of evolutionary design on the organization itself. By harnessing the collective sensing power of the human consciousness available to them, organizations can become not just evolved but evolutionary organisms (Robertson, 2015).

A third holistic approach compatible with the principles of ecological organizing are the "teal organizations" emerging as society evolves into a new stage of maturity, complexity, and consciousness (Laloux, 2014). Teal organizations are seen as living entities, oriented toward realizing their potential, and they are defined by three primary attributes: self-management, based on peer relationships in which people have high autonomy in their domain and are accountable for coordinating with others; wholeness, by creating an environment where people feel free to fully express themselves and in turn bring high levels of energy, passion, and creativity to work; and evolutionary purpose, with agile practices that sense and respond and strategies that reflect what they conclude the world is asking from them. Laloux (2014) distinguishes teal organizations from four preceding types (green, orange, amber, and red) that are all still in use today. Mechanistic bureaucracies are amber organizations, while orange and green organizations incorporate the kinds of evolutionary changes described above; new teal organizations are compatible with the principles of ecological organizing. Like holacracy, these teal organizations have been developing organically through the trial-and-error efforts of people trying to create more effective systems. Since many independent efforts have resulted in strikingly similar approaches, Laloux suggests this is evidence that a coherent new organizational model is emerging. We would argue that these similarities reflect the diffusion of the new paradigm, with a new consciousness leading diverse people in the same transformational direction.

All three of these approaches are being utilized by organizations of varying sizes and types. Some have adopted these approaches fully, others have incorporated only some of the elements, or only in some parts of the organization; for example, many large organizations operate with a mix of agile teams and traditional structures (Rigby et al., 2018). It is not unusual for efforts to implement these approaches to encounter resistance in and from systems still functioning according to conventional principles, and parts of an organization where these new approaches have taken hold can clash with other parts where they haven't. But even though bureaucratic thinking may still dominate the organizational world, agile, holacracy, and teal organizations provide evidence that new ecological forms of organizing are both viable and valuable. Their primary advantage is their adaptability and even agility, which is increasingly considered the vital factor for business success (Holbeche, 2015; Reeves & Deimler, 2011). Going forward, developing this adaptive capacity could be the most significant strategic challenge facing contemporary organizations.

STRATEGIC MANAGEMENT

Adaptive Capacity

Early thinking about bureaucratic organizations conceptualized them as closed systems, essentially autonomous and independent from their environments (Scott, 1981). In contrast, growing environmental turbulence coincided with the emergence of an open systems perspective in organization theory (Katz & Kahn, 1966; Thompson, 1967), as it became clear that organizational effectiveness was a function in part of the congruence between environmental conditions and an organization's structures and processes (Burns & Stalker, 1961; Lawrence & Lorsch, 1967). Growing recognition of the need to respond to environmental contingencies stimulated interest in the role of organizational strategy. Among the first to address this topic was Chandler (1962), who argued that an organization's structure should be driven by its strategy and proposed the multi-divisional structure (M-form) as a way for large corporations to address the need for greater diversification. In contrast to Chandler's general management view of business policy, Ansoff (1965) put more emphasis on a rationalistic and planning-oriented view of strategy, linking it to the idea of organizational long-range planning. Along with Andrews (1971), who emphasized environmental analysis, these theorists helped shift management theory from a deterministic one-best-way approach to the more contingent perspective that organizations need to adapt to their external environment (Furrer, Thomas, & Goussevskaia, 2008).

The early focus on strategy evolved into a more general approach to strategic management (Bracker, 1980), which entails processes and practices related to the organizing of resources for the entire organization as well as how the organization responds to or manages change (Cummings & Daellenbach, 2009). As the field of strategic management matured, there was a transition from a more normative approach towards a more analytical research orientation, focused on identifying features of strategy-making processes and clarifying the link between strategy and performance (Furrer et al., 2008). This led to the development of a widely accepted model for analyzing industry and the definition of a set of generic strategies (Porter, 1980). By helping managers anticipate potential environmental changes and build organizational capacity to respond effectively, strategic management enables organizations to prepare proactively for the future rather than leaving them simply to react when that future arrives.

The growing need for improved adaptive capacity shaped the field of strategic management by giving rise to the resource-based view of the firm (Wernerfelt, 1984). In contrast to an emphasis on environmental analysis as the basis for identifying competitive advantages, strategists shifted their attention to the development and use of a firm's internal resources. In particular, resources that are valuable, rare, and hard to imitate or substitute were recognized as key to sustained competitive advantage (Barney, 1991). For example, with information management becoming a more important strategic issue in organizations, there has been growing attention to the role of organizational knowledge as a primary source of competitive advantage (Pettigrew, Thomas, & Whittington, 2002), along with the learning processes needed to acquire, utilize, and generate new knowledge (Halal, 1998). There has also been increased interest in the role of relationships as another resource that can yield competitive advantage (Cummings & Daellenbach, 2009). Externally, relationships with key stakeholders are a critical focus of strategic management (Freeman, 1984; Svendsen, 1998), with organizational responses to stakeholders' demands determined by their power, legitimacy, and urgency (Mitchell, Agle, & Wood, 1997). Internally, social capital generated through effective teamwork and collaborative relationships is seen as producing an "organizational advantage" by enabling the development of intellectual capital (Nahapiet & Ghoshal, 1998).

More generally, a firm's competitive advantage depends on internal organizational dynamics and the intangible benefits they provide. Teece, Pisano, and Shuen (1997) pointed to the value of honing technological, organizational, and managerial processes so as to be able to identify new opportunities and organize effectively and efficiently to embrace them. For example, strategic planning processes have become more informal and decentralized and less staff driven, enabling greater adaptability and responsiveness to external change (Cummings & Daellenbach, 2009). Given their social complexity, these emergent and autonomous processes are difficult for other firms to mimic and thus can provide an important advantage. The same is true for other socially complex phenomena or "invisible assets" that are not subject to direct management, for example, a firm's culture and technical know-how, its reputation, customer loyalty, and the interpersonal relations among its managers (Barney, 1991; Itami, 1987).

In short, sustained competitive advantage depends on a broad range of organizational, social, and individual phenomena within firms, and the long-term trend towards becoming more organic, with improved adaptive capacity, has been driven by this goal of enhancing competitiveness. While ecological organizing is indeed intended to enable more innovation and adaptability, the goal is not just to become more competitive. Rather, ecological organizing is designed as a collaborative system, in which competitive processes and dynamics are limited to those that have systemic value rather than simply reflecting the self-interested pursuits of particular cells or units. The inherent collaborative orientation of ecological organizing also facilitates effective involvement in organizational ecosystems, where success depends as much on the quality of the collaborative relationships among participating organizations. Thus, operating successfully in an ecosystem context introduces new strategic concerns and challenges beyond those pertinent in a purely competitive environment.

Ecosystem Strategy

As the transition from the Industrial Era into the Information Age has unfolded, observers have noted the resulting shift to a "network society" (Castells, 1996) in which "the world is flat" (Friedman, 2005). One facet of this shift as manifested among organizations is that more and more of them have been getting involved in a diverse array of partnerships, alliances, and networks (Lewis, 1995; Limerick & Cunnington, 1997; Oliver, 1990; Powell, 1990). As a result, the need to manage these interorganizational relationships strategically has become more critical to organizational performance (Das & Teng, 1997). At the same time, there has been growing pressure on businesses to create "shared value," defined as creating economic value in a way that also creates value for society by addressing its needs and challenges (Porter & Kramer, 2012). Kramer and Pfitzer (2016) pointed out that, to advance shared value efforts, businesses need to develop multisector coalitions and initiate collective impact efforts that involve all the players in their ecosystems. Already, many private, public, and nonprofit organizations are engaged in multi-organizational systems in which they work together to serve larger purposes while accomplishing their own objectives. Adner (2017) predicts that ecosystems as arrangements of interdependent value creation will continue to grow in prevalence and importance in the years to come.

The emergence of business ecosystems in particular has raised questions about how firms can function effectively in this context (Moore, 1996). Business ecosystems entail the collaborative arrangements through which firms combine their individual offerings into a coherent, customer-facing solution (Adner, 2006). Many of them have been developed primarily to stimulate and enable more innovation (Adner, 2006; Kanter, 2012). They consist of interlocking networks of partners, suppliers, and customers striving to sustain performance and achieve market success (Moore, 1996). While the boundaries of these ecosystems are fluid, they encompass the full range of organizations from multiple industries that influence the value of a product or service (Iansiti, 2005), or that need to interact in order for a focal value proposition to materialize (Adner, 2017). Rather than being able to operate relatively autonomously, organizations in a business ecosystem are compelled to coordinate their actions with others, and to cooperate in the pursuit of shared objectives.

Business ecosystems are complex adaptive systems (Peltoniemi, 2006), in that they are composed of multiple independent organizations that create complex interdependencies by competing and collaborating with each other in various ways. Like all complex systems, they have emergent properties generated by various types of interactions among their component parts linked to the flow of resources and information (Mars, Bronstein, & Lusch, 2012). Likewise, the multilateral relationships defining the ecosystem are not decomposable to an aggregation of bilateral interactions (Adner, 2017). In other words, the ecosystem as a whole can serve as the unit of analysis, with both competition and evolution taking place not just at the firm level but at the ecosystem level as well. To be successful, ecosystem participants need to coevolve into whatever patterns or relationships are needed at particular times to succeed (Moore, 1996). In turn, the ecosystem can help firms become more resilient to market changes and more responsive to customer needs (Iansiti, 2005). Ultimately, an enriched business ecosystem comprised of symbiotic relationships among participants can create shared value by benefiting consumers, businesses, the economy, and society (Iansiti & Levien, 2004; Kanter, 2012).

Since each member of a business ecosystem ultimately shares the fate of the system as a whole, effective ecosystem management has emerged as a strategic imperative for many firms. Ecosystem strategy is guided by a concern with the competitiveness of the ecosystem as a whole as well as its participants, for whom joint value creation is a general goal (Iansiti & Levian, 2004). Each organization's strategy needs to focus not only on furthering its own interests but also on promoting the ecosystems' overall health. Given the dynamic context, strategy making is best as an iterative process that takes ecosystem risks into account (Adner, 2006). Ecosystem management also requires total system leadership (Moore, 1996), with organizational leaders collaborating to bridge the gaps among their siloed institutions and identify integrated solutions to shared challenges (Kanter, 2012). Participating organizations can play varying roles in the ecosystems, such as a keystone, a dominant player, or a niche actor (Iansiti & Levian, 2004). Aligning the various participants and roles to achieve the focal value proposition, including recognizing and managing key indirect links, is the critical strategic challenge organizational leaders and managers face (Adner, 2017).

The emergence of business ecosystems as a focus of theoretical and strategic attention has had a parallel process in the public sector. As a result of the "reinventing government" and "new public management" trends towards more inclusion in governance processes and greater responsiveness to the public interest, government agencies also started partnering with private and third sector organizations in an array of collaborative relationships and cross-sectoral networks intended to enhance their collective capacity to provide public services more effectively (Goldsmith & Eggers, 2004; Lawless & Moore, 1989; Mandell, 1999; Robertson, 1998). As a result, public management scholars have given considerable attention to the question of what is needed for these network systems to function effectively (Bryson, Crosby, & Stone, 2006; Kickert, Klijn, & Koppenjan, 1997; Milward & Provan, 2006; Page, 2003; Thomson & Perry, 2006).

In addition to policy implementation networks, cross-sectoral, multistakeholder approaches have been established to develop multiparty solutions in contexts where problem complexity and competing interests render traditional, top-down governmental policy-making processes ineffective (Gray, 1997; Imperial, 2005; Innes & Booher, 2003). As the use of these innovative decision making arrangements became more prevalent, labels such as "collaborative governance" (Ansell & Gash, 2008; Emerson, Nabatchi, & Balogh, 2012), "collaborative public management" (Leach, 2006; McGuire, 2006), and "collaborative planning" (Healey, 2006; Margerum, 2002) were adopted to reflect the fact that their purpose was to enable more collaborative decision processes that generated outcomes more acceptable to a wider range of relevant stakeholders. Zadek (2008) argued that "there is no alternative" to global collaborative governance, and that these arrangements through which public and private institutions work together to enhance the provision of public goods could become the common approach to decision making in the future.

Collaborative governance systems are similar to business ecosystems in that a complex array of competitive and collaborative dynamics must be managed successfully in order for an interorganizational network to make progress towards its collective objectives. Further, performance at both the system level and the participant level is important (Provan & Milward, 2001), with the interdependence of the two levels generating the possibility of win–win outcomes that benefit society as well. System leadership is critical, whether as a shared responsibility of the participants, by a dominant organization in the network, or by a lead administrative organization (Provan & Kenis, 2008). On the other hand, these systems cannot be controlled since participation is usually voluntary, meaning they are largely self-organizing with emergent features and unpredictable consequences. They aim to be inclusive with all interests represented, and oriented toward building consensus through deliberative processes (Ansell & Gash, 2008). While collaborative governance theorists have not explicitly adopted an ecosystem perspective to analyze these dynamics and the requirements for success of these systems, these new institutional arrangements being used for public decision making seem to be evolving towards a more ecological form of governance (Robertson & Choi, 2010).

Whether consisting primarily of businesses, or public and nonprofit organizations, or a cross-sectoral mix of organizational types, interorganizational ecosystems by their very nature tend to demonstrate the features of ecological organizing. They are structured holarchically, with self-organizing participation and no centralized control. They entail a complex network of dynamic relationships among diverse participants that aim to generate synergistic, mutually beneficial outcomes. They are guided by a shared purpose to create shared value that motivates participants and helps maintain accountability. They develop by improving their capacity and performance based on feedback and ongoing learning that enables co-evolution with their environment. In short, the four key features of ecological organizing scale up, in the sense that the same ecological principles that define ecological organizing at a micro level (people and groups in organizations) also apply at a macro level (organizations and networks in ecosystems). Adopting the features of ecological organizing internally thus positions an organization to be more effective and successful in its ecosystems, both a competitive and a collaborative advantage.

CONSCIOUS EVOLUTION

For many years now, observers have been noting that the world is changing—quickly, dramatically—and the idea that society is transitioning from the Industrial Era to the Information Age is a concise, convenient way to frame the significance of the shift that is underway. Just as the Industrial Revolution transformed agrarian cultures that had existed for centuries if not millennia, many believe that global society is now in the throes of another cultural shift of similar magnitude. As suggested by the framework of culture discussed earlier, this transformation will necessarily entail changes at three levels: worldview and the taken-for-granted assumptions comprising a dominant theory of reality; primary institutions that reflect and express core cultural values; and practices and patterns of behavior along with the outputs of those activities. There is plenty of evidence in all three levels that a cultural transformation is underway.

We described the foundations of the new paradigm above, arguing that global culture is shifting from a mechanistic to an ecological worldview. This new worldview reflects a better understanding of reality based on contemporary science, while also embracing a more spiritual orientation regarding the essence of life. Because it integrates key ideas from both scientific and spiritual perspectives, this worldview is seen as providing the foundation for a new "integral" culture (Wilber, 1998). Recognizing that life is sacred, it also provides a new vision of development for humanity in the anthropocene that is oriented towards sustaining rather than depleting nature and human community. Growing momentum behind the idea of conscious capitalism, or even a post-capitalist society (Drucker, 1994; Korten, 1999) further reflects awareness that, moving forward, collective human activity needs to be guided by thinking at a higher level of consciousness.

We have argued that organizations, as probably the dominant institution of modern society, are evolving from an old form based on mechanistic principles to a new form based on ecological principles. We believe that the model of ecological organizing we propose is relevant for many different types of organizations, regardless of size or sector. Since it scales naturally, ecological organizing principles are applicable for interorganizational systems, and even systems of systems. With systems at each level driven by a shared purpose to create shared value, sectoral differences would become less meaningful, continuing a blurring of the boundaries that is already underway (Bozeman, 1987). Given the versatility of ecological organizing as a system for making collective decisions and taking collective action, it could be utilized for the various kinds of purposes that collaborative governance mechanisms are being used today (Robertson & Choi, 2010).

As an agile, adaptive organizational system, ecological organizing demonstrates a good fit with environments that are dynamic and complex. Presently, organizations that do not learn to adapt and to be adaptive are disappearing faster than ever (Reeves et al., 2016), and we should expect the environment to continue to "select for" those organizations and organizational forms with more adaptive capacity. This is because the economy itself appears to be in a state of flux, with important changes happening at the fringe that could become more central in the future. For example, by recognizing the inherent limits to economic growth and accounting for energy use by organizational systems, ecological economics provides an ideological alternative to the neoliberal economic theory that dominates the global economy (Daly & Farley, 2004; Krishnan et al., 1995). The availability of cooperative currencies and cryptocurrencies as uncentralized alternatives to a centralized monetary system (Lietaer & Dunne, 2013; Vigna & Casey, 2015), along with crowdsourcing mechanisms for funding projects and borrowing/lending money (Bruton, Khavul, Siegel, & Wright, 2015; Lawton & Maron, 2012), have the potential to reconfigure institutional arrangements in the finance sector. Recent interest in the sharing economy (Botsman & Rogers, 2010; Gansky, 2010) and the caring economy (Eisler, 2007) reflects the possibility of reprioritizing the economy away from a system based on production and consumption to one oriented towards effectively meeting the full range of human needs. The gig economy is driven in part by workers' desire to be more independent and self-sufficient and not subject to the whim of employers concerned only about the bottom line (Mulcahy, 2017). Given the complexity of the global environment, the net effect of these and other potential systemic perturbations is impossible to predict, but the possibility that more radical change is coming should not be discounted (Anderson, 2009; Haskel & Westlake, 2018; Lanier, 2014).

We might anticipate equally significant changes in the government sector as well, given prospects for the emergence of "Government 2.0" (Chun, Shulman, Sandoval, & Hovy, 2010; Eggers, 2004; Nam, 2012; O'Reilly, 2010). This label refers to the systemic changes in how government can function in light of the capabilities provided by highly interactive web 2.0 technologies (Goldsmith & Kleiman, 2017; Tapscott and Williams, 2010). Government 2.0 is "open government" (Lathrop & Ruma, 2010) that incorporates the principles of open source (Raymond, 1999; Roberts, 2011), open data (Attard, Orlandi, Scerri, & Auer, 2015; Sieber & Johnson, 2015), and open innovation (Chesbrough, 2003; Mergel & Desouza, 2013). It enables more and better citizen participation (Linders, 2012; Liu, 2017) and thereby taps into "the wisdom of crowds" (Surowiecki, 2005) to help address societal challenges. More generally, the premise is that government can become a "platform"—by serving as a convener and enabler, or the manager of a marketplace—that allows people inside and outside of government to innovate (O'Reilly, 2010). For example, public organizations can introduce platforms facilitating innovation through interactions with other public organizations, businesses and citizens, and then focus primarily on their orchestration role (Janssen & Estevez, 2013). To support these efforts, policy makers should be guided by the goal of intentionally constructing open government ecosystems (Harrison, Pardo, & Cook, 2012). Coupled with the availability of "big data" (Mergel, Rethemeyer, & Isset, 2016) and the growth of the "internet of things" (Bunz & Meikle, 2018), we can expect the development of "smart cities" (Townsend, 2013) in which the integration of all these new capabilities will radically transform the nature of civic life.

The diffusion of the new paradigm worldview along with the significant institutional changes already in progress are generating, and being generated by, changes in the practices and patterns of activity of millions of people on the planet. Here too there are signs of a shift in attitudes and behaviors that comport with the deeper cultural change unfolding. Elgin and LeDrew (1997) integrated findings from a number of comprehensive global and U.S. surveys to conclude that a new global culture and consciousness had taken root, with this change in consciousness demonstrated by two primary features: a further awakening of the human capacity to be self-reflective and the ecological perspective that the Earth and the cosmos are interconnected living systems. Likewise, Ray and Anderson (2000) estimated that as many as 50 million adults in the U.S. and 80–90 million adults in Western Europe could be identified as "cultural creatives" who care intensely about a range of social issues, including the environment and stopping corporate globalization, spirituality and personal growth, and peace and social justice.

Many of these people are socially engaged, living their values and creating social innovations intended to improve the world. For example, Hawken (2007) estimated that there are hundreds of thousands of small organizations around the world devotedly working to make things better in some specific way in some particular place. In short, global society is now populated by millions of "imaginal cells" (Hubbard, 1998) who are enacting this culture change through their thoughts, words, and deeds.

Practices also include technologies, and the capabilities and activities they require and enable, and a host of new technologies are poised to have significant consequences for the future evolution of civilization (Diamandis & Kotler, 2020). These include artificial intelligence, especially when coupled with robotics, as the integration of these technologies is producing machines more capable than human beings at many sophisticated tasks. Quantum computing, with its orders of magnitude greater computing power, will have unimaginable consequences once the technology becomes operationally viable. The inevitable diffusion of desktop 3D printing will further eliminate many jobs as many products will be produced by users on-demand at home rather than by workers in manufacturing facilities somewhere else in the world. Genetic engineering will open up possibilities for more effective healthcare treatments that extend life even longer, and also for creating "designer babies" that match parents' particular preferences. With more healthy, active people and a greatly reduced need for employees, it may be untenable to base the economy on the core premise that one must "work" in order to earn money to acquire the necessities of life. There have already been experiments with the distribution of some form of "universal basic income," based on the idea that everyone should have a basic income that covers the cost of essentials like food and shelter.

While many other revolutionary technologies could be identified here, a key point is that the paradigm change is happening more quickly and more visibly at the level of practices than at the worldview or institutional levels. This is because people around the world are working to mitigate the worst effects of the old paradigm and its increasingly problematic economic, political, and organizational systems, and to identify, implement, and disseminate innovative approaches based on contemporary beliefs and values about what is meaningful and important. The new paradigm, and ecological organizing, is aligned with core human values held by people of all ages, races, religions, and cultures. These include the belief in equality and democracy and the pursuit of social justice; the emphasis on relationships and being connected to others in collaborative efforts; the acknowledgement of spirituality as an important source of meaning and fulfillment; and the focus on learning and growth as key to personal and systemic development. In contrast to the values of hierarchical inequality, individualistic self-interest, scientific materialism, and rational efficiency, these new paradigm ideals provide a powerful, attractive vision for the future evolution of society.

Along with many others, we believe that human civilization is in the midst of a cultural transformation that will eventually lead to a very different kind of society. Neither state nor market in their current manifestations are demonstrating the capacity to guide humanity onto a path of peaceful, sustainable development; indeed, the dynamics in both systems are oriented primarily toward competition and control, which undermine the collaborative ethos needed to address the complex challenges facing society (Robertson, 1999). Collaboration is the raison d'être for ecological organizing, and its four features create system dynamics that make collaboration more viable and productive. The result is organizations empowered by people working together to create shared value and make the world a better place. Rather than competing over scarce resources, this collaborative system would naturally generate abundance (Diamandis & Kotler, 2012; McKnight & Block, 2010) and thus improve the overall quality of life on the planet.

The holarchical structure of the universe, and the evolutionary trajectory of life on this planet, both reflect the "transcend and include" nature of systems as we currently understand them. In terms of the physical universe, larger systems include smaller systems but also have emergent properties by which they transcend these smaller systems. In evolution, more complex life forms include features of the less complex life forms from which they evolved, but they also transcend those simpler systems by developing new skills and capabilities. Just as industrialized cultures transcended their agrarian predecessors, we should assume that the new ecological paradigm will transcend the mechanistic paradigm of the Industrial Age. And just as industrialization was stimulated by a cultural "enlightenment" of society, the current shift into the Information Age is being stimulated by a cultural "awakening" to a new level of conscious awareness. The new paradigm reflects humanity's growing understanding of our interconnectedness (Barabási, 2002), with each other and with all of life, giving rise to a growing sense of urgency about the need to protect our planetary life support system.

Elgin (1993) suggested that humanity is transitioning into an "era of reconciliation" driven by this shift in our collective consciousness. The idea that consciousness exists on a spectrum has a long history (Wilber, 1977), and it is not uncommon to refer to the notion of raising the consciousness of a particular person or group of people. Likewise, we can perceive qualitative differences in human consciousness from that of the animals from which we evolved, and might even recognize the Enlightenment as having raised the consciousness of Western culture. But the idea that we are living through a period of consciousness raising for humanity as a whole, with a corresponding transformation of global culture, is not widely considered.

One way to characterize this shift in consciousness is that we can now recognize our roles as co-creators of the future. The future is not something that arrives independently of the actions we have taken in the past. The nature of human culture tomorrow depends on the choices we make today.

The concept of conscious evolution (Hubbard, 1998; McWaters, 1982) points to the fact that human beings now have the opportunity and responsibility to make conscious decisions about if and how they will contribute to the evolution of society. It also suggests that humanity, collectively, has the opportunity and responsibility to make conscious decisions about how we want society to evolve. At present, society is populated and dominated by large organizations that pursue their narrow self-interests without much regard for the evolutionary impact of their actions. They do this because it is what they were designed and intended to do, given the values and logic of the mechanistic mindset at the time the bureaucratic model was developed. But the pursuit of narrow self-interest is anachronistic in an interconnected, information-rich environment, where there is a premium on being mindful of the effects one's actions have on others. Ecological organizing expects and rewards cooperative, collaborative activity at all levels of the holarchy, with the net effect being organizational systems that are conducive to operating in ways that effectively benefit society. Rather than maintaining a path of unconscious evolution, "developing" in an unsustainable way that most people do not like, we believe that ecological organizing can help global society consciously evolve to the next stage of human civilization.

REFERENCES

Aburdene, P. (2005). *Megatrends 2010: The rise of conscious capitalism.* Charlottesville, VA: Hampton Roads.

Ackoff, R. L. (1994). *The democratic corporation: A radical prescription for recreating corporate America and rediscovering success.* New York, NY: Oxford University Press.

Ackoff, R. L. (1999). *Re-creating the corporation: A design of organizations for the 21st century.* New York, NY: Oxford University Press.

Adner, R. (2006). Match your innovation strategy to your innovation ecosystem. *Harvard Business Review, 84*(4), 98–107.

Adner, R. (2017). Ecosystem as structure: An actionable construct for strategy. *Journal of Management, 43*(1), 39–58.

Anderson, C. (2009). *Free: The future of a radical price.* New York, NY: Hyperion.

Anderson, R. C. (1998). *Mid-course correction: Toward a sustainable enterprise: The Interface model.* Atlanta, GA: Perengrinzilla.

Andrews, K. R. (1971). *The concept of corporate strategy.* New York, NY: Dow Jones-Irwin.

Ansell, C., & Gash, A. (2008). Collaborative governance in theory and practice. *Journal of Public Administration Research and Theory, 18*(4), 543–571.

Ansoff, H. I. (1965). *Corporate strategy.* Homewood, IL: Dow Jones-Irwin.

Antonioni, D. (1996). Designing an effective 360-degree appraisal feedback process. *Organizational Dynamics, 25*(2), 24–38.

Argyris, C. (1957). The individual and the organization: Some problems of mutual adjustment. *Administrative Science Quarterly, 2*(1), 1–24.

Argyris. C. (1970). *Intervention theory and method.* Reading, MA: Addison-Wesley.

Argyris, C. (1977). Double loop learning in organizations. *Harvard Business Review, 55*(5), 115–125.

Argyris, C. (1991). Teaching smart people how to learn. *Harvard Business Review, 69*(3), 99–109.

Ashkenas, R., Ulrich, D., Jick, T., & Kerr, S. (1995). *The boundaryless organization: Breaking the chains of organizational structure.* San Francisco, CA: Jossey-Bass.

Attard, J., Orlandi, F., Scerri, S., & Auer, S. (2015). A systematic review of open government data initiatives. *Government Information Quarterly, 32*(4), 399–418.

Ayres, R. U., & Ayres, L. (Eds.). (2002). *A handbook of industrial ecology.* Northampton, MA: Edward Elgar.

Barabási, A.-L. (2002). *Linked: How everything is connected to everything else and what it means for business, science, and everyday life.* Cambridge, MA: Perseus.

Barnard, C. I. (1938). *The functions of the executive.* Cambridge, MA: Harvard University Press.

Barney, J. (1991). Firm resources and sustained competitive advantage. *Journal of Management, 17*(1), 99–120.

Barrett, J., & Scott, A. (2001). The ecological footprint: A metric for corporate sustainability. *Corporate Environmental Strategy, 8*(4), 316–325.

Barrett, R. (1998). *Liberating the corporate soul: Building a visionary organization.* Boston, MA: Butterworth-Heinemann.

Barzelay, M. (1992). *Breaking through bureaucracy: A new vision for managing in government.* Berkeley: University of California Press.

Beckhard, R. (1969). *Organization development: Strategies and models.* Reading, MA: Addison-Wesley.

Benett, A., O'Reilly, A., Gobhai, C., & Welch, G. (2009). *Good for business: The rise of the conscious corporation.* New York, NY: St. Martin's Press.

Benioff, M., & Southwick, K. (2004). *Compassionate capitalism: How corporations can make doing good an integral part of doing well.* Newburyport, MA: Career Press.

Bennett, M., & James, P. (Eds.). (2017). *The green bottom line: Environmental accounting for management, current practice and future trends.* Abingdon-on-Thames, England: Routledge.

Bennis, W. G. (1965). Theory and method in applying behavioral science to planned organizational change. *Journal of Applied Behavioral Science, 1*(4), 337–360.

Bennis, W. G. (1969). *Organization development: Its nature, origins, and prospects.* Reading, MA: Addison-Wesley.

Benveniste, G. (1994). *The twenty-first century organization: Analyzing current trends and imagining the future.* San Francisco, CA: Jossey-Bass.

Berger, P. L., & Luckmann, T. (1966). *The social construction of reality: A treatise in the sociology of knowledge.* Garden City, NY: Doubleday.

Bergquist, W. (1993). *The postmodern organization: Mastering the art of irreversible change.* San Francisco, CA: Jossey-Bass.

Bhat, V. N. (1996). *The green corporation: The next competitive advantage.* Westport, CT: Quorum Books.

Blake, R. R., & Mouton, J. S. (1966). *The managerial grid: Key orientations for achieving production through people.* Houston, TX: Gulf.

Block, P. (1993). *Stewardship: Choosing service over self-interest.* San Francisco, CA: Berrett-Koehler.

Bohm, D. (1980). *Wholeness and the implicate order.* London, England: Routledge & Kegan Paul.

Bohm, D. (1996). *On dialogue.* London, England: Routledge.

Bolman, L. G., & Deal, T. E. (1995). *Leading with soul: An uncommon journey of the spirit.* San Francisco, CA: Jossey-Bass.

Booth, A. L., & Jacobs, H. L. (1990). Ties that bind: Native American beliefs as a foundation for environmental consciousness. *Environmental Ethics, 12*(1), 27–43.

Botsman, R., & Rogers, R. (2010). *What's mine is yours: The rise of collaborative consumption.* New York, NY: HarperCollins.

Bowman, T. J. (2008). An ideal type of spiritually informed organizations: A sociological model. *Journal of Management, Spirituality & Religion, 5*(3), 293–320.

Bozeman, B. (1987). *All organizations are public: Bridging public and private organizational theories.* San Francisco, CA: Jossey-Bass.

Bracker, J. (1980). The historical development of the strategic management concept. *Academy of Management Review, 5*(2), 219–224.

Bradford, D. L., & Cohen, A. R. (1984). *Managing for excellence: The guide to developing high performance in contemporary organizations.* New York, NY: Wiley.

Bragdon, J. H. (2016). *Companies that mimic life: Leaders of the emerging corporate renaissance.* Saltair, England: Greenleaf.

Brief, A. P., & Motowidlo, S. J. (1986). Prosocial organizational behaviors. *Academy of Management Review, 11*(4), 710–725.

Briskin, A. (1996). *The stirring of soul in the workplace.* San Francisco, CA: Jossey-Bass.

Brockner, J. (1996). Understanding the interaction between procedural and distributive justice: The role of trust. In R. M. Kramer & T. R. Tyler (Eds.), *Trust in organizations: Frontiers of theory and research* (pp. 390–413). Thousand Oaks, CA: SAGE.

Brown, T., & Wyatt, J. (2010). Design thinking for social innovation. *Stanford Social Innovation Review, 8*(1), 31–35.

Brudney, J. L., Hebert, F. T., & Wright, D. S. (1999). Reinventing government in the American states: Measuring and explaining administrative reform. *Public Administration Review, 59*(1), 19–30.

Bruton, G., Khavul, S., Siegel, D., & Wright, M. (2015). New financial alternatives in seeding entrepreneurship: Microfinance, crowdfunding, and peer-to-peer innovations. *Entrepreneurship Theory and Practice, 39*(1), 9–26.

Bryson, J. M., & Anderson, S. R. (2000). Applying large-group interaction methods in the planning and implementation of major change efforts. *Public Administration Review, 60*(2), 143–162.

Bryson, J. M., Crosby, B. C., & Stone, M. M. (2006). The design and implementation of cross-sector collaborations: Propositions from the literature. *Public Administration Review, 66*(s1), 44–55.

Bunker, B. B., & Alban, B. T. (1997). *Large group interventions: Engaging the whole system for rapid change.* San Francisco, CA: Jossey-Bass.

Burns, T., & Stalker, G. M. (1961). *The management of innovation.* London, England: Tavistock.

Bunz, M., & Meikle, G. (2018). *The internet of things.* Cambridge, England: Polity Press.

Capra, F. (1991). *The tao of physics* (3rd ed.). Boston, MA: Shambhala.

Capra, F. (1996). *The web of life: A new scientific understanding of living systems.* New York, NY: Anchor Books.

Capra, F. (2002). *The hidden connections: Integrating the biological, cognitive, and social dimensions of life into a science of sustainability.* New York, NY: Doubleday.

Carroll, A. B. (1999). Corporate social responsibility: Evolution of a definitional construct. *Business & Society, 38*(3), 268–295.

Castells, M. (1996). *The rise of the network society.* Cambridge, MA: Blackwell.

Chandler, A. R. (1962). *Strategy and structure: Chapters in the history of the industrial enterprise.* Cambridge, MA: MIT Press.

Chesbrough, H. (2003). *Open innovation: The new imperative for creating and profiting from technology.* Boston, MA: Harvard Business School.

Choo, C. W., & Bontis, N. (Eds.). (2002). *The strategic management of intellectual capital and organizational knowledge.* Oxford, England: Oxford University Press.

Chouinard, Y., Ellison, J., & Ridgeway, R. (2011). The sustainable economy. *Harvard Business Review, 89*(10), 52–62.

Chun, S., Shulman, S., Sandoval, R., & Hovy, E. (2010). Government 2.0: Making connections between citizens, data and government. *Information Polity, 15*(1/2), 1–9.

Clark, M. E. (1995). Changes in Euro-American values needed for sustainability. *Journal of Social Issues, 51*(4), 63–82.

Cleveland, H. (1985). The twilight of hierarchy: Speculations on the global information society. *Public Administration Review, 45*(1), 185–195.

Cleveland, H. (2000). The future is uncentralized. *Public Administration Review, 60*(4), 293–297.

Cohen, A. R., & Bradford, D. L. (1989). Influence without authority: The use of alliances, reciprocity, and exchange to accomplish work. *Organizational Dynamics, 17*(3), 4–17.

Cohen, S., & Brand, R. (1993). *Total quality management in government: A practical guide for the real world.* San Francisco, CA: Jossey-Bass.

Cohen, S. G. (1993). New approaches to teams and teamwork. In J. R. Galbraith, E. E. Lawler III, & Associates (Eds.), *Organizing for the future: The new logic for managing complex organizations* (pp. 194–226). San Francisco, CA: Jossey-Bass.

Cohen, S. G., Ledford, G. E., Jr., & Spreitzer, G. M. (1996). A predictive model of self-managing work team effectiveness. *Human Relations, 49*(5), 643–676.

Collins, D. (1997). The ethical superiority and inevitability of participatory management as an organizational system. *Organization Science, 8*(5), 489–507.

Collins, J. C., & Porras, J. I. (1994). *Built to last: Successful habits of visionary companies.* New York, NY: HarperCollins.

Comfort, L. K. (1994). Self-organization in complex systems. *Journal of Public Administration Research and Theory, 4*(3), 393–410.

Conger, J. A., & Associates (Eds.). (1994). *Spirit at work: Discovering the spirituality in leadership.* San Francisco, CA: Jossey-Bass.

Cook, W. J., Jr. (2000). *The evolving corporation: A humanist interpretation.* Westport, CT: Quorum Books.

Cotton, J. L. (1993). *Employee involvement: Methods for improving performance and work attitudes.* Newbury Park, CA: SAGE.

Culbert, S. A., & McDonough, J. J. (1985). How reality gets constructed in an organization. In R. Tannenbaum, N. Margulies, F. Massarik, & Associates (Eds.), *Human systems development* (pp. 122–142). San Francisco, CA: Jossey-Bass.

Cummings, S., & Daellenbach, U. (2009). A guide to the future of strategy? The history of long range planning. *Long Range Planning, 42*(2), 234–263.

Cummings, T., & Srivastva, S. (1977). *Management of work: A sociotechnical systems approach.* San Diego, CA: Pfeiffer & Company.

Dachler, H. P., & Wilpert, B. (1978). Conceptual dimensions and boundaries of participation in organizations. *Administrative Science Quarterly, 23*(1), 1–39.

Dalio, R. (2017). *Principles: Life and work.* New York, NY: Simon & Schuster.

Daly, H. E., & Cobb, J. B., Jr. (1994). *For the common good: Redirecting the economy toward community, the environment, and a sustainable future* (2nd ed.). Boston, MA: Beacon Press.

Daly, H. E., & Farley, J. (2004). *Ecological economics: Principles and applications.* Washington, DC: Island Press.

Das, T. K., & Teng, B. (1997). Sustaining strategic alliances: Options and guidelines. *Journal of General Management, 22*(4), 49–64.

Davidow, W. H., & Malone, M. S. (1993). *The virtual corporation: Structuring and revitalizing the corporation for the 21st century.* New York, NY: HarperBusiness.

Davis, L. E. (1977). Enhancing the quality of working life: Developments in the United States. *International Labour Review, 116*(1), 53–65.

de Geus, A. (1997). *The living company.* Boston, MA: Harvard Business School Press.

de Quincey, C. (2002). *Radical nature: Rediscovering the soul of matter.* Montpelier, VT: Invisible Cities Press.

Deal, T., & Kennedy, A. (1982). *Corporate cultures: The rites and rituals of corporate life.* Reading, MA: Addison-Wesley.

Deming, W. E. (1986). *Out of the crisis.* Cambridge, MA: Massachusetts Institute of Technology, Center for Advanced Engineering Study.

Denhardt, R. B. (1984). *Theories of public organization.* Belmont, CA: Brooks/Cole.

Denning, S. (2018). *The age of agile: How smart companies are transforming the way work gets done.* New York, NY: AMACOM.

Diamandis, P. H., & Kotler, S. (2012). *Abundance: The future is better than you think.* New York, NY: Free Press.

Diamandis, P. H., & Kotler, S. (2020). *The future is faster than you think: How converging technologies are transforming business, industries, and our lives.* New York, NY: Simon & Schuster.

Donaldson, T., & Preston, L. E. (1995). The stakeholder theory of the corporation: Concepts, evidence, and implications. *Academy of Management Review, 20*(1), 65–91.

Drucker, P. F. (1988). The coming of the new organization. *Harvard Business Review, 66*(1), 45–53.

Drucker, P. F. (1994). *The post-capitalist society.* New York, NY: HarperBusiness.

Druskat, V. U., & Wolff, S. B. (2001). Building the emotional intelligence of groups. *Harvard Business Review, 79*(3), 80–91.

Dyer, W. G. (1977). *Team building: Issues and alternatives.* Reading, MA: Addison-Wesley.

Eccles, R. G., Perkins, K. M., & Serafeim, G. (2012). How to become a sustainable company. *Sloan Management Review, 53*(4), 43.

Eggers, W. D. (2004). *Government 2.0: Using technology to improve education, cut red tape, reduce gridlock, and enhance democracy.* Lanham, MD: Rowman & Littlefield.

Egri, C. P., & Frost, P. J. (1991). Shamanism and change: Bringing back the magic in organizational transformation. In R. W. Woodman & W. A. Pasmore (Eds.), *Research in organizational change and development* (Vol. 5; pp. 175–221). Greenwich, CT: JAI Press.

Eisler, R. (2007). *The real wealth of nations: Creating a caring economics.* Oakland, CA: Berrett-Koehler.

Elden, M. (1985). Democratizing organizations: A challenge to organization development. In R. Tannenbaum, N. Margulies, F. Massarik, & Associates (Eds.), *Human systems development* (pp. 198–223). San Francisco, CA: Jossey-Bass.

Elgin, D. (1993). *Awakening earth: Exploring the evolution of human culture and consciousness.* New York, NY: Morrow.

Elgin, D., & LeDrew, C. (1997). *Global consciousness change: Indicators of an emerging paradigm.* Sausalito, CA: Institute of Noetic Sciences.

Elkington, J. (1997). *Cannibals with forks: The triple bottom line of 21st century business.* North Mankato, MN: Capstone.

Emerson, K., Nabatchi, T., & Balogh, S. (2012). An integrative framework for collaborative governance. *Journal of Public Administration Research and Theory, 22*(1), 1–29.

Emery, F. E., & Trist, E. L. (1965). The causal texture of organizational environments. *Human Relations, 18*(1), 21–32.

Epstein, M. J. (1996). Improving environmental management with full environmental cost accounting. *Environmental Quality Management, 6*(1), 11–22.

Epstein, M. J. (2008). *Making sustainability work: Best practices in managing and measuring corporate social, environmental, and economic impacts.* San Francisco, CA: Berrett-Koehler.

Evered, R. D., & Selman, J. C. (1989). Coaching and the art of management. *Organizational Dynamics, 18*(2), 16–32.

Fairholm, G. W. (1997). *Capturing the heart of leadership: Spirituality and community in the new American workplace.* Westport, CT: Quorum Books.

Fayol, H. (1949). *General and industrial management.* London, England: Pitman.

Ferlie, E., Ashburner, L., Fitzgerald, L., & Pettigrew, A. (1996). *The new public management in action.* Oxford, England: Oxford University Press.

Folger, R., & Konovsky, M. A. (1989). Effects of procedural and distributive justice on reactions to pay raise decisions. *Academy of Management Journal, 32*(1), 115–130.

Fradette, M., & Michaud, S. (1998). *The power of corporate kinetics: Create the self-adapting, self-renewing, instant-action enterprise.* New York, NY: Free Press.

Freeman, R. E. (1984). *Strategic management: A stakeholder approach.* Boston, MA: Pitman.

Freer, A., & Robertson, P. J. (2020). Organizational spiritual maturity: A goal of positive leaders and direction for change. In S. K. Dhiman & J. Marques (Eds.), *New horizons in positive leadership and change* (pp. 103-126). New York, NY: Springer.

Frenay, R. (2006). *Pulse: The coming age of systems and machines inspired by living things.* New York, NY: Farrar, Straus and Giroux.

French, W. L., & Bell, C. H., Jr. (1973). *Organization development: Behavioral science interventions for organization improvement.* Englewood Cliffs, NJ: Prentice-Hall.

Freudenthal, G. (1986). *Atom and individual in the age of Newton: On the genesis of the mechanistic worldview.* Dordrecht, Netherlands: D. Reidel.

Friedlander, F., & Brown, L. D. (1974). Organization development. *Annual Review of Psychology, 25,* 313–341.

Friedman, T. L. (2005). *The world is flat.* New York, NY: Farrar, Straus and Giroux.

Fry, L. W. (2003). Toward a theory of spiritual leadership. *Leadership Quarterly, 14*(6), 693–727.

Fulmer, E. (2000). *Shaping the adaptive organization: Landscapes, learning, and leadership in volatile times.* New York, NY: AMACOM.

Furrer, O., Thomas, H., & Goussevskaia, A. (2008). The structure and evolution of the strategic management field: A content analysis of 26 years of strategic management research. *International Journal of Management Reviews, 10*(1), 1–23.

Galbraith, J. R. (1994). *Competing with flexible lateral organizations.* Reading, MA: Addison-Wesley.

Gansky, L. (2010). *The mesh: Why the future of business is sharing.* London, England: Penguin.

Gersick, C. J. G. (1991). Revolutionary change theories: A multilevel exploration of the punctuated equilibrium model. *Academy of Management Review, 16*(1), 10–36.

Giacalone, R. A., & Jurkiewicz, C. L. (Editors). (2002.) *Handbook of workplace spirituality and organizational performance.* Armonk, NY: M. E. Sharpe.

Gibson, P. (1982). *Quality circles: An approach to productivity improvement.* New York, NY: Pergamon Press.

Gladwin, T. N., Kennelly, J. J., & Krause, T.-S. (1995). Shifting paradigms for sustainable development: Implications for management theory and research. *Academy of Management Review, 20*(4), 874–907.

Gleick, J. (1987). *Chaos: Making a new science.* New York, NY: Viking.

Goldsmith, S., & Eggers, W. D. (2004). *Governing by network: The new shape of the public sector.* Washington, DC: Brookings Institution Press.

Goldsmith, S., & Kleiman, N. (2017). *A new city O/S: The power of open, collaborative, and distributed governance.* Washington, DC: Brookings Institution Press.

Goleman, D. (1995). *Emotional intelligence.* New York, NY: Bantam Books.

Gore, A. (1993). *From red tape to results: Creating a government that works better & costs less: Report of the national performance review.* Washington, DC: Office of the Vice President, U.S. Government Printing Office.

Gould, S. J. (2002). *The structure of evolutionary theory.* Cambridge, MA: Belknap Press of Harvard University Press.

Gouldner, A. (1960). The norm of reciprocity: A preliminary statement. *American Sociological Review, 25*(2), 161–178.

Graham, J. W. (1991). An essay on organizational citizenship behavior. *Employee Responsibilities and Rights Journal, 4*(4), 249–270.

Grant, A. M. (2014). *Give and take: Why helping others drives our success.* London, England: Penguin.

Gray, B. (1997). *Collaborating: Finding common ground for multiparty problems.* San Francisco, CA: Jossey-Bass.

Greenleaf, R. K. (1977). *Servant leadership: A journey into the nature of legitimate power and greatness.* New York, NY: Paulist Press.

Gregerson, H., & Sailer, L. (1993). Chaos theory and its implications for social science research. *Human Relations, 46*(7), 777–803.

Grossman, L. K. (1995). *The electronic republic: Reshaping democracy in the information age.* New York, NY: Viking.

Guastello, S. J. (1995). *Chaos, catastrophe, and human affairs: Applications of nonlinear dynamics to work, organizations, and social evolution.* Mahwah, NJ: Erlbaum.

Gulick, L., & Urwick, L. (Eds.). (1937). *Papers on the science of administration.* New York, NY: Institute of Public Administration, Columbia University.

Hackman, J. R., Oldham, G., Janson, R., & Purdy, K. (1975). A new strategy for job enrichment. *California Management Review, 17*(4), 57–71.

Haigh, N., & Hoffman, A. (2012). Hybrid organizations: The next chapter in sustainable business. *Organizational Dynamics, 41*(2), 126–134.

Halal, W. E. (1996). *The new management: Democracy and enterprise are transforming organizations.* San Francisco, CA: Berrett-Koehler.

Halal, W. E. (1998). *The infinite resource: Creating and leading the knowledge enterprise.* San Francisco, CA: Jossey-Bass.

Hamel, G. (2011). First, let's fire all the managers. *Harvard Business Review, 89*(12), 48–60.

Hammer, M., & Champy, J. (1993). *Reengineering the corporation: A manifesto for business revolution.* New York, NY: HarperBusiness.

Handy, C. (1994). *The age of paradox.* Boston, MA: Harvard Business School Press.

Hansen, J. L., & Christensen, P. A. (1995). *Invisible patterns: Ecology and wisdom in business and profit.* Westport, CT: Quorum Books.

Harder, J. W., & Robertson, P. J. (2007). Leading a living organization. *Human Factor,* Nov. 2006–Feb. 2007, 18–23.

Harder, J. W., Robertson, P. J., & Woodward, H. (2004). The spirit of the new workplace: Breathing life into organizations. *Organizational Development Journal, 22*(2), 79–103.

Harman, W. W. (1998). *Global mind change: The promise of the 21st century* (2nd ed.). San Francisco, CA: Berrett-Koehler.

Harris, L. C., & Crane, A. (2002). The greening of organizational culture: Management views on the depth, degree and diffusion of change. *Journal of Organizational Change Management, 15*(3), 214–234.

Harrison, T. M., Pardo, T. A., & Cook, M. (2012). Creating open government ecosystems: A research and development agenda. *Future Internet, 4*(4), 900–928.

Hartmann, T. (1998). *The last hours of ancient sunlight: Waking up to personal & global transformation.* New York, NY: Harmony Books.

Haskel, J., & Westlake, S. (2018). *Capitalism without capital: The rise of the intangible economy.* Princeton, NJ: Princeton University Press.

Hatch, M. J. (1993). The dynamics of organizational culture. *Academy of Management Review, 18*(4), 657–693.

Hawken, P. (2007). *Blessed unrest: How the largest movement in the world came into being and why no one saw it coming.* New York, NY: Penguin.

Hawken, P., Lovins, A., & Lovins, L. H. (1999). *Natural capitalism: Creating the next industrial revolution.* Boston, MA: Little, Brown.

Hawley, J. (1993). *Reawakening the spirit in work: The power of dharmic management.* San Francisco, CA: Berrett-Koehler.

Healey, P. (2006). *Collaborative planning: Shaping places in fragmented societies* (2nd ed.). Basingstoke, England: Palgrave Macmillan.

Henderson, H. (1996). *Building a win-win world: Life beyond global economic warfare.* San Francisco, CA: Berrett-Koehler.

Henderson, H. (2006). *Ethical markets: Growing the green economy.* White River Junction, VT: Chelsea Green.

Herzberg, F. (1966). *Work and the nature of man.* Cleveland, OH: World.

Hock, D. (1999). *Birth of the chaordic age.* San Francisco, CA: Berrett-Koehler.

Holbeche, L. (2015). *The agile organization: How to build an innovative, sustainable and resilient business.* London, England: Kogan Page.

Holland, L. (2003). Can the principle of the ecological footprint be applied to measure the environmental sustainability of business? *Corporate Social Responsibility and Environmental Management, 10*(4), 224–232.

Hood, C. (1991). A public management for all seasons? *Public Administration, 69*(1), 3–19.

Hopwood, A., Unerman, J., & Fries, J. (Eds). (2010). *Accounting for sustainability: Practical insights.* London, England: Earthscan.

Horibe, F. (1999). *Managing knowledge workers: New skills and attitudes to unlock the intellectual capital in your organization.* New York, NY: Wiley.

Houghton, J. D., Neck, C. P., & Krishnakumar, S. (2016). The what, why, and how of spirituality in the workplace revisited: A 14-year update and extension. *Journal of Management, Spirituality & Religion, 13*(3), 177–205.

Howard, S. (2002). A spiritual perspective on learning in the workplace. *Journal of Managerial Psychology, 17*(3), 230–242.

Hubbard, B. M. (1998). *Conscious evolution: Awakening the power of our social potential.* Novato, CA: New World Library.

Huber, G. P. (1991). Organizational learning: The contributing processes and literatures. *Organization Science, 2*(1), 88–115.

Iansiti, M., & Levien, R. (2004). Strategy as ecology. *Harvard Business Review, 82*(3), 68–78.

Imperial, M. T. (2005). Using collaboration as a governance strategy: Lessons from six watershed management programs. *Administration & Society, 37*(3), 281–320.

Ingraham, P. W., Thompson, J. R., & Sanders, R. P. (Editors). (1998). *Transforming government: Lessons from the reinvention laboratories.* San Francisco, CA: Jossey-Bass.

Innes, J. E., & Booher, D. E. (2003). Collaborative policymaking: governance through dialogue. In M. A. Hajer & H. Wagenaar (Eds.), *Deliberative policy analysis: Understanding governance in the network society* (pp. 3–59). Cambridge, England: Cambridge University Press.

Isaacs, W. (1999). *Dialogue and the art of thinking together: A pioneering approach to communicating in business and in life.* New York, NY: Doubleday.

Isaak, R. (1999). *Green logic: Ecopreneurship, theory and ethics.* West Hartford, CT: Kumarian Press.

Itami, H. (1987). *Mobilizing invisible assets.* Cambridge, MA: Harvard University Press.

Jablonski, J. R. (1992). *Implementing TQM: Competing in the nineties through total quality management.* San Diego, CA: Pfeiffer & Company.

Janov, J. (1994). *The inventive organization: Hope and daring at work.* San Francisco, CA: Jossey-Bass.

Janssen, M., & Estevez, E. (2013). Lean government and platform-based governance—Doing more with less. *Government Information Quarterly, 30*(s1), S1–S8.

Jantsch, E. (1980). *The self-organizing universe.* New York, NY: George Braziller.

Jones, V. (2008). *The green collar economy: How one solution can fix our two biggest problems.* New York, NY: HarperCollins.

Kamensky, J. M. (1996). Role of the "reinventing government" movement in federal management reform. *Public Administration Review, 56*(3), 247–255.

Kanter, R. M. (2012). Enriching the ecosystem. *Harvard Business Review, 90*(3), 140–147.

Kantur, D., & İşeri-Say, A. (2012). Organizational resilience: A conceptual integrative framework. *Journal of Management & Organization, 18*(6), 762–773.

Kaplan, R. S., & D. P. Norton. (1996). *The balanced scorecard: Translating strategy into action.* Boston, MA: Harvard Business School Press.

Kates, R. W., Parris, T. M., & Leiserowitz, A. A. (2005). What is sustainable development? Goals, indicators, values, and practice. *Environment, 47*(3), 8–21.

Katz, D., & Kahn, R. L. (1966). *The social psychology of organizations.* New York, NY: Wiley.

Kauffman, S. (1995). *At home in the universe: The search for laws of self-organization and complexity.* New York, NY: Oxford University Press.

Keeley, M. (1984). Impartiality and participant-interest theories of organizational effectiveness. *Administrative Science Quarterly, 29*(1), 1–25.

Kelly, K. (1998). *New rules for the new economy: 10 radical strategies for a connected world.* New York, NY: Viking.

Kickert, W. J. M., Klijn, E.-H. , & Koppenjan, J. F. M. (1997). *Managing complex networks: Strategies for the public sector.* Thousand Oaks, CA: SAGE.

Koehler, J. W., & Pankowski, J. M. (1996). *Teams in government: A handbook for team-based organizations.* Delray Beach, FL: St. Lucie.

Koestler, A. (1967). *The ghost in the machine.* London, England: Hutchinson.

Kolodinsky, R. W., Giacalone, R. A., & Jurkiewicz, C. L. (2008). Workplace values and outcomes: Exploring personal, organizational, and interactive workplace spirituality. *Journal of Business Ethics, 81*(2), 465–480.

Korsgaard, M. A., Schweiger, D. M., & Sapienza, H. J. (1995). Building commitment, attachment, and trust in strategic decision-making teams: The role of procedural justice. *Academy of Management Journal, 38*(1), 60–84.

Korten, D. C. (1999). *The post-corporate world: Life after capitalism.* San Francisco, CA: Berrett-Koehler.

Korten, D. C. (2007). *The great turning: From empire to earth community.* San Francisco, CA: Berrett-Koehler.

Korten, D. C. (2015). *Change the story, change the future: A living economy for a living earth.* Oakland, CA: Berrett-Koehler.

Kramer, M. R., & Pfitzer, M. W. (2016). The ecosystem of shared value. *Harvard Business Review, 94*(10), 80–89.

Krishnan, R., Harris, J. M., & Goodwin, N. R. (Eds.). (1995). *A survey of ecological economics.* Washington, DC: Island Press.

Laloux, F. (2014). *Reinventing organizations: A guide to creating organizations inspired by the next stage in human consciousness.* Brussels, Belgium: Nelson Parker.

Lane, J.-E. (2000). *New public management.* London, England: Routledge.

Lanier, J. (2013). *Who owns the future?* New York, NY: Simon & Schuster.

Laszlo, E. (2001). *Macroshift: Navigating the transformation to a sustainable world.* San Francisco, CA: Berrett-Koehler.

Laszlo, E. (2003). *The connectivity hypothesis: Foundations of an integral science of quantum, cosmos, life, and consciousness.* Albany: State University of New York Press.

Lathrop, D., & Ruma, L. (Eds.). (2010). *Open government: Collaboration, transparency and participation in practice.* Sebastopol, CA: O'Reilly Media.

Lavine, M. (2014). Paradoxical leadership and the competing values framework. *Journal of Applied Behavioral Science, 50*(2), 189–205.

Lawler, E. E., III. (1992). *The ultimate advantage: Creating the high-involvement organization.* San Francisco, CA: Jossey-Bass.

Lawler, E. E., III. (1997). *From the ground up: Six principles for building the new logic corporation.* San Francisco, CA: Jossey-Bass.

Lawless, M. W., & Moore, R. A. (1989). Interorganizational systems in public service delivery: A new application of the dynamic network framework. *Human Relations, 42*(12), 1167–1184.

Lawrence, P. R., & Lorsch, J. W. (1967). *Organization and environment.* Boston, MA: Division of Research, Harvard Business School.

Lawton, K., & Maron, D. (2013). *The crowdfunding revolution: How to raise venture capital using social media.* New York, NY: McGraw-Hill.

Leach, W. D. (2006). Collaborative public management and democracy: Evidence from western watershed partnerships. *Public Administration Review, 66*(s1), 100–110.

LeMay, M. (2018). *Agile for everybody: Creating fast, flexible, and customer-first organizations.* Sebastopol, CA: O'Reilly Media.

Lemkow, A. F. (1990). *The wholeness principle: Dynamics of unity within science, religion, & society.* Wheaton, IL: Theosophical.

Lengnick-Hall, C. A., Beck, T. E., & Lengnick-Hall, M. L. (2011). Developing a capacity for organizational resilience through strategic human resource management. *Human Resource Management Review, 21*(3), 243–255.

Lepsinger, R., & Lucia, A. D. (1997). *The art and science of 360-degree feedback.* San Francisco, CA: Jossey-Bass.

Lerner, M. (1996). *The politics of meaning: Restoring hope and possibility in an age of cynicism.* Boston, MA: Addison-Wesley.

Levitt, B., & March, J. G. (1988). Organizational learning. *Annual Review of Sociology, 14*, 319–340.

Lewandowski, M. (2016). Designing the business models for circular economy—Towards the conceptual framework. *Sustainability, 8*(1), 43–71.

Lewin, R. (1992). *Complexity: Life at the edge of chaos.* New York, NY: Macmillan.

Lewis, J. D. (1995). *The connected corporation: How leading companies win through customer-supplier alliances.* New York, NY: Free Press.

Lewis, S. L., & Maslin, M. A. (2015). Defining the anthropocene. *Nature, 519*(7542), 171–180.

Lietaer, B., & Dunne, J. (2013). *Rethinking money: How new currencies turn scarcity into prosperity.* San Francisco, CA: Berrett-Koehler.

Limerick, D., & Cunnington, B. (1997). *Managing the new organization: A blueprint for networks and strategic alliances.* San Francisco, CA: Jossey-Bass.

Linden, R. (1994). *Seamless government: A practical guide to re-engineering in the public sector.* San Francisco, CA: Jossey-Bass.

Linders, D. (2012). From e-government to we-government: Defining a typology for citizen coproduction in the age of social media. *Government Information Quarterly, 29*(4), 446–454.

Lipnack, J., & Stamps, J. (1994). *The age of the network: Organizing principles for the 21st century.* Essex Junction, VT: Oliver Wight.

Lipton, B. H. (2005). *The biology of belief: Unleashing the power of consciousness, matter and miracles.* Santa Rosa, CA: Mountain of Love/Elite Books.

Liu, H. K. (2017). Crowdsourcing government: Lessons from multiple disciplines. *Public Administration Review, 77*(5), 656–667.

Louis, M. R. (1983). Organizations as culture-bearing milieux. In L. R. Pondy, P. J. Frost, G. Morgan, & T. C. Dandridge (Eds.), *Organizational symbolism* (pp. 39–54). Greenwich, CT: JAI Press.

Lovelock, J. (1988). *The ages of Gaia: A biography of our living earth.* New York, NY: Norton.

Lynn, L. E., Jr. (1998). The new public management: How to translate a theme into a legacy. *Public Administration Review, 58*(3), 231–237.

Mackey, J., & Sisodia, R. (2013). *Conscious capitalism: Liberating the heroic spirit of business.* Boston, MA: Harvard Business School.

Mandell, M. P. (1999). Community collaborations: Working through network structures. *Policy Studies Review, 16*(1), 42–64.

Mander, J., & Goldsmith, E. (Eds.). (1996). *The case against the global economy: And for a turn toward the local.* San Francisco, CA: Sierra Club Books.

Manz, C. C., & H. P. Sims, Jr. (1993). *Business without bosses: How self-managing teams are building high-performing companies.* New York, NY: Wiley.

March, J. G., & Simon, H. A. (1958). *Organizations.* New York, NY: John Wiley & Sons.

Marcic, D. (1997). *Managing with the wisdom of love: Uncovering virtue in people and organizations.* San Francisco, CA: Jossey-Bass.

Margerum, R. D. (2002). Collaborative planning: Building consensus and building a distinct model for practice. *Journal of Planning Education and Research, 21*(3), 237–253.

Marion, R. (1999). *The edge of organization: Chaos and complexity theories of formal social systems.* Thousand Oaks, CA: SAGE.

Marques, J., Dhiman, S., & King, R. (2007). *Spirituality in the workplace: What it is, why it matters, how to make it work for you.* Fawnskin, CA: Personhood Press.

Mars, M. M., Bronstein, J. L., & Lusch, R. F. (2012). The value of a metaphor: Organizations and ecosystems. *Organizational Dynamics, 41*(4), 271–280.

Martin, R. (2009). *The design of business: Why design thinking is the next competitive advantage.* Boston, MA: Harvard Business School.

Maslow, A. (1954). *Motivation and personality.* New York, NY: Harper & Row.

Maturana, H. R., & Varela, F. G. (1980). *Autopoiesis and cognition: The realization of the living.* Boston, MA: D. Reidel.

Maynard, H. B., Jr., & Mehrtens, S. E. (1993). *The fourth wave: Business in the 21st century.* San Francisco, CA: Berrett-Koehler.

McDonough, W., & Braungart, M. (2010). *Cradle to cradle: Remaking the way we make things.* New York, NY: North Point Press.

McGaa, E. (2004). *Nature's way: Native wisdom for living in balance with the earth.* San Francisco, CA: Harper.

McGregor, D. (1960). *The human side of enterprise.* New York, NY: McGraw-Hill.

McGuire, M. (2006). Collaborative public management: Assessing what we know and how we know it. *Public Administration Review, 66*(s1), 33–43.

McInerney, F., & White, S. (1995). *The total quality corporation: How 10 major companies added to profits and cleaned up the environment in the 1990s.* New York, NY: Truman Talley Books/Dutton.

McKibben, B. (2007). *Deep economy: The wealth of communities and the durable future.* New York, NY: Henry Holt and Company.

McKnight, J., & Block, P. (2010). *The abundant community: Awakening the power of families and neighborhoods.* San Francisco, CA: Berrett-Koehler.

McLagan, P., & Nel, C. (1997). *The age of participation: New governance for the workplace and the world.* San Francisco, CA: Berrett-Koehler.

McLaughlin, C., & Davidson, G. (1994). *Spiritual politics: Changing the world from the inside out.* New York, NY: Ballantine Books.

McTaggart, L. (2002). *The field: The quest for the secret force of the universe.* New York, NY: HarperCollins.

McWaters, B. (1982). *Conscious evolution: Personal and planetary transformation.* San Francisco, CA: Evolutionary Press.

Meadows, D. H., Meadows, D. L., Randers, J., & Behrens, W.W., III. (1972). *The limits to growth: A report for the Club of Rome's Project on the Predicament of Mankind.* New York, NY: Universe Books.

Meeker-Lowry, S. (1988). *Economics as if the earth really mattered.* Philadelphia, PA: New Society.

Melé, D. (2005). Exploring the principle of subsidiarity in organisational forms. *Journal of Business Ethics, 60*(3), 293–305.

Mergel, I., & Desouza, K. C. (2013). Implementing open innovation in the public sector: The case of Challenge.gov. *Public Administration Review, 73*(6), 882–890.

Mergel, I., Gong, Y., & Bertot, J. (2018). Agile government: Systematic literature review and future research. *Government Information Quarterly, 35*(2), 291–298.

Mergel, I., Rethemeyer, R. K., & Isett, K. (2016). Big data in public affairs. *Public Administration Review, 76*(6), 928–937.

Merry, U. (1995). *Coping with uncertainty: Insights from the new sciences of chaos, self-organization, and complexity.* Westport, CT: Praeger.

Metzner, R. (1999). *Green psychology: Transforming our relationship to the earth.* Rochester, VT: Park Street Press.

Miles, R. E., Snow, C. C., Mathews, J. A., Miles, G., & Coleman, H. J., Jr. (1997). Organizing in the knowledge age: Anticipating the cellular form. *Academy of Management Executive, 11*(4), 7–24.

Miller, K. I., & Monge, P. R. (1986). Participation, satisfaction, and productivity: A meta-analytic review. *Academy of Management Journal, 29*(4), 727–753.

Milliman, J., Ferguson, J., Trickett, D., & Condemi, B. (1999). Spirit and community at Southwest Airlines: An investigation of a spiritual values-based model. *Journal of Organizational Change Management, 12*(3), 221–233.

Milward, H. B., & Provan, K. G. (2006). *A manager's guide to choosing and using collaborative networks.* Washington, DC: IBM Center for the Business of Government.

Mitchell, R. K., Agle, B. R., & Wood, D. J. (1997). Toward a theory of stakeholder identification and salience: Defining the principle of who and what really counts. *Academy of Management Review, 22*(4), 853–886.

Mitroff, I. I., & Denton, E. A. (1999). *A spiritual audit of corporate America: A hard look at spirituality, religion, and values in the workplace.* San Francisco, CA: Jossey-Bass.

Mohrman, S. A., Cohen, S. G., & Mohrman, A. M., Jr. (1995). *Designing team-based organizations: New forms for knowledge work.* San Francisco, CA: Jossey-Bass.

Mohrman, S. A., & Cummings, T. G. (1989). *The self-designing organization.* Reading, MA: Addison-Wesley.

Moon, M. J., & deLeon, P. (2001). Municipal reinvention: Managerial values and diffusion among municipalities. *Journal of Public Administration Research and Theory, 11*(3), 327–351.

Moore, J. F. (1996). *The death of competition: Leadership and strategy in the age of business ecosystems.* New York, NY: HarperBusiness.

Moorman, R. H. (1991). Relationship between organizational justice and organizational citizenship behaviors: Do fairness perceptions influence employee citizenship? *Journal of Applied Psychology, 76*(6), 845–855.

Morowitz, H. J. (2002). *The emergence of everything: How the world became complex.* Oxford, England: Oxford University Press.

Mulcahy, D. (2017). *The gig economy: The complete guide to getting better work, taking more time off, and financing the life you want!* New York, NY: AMACOM.

Murray, A., Skene, K., & Haynes, K. (2017). The circular economy: An interdisciplinary exploration of the concept and application in a global context. *Journal of Business Ethics, 140*(3), 369–380.

Nadeau, R., & Kafatos, M. (1999). *The non-local universe: The new physics and matters of the mind.* New York, NY: Oxford University Press.

Naess, A. (1973). The shallow and the deep, long-range ecology movement. A summary. *Inquiry, 16*(1/4), 95–100.

Nahapiet, J., & Ghoshal, S. (1998). Social capital, intellectual capital, and the organizational advantage. *Academy of Management Review, 23*(2), 242–266.

Nam, T. (2012). Suggesting frameworks of citizen-sourcing via Government 2.0. *Government Information Quarterly, 29*(1), 12–20.

Newton, R. G. (2009). *From clockwork to crapshoot: A history of physics.* Cambridge, MA: Harvard University Press.

Nirenberg, J. (1993). *The living organization: Transforming teams into workplace communities.* Burr Ridge, IL: Irwin Professional.

Nonaka, I. (1994). A dynamic theory of organizational knowledge creation. *Organization Science, 5*(1), 14–37.

Nutt, P. C. (1984). Types of organizational decision processes. *Administrative Science Quarterly, 29*(3), 414–450.

Oliver, C. (1990). Determinants of interorganizational relationships: Integration and future directions. *Academy of Management Review, 15*(2), 241–265.

Olson, R. L. (1995). Sustainability as a social vision. *Journal of Social Issues, 51*(4), 15–35.

Organ, D. W. (1988). *Organizational citizenship behavior: The good soldier syndrome.* Lexington, MA: Lexington Books.

O'Reilly, T. (2010). Government as a platform. In D. Lathrop & L. Ruma (Eds.), *Open government: Collaboration, transparency, and participation in practice* (pp. 11–39). Cambridge, MA: O'Reilly Media.

Orlitzky, M., Schmidt, F. L., & Rynes, S. L. (2003). Corporate social and financial performance: A meta-analysis. *Organization Studies, 24*(3), 403–441.

Orth, C. D., Wilkinson, H. E., & Benfari, R. C. (1987). The manager's role as coach and mentor. *Organizational Dynamics, 15*(4), 66–74.

Osborne, D., & Gaebler, T. (1992). *Reinventing government: How the entrepreneurial spirit is transforming the public sector.* Reading, MA: Addison-Wesley.

O'Sullivan, E., & Taylor, M. M. (Eds.). (2004). *Learning toward an ecological consciousness: Selected transformative practices.* New York, NY: Palgrave Macmillan.

Ouchi, W. G. (1981). *Theory Z: How American business can meet the Japanese challenge.* Reading, MA: Addison-Wesley.

Overman, E. S. (1996). The new science of management: Chaos and quantum theory and method. *Journal of Public Administration Research and Theory, 6*(1), 75–89.

Owen, H. (1987). *Spirit: Transformation and development in organizations.* Potomac, MD: Abbott.

Page, S. (2003). Entrepreneurial strategies for managing interagency collaboration. *Journal of Public Administration Research and Theory, 13*(3), 311–339.

Parker, B. R. (1996). *Chaos in the cosmos: The stunning complexity of the universe.* New York, NY: Plenum Press.

Pascale, R. T. (1999). Surfing the edge of chaos. *Sloan Management Review, 40*(3), 83–94.

Pascale, R. T., & Athos, A. G. (1981). *The art of Japanese management.* New York, NY: Simon & Schuster.

Pasternack, B., & Viscio, A. (1998). *The centerless corporation: A new model for transforming your organization for growth and prosperity.* New York, NY: Simon & Schuster.

Pavlovich, K., & Corner, P. D. (2014). Conscious enterprise emergence: Shared value creation through expanded conscious awareness. *Journal of Business Ethics, 121*(3), 341–351.

Peltoniemi, M. (2006). Preliminary theoretical framework for the study of business ecosystems. *Emergence: Complexity and Organization, 8*(1), 10–19.

Peters, T. (1987). *Thriving on chaos: Handbook for a management revolution.* New York, NY: Knopf.

Peters, T. J., & Waterman, R. H., Jr. (1982). *In search of excellence: Lessons from America's best run companies.* New York, NY: Harper & Row.

Pettigrew, A., Thomas, H., & Whittington, R. (2002). Strategic management: The strengths and limitations of a field. In A. Pettigrew, H. Thomas, & R. Whittington (Eds.), *Handbook of strategy and management* (pp. 3–30). London, England: SAGE.

Pink, D. H. (2009). *Drive: The surprising truth about what motivates us.* New York, NY: Riverhead Books.

Pfeffer, J. (1980). Management as symbolic action: The creation and maintenance of organizational paradigms. In L. L. Cummings & B. M. Staw (Eds.), *Research in organizational behavior,* Vol. 3 (pp. 1–52). Greenwich, CT: JAI Press.

Pfeffer, J. (1998). *The human equation: Building profits by putting people first.* Boston, MA: Harvard Business School Press.

Pfeffer, J., & Salancik, G. R. (1978). *The external control of organizations: A resource dependence perspective.* New York, NY: Harper & Row.

Pinchot, G., & Pinchot, E. (1994). *The end of bureaucracy & the rise of the intelligent organization.* San Francisco, CA: Berrett-Koehler.

Pondy, L. R., & Mitroff, I. I. (1979). Beyond open system models of organization. *Research in organizational behavior* (Vol. 1; pp. 3–39). Greenwich, CT: JAI Press.

Porter, M. E. (1980). *Competitive strategies: Techniques for analyzing industries and competitors.* New York, NY: Free Press.

Porter, M. E., & Kramer, M. R. (2019). Creating shared value. *Harvard Business Review, 89*(1/2), 62–77.

Powell, W. W. (1990). Neither market nor hierarchy: Network forms of organization. In B. M. Staw & L. L. Cummings (Eds.), *Research in organizational behavior* (Vol. 12; pp. 295–336). Greenwich, CT: JAI Press.

Prigogine, I., & Stengers, I. (1984). *Order out of chaos: Man's new dialogue with nature.* New York, NY: Bantam Books.

Provan, K. G., & Kenis, P. (2008). Modes of network governance: Structure, management, and effectiveness. *Journal of Public Administration Research and Theory, 18*(2), 229–252.

Provan, K. G., & Milward, H. B. (2001). Do networks really work? A framework for evaluating public-sector organizational networks. *Public Administration Review 61*(4), 414–423.

Purser, R. E., & Cabana, S. (1998). *The self-managing organization: Transforming the work of teams for real impact.* New York, NY: Free Press.

Quinn, R. E. (1988). *Beyond rational management: Mastering the paradoxes and competing demands of high performance.* San Francisco, CA: Jossey-Bass.

Quinn, R. E., & Spreitzer, G. M. (1997). The road to empowerment: Seven questions every leader should consider. *Organizational Dynamics, 26*(2), 37–49.

Ray, P. H., & Anderson, S. R. (2000). *The cultural creatives: How 50 million people are changing the world.* New York, NY: Harmony Books.

Raymond, E. S. (1999). *The cathedral and the bazaar: Musings on Linux and open source by an accidental revolutionary*. Sebastopol, CA: O'Reilly & Associates.

Reeves, M., & Deimler, M. (2011). Adaptability: The new competitive advantage. *Harvard Business Review, 89*(7/8), 134–141.

Reeves, M., Levin, S., & Ueda, D. (2016). The biology of corporate survival. *Harvard Business Review, 94*(1/2), 47–55.

Rigby, D. K., Sutherland, J., & Takeuchi, H. (2016). Embracing agile. *Harvard Business Review, 94*(5), 40–50.

Roberts, N. C. (2011). Beyond smokestacks and silos: Open-source, web-enabled coordination in organizations and networks. *Public Administration Review, 71*(5), 677–693.

Robertson, B. J. (2015). *Holacracy: The new management system for a rapidly changing world*. New York, NY: Henry Holt & Company.

Robertson, P. J. (1998). Interorganizational relationships: Key issues for integrated services. In J. McCroskey & S. D. Einbinder (Eds.), *Communities and universities: Remaking professional and interprofessional education for the next century* (pp. 67–87). Westport, CT: Greenwood.

Robertson, P. J. (1999). Collaborative organizing: An 'ideal type' for a new paradigm. In R. W. Woodman & W. A. Pasmore (Eds.), *Research in organizational change and development* (Vol. 12; pp. 205–267). Greenwich, CT: JAI Press.

Robertson, P. J., & Choi, T. (2010). Ecological governance: Organizing principles for an emerging era. *Public Administration Review, 70*(s1), s89–s99.

Roethlisberger, F. J., & Dickson, W. J. (1939). *Management and the worker*. Cambridge, MA: Harvard University Press.

Rothschild, J., & Russell, R. (1986). Alternatives to bureaucracy: Democratic participation in the economy. *Annual Review of Sociology, 12*, 307–328.

Rousseau, D. (1995). *Psychological contracts in organizations: Understanding written and unwritten agreements*. Thousand Oaks, CA: SAGE.

Russell, P. (1998). *Waking up in time: Finding inner peace in times of accelerating change*. Novato, CA: Origin Press.

Sanders, T. I. (1998). *Strategic thinking and the new science: Planning in the midst of chaos, complexity, and change*. New York, NY: Free Press.

Schein, E. H. (1969). *Process consultation*. Reading, MA: Addison-Wesley.

Schein, E. H. (1985). *Organizational culture and leadership*. San Francisco, CA: Jossey-Bass.

Schmidt, W. H., & Finnigan, J. P. (1992). *The race without a finish line: America's quest for total quality*. San Francisco, CA: Jossey-Bass.

Schwartz, G. E. R., & Russek, L. G. S. (1999). *The living energy universe: A fundamental discovery that transforms science and medicine*. Charlottesville, VA: Hampton Roads.

Scott, W. R. (1981). *Organizations: Rational, natural, and open systems*. Englewood Cliffs, NJ: Prentice-Hall.

Semler, R. (1993). *Maverick! The success story behind the world's most unusual workplace*. New York, NY: Warner Books.

Senge, P. M. (1990). *The fifth discipline: The art & practice of the learning organization*. New York, NY: Doubleday.

Senge, P., Smith, B., Kruschwitz, N., Laur, J., & Schley, S. (2008). *The necessary revolution: How individuals and organizations are working together to create a sustainable world.* New York, NY: Doubleday.

Seybold-Clegg, J. (2007). *Toward a theology of work: Spirituality in the corporate world.* South Bend, IN: Victoria Press.

Shonk, J. H. (1992). *Team-based organizations: Developing a successful team environment.* Homewood, IL: Business One Irwin.

Shrivastava, P. (1995). The role of corporations in achieving ecological sustainability. *Academy of Management Review, 20*(4), 936–960.

Sieber, R. E., & Johnson, P. A. (2015). Civic open data at a crossroads: Dominant models and current challenges. *Government Information Quarterly, 32*(3), 308–315.

Simon, H. A. (1946). The proverbs of administration. *Public Administration Review, 6*(1), 53–67.

Simon, H. A. (1957). *Administrative behavior* (2nd ed.). New York, NY: Macmillan.

Sinek, S. (2009). *Start with why: How great leaders inspire everyone to take action.* New York, NY: Penguin.

Smircich, L., & Morgan, G. (1982). Leadership: The management of meaning. *Journal of Applied Behavioral Science, 18*(3), 257–273.

Socolow, R., Andrews, C., Berkhout, F., & Thomas, V. (Eds.). (1994). *Industrial ecology and global change.* Cambridge, England: Cambridge University Press.

Stacey, R. D. (1996). *Complexity and creativity in organizations.* San Francisco, CA: Berrett-Koehler.

Stead, W. E., & Stead, J. G. (1994). Can humankind change the economic myth? Paradigm shifts necessary for ecologically sustainable business. *Journal of Organizational Change Management, 7*(4), 15–31.

Stewart, T. A. (1997). *Intellectual capital: The new wealth of organizations.* New York, NY: Doubleday/Currency.

Strebel, P. (Ed.). (2000). *Focused energy: Mastering bottom-up organization.* Chichester, England: Wiley.

Strogatz, S. (2003). *Sync: How order emerges from chaos in the universe, nature, and daily life.* New York, NY: Hyperion Books.

Strong, M. (2009). *Be the solution: How entrepreneurs and conscious capitalists can solve all the world's problems.* Hoboken, NJ: John Wiley & Sons.

Surowiecki, J. (2005). *The wisdom of crowds.* New York, NY: Anchor Books.

Sutcliffe, K. M., & Vogus, T. J. (2003). Organizing for resilience. In K. Cameron, J. E. Dutton, & R. E. Quinn (Eds.), *Positive organizational scholarship* (pp. 94–110). San Francisco, CA: Berrett-Koehler.

Svendsen, A. (1998). *The stakeholder strategy: Profiting from collaborative business relationships.* San Francisco, CA: Berrett-Koehler.

Talbot, M. (1991). *The holographic universe.* New York, NY: HarperCollins.

Tannenbaum, R., & Davis, S. A. (1969). Values, man, and organizations. *Industrial Management Review, 10*(2), 67–83.

Tapscott, D., & Williams, A. D. (2010). *Macrowikinomics: Rebooting business and the world.* New York, NY: Penguin.

Taso, F. C., & Laszlo, C. (2019). *Quantum leadership: New consciousness in business.* Stanford, CA: Stanford University Press.

Taylor, F. W. (1911). *The principles of scientific management.* New York, NY: Harper.

Taylor, J. C. (1975). The human side of work: The socio-technical approach to work system design. *Personnel Review, 4*(3), 17–22.

Teece, D. J., Pisano, G., & Shuen, A. (1997). Dynamic capabilities and strategic management. *Strategic Management Journal, 18*(7), 509–533.

Teng, J. T., Grover, V., & Fiedler, K. D. (1994). Business process reengineering: Charting a strategic path for the information age. *California Management Review, 36*(3), 9–31.

Thompson, J. D. (1967). *Organizations in action.* New York, NY: McGraw-Hill.

Thomson, A. M., & J. L. Perry. (2006). Collaboration processes: Inside the black box. *Public Administration Review, 66*(s1), 20–32.

Tornow, W., & London, M. (1998). *Maximizing the value of 360-degree feedback: A process for successful individual and organizational development.* San Francisco, CA: Jossey-Bass.

Townsend, A. M. (2013). *Smart cities: Big data, civic hackers, and the quest for a new utopia.* New York, NY: W.W. Norton.

Tracy, L. (1989). *The living organization: Systems of behavior.* New York, NY: Praeger.

Trice, H. M., & Beyer, J. M. (1984). Studying organizational cultures through rites and ceremonials. *Academy of Management Review, 9*(4), 653–669.

Tushman, M. L., & O'Reilly III, C. A. (1996). Ambidextrous organizations: Managing evolutionary and revolutionary change. *California Management Review, 38*(4), 8–29.

Tushman, M. L., & Romanelli, E. (1985). Organizational evolution: A metamorphosis model of convergence and reorientation. In L. L. Cummings & B. S. Staw (Eds.), *Research in organizational behavior* (Vol. 7; pp. 171–222). Greenwich, CT: JAI Press.

Uhl, C. (2004). *Developing ecological consciousness: Path to a sustainable world.* Lanham, MD: Rowman & Littlefield.

Uhl-Bien, M., Marion, R., & McKelvey, B. (2007). Complexity leadership theory: Shifting leadership from the industrial age to the knowledge era. *Leadership Quarterly, 18*(4), 298–318.

Ulanowicz, R. E. (1997). *Ecology, the ascendent perspective.* New York, NY: Columbia University Press.

Van Beurden, P., & Gössling, T. (2008). The worth of values – A literature review on the relation between corporate social and financial performance. *Journal of Business Ethics, 82*(2), 407–424.

Vigna, P., & Casey, M. J. (2015). *The age of cryptocurrency: How bitcoin and digital money are challenging the global economic order.* New York, NY: St. Martin's Press.

Waddock, S. (2009). Making a difference? Corporate responsibility as a social movement. *Journal of Corporate Citizenship, 33*(Spring), 35–46.

Wagner-Marsh, F., & Conley, J. (1999). The fourth wave: The spiritually-based firm. *Journal of Organizational Change Management, 12*(4), 292–302.

Waldroop, J., & Butler, T. (1996). The executive as coach. *Harvard Business Review, 74*(6), 111–117.

Waldrop, M. M. (1992). *Complexity: The emerging science at the edge of order and chaos.* New York, NY: Simon & Schuster.

Walton, R. E. (1969). *Interpersonal peacemaking; Confrontations and third-party consultation.* Reading, MA: Addison-Wesley.

Weber, M. (1947). *The theory of social and economic organization.* Glencoe, IL: Free Press.

Weick, K. E. (1979). Cognitive processes in organizations. In B. S. Staw (Ed.), *Research in organizational behavior* (Vol. 1; pp. 41–74). Greenwich, CT: JAI Press.

Weisbord, M. R., & Janoff, S. (1995). *Future search: An action guide to finding common ground in organizations & communities.* San Francisco, CA: Berrett-Koehler.

Wernerfelt, B. (1984). A resource-based view of the firm. *Strategic Management Journal, 5*(2), 171–180.

Wheatley, M. J. (1992). *Leadership and the new science: Learning about organization from an orderly universe.* San Francisco, CA: Berrett-Koehler.

Whiteman, G., Walker, B., & Perego, P. (2013). Planetary boundaries: Ecological foundations for corporate sustainability. *Journal of Management Studies,* 50(2), 307–336.

Wilber, K. (1977). *The spectrum of consciousness.* Wheaton, IL: Quest Books.

Wilber, K. (1995). *Sex, ecology and spirituality: The evolution of spirit.* Boston, MA: Shambhala.

Wilber, K. (1998). *The marriage of sense and soul. Integrating science and religion.* New York, NY: Random House.

Wilber, K. (2000). *A theory of everything: An integral vision for business, politics, science, and spirituality.* Boston, MA: Shambhala.

Williamson, M. (1997). *The healing of America.* New York, NY: Simon & Schuster.

Wolf, F. A. (1996). *The spiritual universe: How quantum physics proves the existence of the soul.* New York, NY: Simon & Schuster.

Wolfe, N. (2011). *The living organization: Transforming business to create extraordinary results.* Irvine, CA: Quantum Leaders.

Woodhouse, M. B. (1996). *Paradigm wars: Worldviews for a new age.* Berkeley, CA: Frog.

World Commission on Environment and Development. (1987). *Our common future.* Oxford, England: Oxford University Press.

Zadek, S. (2008). Global collaborative governance: There is no alternative. *Corporate Governance, 8*(4), 374–388.

Zeleny, M. (1997). Autopoiesis and self-sustainability in economic systems. *Human Systems Management, 16*(4), 251–262.

Zohar, D. (1990). *The quantum self: Human nature and consciousness defined by the new physics.* New York, NY: Morrow.

Zohar, D. (1997). *Rewiring the corporate brain: Using the new science to rethink how we structure and lead organizations.* San Francisco, CA: Berrett-Koehler.

Zohar, D., & Marshall, I. (1994). *The quantum society: Mind, physics, and a new social vision.* New York, NY: Morrow.

Zucker, L. G. (1983). Organizations as institutions. In S. B. Bacharach (Ed.), *Research in the sociology of organizations* (Vol. 2; pp. 1–47). Greenwich, CT: JAI Press.

CHAPTER 2

HAVE YOU SEEN CORPORATE CULTURAL RESPONSIBILITY?

Prospects of a New Construct for Corporations Operating Across Communities

W. G. (Will) Zhao
Kyle Neabel
Jingjing Du

ABSTRACT

Existing literature on corporate social responsibility (CSR) has been curiously silent about the relevance of culture. This chapter argues that, as a key concept in strategy and organization, culture needs to be de-trivialized and its breadth and depth highlighted in the studies and practice of CSR and beyond. Particularly, this chapter advances a community-based conceptualization of corporate cultural responsibility (CCR) and seeks to demonstrate CCR both as an integral part of CSR and as a promising generic construct in strategy and organization. The applications and implications of this new construct are explored.

Cultural Values in Strategy and Organization, pages 65–82

INTRODUCTION

Corporate social responsibility (CSR) is a prominent construct in strategy and organization that captures a host of activities and considerations corporations take to further the social good (McWilliams, Siegel, & Wright, 2006; van Marrewijk, 2013) and to meet the expectations of their stakeholders in the areas of governance, environment, work conditions, social justice, and so forth (Carroll, 1999; Garriga & Melé, 2013; Perrini, 2006; Porter & Kramer, 2006). Recently, however, scholars have highlighted culture as a neglected dimension for CSR (Maon & Lindgreen, 2015), arguing that CSR cannot adequately explain how corporations' business models, activities and outcomes may affect the value systems and enduring beliefs of the group of people corporations interact with.

Cultural values have been understood as having an important bearing on the functioning and practices of businesses and other organizations (Gehman, Treviño, & Garud, 2013; Hofstede, 1983). However, although cultural values and culture often feature in existing strategy research, as evidenced by the proliferation of studies on the role of cultural values in business success and failures *for the former construct* (e.g., Ang & Inkpen, 2008; Chipulu et al., 2014) and those on corporate culture and organizational culture *for the latter* (Kotter & Heskett, 2001; Sheridan, 1992), little attention has been granted to corporations' bearing on culture. In other words, in strategy and organization studies in general, and particularly in the much-studied field of CSR, culture has usually been placed on the independent variable side and rarely on the dependent variable side.

Recent research in CSR has begun to take seriously the cultural impacts of corporations from. A notable attempt is Maon and Lindgreen's (2015) conceptualization of corporate cultural responsibility (CCR), which captures

> the extent to which a corporation voluntarily develops its activities in a manner that recognizes and ensures the conscious consideration, respect, and defense of the systems of values and beliefs underlying and accompanying the myriad of behaviors and practices that represent extant cultures in the various settings in which the corporation operates. (p. 759)

In their conceptual work largely informed by international management studies, they move the McDonaldization–fragmentation–hybridization debate (Friedman, 1990; Husted, 2002) to the corporate level, drawing attention to the "the actual influence of business models and corporate practices on extant cultures" (Maon & Lindgreen, 2015, p. 758), and delineating three potential CCR stances with which corporate interact with target cultures, that is, cultural destructiveness, cultural carelessness, and cultural prowess.

This pioneering CCR study highlighted the importance of cultural considerations in corporations' selecting markets and operating in them. This view is in line with dominant international business insights whereby culture and cultural values are seen as a means of increasing foreign market share and creating a source of competitive advantage. We concur with Maon and Lindgreen's (2015) suggestion that culture should be brought back into the discussion of CSR. To us, this extension of CSR to include cultural considerations holds the potential to change the orientation of CSR from a generic social orientation to a more fine-grained and more complex social orientation.

Nevertheless, while we champion the emergence of CCR in the scholarly discussions in the field of CSR, which, at its core, centers on businesses taking actions that appear to further some social good, beyond the interests of the corporation and that which is required by law (McWilliams et al., 2006), we argue that CCR holds the potential to be a more generic strategy concept that has relevance beyond corporations operating across national borders. We believe that, despite the importance of culture in international management, culture, regardless of national borders, should be one of the key drivers of these ever-expanding requirements for corporate responsibility (Carroll, 1999).

Culture is a broad concept. Hofstede (1993) defines culture as the collective programming of the mind which distinguishes one group or category of people from another. Other scholars have identified its material, tangible aspect (Cohen, 2009), in addition to its less tangible, more subjective aspect (Triandis & Gelfand, 2012). Today the meaning of the word "culture" in our field is typically connected to symbols, myths, languages, beliefs, values, norms, rituals, attitudes, and artifacts. To us, the value of CCR lies above all in its usefulness for analyzing any cultural group, rather than treating a country as the preferred unit of analysis. Without expanding its unit of analysis beyond the scope of national cultures, the broadly conceived CCR is to be narrowly applied, with its connection to CSR remaining loose, for example, regarded as a complementary dimension of CSR in the context of international management.

One of our key assumptions is that culture is remarkably borderless in nature. Focusing on national boundaries can easily lead to a neglect of the specific beliefs, needs, claims, and expectations of different cultural groups within national boundaries—neglect that has plagued traditional CSR research. This oversimplification of culture and its potential scope of application may not allow researchers to readdress the culture "gap" in current CSR research. In practice, overemphasizing national culture as the only viable unit of analysis can also lead to a failure to understand why CSR efforts, at home or abroad, are not being rewarded or simply acknowledged.

The main purpose of this chapter is to, therefore, substantiate the discussion on the conceptualization and implications of CCR both as previously trivialized CSR element and as a generic construct for strategy and organization, and in doing so advance the nascent literature of CCR and add to the abovementioned culture-as-dependent variable perspective. This work contributes to the growing literature of CCR and to CSR, strategy, and organization research and practice in general in a number of important ways.

First, this chapter constitutes a useful reminder of the nature and complexity of culture in the context of CSR and that of strategy and organization. Our treatment of CCR demonstrates that culture and cultural values are neither vague nor irrelevant abstractions for management. Incorporating CCR into the debates around CSR shows the multifaceted nature of the environment in which contemporary corporations operate. Understanding CCR and its interaction with business operations is an important part of CSR, more than being merely a cultural add-on. The scope of CCR also suggests broader social concerns, requiring corporations to consider how they can address the vulnerabilities of certain cultures while managing rising expectations from specific communities and from the society as a whole on businesses and other organizations.

Second, not only is this chapter one of the earliest studies in English on the topic of CCR, it also develops and illustrates the construct of CCR with a generic understanding of culture. We diversify the unit of analysis of CCR and explicate the nature of CCR in a way that is both sufficiently generic and empirically relevant. Earlier work (Maon & Lindgreen, 2015) laid important groundwork in clarifying culture as a key dimension of CSR. However, the more comprehensive theoretical and practical implications of culture on the day-to-day strategy and organization of contemporary corporations have yet to be explored. We argue that, given the broad scope of culture, the conceptualization of CCR, and subsequent empirical inquiries of CCR, should not be limited to cross-national cultural encountering that typically involves host country and home country cultures. Specifically, we formally expand the empirical scope of CCR from countries to communities, which, in our conceptualization, could still accommodate cross-border (host country culture vs. home country culture) scenarios in addition to intra-border ones (e.g., local community culture vs. outsider culture). In this vein, our conceptualization of CCR has greater empirical implications for strategy and organization than the original CCR thinking implies.

From a managerial perspective, a broader understanding of CCR, cultural values, and culture can not only provide much-needed CSR guidance on corporations but also, as we will discuss in this chapter, offer a clearer logic on corporations' strategy and organization as they operate across communities.

The remainder of this chapter is organized as follows. After making the case for further engaging culture in CSR, we will put forth our community-based view of CCR. We will then discuss two different stances of our expanded CCR, which we call "cultural vigilance" and "cultural nonchalance," and highlight the benefits and consequences associated with CCR. Next, we will showcase the empirical relevance of our CCR construct by it to one important tandem of strategic concepts, that is, "strategic fit" (Chorn, 1991; Zajac, Kraatz, & Bresser, 2000) and "liability of foreignness" (Mezias, 2002; Zaheer, 1995). Specifically, we will show how CCR can be used in expanding the scope of the applicability of these concepts beyond their traditional international management scope. We will end this chapter with discussions of its implications and outline some future directions.

CULTURAL VALUES, CULTURE, AND COMMUNITY: TOWARDS A GENERIC CONCEPTUALIZATION OF CCR

In this section, we will provide some clarification on cultural values and culture as well as their effect(s) on the day-to-day operations of corporations. We will demonstrate that culture, as ingrained in values, beliefs, and practices of different communities, has important implications for the strategy, operations, and ultimately performance and legitimacy among the communities in which corporations hope to operate.

Cultural Values, Culture and Community as Proxy for Cultural Groups

Since Hofstede's seminal work on international differences among work-related values (Hofstede, 1983; Sorge & Hofstede, 1983), generations of scholars have been exploring the concept of cultural values. Hofstede's work, while having marshaled tremendous supports, was also regarded by many critics as having "far too loose" criteria for acceptable evidence (McSweeney, 2002, p. 112).

Part of the reason perhaps emanates from difficulty in transposing the lay understanding of cultural values to an empirical construct that has broader applicability across different sub-disciplines of management. As scholars concede (Caprar, Devinney, Kirkman, & Caligiuri, 2015, p. 1014), "It is hard to argue that cultural values would pass common construct requirements, such as the need to be coherently defined, with specified scope conditions and clearly mapped relationships with other constructs." This, therefore, requires researchers to pre-determine the central themes regarding cultural values before any workable definitions can be posited.

Therefore, in light of the previously mentioned culture-as-dependent-variable perspective, in this chapter, the notion of cultural values is understood as more stable, long-lasting beliefs about what is important for a cultural group. Cultural groups in this sense consist of individuals sharing similar values, beliefs, language, attitudes, norms, symbols, artifacts and myths (Parboteeah & Cullen, 2003). This is essentially what Hofstede means when he defines culture as "collective programming of the mind which distinguishes one group or category of people from another" (Hofstede, 1993, p. 89). While Hofstede's original focus was on national culture, Craig and Douglas (2006) argue that culture can be subdivided within a nation. Upholding this distinction, we now turn to the concept of community, that is, our proxy construct for cultural groups.

Cultures are markers for a community, as well as what makes the community (Bechky, 2003; Berry, 1997; Craig & Douglas, 2006; Maon & Lindgreen, 2015). In the sociological tradition, a community is a social group that has similar values and norms, loyalty, face-to-face interactions and share a mutual geography (Adler, 2015). Community takes many forms in the literature of strategy and organization. Most relevant to our perspective perhaps is the view of community as a highly diverse group of both individuals and organizations, who have various and sometimes even conflicting demands, and who are embedded in complex network structures and cultural systems "within a large coverage boundary" (Liu, Eng, & Ko, 2013, p. 469). In this chapter, this "coverage boundary" delineates our minimalist definition of community as people with shared values and often with a shared language.

Language is an important cultural element in our discussion as it is critical to knowledge sharing in a community (Bechky, 2003; Liu et al., 2013). If culture is a collection of cultural tools to be used to achieve objectives for the individual (Rindova, Dalpiaz, & Ravasi, 2011), then among the elements that make up these toolkits are language, symbols, etc. that come from a broader cultural repertoire (Rindova et al., 2011). Indeed, as research highlights, "language is the vehicle for culture; cultural values are reflected in the language spoken" (Selmier, Newenham-Kahindi, & Oh, 2015, pp. 487–488). For instance, communities in bilingual or multilingual countries such as Canada, Finland, and Switzerland often define their cultural identities through language (Oakes & Warren, 2007; Pigott & Kalbach, 2005).

This community-based view would point us to the relationship between different groups for which culture is an integral part of their series of decisions and behaviors that characterize their daily organizational lives. For corporations, doing business across communities means interacting with encountering different cultures. As corporations move into new markets and new areas of activity—whether home or abroad—they must cross countless cultural boundaries, which entails unpacking what is taken for granted in the business environment of a particular community. While some assumptions are usually clear to insiders, they are not so clear to outsiders who lack the common experience of the former.

A caveat is that membership of communities is not always stable, even when communities are defined by shared cultural values and language. As one country's culture can be further divided and subdivided into many different cultures (Craig & Douglas, 2006), the border becomes a largely irrelevant construct. Similarly, individuals in one community can identify with other communities, for instance, immigration to different communities or even multicultural societies (Berry, 1997; Cleveland & Xu, 2019).

Community-Based View of CCR and Two Associated Stances

CSR research continues to emphasize the importance of corporate social decision making and how businesses manage this through different socially oriented practices (Flammer, 2013; Ioannou, Serafeim, & Link, 2013). Operating across communities, whether between countries or regions, is becoming common practice for contemporary corporations. In communities, corporations are expected to make socially responsible choices about where they think they will develop or manage important relationships.

Being culturally informed when creating a strategy is critical to the creation or destruction of economic value (Maurer, Bansal, & Crossant, 2011). In their research regarding CSR and legitimacy, Panwar, Paul, Nybakk, Hansen, and Thompson (2014, p. 481) state that "legitimacy of CSR actions is indeed influenced by the actions of the corporation but also is rooted in the basic cultural values of a society and the ideologies of evaluators." Despite the implications of culture in and for the study of strategy and organization, the role of culture in CSR remains opaque and poses a serious challenge to CSR practices.

Maon and Lindgreen's work (2015) provides an important starting point for bridging this gap. Their treatment of CCR includes a survey of three corporate cultural stances. The first stance was *cultural destructiveness,* where an organization acts in a way that actively destroys or harms a culture, either through the corporation thinking their culture is superior or their profits are more important. The second stance is *cultural carelessness,* in which an organization acts in a way that they neglect or overlook the consequences of their actions on the culture. The third stance is *cultural prowess,* where an organization acts or attempts to act in a way that does not harm and, in some cases, benefits the culture.

While CSR targeted at non-culture-specific stakeholders has obvious value, how this value is achieved in reality still requires that corporations have a fine-grained understanding of the expectations, claims, and concerns of specific cultural groups. We concur with the insights of Maon and Lindgreen (2015), yet we seek to further stress that the "borderless" nature of culture needs to be acknowledged and highlighted as it potentially will allow researchers and practitioners to better appreciate how and why culture is and CCR should be involved in every aspect of strategy and organization for a corporation.

To us, the use of a country as a unit of analysis can be controversial because the overlap between country and culture is not taken for granted. Countries and cultures may overlap substantially, to some extent, or not at all. This points us to the core of CCR investigations, viz cultural groups, rather than nationalities. Focusing on international differences means largely ignoring the possibility that CCR can also be seen as a phenomenon that involves cultures of communities.

Our community based CCR conceptualization rests upon the fact that most corporations operate in their broader competitive environment populated and demarcated by various communities. Corporations therefore need to consider a range of potentially very different needs, from showing respect to the identity of specific communities to joining cultural movements, to paying close attention to cultural particularities to avoiding stigmatization. Below, we apply this community-based view in revisiting the different stances of CCR entailed in previous research (Maon & Lindgreen, 2015). In light of our borderless generic conceptualization of CCR, we transpose the three original stances into two categories of corporations' attitude and actions towards the communities they interact with and operate in, that is, one stance of *cultural nonchalance*, and the other which we identify as *cultural vigilance.*

Cultural Nonchalance

Corporations that exhibit a degree of indifference to local culture are not rare. In operating internationally, some corporations may put forth policies and practices that deliberately undermine existing cultural values in the target market, possibly due to top management's belief that the cultural values they convey are superior and should be imposed on their host environment, or due to the corporation's profit-orientation objectives (Maon & Lindgreen, 2015).

In our view, both reasons are in line with Milton Friedman's argument that the only social responsibility a business has is to increase its profits as much as possible in a manner that it conforms to society (Friedman, 2007). It is, therefore, feasible to combine these two since both stances take the idea of causing either directly or indirectly to another culture through the corporation's active strategy. The CCR stance that captures the above scenarios is termed *cultural nonchalance* in this study. In essence, cultural nonchalance is where corporations fail to consider the harm they might cause or be ignorant of the damage they are causing in a community, and will also include those strategies that indirectly caused harm to a community's culture. On top of this, corporations may passively cause harm to another culture when there is a lack of effort to understand a community's culture.

Cultural Vigilance

Corporations need to have stronger cultural awareness for their activities. Often, companies recognize cultural differences and their intrinsic values and strive to develop and demonstrate respect for and support for the cultural identity of the environment in which they operate (Maon & Lindgreen, 2015). Similar to "cultural prowess" in Maon and Lindgreen's work, our view on enhanced cultural awareness, which we term as *cultural vigilance* describe a corporation being aware of the culture they are entering into. They continuously self-evaluate their cultural awareness and follow cultural dynamics, which form the basis of their activities.

In our view, cultural vigilance includes a corporation's attempts to make amends to the damage or creates a plan that considers the target community. One example is Halal food: cultural pressure has undoubtedly prompted food companies operating in these communities to adapt their food procurement policies, enhancing the transparency in the composition of their products.

Unlike existing literature would suggest, our CCR perspective does not assume communities as passive. Corporations that have not been thoughtful and attentive in dealing with issues related to cultural norms often will face consequences associated with their activities. Communities may be constituents or activists, who try to avoid the damaging effects of corporations' operations. Activism can be seen even within an organization when the interest of select people or communities at large is felt to be encroached. For instance, LGBT communities within a corporation will actively fight for their rights (Briscoe & Gupta, 2016), shifting the organization to shift their direction from cultural nonchalance towards practicing cultural vigilance.

INTEGRATING CCR IN TO STRATEGY: AN ILLUSTRATION OF STRATEGIC FIT AND FOREIGNNESS

We have discussed in the above sections the extension of CCR into a borderless, community-based construct. We have not, however, discussed the generic nature of our CCR conceptualization. In order to further demonstrate the usefulness of CCR as a generic construct for strategy and organization, below we apply our extended CCR framework to examining an important construct tandem in international management "strategic fit" and "liability of foreignness," and demonstrate how the community-based view of culture could allow these constructs to take on borderless, generic nature.

The term *strategic fit* describes how a strategy needs to align with its external environment and how the internal organization needs to fit properly with the strategy. Such alignments with the external environment and internal organization are deemed as the primary task of the top management of any organization (Channon & McGee, 2015).

Foreignness can be an important factor for an organization's failure in aligning its strategy with its internal and external environments. For example, companies such as Disney in Europe and General Motors in Japan faced difficulties when expanding into foreign markets, hence the need for a revised strategic approach.

The degree of internationalization, the experience of the host country, and the institutional distance are the three dimensions that determine Foreignness. Internationalization refers to the degree to which a corporation participates in international activities (Mitchell, Shaver, & Yeung, 1992). Host country experience is the knowledge gained by a corporation in a particular country context, which is found to be dependent on the time spent in the country and the range of activities such as sales, distribution, manufacturing, and services. Institutional distance is concerned with the different institutional characteristics between two countries (Phillips, Tracey, & Karra, 2009), which encompasses regulatory, cognitive, and normative systems in each country.

Conventional wisdom on international strategy suggests that the higher the degree of internationalization, the better the ability of multinational companies to correctly assess its strategic fit prospect in the new environment (Roth, 1988). As a corporation gains experience in internationalization, it is better able to assess the fit between itself and the host environment, as it builds the capacity to learn and operate in new environments (Delios & Beamish, 1999). The literature on host country experience finds that companies with more host country experience are expected to be less negatively affected by foreignness and have greater strategic fit as they continue to expand their internationalization activities locally (Zaheer & Mosakowski, 1997).

Institutional distance in the existing literature is depicted as adverse to strategic fit, that is, the larger the institutional distance, the worse the strategic fit (Brannen, 2004) as there exist many obstacles for transfer "hard" organizational resources hard and "soft" organizational practices based on values and meaning (Kostova, 1999).

In what follows, we will inject our community-based understanding of culture in CCR to the discussion of foreignness and strategic fit.

Fit and Foreignness in the Light of CCR

Can business success be achieved when a strategy is "fitting"? Some people may be inclined to say "Yes," but it certainly is not automatic. In light of CCR, "fitting" attempts could be made by recognizing the environmental and organizational factors and applying a strategy that matches to create a strategic fit (Zajac et al., 2000) with the communities that the corporations operate in. When seen with the community lens, the concept of strategic fit is taken from the international level and can be applied to businesses that wish to expand within or beyond national borders. Knowing this, we now look at the multiple forms of communities.

The first scenario will be national culture-to-national culture, where an organization goes international and can face a high degree of foreignness (Brannen, 2004). As the corporation trying to expand would need to have a high level of cultural vigilance, experience with the host country's culture and an understanding of how the institutions may differ. An example could be a Canadian non-profit trying to tackle issues in a developing nation. If the non-profit fails to recognize that the host country's values and norms regarding receiving help, then the corporation might be embarrassed by its activities or even cause harm to those communities. Therefore, not identifying the distance between the institutions leads the non-profit to practice cultural nonchalance.

The next scenario is a local community-to-local community, where an organization attempts to expand within its home nations borders. The degree of foreignness, which can be high or low, depends on the size and levels of multiculturalism within the nation. However, the level of adaptation should be high due to regular interaction between the two different communities. In a similar sense, experience with the host community should also be high because of the regular interactions. Lastly, there should also be a smaller distance between institutions, since the home and host communities share a government, and potentially a language. An example of this scenario is how Tim Hortons, a popular coffee and doughnut chain, made the strategic choice to drop the apostrophe from all of the spellings of its brand name because of their operation in Québec. This choice reflects Tim Hortons's cultural vigilance and conforming to a more French-looking name to help become more successful in Québec. The reason these changes were due to the Office Québécios de la Langue Française enforcement of the French language laws in the province of Quebec. Demonstrating that even though there are similar institutions in both Ontario (where Tim Hortons is from) and Quebec, regulatory institutions still held a small distance. Furthermore, this small distance allows a major transfer of capabilities that the corporation can use in both the host and home communities (van den Waeyenberg & Hens, 2012).

Communities have important expectations about the products or services corporations offer. For example, if a corporation offers some kind of free service in the name of social responsibility, this strategy works only if the cultural community has a need for that free service. Similarly, it may be in the public interest and socially responsible for a corporation to sell more vegan food, yet, similar to the previous example on Halal food, this is only effective if the community is interested in buying more vegan food.

Culturally vigilant businesses can build relationships with communities, leveraging increasing assets and capacities, for example, through highly visible cultural donations, such as corporate donations of profits to a cultural community. Indeed, the links between CSR and business success have been studied and identified. Scholars often equate "good responsibility" to "good business" in the long run. However, from the CCR perspective, this strategy can often be self-defeating. In our view, it makes sense to increase socially responsible activities if corporate interests (i.e., profits) and the interests of cultural groups are aligned, but if they are not, then the quest for social responsibility is unlikely to succeed.

DISCUSSION AND CONCLUSION

We consider this broader view of CCR we proposed in this study to be novel and analytically flexible (with the community as its unit of analysis). It is also suggested that the existence, salience or lack of salience of certain cultural considerations may help to explain the pressures (or lack thereof) of traditional CSR in the face of different cultural groups. While it is not intended to provide a "catch-all" conceptualization, this study provides a new way of explaining the impact of culture and culture values on the operations of corporations across communities. This chapter makes a few meaningful contributions to the emergence debate around CCR, and to the research and practices related to culture, CSR, and, more globally, to strategy and organization.

CCR as a Concept That Complements (and Substantiates) CSR

As a key construct in the field of strategy and organization, culture has not been fully elaborated or theorized in CSR. While there are many ways to understand the impact of culture on social responsibility and on strategic and organizational practices, much existing research on CSR presupposes cultural consistency for CSR initiatives, and few frameworks can capture the breadth and multi-layered nature of culture. The aim of this chapter was to invoke the concepts of culture and cultural values in order to further inject the cultural considerations into CSR. Understanding the complex interactions among various aspects of culture and how they affect the day-to-day operations of an organization is one of the contributions this study makes, as one of the earliest contributions on the topic of CCR.

As pointed out in the introduction, research on CSR has only recently begun to recognize a need to engage the culture and cultural values. The role of culture in CSR, nevertheless, remains opaque and poses a serious challenge to the theory and practice of CSR. This chapter argues that CSR practices work only if cultural groups also recognize such responsibility that is if there is a tacit understanding between corporations and communities about what it means to be socially responsible. It can even be further pointed out that what is really needed is social responsibility in the eyes of various cultural groups in order for CSR to play its role.

CCR as a Generic Construct

This study synthesizes insights from a variety of literature on culture, cultural values, strategy, and organization, and applies such an integrated understanding to expanding existing conceptualization of CCR into a generic construct. Existing CCR conceptualization (Maon & Lindgreen, 2015) prioritizes international operations, which we believe falls short of the promise that CCR hopes as a borderless, generic construct for strategy and organization. In addition to the cultural differences between individual countries, CCR is considered here to pertain to the relations between any cultural groups. In other words, this chapter attempts to develop a more comprehensive and multi-level concept of CCR than has been proposed in previous literature, and thus extends the explanatory power of CCR to that beyond what international management would allow.

The empirical scope of CCR in our conceptualization is broad and could still accommodate cross-border (host country culture vs. home country culture) scenarios, in addition to intra-border ones (e.g., local community culture vs. outsider culture). In this sense, we show that CCR has created opportunities for "accountability" in the cultural sphere, where corporations can strive to become the "glue" for communities of different cultures. Cultural awareness is no longer achieved primarily in relations with a foreign country or in international management, but rather in the day-to-day functioning of any corporation operating across communities.

Managerial Implications

In addition to the above theoretical contributions, another major contribution of this chapter is to explain why a complementary cultural perspective can add value to the practice of CSR. As mentioned above by Maon and Lindgreen (2015), cultural distinctiveness, initially trivialized in the picture of corporations' creating social value, has recently become part of many corporations' primary concerns. Wal-Mart, KFC, and many others are responding to expectations for enhanced cultural awareness, or cultural vigilance. In addition, it appears that other stakeholders such as governments and the media are increasingly putting pressure on CSR to become culturally sensitive members of society.

Our conceptualization has some more practical implications for managers, decision makers, and "culturally responsible" actors. For instance, business practitioners interested in projects related to CCR can use this detailed discussion as a framework to determine the appropriate response to cultural needs. In addition, considering the logic of CCR being largely independent of national boundaries, this framework can help identify culture-oriented initiatives in CSR and beyond, and evaluate if and how they work (or may work) within and outside community boundaries.

Future Directions

In summary, the study represents an exploration of what CCR means, how CCR is analyzed, how it complements CSR, and how it serves as a more generic construct in strategy and organization. Here, we outline a few possible directions to diversify CCR research.

Future research could consider the relationship between cultural groups and political systems. Matten and Moon (2008) argue that the institutional environment of any government determines the extent to which companies are involved in responsibility issues. Many governments have largely legislated on cultural issues, for example, language bills in Canada. An interesting question is, therefore, whether CCR would be more (or less) explicitly expressed through market relations if governments adopted a laissez-faire approach?

As a generic construct, CCR provides researchers with an opportunity to describe, explain, and even predict business consequences. Large corporations often have comprehensive product ranges that target diverse customers. While the vast majority of CSR activities usually involve cross-communities operations, there might be important differences in the CCR capabilities between companies of different sizes and nature. Research on whether CCR translates into rewards has an attractive prospect, and can potentially help us better appreciate the puzzle of "doing better by doing good." Future research, for starters, may provide further explanation and prediction of CCR, such as goodwill, performance, and so on.

ACKNOWLEDGMENTS

The authors are grateful for Michelle Henderson's excellent assistance in the initial literature review on cultural values. Heartfelt thanks are extended to Dr. T. K. Das for his valuable and constructive suggestions that greatly benefited the revision of this study. The first author also wishes to express his very great appreciation to his colleagues at SCANCOR-Stanford for comments on an earlier version of this research.

REFERENCES

Adler, P. S. (2015). Community and innovation: From Tönnies to Marx. *Organization Studies, 36*(4), 445–471.

Ang, S., & Inkpen, A. C. (2008). Cultural intelligence and offshore outsourcing success: A framework of firm-level intercultural capability. *Decision Sciences, 39*(3), 337–358.

Bechky, B. A. (2003). Sharing meaning across occupational communities: The transformation of understanding on a production floor. *Organization Science, 14*(3), 312–330.

Berry, J. W. (1997). Immigration, acculturation and adaptation. *Applied Psychology, 46*(1), 5–68.

Brannen, M. Y. (2004). When Mickey loses face: Recontextualization, semantic fit, and the semiotics of foreignness. *Academy of Management Review, 29*(4), 593–616.

Briscoe, F., & Gupta, A. (2016). Social activism in and around organizations. *Academy of Management Annals, 10*(1), 671–727.

Caprar, D. V., Devinney, T. M., Kirkman, B. L., & Caligiuri, P. (2015). Conceptualizing and measuring culture in international business and management: From challenges to potential solutions. *Journal of International Business Studies, 46*(9), 1011–1027.

Carroll, A. B. (1999). Corporate social responsibility. *Business & Society, 38*(3), 268–295.

Channon, D. F., & McGee, J. (2015). Strategic fit. In C. L. Cooper, J. McGee, & T. Sammut (Eds.), *Wiley encyclopedia of management* (Vol. 12; pp. 1–2). Hoboken, NJ: Wiley.

Chipulu, M., Ojiako, U., Gardiner, P., Williams, T., Mota, C., Maguire, S., . . . Marshall, A. (2014). Exploring the impact of cultural values on project performance. *International Journal of Operations & Production Management, 34*(3), 364–389.

Chorn, N. H. (1991). The "alignment" theory: Creating strategic fit. *Management Decision, 29*(1), 20–24.

Cleveland, M., & Xu, C. (2019). Multifaceted acculturation in multiethnic settings. *Journal of Business Research, 103*, 250–260.

Cohen, A. B. (2009). Many forms of culture. *American Psychologist, 64*(3), 194–204.

Craig, C. S., & Douglas, S. P. (2006). Beyond national culture: Implications of cultural dynamics for consumer research. *International Marketing Review, 23*(3), 322–342.

Delios, A., & Beamish, P. W. (1999). Geographic scope, product diversification, and the corporate performance of Japanese firms. *Strategic Management Journal, 20*(8), 711–727.

Flammer, C. (2013). Corporate social responsibility and shareholder reaction: The environmental awareness of investors. *Academy of Management Journal, 56*(3), 758–781.

Friedman, J. (1990). Being in the World: Globalization and localization. *Theory, Culture & Society*, 7(2/3), 311–328.

Friedman, M. (2007). The social responsibility of business is to increase its profits. In W. C. Zimmerli, M. Holzinger, & K. Richter (Eds.), *Corporate ethics and corporate governance* (pp. 173–178). Heidelberg, Germany: Springer Berlin.

Garriga, E., & Melé, D. (2013). Corporate social responsibility theories: Mapping the territory. In *Citation Classics from the Journal of Business Ethics* (pp. 69–96). Dordrecht, Netherlands: Springer Netherlands.

Gehman, J., Treviño, L. K., & Garud, R. (2013). Values work: A process study of the emergence and performance of organizational values practices. *Academy of Management Journal, 56*(1), 84–112.

Hofstede, G. (1983). The cultural relativity of organizational practices and theories. *Journal of International Business Studies, 14*(2), 75–89.

Hofstede, G. (1993). Cultural constraints in management theories. *Academy of Management Perspectives*, 7(1), 81–94.

Husted, B. W. (2002). Cultural Balkanization and hybridization in an era of globalization: Implications for international business research. In M. Kotabe & P. Aulakh (Eds.), *Emerging issues in international business research* (pp. 81–95). Northempton, MA: Edward Elgar.

Ioannou, I., Serafeim, G., & Link, C. (2013). Corporate social responsibility and access to finance. *Strategic Management Journal, 35*(1), 1–23.

Kostova, T. (1999). Transnational transfer of strategic organizational practices: a contextual perspective. *Academy of Management Review, 24*(2), 308–324.

Kotter, J. P., & Heskett, J. L. (2001). *Corporate culture and performance.* New York, NY: Free Press.

Liu, G., Eng, T.-Y., & Ko, W.-W. (2013). Strategic direction of corporate community involvement. *Journal of Business Ethics, 115*(3), 469–487.

Maon, F., & Lindgreen, A. (2015). Reclaiming the child left behind: The case for corporate cultural responsibility. *Journal of Business Ethics, 130*(4), 755–766.

Matten, D., & Moon, J. (2008). "Implicit" and "explicit" CSR: A conceptual framework for a comparative understanding of corporate social responsibility. *Academy of Management Review, 33*(2), 404–424.

Maurer, C. C., Bansal, P., & Crossan, M. M. (2011). Creating economic value through social values: Introducing a culturally informed resource-based view. *Organization Science, 22*(2), 432–448.

McSweeney, B. (2002). Hofstede's model of national cultural differences and their consequences: A triumph of faith – a failure of analysis. *Human Relations, 55*(1), 89–118.

McWilliams, A., Siegel, D. S., & Wright, P. M. (2006). Corporate social responsibility: Strategic implications. *Journal of Management Studies, 43*(1), 1–18.

Mezias, J. M. (2002). How to identify liabilities of foreignness and assess their effects on multinational corporations. *Journal of International Management, 8*(3), 265–282.

Mitchell, W., Shaver, J. M., & Yeung, B. (1992). Getting there in a global industry: Impacts on performance of changing international presence. *Strategic Management Journal, 13*(6), 419–432.

Oakes, L., & Warren, J. (2007). *Language, citizenship and identity in Quebec.* Basingstoke, England: Palgrave Macmillan.

Panwar, R., Paul, K., Nybakk, E., Hansen, E., & Thompson, D. (2014). The legitimacy of CSR actions of publicly traded companies versus family-owned companies. *Journal of Business Ethics, 125*(3), 481–496.

Parboteeah, K. P., & Cullen, J. B. (2003). Social institutions and work centrality: explorations beyond national culture. *Organization Science, 14*(2), 137–148.

Perrini, F. (2006). Review of corporate social responsibility: Doing the most good for your company and your cause by P. Kotler & Nancy Lee (Eds.), Hoboken, New Jersey: Wiley, 2005. *Academy of Management Perspectives, 20*(2), 90–93.

Phillips, N., Tracey, P., & Karra, N. (2009). Rethinking institutional distance: Strengthening the tie between new institutional theory and international management. *Strategic Organization, 7*(3), 339–348.

Pigott, B., & Kalbach, M. (2005). Language effects on ethnic identity in Canada. *Canadian Ethnic Studies Journal, 32*(2), 3–18.

Porter, M. E., & Kramer, M. R. (2006). Strategy and society: The link between competitive advantage and corporate social responsibility. *Harvard Business Review, 84*(12), 78–92.

Rindova, V., Dalpiaz, E., & Ravasi, D. (2011). A cultural quest: A study of organizational use of new cultural resources in strategy formation. *Organization Science, 22*(2), 413–431.

Roth, K. (1988). The multinational mission: Balancing local demands and global vision. *Journal of International Business Studies, 19*(2), 304–306.

Selmier, W. T., II, Newenham-Kahindi, A., & Oh, C. H. (2015). "Understanding the words of relationships": Language as an essential tool to manage CSR in communities of place. *Journal of International Business Studies, 46*(2), 153–179.

Sheridan, J. E. (1992). Organizational Culture and Employee Retention. *Academy of Management Journal, 35*(5), 1036–1056.

Sorge, A., & Hofstede, G. (1983). Culture's consequences: International differences in work-related values. *Administrative Science Quarterly, 28*(4), 625.

Triandis, H. C., & Gelfand, M. (2012). Subjective culture. In V. S. Ramachandran (Ed.), *Encyclopedia of human behavior* (2nd ed.; pp. 544–550). London, England: Academic Press.

van den Waeyenberg, S., & Hens, L. (2012). Overcoming institutional distance: Expansion to base-of-the-pyramid markets. *Journal of Business Research, 65*(12), 1692–1699.

van Marrewijk, M. (2013). Concepts and definitions of CSR and corporate sustainability: Between agency and communion. In A. C. Michalos & D. C. Poff (Eds.), *Citation classics from the Journal of Business Ethics* (pp. 641–655). Dordrecht, Netherlands: Springer Netherlands.

Zaheer, S. (1995). Overcoming the liability of foreignness. *Academy of Management Journal, 38*(2), 341–363.

Zaheer, S., & Mosakowski, E. (1997). The dynamics of the liability of foreignness: A global study of survival in financial services. *Strategic Management Journal, 18*(6), 439–463.

Zajac, E. J., Kraatz, M. S., & Bresser, R. K. F. (2000). Modeling the dynamics of strategic fit: A normative approach to strategic change. *Strategic Management Journal, 31*(4), 429–453.

CHAPTER 3

MANAGING CULTURAL INTEGRATION IN MERGERS AND ACQUISITIONS

José-Luis Rodríguez-Sánchez
Eva-María Mora-Valentín
Marta Ortiz-de-Urbina-Criado

ABSTRACT

The main challenge for companies in the mergers and acquisitions (M&A) process is cultural integration management. Cultural integration management generates uncertainty, tension, and loss of motivation within human resources (HR). There is no strategy for avoiding these effects, but appropriate management of cultural integration can help to reduce them significantly. Therefore, in the context of mergers and acquisitions processes, the importance of cultural factors in human resources management needs to be analyzed. The objective of this chapter is to explain the key factors of cultural integration management in mergers and acquisitions processes. After reviewing the previous literature about this topic, a three-stage theoretical model has been developed, grouping the relevant factors of cultural integration for each stage of the mergers and acquisitions process. In the first stage (planning–cultural analysis), firms need to analyze due diligence, cultural

Cultural Values in Strategy and Organization, pages 83–108

similarities, degree of compatibility and the communication process. In the second stage (integration–cultural fit), companies must manage cultural resistance, and the firms' integration through human resources involvement and by retaining valuable human resources. In the final stage (implementation–cultural endstate), it is analyzed to assess psychological state, the cultural endstate targeted and communication effectiveness. The main conclusion is "organizational culture is one of the decisive factors to be considered for the success of cultural integration in mergers and acquisitions processes."

INTRODUCTION

An issue that has aroused great interest from the perspective of strategic management of companies and the industrial economy, is the mergers and acquisitions (M&A) process, and its consequences for companies (Martínez Caraballo, 2006). Competition between organizations in a globalized business environment, the economic context of instability and uncertainty, and the numerous changes suffered by different sectors and countries make M&A processes a strategic operation that is essential for the survival and growth of companies (DeOrtentiis, Summers, Ammeter, Douglas, & Ferris, 2013).

According to Maimunah, Nordahlia, and Zoharah (2018), the reasons M&A is a relevant operation for the future of businesses are (a) cost reduction via the synergies generated; (b) ability to share technology, skills, and talent; (c) entry in new markets; and (d) increasing the company's competitiveness to gain market share.

The large number of M&As carried out historically should be no surprise, due to the belief that they are a fast and easy way to achieve growth objectives. M&As have high acceptance in the recent economy (Rodríguez-Sánchez, Ortiz-de-Urbina-Criado, & Mora-Valentín, 2019). Despite the uncertainty generated by political events and the process of globalization which the business environment has experienced in the last 70 years, M&A activity has stayed robust, reaching a total of 38,070 operations in 2016.[1] The number of M&A operations was 38,128 in 2013; 41,240 in 2014; 40,368 in 2015; and 38,070 in 2016. The volume measured in US$M reached $2,787,278 in 2013; $3,619,171 in 2014; $4,656,933 in 2015; and $3,902,128 in 2016 (Becker, 2017).

Despite these figures, in practice, there are many M&As that do not generate value for the parent company (Gomes, Angwin, & Tarba, 2013), which means objectives are not completed, better financial results are not obtained, competitive position is lost and, most worrying, valuable human resources (HR) are lost (Bastida, 2007). Managing activities like due diligence, negotiation, financing, and HR integration or managing organizational culture can help achieve the synergies expected from M&A processes (Magano & Adele, 2017).

Traditionally, in M&A processes hard factors (economic, financial, and legal) have been considered most significant to the success of the operation, without keeping in mind that soft factors (cultural integration, HR management, communication, and leadership) are intangible elements that affect the results (Pascual de Blas, 2006). Thus, HR management leaves its operational support role (Rodríguez-Sánchez, Mora-Valentín, & Ortiz-de-Urbina-Criado, 2019), to influence key questions like business strategy and creating competitive advantage (Bhaskar, 2012).

In M&A, HR is acquired in addition to other resources, so problems related to organizational culture arise both before and after the process of integration, and do not affect just one company. When two or more companies unite, one may change more than the other, but both change. The expected success will only be achieved if the change is assimilated. Companies have begun to understand that the consideration of HR is critical to ensure the success of the process, and to attain the expected value. Lack of planning, poor communication, and a reactive approach to dealing with multiple HR problems, have been some of the reasons for the failure of M&As (Castro Casal & Neira Fontela, 2002).

The consideration of factors like final desired cultural state (strategy, organization, processes, and HR), integrated communication (shareholders, clients, employees, providers, and institutions), and retention of valuable HR (leadership, knowledge, capacity, and competency) has been of vital importance in successful M&A processes (Pascual de Blas, 2006). In this context, the objective of this chapter is to realize a theoretical analysis of all aspects related to the management of organizational culture in M&A processes. Once the literature has been analyzed, a model with three stages of M&A is proposed, in which the cultural management factors that are decisive for the process to be successful are identified.

LITERATURE REVIEW: CULTURAL VALUES IN MERGERS AND ACQUISITIONS

To analyze the literature about cultural integration management in M&A processes, a review of the literature considering previously published studies about the topic has been done. Since a review of the literature should be made in an objective, rigorous, and meticulous way (Manterola, Vial, Pineda, & Sanhueza, 2009), a search process has been defined (see Figure 3.1) that permits (a) identification of existing studies, (b) analysis of their usefulness and relevance in a specific research topic, and (c) gathering several studies conducted independently, at times with opposite results, and synthesizing their implications.

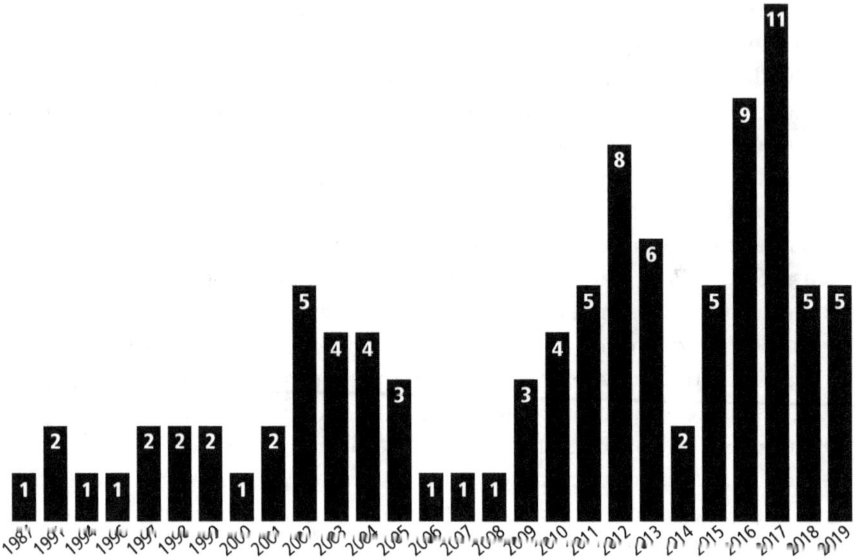

Figure 3.1 Historical evolution of documents.

The information search strategy has been carried out using two bibliographic databases: (a) Web of Science (WoS) and (2) Scopus. They are the most prestigious databases in the field of social sciences, especially in business and economics. As inclusion criteria, articles and reviews have been selected. The period specified is all references to the topic published up to 2019. The document search was carried out on July 6, 2019 with the protocol that is included in Table 3.1.

The number of documents obtained is 54 in WoS and 72 in Scopus. All the results obtained in the search have been reviewed to eliminate duplicates, to confirm they fit the subject matter of the study, and those with no identified authors have been discarded. The final sample is 96 documents (51 in WoS and 65 in Scopus, with 20 documents that were duplicated in both databases).

Next, a descriptive analysis of the previous literature has been done. Figure 3.1 details the year of the publications obtained and their historical evolution. It can be observed that the first publication related to the subject of the study was in 1987, found in the Scopus database and published in the *Journal of Management in Engineering* by Barnhart (1987). Until the beginning of the 2000s, research centered on subjects relative to the functioning of the company, the search for cost effectiveness and productivity, and strategy, leaving the management of organizational culture relegated to the background.

From 2009 to the present one can observe an increase in the number of documents related to the subject of the study. This could be due to the period

TABLE 3.1 Search Protocol

Databases	WoS	Scopus
Geographical Scope	Global scientific production	Global scientific production
Characteristics	*Quality indicators:* JCR impact factor Immediacy index Times cited Quartile	*Quality indicators:* SJR impact factor Times cited Quartile
Documents Searched	Topic	Article title, abstract, keywords
Inclusion Criteria	Articles Reviews	Articles Reviews
Data Range	All years to 2019	All years to 2019
Search Date	June 7, 2019	June 7, 2019
Search Terms	(Merger* and acquisition* OR "M&A" OR merger*) AND ("Human Resource*" OR "HR") AND "Cultur*"	(Merger* and acquisition* OR "M&A" OR merger*) AND ("Human Resource*" OR "HR") AND "Cultur*"
Number of Documents	54	72
Filtered Process	Duplicates Not identify the authors Not related to the topic	Duplicates Not identify the authors Not related to the topic
Final Number of Documents	51	65

of crisis in the global economy at the time, in which companies and problems of management that hindered the achievement of expected results, began to be studied in depth. In this period, the organizational culture of the company was put to the test due to the drastic and continuous strategic decisions that had to be made. It is at this moment that M&A operations have greater relevance to be considered operations of external growth, commonly used by companies to change and to face new market situations.

Over the years, organizational culture has been gaining greater importance for companies because it is a very important factor when implementing any strategy that directly affects the achievement of the desired sustainable competitive advantage. Further, it is a tool that permits companies to attract, select, and retain valuable people who fit the established organizational culture.

It is noted that the number of publications regarding the organizational culture of the company has increased since 2009. In this positive trend of interest in the research subject, the years 2012, 2016, and 2017 stand out

TABLE 3.2 List of Journals With the Most References in the Research Area

Journal	Number of Documents
Human Resource Management	7
International Journal of Human Resource Management	7
Industrial and Commercial Training	6
Journal of Organizational Change Management	4
Human Resource Development International	3
Career Development International	2
Harvard Business Review	2
International Journal of Human Resources Development and Management	2
Journal of Management and Organization	2
Journal of Nursing Management	2
Multinational Business Review	2
Thunderbird International Business Review	2

with the largest number of documents. Twenty-nine percent of the articles on the subject were published in these 3 years.

Table 3.2 shows the journals that have published work on this theme. We highlight *Human Resource Management* located in Q2 in Journal Citation Report™ (JCR) and in Q1 in *Scimago Journal & Country Rank* (SJR), and the *International Journal of Human Resource Management* located in Q2 in JCR and Q1 in SJR, as the journals that publish the most on this subject, each with seven documents. It should be noted that work on this theme has been published in 67 journals, but 55 of them have only published one article. There are five journals that have published more than two articles, accumulating 27 publications between them. Three of the journals belong to the area of human resources management, one to the area of organization studies, and another to the area of learning and development. This shows that these are works that can be published both in specific journals of human resources and more generic journals on management.

THEORETICAL MODEL FOR MANAGING CULTURAL FACTORS IN MERGERS AND ACQUISITIONS

In the context of M&A processes it is necessary to highlight the importance of cultural factors in the management of HR. Haberberg and Rieple (2008) identify three types of risks that determine the choice of the most appropriate method for each situation. First, the financial risk that the company won't be profitable enough, which is high in M&A. Second, the market risk related to the possibility that the company won't secure entry into a certain market or won't achieve the expected success, which is low in M&A. Third, cultural risk, which is also high and is related to the possibility of failure due to lack of organizational fit or HR integration problems.

On the other hand, little consideration has been shown for cultural integration in M&A. Therefore, following the model of the three stages of M&A—planning, integration, and implementation—of Rodríguez-Sánchez, Ortiz-de-Urbina-Criado, and Mora-Valentín (2015), the factors of cultural integration considered most relevant for the success of M&A according to the existing literature, have been grouped in each stage (see Table 3.3).

First Stage: Planning–Cultural Analysis

Before beginning any M&A process, and its subsequent cultural integration, it is essential to analyze the HR characteristics of both companies to

TABLE 3.3 Cultural Management Model in Three Stages of M&A

PLANNING Cultural Analysis	INTEGRATION Cultural Fit	IMPLEMENTATION Cultural Endstate
HR due diligence Hard and soft factors Reputation (Bastida, 2007; Das & Teng, 2002)	Cultural resistance Cultural separation Countercultural movements (Lucenko, 2000; Martín Bello, 1997)	Psychological state Flexible mentality Change possibility (Cartwright & Cooper, 1992; Martín Bello, 1997)
Cultural similarities vs differences Industry Size Technologies (Bower, 2001; Castro Casal, 2003)	Retaining valuable employees Lost experience Valuable knowledge (Lucenko, 2000; McCann & Gilkey, 1990)	Desired final cultural state Parent vs. target change HR Autonomy Training and development (Marks & Mirvis, 2010, 2011; Martínez Caraballo, 2006)
Degree of compatibility Friendliness vs hostility Degree of integration (Marks & Mirvis, 2011; Neira Fontela, 1992)	HR participation Personal relationships Teamwork (Goulet & Schweiger, 2006; Larsson & Finkelstein, 1999)	Differentiation Sustainability Work climate (Leite, 2009; Schimnke, Ambrose, & Neubaum, 2005)
Communication (I) Process design Message channel (Lin, Hung, & Li, 2006)	Communication (II) Message truth and frequency Two-way communication (Carrio, 2009)	Communication (III) Message understanding Effectiveness (Appelbaum & Gandell, 2003)

identify cultural differences and decide whether the two organizations are culturally compatible (Marks & Mirvis, 2011).

The planning stage is critical for the success of the M&A process because in it we select the target company. Traditionally, companies have focused importance only on tangible factors (strategic, financial, and legal) because of the difficulty or time required for a correct evaluation of intangible factors. When M&A don't achieve the expected results, one of the intangible factors that contributes to this failure is the organizational culture of the participating companies (Napier, 1989).

Regardless of how well the other two stages are planned and developed, the selection of a culturally incompatible company decreases the possibility of success (Schuler & Jackson, 2001). The evaluation of candidates can be limited by the inability to develop a comprehensive list of areas to be examined, by lack of information or by the decision not to provide the desired data (Castro Casal & Neira Fontela, 1994).

The director of the process together with the HR specialists should analyze and evaluate the organizational culture of the participating companies (Andrews & Bradsher, 2000). When the right partner has been selected and the M&A process is launched, management should take a proactive approach to cultural management problems and propose an HR due diligence plan to understand the organizational culture and characteristics of all the HR of the target company as much as possible. During the development of an HR due diligence plan, it is necessary to go deep into aspects related to employees (job security, impact on their position, or salaries), unions (policies or stability), consultants (contracts, temporary staff or recruitment needs), insured mutuals (transfer of plans), and financial entities (transfer of funds or consolidation of plans; Bastida, 2007).

In HR due diligence we should analyze the cultural factors that can affect the achievement of the objectives (Bramson, 2000). Some factors are easy to identify, like contracts, salary tables or statistical data. But you must also evaluate the intangible factors, identifying strengths and weaknesses, cultural compatibilities, and recognizing valuable employees to determine potential risks (Pascual de Blas, 2006). The evaluation of these intangibles is complicated and expensive because it requires a well-planned and developed strategy plus time to interact with HR (Harding & Rouse, 2007).

Once the characteristics of the target companies have been analyzed, we must select one of them. The cultural factors detected as determinants to select the right partner are cultural similarity versus difference, reputation, degree of cultural compatibility, and the communication plan for all employees (HRs) involved.

For Abrahamson and Fombrun (1994), the cultures of two organizations tend to be similar when they operate in homogeneous industries, are similar in size, use the same technologies, or are ordered with the same structural HR configuration. In contrast, the cultures of companies that are in heterogeneous industries show greater differences. Buono and Bowditch (1989) state that adjusting cultural differences between companies in the same industry is easier, although divergences between organizations in the same sector create difficulties.

Martin, Feldman, Hatch, and Sim (1983) defend cultural uniqueness, describing companies as idiosyncratic inventions that reflect the unique personalities and experiences of the employees working in them. Organizational culture reflects the circumstances of the company's creation, the personalities of its founders, and the circumstances of its growth (Schein, 1983). For Bower (2001), culture is specific in each company, constituting a differentiating element between organizations and units inside the same organization.

Differences in organizational culture, understood as what members of an organization think about, what they do and why they do it (Bower, 2001), and what they consider appropriate business practices (Schein, 1983), can generate anxiety, distrust, and feelings of hostility (Castro Casal, 2003). They influence the levels of commitment, cooperation, satisfaction, and productivity of the employees of the target company (Marks, 2000).

Reputation is the result of direct interactions maintained in the past, of past common partners, or the image of the company in the market. Reputation can improve collective strengths because partners will be more willing to provide key resources (Das & Teng, 2002). Zaheer, McEvily, and Perrone (1998) found that trust between companies reduces negotiation costs, which increases collective strengths. In addition, improving reputation reduces conflict between partners.

To identify the degree of compatibility between companies, it is essential to describe and evaluate the values, attitudes, beliefs, and group norms of the companies (Marks & Mirvis, 2011). The degree of cultural incompatibility depends on the characteristics of each part, which makes a correct assessment of HR in the initial planning phase essential for a successful integration process (Martín Bello, 1997). The parent company does not usually spend enough time to study the characteristics of each culture (Marks & Mirvis, 2011). However, the analysis of the culture of each company has been accepted as a key aspect to initiate the M&A process, and the level of cultural compatibility facilitates or hinders the opportunities to integrate properly. Neira Fontela (1992) identifies five dimensions to decide if the two companies are culturally compatible: strategic purpose of the M&A, business effectiveness and efficiency level, degree of friendship versus hostility, desired level of integration, and HR impact (managers and employees).

Most conflicts that occur between people participating in the M&A process have their origin in the lack of compatibility of the participating cultures (Castro Casal & Neira Fontela, 2002). Cultural clashes occur when people must work together without understanding the culture of their colleagues. The main causes of failure in M&A are associated with culture shock caused by incompatibility, and these cultural clashes undergo a process of evolutionary development that is composed of four stages: perception of differences, magnification of differences, stereotypes, and humiliations (Appelbaum, Karelis, Le Henaff, & McLaughlin, 2017).

Many of the studies about M&A recognize that cultural incompatibility is a determining problem (Cartwright & Cooper, 1992; Castro Casal, 2003). It is a very difficult aspect to manage especially in the first moments of the process when everyone wants to gain respect and demonstrate that their own culture is the best (Yu, Wang, Lin, & Li, 2005). People who are not able to adapt to the new culture can leave the company or actively oppose the change. The "us versus them" attitude hinders the implementation of the organizational changes and procedures necessary to achieve synergies (Lane, Cannella, & Lubatkin, 1999).

To address the negative feelings like stress, lack of trust, or uncertainty that people experience at the announcement of an M&A process, information about specific aspects like job loss, changes in compensation, benefit programs and career plans, or geographical relocations must be provided in a clear and concise way (Schweiger & DeNisi, 1991). Therefore, the communication plan addressed to the employees of both organizations is a key factor, since a direct relationship must be established with the aims of generating enthusiasm, ensuring a consistent and positive message, dispelling doubts and fears, and making people feel that they are a crucial part of the integrated company and the M&A process (Appelbaum & Gandell, 2003). The manner and steps in which the integration will be carried out, execution deadlines, employees' new functions and what is expected of each of them must be explained with clarity and certainty. In the study of Lin, Hung, and Li (2006) about employees of acquired banks, 48.6% showed confusion about changes and procedures, 38.9% considered the work environment unstable and 22.2% said there was no change in planning. The characteristics of a good communication plan during the planning phase are summarized in Figure 3.2.

From the start, we should speak in terms of the new entity to facilitate an open attitude to the cultural unity of the companies. A frequent problem is rumors about bad experiences suffered in the process (Bramson, 2000). The rumors usually focus on negative, and often quite imprecise, information provoking anxiety and tension. To avoid these rumors, it is advisable to first use internal media such as the corporate magazine, specific M&A memos, the intranet or interpersonal media (Neira Fontela, Castro Casal, & Álvarez, 1994). Then communicate externally through television, radio, or the press since it can reduce shock and increase confidence in subsequent communications (Castro Casal & Neira Fontela, 2002).

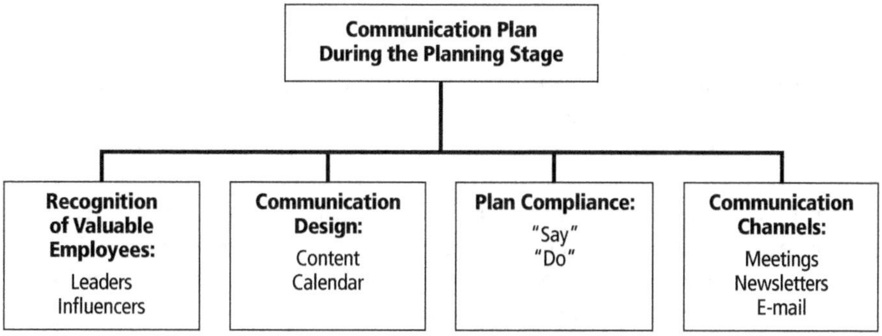

Figure 3.2 Communication plan during planning.

The main problem of communication in the first stage is the need for the organizations to maintain the confidentiality of the negotiations and the process, for example, in listed companies. These companies must delay the start of the communication plan, implementing actions that do not involve profuse jargon and proceeding with absolute caution (Santamaría Zurdo, 2004).

Second Stage: Integration–Cultural Fit

In the integration stage, the companies start to work together, having to manage aspects like the change process, restructuring, and the adjustment between HR and business strategies of both companies. Therefore, the integration stage is oriented to the analysis of the cultural fit of the companies. In this process of cultural change and restructuring, the employees have feelings that provoke a cultural resistance that may be active via quitting voluntarily, or passive through absenteeism or disobedience (Lucenko, 2000). This cultural resistance causes psychological erosion, loss of autonomy, problems of adaptation to the new environment, and confusion of values and identity (Vosse & Aliyu, 2018).

According to Gunkel, Schlaegel, Rossteutscher, and Wolff (2015), cultural resistance can be analyzed from an individual perspective (psychological level) or a collective perspective (organizational level). First, the psychological perspective identifies problems like the antagonism of "us versus them," condescending attitudes, distrust, tension, and hostility (Astrachan, 1990). Mark and Mirvis (1986) describe "merger syndrome," where people in the target company start negative rumors and restrict communication with their new co-workers. These barriers negatively affect the ability and predisposition of staff to understand, adhere to, or adopt the norms of a foreign culture, leading to so-called cultural separation.

This cultural separation occurs when people try to preserve their own values and behavior patterns, remaining aloof and independent from the other group (Martínez Caraballo, 2006). Cartwright and Cooper (1992) showed that two companies, 3 years after a merger, still maintained indications of their old cultures thus giving cultural incongruities to the new integrated organization. Buono, Bowditch, and Lewis (1985) state that within the same M&A process, employees can acculturate differently, because each person has different characteristics and thinking. The leader and his team must identify the people who, due to personal or contextual circumstances, are more resistant to change to manage them with care.

Second, the collective perspective refers to cultural clashes of the organizations due to people in each company trying to maintain their routines or traditional values. Normally, the target company is obligated to change its cultural traditions more rapidly, generating conflicts that cause countercultural movements (Martín Bello, 1997).

A key factor in countercultural movements is having a lower entry status than before the acculturation, causing people to stay rooted in their culture of origin, generating subcultures that support values contrary to the dominant culture, which they oppose and challenge (Martin & Siehl, 1983). There are three forms of countercultural movements: (a) direct opposition to the dominant values of the company, (b) opposition to the power structures of the dominant culture, and (c) opposition to the structural relationships of the dominant culture.

These countercultures cause a decrease in employee motivation and productivity (Martín Bello, 2011). Employees dissatisfied with the M&A of their company can be uncomfortable with colleagues from the other company, blame their own management, and make it difficult to communicate with M&A colleagues (Buono et al., 1985). The evolution of staff resistance and its consequences is shown in Figure 3.3.

Resistance to and rejection of cultural change cause voluntary resignations and loss of valuable personnel, which is much more frequent in managers or middle managers of the target company. Fulmer and Gilkey (1988) showed that in 50% of the 150 companies studied, senior managers left in the first year after the M&A agreement was signed, and this figure increased to 75% in the second year. It also involves the loss of experience and valuable knowledge, while a feeling of being losers in those that stay can cause dysfunctional behaviors in the new organization (McCann & Gilkey, 1990).

A fundamental factor for successful cultural adaptation and fit for both companies is equal participation of parent and target company employees in the change process. This participation entails a reduction in psychological problems (stress, anxiety, confusion or a feeling of incompetence) experienced during the process (Marks, 2000) and a more successful integration of functional areas, facilitating alliances and collaborative work

Figure 3.3 Evolution and consequences of employee resistance.

environments that achieve the expected synergies (Larsson & Finkelstein, 1999). Some actions that encourage employee participation are:

- Promote the exchange of information and the development of personal relationships between employees of the parent and target companies. Seminars, training activities, and guided tours can help reduce tension (Goulet & Schweiger, 2006).
- Give control and ability to manage activities, presenting the possible benefits the changes can have when completed (Schweiger & Goulet, 2000).
- Identify valuable personnel to promote the cultural integration process and give them support and rewards. They are known as "integration entrepreneurs" and it is necessary to evaluate their abilities and place them in the most appropriate position (Kay & Shelton, 2000). To produce competitive advantage, the parent company should transfer employees from the target company who have skills and abilities superior to competitors, negotiating financial agreements (Weber & Tarba, 2010).
- Promote joint work by the leaders of both companies on proposals for organization, processes, and people in the new organization.
- Establish communication processes in which leaders must be able to communicate on all levels with authority (Ashkenas, DeMonaco, & Francis, 1998).

At this stage, it is also essential to define a good communication plan establishing high levels of information and ensuring that people perceive

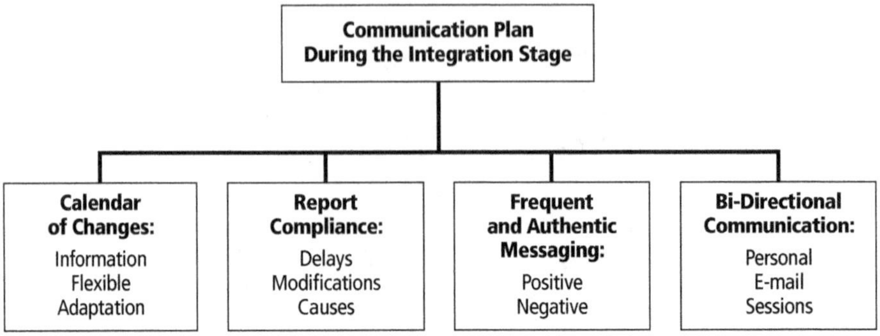

Figure 3.4 Communication plan characteristics during integration.

the truth of the message to give certainty both inside and outside the organization (Carrio, 2009).

It is fundamental to communicate the new culture and increase employee trust in management using two-way communication, giving employees the opportunity to express their doubts, suggestions, and difficulties (see Figure 3.4).

Third Stage: Implementation–Cultural Endstate

Once the employees of both companies are integrated, joint work and settlement in the new entity begins. All the actions implemented in the integration stage, like the new structure, new processes, or cultural modifications start to take effect and we must evaluate the proper functioning of the organization, to detect possible problems and solve them.

This period is characterized by layoffs, power struggles, resignations, and absenteeism (Siehl & Smith, 1990). People feel confusion between their old cultural reality and the final cultural state desired by the management of the new integrated organization. As the new entity starts up and consolidates, restructuring, readjustment and implementation problems arise due to changes in operations and employee competencies (Fapohunda, 2012). These problems will have different degrees of intensity depending on the type of M&A. Buono and Bowditch (1989) pointed out that it is necessary for at least two years to have elapsed since the integration to begin to evaluate the cultural modifications of the new structure, as well as to detect problems or consequences relevant to the progress of the new entity. According to Pritchett (1996), while in friendly M&As 5 to 7 years must pass before employees feel integrated, in hostile M&As it can take up to ten years to achieve cultural unity.

In this stage, all the people in the organization may experience different thoughts or psychological states ranging from disorientation or disintegration to discovery (Appelbaum et al., 2017). Since employee mentality is dynamic, flexible, and changes with time depending on the context and situation, in this period it should be ensured that the employees who initially had doubts about the need for cultural change end up considering the new culture necessary and valuable (Martín Bello, 1997). It is crucial to identify the phases in which employees are most vulnerable, and their feelings intensify.

From the start of the third stage, we must identify, clarify, and communicate the final cultural state desired by the organization. Marks and Mirvis (2010, 2011) identify the different cultural endstates available depending on the degree of change of the participating companies (see Figure 3.5). To reduce the complexity of the transition, we must determine the situation and functions of each employee to facilitate the coordination and simplification of the process. The degree of convergence between HR management practices in different national cultures and the necessary degree of adaptation to local conditions and cultures is crucial (Brewster, 2005).

The employees of the parent organization are prone to show arrogant behavior and often consider that their company's practices, styles, and values are better. This leads them to believe that the way their company operates is correct, superior, and cannot be improved. This behavior leads to an attitude of rejection toward the employees of the target company (Jemison & Sitkin, 1986). Management must prepare parent company employees for change, demonstrating that the procedures, styles and values of the target company

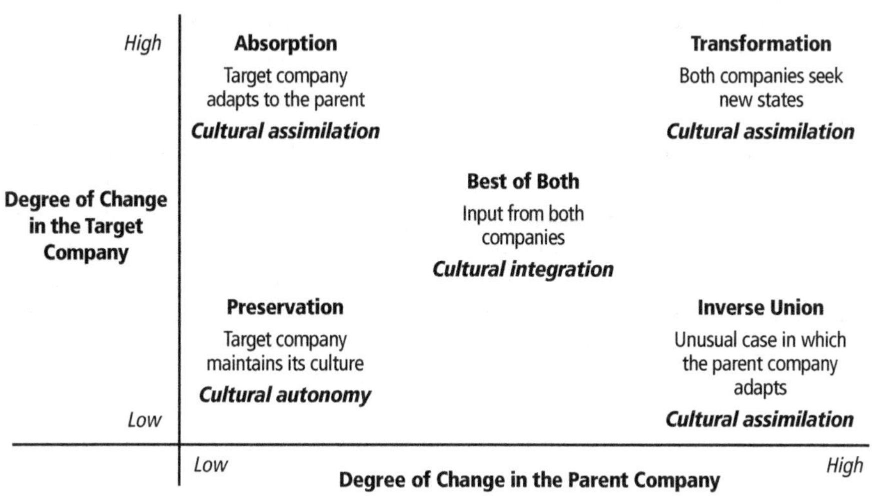

Figure 3.5 Cultural endstates. *Source*: Adapted from Mark and Mirvis (2010, 2011).

can be valid and encouraging them to learn from colleagues (Marks & Mirvis, 1986). People should be convinced that absorption (where the target company is culturally adapting to the parent) is only one option and is not always the most appropriate to achieve the expected results.

During this third stage of implementation for the correct evolution and control of the desired final cultural state, two key HR factors appear that we must manage efficiently: autonomy and cultural learning. Focus on these factors must be proactive since it is a stage where potential HR management problems that have appeared during previous stages of the M&A process can be corrected if they are detected in time.

People with autonomy are those who can control their work situation. This autonomy is good for both the worker and the company. People who can make decisions about their professional activities are less likely to feel undervalued and demotivated. Further, this autonomy gives more responsibility and the person feels closer to the organization, which increases their motivation and makes them more efficient. A worker with autonomy has a greater predisposition to participate in the M&A respecting other cultures and encouraging the achievement of the correct integration.

Additionally, people who have more autonomy are more satisfied and innovative, which helps the company to be more competitive. Hambrick and Cannella (1993) state that if senior executives have high status and autonomy in their work, rates of resignation in the year following the integration process diminish. But parent companies often decrease status and reduce autonomy, increasing control once the M&A has been established causing the deterioration of the senior executives' positions, which increases rates of resignation from the fourth year (Martínez Caraballo, 2006).

We must emphasize that complete autonomy and independence for employees, and especially for executives of the target company, is not the solution to achieve the correct cultural integration (Schweiger & Goulet, 2005). The solution is to achieve a state of parity between the parent company and the target company. Thus, we avoid the negative effects of eliminating autonomy by sharing power and responsibility. It is important to clarify that the management of HR factors must be permanent and constant over time. This is due to the open and flexible mentality of people. It has been shown that sometimes the problem is eliminated initially, but in the long term the organization fails to achieve true cultural integration, or to make employees feel a shared identity (Olie, 1994). Autonomy and culture are strongly related, and the correct management of autonomy helps build a strong organizational culture that respects the work of the employees, which creates a sense of security.

Another critical factor to reach the desired cultural state is the process of training and development. To develop the knowledge and skills necessary for good performance in new jobs, training, education, and practice are essential (Schuler & Jackson, 2001). Training plays a key role in the development of two main sources of the company's competitive advantage: its employees and its organizational knowledge (Serrano Segura & Barba Aragón, 2012).

Training should extend to new technologies, systems, and work processes, and can be complemented with manuals and databases with updated information (Gomes, Weber, Brown, & Tarba, 2011). To minimize cultural conflict, cultural understanding and learning play an essential role in raising awareness of cultural dynamics (Pablo, Sitkin, & Jemison, 1996).

The company's previous experience in M&A processes facilitates the creation of learning policies and practices. Forums to exchange information and the intranet are tools to improve the exchange of knowledge (Metha, 2000). Learning from previous experience in cultural integration processes, and from all the new employees available to the organization is a significant opportunity to attain competitive advantage and differentiation from competitors. Schweiger and Goulet (2000) established three levels of cultural learning during an M&A and found important relationships between these levels and the cultural integration of the companies (see Table 3.4).

Schweiger and Goulet (2000) state that the first objective of learning is to know the perceptions and stereotypes between companies to be able to eliminate them. The second is to encourage dialog to reach the desired cultural state. We should pose three open questions to the employees and act according to their perceptions: "How do they see their organizational culture?"; "How do they see the culture of the other company?"; and "How do they think the other company sees their culture?"

This process should enrich the dialogue, obtaining the maximum feedback possible from the employees (Goulet & Schweiger, 2006).

TABLE 3.4 Levels of Cultural Learning
None
No activities to manage learning
Reduced level of learning
Consequence: cultural integration failure
Superficial
Presentations, official communications or memos
Cultural stereotypes are usually not clarified nor eliminated
Consequence: effects opposite to those desired, and greater conflict between employees
Deep
Conversations, educational workshops, employee participation
More teamwork, cooperation, and commitment
Consequence: understanding and implementation of the desired cultural state

Inter-organizational learning supports greater communication, cooperation, and commitment among employees. Both parties learn not only about their colleague, but also about themselves by understanding the explicit values of each company as well as the implicit values behind them (Schweiger & Goulet, 2005). It is critical that at the end of the M&A process, the new culture is composed of the strengths of both the parent and target company cultures (Mayo & Hadaway, 1994). The employees of both companies will be more receptive to this change if they feel they have been involved and relevant during the integration.

Organizational culture is a source of sustainable competitive advantage due to complexity, uniqueness and opacity with respect to the outside. Therefore, although it constitutes a source of differentiation, it is necessary to ensure that the new employees are involved in its implementation (Rego, Ribeiro, & Cunha, 2010). Implementation activities are best carried out if there is a good climate. This positive climate is created thanks to the dedication of the workers. We must activate a motivating process where the organizational culture becomes especially important. In this way, workers will generate a feeling of well-being that will influence their attitudes and behaviors, providing certain value (Bayona, Goñi, & Madorrán, 2000).

During the implementation stage, if an ethical organizational culture that transmits good morality is perceived, the response from the employees is positive. Schimnke, Ambrose, and Neubaum (2005) understand that the congruence that exists between beliefs, norms, and organizational values and individuals is a highly influential aspect in the employee's work response. However, for these to exist, the worker himself needs pleasant contextual conditions, like those in a work environment with a satisfactory work climate (Wei & Clegg, 2014).

A factor closely related to the training and development process, since it directly affects success, is the way in which the communication plan of this third stage is executed (Figure 3.6). Proper cultural learning is impossible

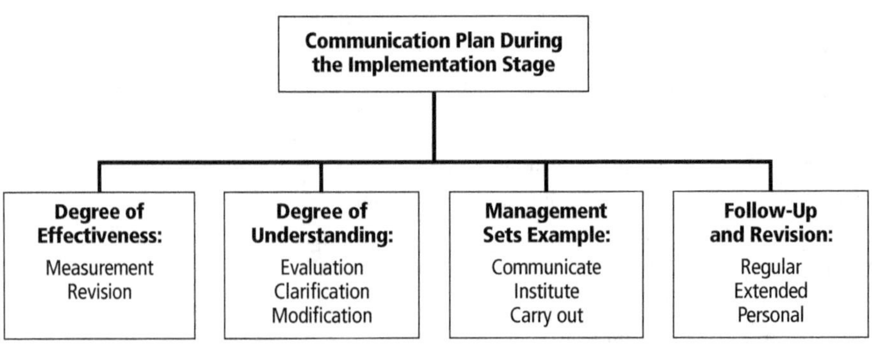

Figure 3.6 Communication plan characteristics during implementation.

if we do not develop clear, effective, and proactive communication. Regarding the content of the message, care should be taken with the language to ensure understanding. In transnational M&As, employees of the target company may not share the same language, leading to lack of understanding and low effectiveness of the communication plan (Vaara, 2003).

CONCLUSIONS

From a management perspective, it is necessary to go beyond strategic and financial considerations per se and examine the organizational dynamic and HR problems that emerge in M&A processes. Organizational culture is one of the determining factors to keep in mind for the success of cultural integration in M&A processes. The employees of the target company observe that their culture changes faster than that of their co-workers, leading them to resist the change. Not managing cultural differences can cause problems from lack of communication and understanding among personnel.

Cultural management generates uncertainty, tension, and loss of motivation in employees. No formula exists to avoid these effects, but there are specific ways to reduce them significantly. These pathways have a common objective: to recover and reinforce employee commitment, taking organizational and cultural uniqueness into account. It is essential to consider the characteristics of the people who will participate in the M&A and make the resulting company bigger and better. We must have a tight workforce with motivated, high performers who have significant potential.

The new organization can maintain the strengths of the parent culture, but is also able to improve, adding new elements from the culture of the target company. It is a complex task because of the need to overcome the barriers opposing the cultural change, for example, workers who feel their jobs or career development are threatened.

The literature review shows that most studies tend to analyze only one of the stages of the M&A process or a single cultural factor. Therefore, the main contribution of this chapter is the proposed theoretical model that includes, for each of the three stages of M&A, all the factors that are decisive for the cultural integration of the participating organizations.

In the first stage (planning–cultural analysis), companies must analyze the reasons for an M&A and define the profile of the target company. Special attention must be paid to the design of an action plan (integration plan, communication and learning process), with knowledge of the companies' employees to assess and analyze differences, similarities, and cultural compatibilities. Lack of cultural management in the planning stage causes problems to appear in later stages. To remedy these problems afterwards, time and resources will have to be invested. A proactive approach at the start of the M&A avoids certain problems. For example, the most notable and important problem—selecting a target company with an incompatible culture. An in-depth analysis of HR characteristics during due diligence avoids this problem.

In the second stage (integration–cultural fit), we must manage the companies' integration directing the change process, restructuring and fit between the cultures of both companies. Among the HR activities conducted at this stage, several stand out. They include management of resistance to cultural change, initiating HR policies that assist the restructuring process, creating the new culture and motivating employees through their participation in the M&A process.

In the third stage (implementation–cultural endstate), we face the necessity of reviewing and assessing the implementation of new policies and strategies during earlier stages. Culturally the objective is to change the minds of those employees who view the process with fear and negativity, leveraging the flexible employee mentality. Additionally, providing HR professionals with autonomy to manage cultural factors like reward systems, or learning programs will be essential to reach the desired final cultural state.

At a practical level, for cultural integration, it is important to avoid rumors that tend to focus on vague, negative information thus causing stress and confusion. The information gathered during the three stages of the communication process should be transcribed, analyzed and transformed into action plans. If employees see that the information provided has been used to carry out actions that continually improve the organization, they will enter a state of certainty and participation that is very beneficial for achieving the expected results.

Another fundamental aspect is the organizational culture fit model proposed by management. The new hierarchical structure (organization chart) resulting from the merger should be assessed. The main problem is layoffs due to overlapping positions and grouping criteria. Managers must select, promote, and reward valuable personnel with fair criteria and give a clear explanation to avoid dysfunctional behaviors from the rest of the people affected.

Finally, management must promote the development of personal relationships between employees of the parent and target companies with practices like seminars, training activities, or guided tours. These actions help to reduce tension, generating collaborative work environments and avoiding cultural shocks among participants.

It can be considered, based on what has been stated throughout the chapter, that it is necessary to conduct new studies to improve cultural management in M&A and analyze its influence on the success of these processes. Carrying out case studies of cultural management analyzing the three stages of the M&A process to better understand it is interesting as a line of future research.

It would also be interesting to analyze the influence of HR management in the success of different types of M&As. In this sense, it is necessary to analyze which HR factors are more determining in each type of M&A, as well as the significant differences in HR management according to the industrial sector to which the companies belong.

NOTE

1. Some of the most relevant M&A operations mentioned in a study by Becker (2017) are the acquisition of the American *Mosanto* by the German *Bayer* for US$66.3 billion (bn), the acquisition of shares in the American *Reynolds American Tobacco* by *British American Tobacco* for US$58.1 bn, the acquisition of the Dutch *NXP Semiconductors*, by the American *Qualcomm* for US$47 bn, the acquisition of the Swiss *Syngenta* by the Chinese *Chenchina* for US$46.9 bn, the acquisition of the American *Spectra Energy* by *Canadian Enbridge* for US$43 bn and the acquisition of the German *Linde AG* by the American *Praxair* for US$42.5 bn.

ACKNOWLEDGMENTS

This chapter has been supported by Project ECO2015-67434-R (MINECO/FEDER) of Spanish Ministry of Economy and Competitiveness (Spain) and the project RTI2018-097447-B-I00 of the Ministry of Science, Innovation and Universities (Spain).

REFERENCES

Abrahamson, E., & Fombrun, C. J. (1994). Macrocultures: Determinants and consequences. *The Academy of Management Review, 19*(4), 728–755.

Andrews, E., & Bradsher, K. (2000, November 26). This 1998 model is looking more like a lemon. *The New York Times.* Retrieved from https://www.nytimes.com/2000/11/26/business/this-1998-model-is-looking-more-like-a-lemon.html

Appelbaum, S., & Gandell, J. (2003). A cross method analysis of the impact of culture and communications upon a health care merger. *Journal of Management Development, 22*(5), 370–409.

Appelbaum, S., Karelis, C., Le Henaff, A., & McLaughlin, B. (2017). Resistance to change in the case of mergers and acquisitions: Part 1. *Industrial and Commercial Training, 49*(2), 87–92.

Ashkenas, R. N., DeMonaco, L. J., & Francis, S. (1998). Making the deal real: How GE capital integrates acquisitions. *Harvard Business Review, 76*(1), 165–178.

Astrachan, J. H. (1990). *Mergers, acquisitions, and employee anxiety: A study of separation anxiety in a corporate context.* New York, NY: Praeger.

Barnhart, G. (1987). Common critical success factors for integrating mergers and acquisitions. *Journal of Management in Engineering, 3*(1), 38–46.

Bastida, M. (2007). La gestión del capital humano como activo intangible en las fusiones y adquisiciones [Human capital management as an intangible asset in mergers and acquisitions]. *Harvard Deusto Finanzas y Contabilidad* [*Harvard Deusto Finance and Accounting*], *78*, 20–31.

Bayona, C., Goñi, S., & Madorrán, C. (2000). Compromiso organizacional: Implicaciones para la gestión estratégica de los recursos humanos [Organizational commitment: Implications for the strategic human resources management]. *Revista Europea de Dirección y Economía de la Empresa* [*European Journal of Management and Business Economics*], *9*, 139–149.

Becker, C. (2017). *Estudio sobre fusiones y adquisiciones 2017* [*Mergers and acquisitions report 2017*]. Santiago, Chile: PricewaterhouseCoopers.

Bhaskar, A. U. (2012). HR as business partner during mergers and acquisitions. *Human Resource Management International Digest, 20*(2), 22–23.

Bower, J. L. (2001). Not all M&As are alike and that matters. *Harvard Business Review, 79*(3), 92–101.

Bramson, R. N. (2000). HR's role in mergers and acquisitions. *Training & Development, 54*(10), 59.

Brewster, C. (2005). *Comparing HRM policies and practices across geographical borders.* Camberley, England: Edward Elgar.

Buono, A. F., & Bowditch, J. L. (1989). *The human side of mergers and acquisitions: Managing collisions between people, cultures and organizations.* San Francisco, CA: Jossey-Bass.

Buono, A. F., Bowditch, J. L., & Lewis, J. W. (1985). When cultures collide: The anatomy of a merger. *Human Relations, 28*(5), 477–500.

Carrio, M. (2009). Fusiones: El contrato, los recursos humanos, los errores, la estrategia... todas las claves para integrar sin traumas dos pymes de diferentes culturas [Mergers: the contract, human resources, mistakes, strategy... all the keys to integrate two SMEs from different cultures without trauma]. *Emprendedores: Las Claves de la Economía y el Éxito Profesional* [*Entrepreneurs: The Keys to Economy and Professional Success*], *141*, 44–48.

Cartwright, S., & Cooper, C. L. (1992). *Mergers and acquisitions: The human factor.* Oxford, England: Butterworth-Heinemann.

Castro Casal, C. (2003). Dirección del conflicto cultural en fusiones y adquisiciones [The cultural conflict management in mergers and acquisitions]. *Investigaciones Europeas de Dirección y Economía de la Empresa* [*European Research on Management and Business Economics*], *9*(2), 129–150.

Castro Casal, C., & Neira Fontela, E. (1994). Los procesos de fusión/adquisición de empresa: Razones, fuentes de información e importancia de los recursos humanos [Merger/acquisition company processes: Reasons, sources of information and human resources importance]. *Boletín de Estudios Económicos* [*Economic Studies Bulletin*], *49*(152), 267–284.

Castro Casal, C., & Neira Fontela, E. (2002). Gestión de la ansiedad de los recursos humanos en procesos de fusión y adquisición [Human resources anxiety management in merger and acquisition processes]. *AEDIPE: Revista de la Asociación Española de Dirección de Personal* [*AEDIPE: Journal of the Spanish Association of Personnel Management*], *23*, 30–38.

Das, T. K., & Teng, B. S. (2002). The dynamics of alliance conditions in the alliance development process. *Journal of Management Studies, 39*(5), 725–746.

DeOrtentiis, P. S., Summers, J. K., Ammeter, A. P., Douglas, C., & Ferris, G. (2013). Cohesion and satisfaction as mediators of the team trust – team effectiveness relationship. *Career Development International, 18*(5), 521–543.

Fapohunda, T. M. (2012). The human resource management challenges of post-consolidation mergers and acquisitions in Nigeria`s banking industry. *International Business Management, 6*(1), 68–74.

Fulmer, R., & Gilkey, R. (1988). Blending corporate families: Management and organization development in a post-merger environment. *Academy of Management Executive, 2*(4), 275–283.

Gomes, E., Angwin, D. N., & Tarba, S. Y. (2013). Critical success factors through the mergers and acquisitions process: Revealing pre and post M&A connections for improvement performance. *Thunderbird International Business Review, 55*(6), 13–35.

Gomes, E., Weber, Y., Brown, C., & Tarba, S. Y. (2011). *Mergers, acquisitions & strategic alliances: Understanding the process.* London, England: Palgrave MacMillan.

Goulet, P. K., & Schweiger, D. M. (2006). Managing culture and human resources in mergers and acquisitions. In G. K. Stahl & I. Björkman (Eds.), *Handbook of research in international human resource* (pp. 405–431). Camberley, England: Edward Elgar.

Gunkel, M., Schlaegel, C., Rossteutscher, T., & Wolff, B. (2015). The human aspect of cross-border acquisition outcomes: The role of management practices, employee emotions, and national culture. *International Business Review, 24*(3), 394–408.

Haberberg, A., & Rieple, A. (2008). *Strategic management. Theory and application.* Oxford, England: Oxford University Press.

Hambrick, D. C., & Cannella, A. A. (1993). Relative standing: A framework for understanding departures of acquired executives. *Academy of Management Journal, 36*(4), 733–762.

Harding, D. P., & Rouse, T. (2007). Human due diligence. *Harvard Business Review, 85*(4), 105–113.

Jemison, D. B., & Sitkin, S. B. (1986). Corporate acquisitions: A process perspective. *Academy of Management Review, 11*(1), 145–163.

Kay, I. T., & Shelton, M. (2000). The people problems in mergers. *The McKinsey Quarterly, 4*, 29–37.

Lane, P. J., Cannella, A. A., & Lubatkin, M. H. (1999). Ownership structure and corporate strategy: One question viewed from two different worlds. *Strategic Management Journal, 20*(12), 1077–1086.

Larsson, R., & Finkelstein, S. (1999). Integrating strategic, organizational, and human resource perspectives on mergers and acquisitions: A case survey of synergy realization. *Organization Science, 10*(1), 1–26.

Leite, D. (2009). A análise da cultura organizacional de uma instituição do setor hoteleiro [The organizational culture analysis of a hotel sector institution]. *Psicología IESB* [*IESB Psychology*], *1*(21), 21–33.

Lin, B. W., Hung, S. C., & Li, P. C. (2006). Mergers and acquisitions as a human resource strategy. *International Journal of Manpower, 27*(2), 126–142.

Lucenko, K. (2000). Strategies for growth. *Across the Board, 37*(8), 63.

Magano, K. D., & Adele, T. (2017). Organisational change and the psychological contract at a pharmaceutical company. *SA Journal of Human Resources Management, 15*(a920), 1–10.

Maimunah, I., Nordahlia, U. B., & Zoharah, O. (2018). The influence of organizational culture and organizational justice on group cohesion as perceived by merger and acquisition employees. *Organizations and Markets in Emerging Economies, 9*(2), 233–250.

Manterola, C., Vial, M., Pineda, V., & Sanhueza, A. (2009). Systematic review of literature with different types of design. *International Journal Morphology, 27*(4), 1179–1186.

Marks, M. L. (2000). Mixed signals: Don´t stay merger when you mean acquisition. *Across the Board, 37*(5), 21–27.

Marks, M. L., & Mirvis, P. H. (1986). The merger syndrome-when companies combine, a clash of cultures can turn potentially good business alliances into financial disasters. *Psychology Today, 20*(10), 36–42.

Marks, M. L., & Mirvis, P. H. (2010). *Joining forces: Making one plus one equal three in mergers, acquisitions, and alliances.* San Francisco, CA: Jossey-Bass.

Marks, M. L., & Mirvis, P. H. (2011). A framework for the human resources role in managing culture in mergers and acquisitions. *Human Resource Management, 50*(5), 651–670.

Martin, J., & Siehl, C. (1983). Organizational culture and counterculture: An uneasy symbiosis. *Organizational Dynamics, 12*(2), 52–64.

Martin, J., Feldman, M. S., Hatch, M. J., & Sim B. (1983). The uniqueness paradox in organizational stories. *Administrative Science Quarterly, 28*(3), 438–453.

Martín Bello, J. C. (1997). Cultura organizacional en fusiones y adquisiciones empresariales [Organizational culture in mergers and acquisitions]. *Serie Estudios – Instituto Universitario de la Empresa* [*Studies Series–University Institute of Business*], *31*, 1–26.

Martínez Caraballo, N. (2006). Los recursos humanos en los procesos de fusión y adquisición [Human resources in merger and acquisition processes]. *Intangible Capital, 2*(12), 236–258.

Mayo, A., & Hadaway, T. (1994). Cultural adaptation – The ICL-Nokia-data merger 1991-2. *Journal of Management Development, 13*(2), 59–71.

McCann, J. E., & Gilkey, R. (1990). *Fusiones y adquisiciones de empresas* [*Mergers and acquisitions*]. Madrid, Spain: Díaz de Santos.

Metha, S. N. (2000). Lucent`s new spin. *Fortune, August*(3), 30–31.

Napier, N. K. (1989). Mergers and acquisitions, human resources issues and outcomes: A review and suggested typology. *Journal of Management Studies, 26*(3), 271–289.

Neira Fontela, E. (1992). Un modelo para evaluar el impacto sobre los recursos humanos de las fusiones/adquisiciones [A model to assess the mergers/acquisitions impact on human resources]. *Revista Europea de Dirección y Economía de la Empresa [European Journal of Management and Business Economics], 1*(1), 91–98.

Neira Fontela, E., Castro Casal, C., & Álvarez, D. (1994). Recursos humanos y procesos de concentración empresarial: Un estudio empírico comparado España–Reino Unido [Human resources and business concentration processes: An empirical study comparing Spain–United Kingdom]. *Revista Europea de Dirección y Economía de la Empresa [European Journal of Management and Business Economics], 3*(3), 137–149.

Olie, R. (1994). Shades of culture and institutions in international mergers. *Organization Studies, 15*(3), 381–405.

Pablo, A. L., Sitkin, S. B., & Jemison, D. B. (1996). Acquisition decision-making processes: The central role of risk. *Journal of Management, 22*(5), 723–746.

Pascual de Blas, J. (2006). Gestión del capital humano en todo el proceso de fusión/adquisición para asegurar el valor esperado por el accionista [Human capital management in merger/acquisition process to ensure the shareholder value expected]. *Revista APD: Asociación para el Progreso de la Dirección [APD Journal: Association for Management Progress], 9*(6), 73–77.

Pritchett, P. (1996). *After the merger: Managing the shockwaves.* New York, NY: Dow Jones-Irwin.

Rego, A., Ribeiro, N., & Cunha, M. P. (2010). Perceptions of organizational virtuousness and happiness as predictors of organizational citizenship behaviors. *Journal of Business Ethics, 9*(2), 215–235.

Rodríguez-Sánchez, J.-L., Ortiz-de-Urbina-Criado, M., & Mora-Valentín, E.-M. (2015). Human resources management and mergers and acquisitions: Perspectives and challenges. In W. D. Nelson (Ed.), *Advances in business and management* (Vol. 7; pp. 67–87). New York, NY: Nova.

Rodríguez-Sánchez, J.-L., Ortiz-de-Urbina-Criado, M., & Mora-Valentín, E.-M. (2019). Thinking about people in mergers and acquisitions processes. *International Journal of Manpower, 40*(4), 643–657.

Rodríguez-Sánchez, J.-L., Mora-Valentín, E.-M., & Ortiz-de-Urbina-Criado, M. (2019). Human resource management in merger and acquisition planning. *Journal of Organizational Change Management, 33*(1), 16–28.

Santamaría Zurdo, A. (2004). El nuevo rol de los recursos humanos en los procesos de fusión: Un concepto innovador de cultura corporativa [The new human resources role in merger processes: An innovative concept of corporate culture]. *Estudios Financieros: Revista de Trabajo y Seguridad Social [Financial Studies: Journal of Work and Social Security], 260,* 147–224.

Schein, E. H. (1983). The role of the founder in creating organizational culture. *Organizational Dynamics, 12*(1), 13–28.

Schimnke, M., Ambrose, M. L., & Neubaum, D. O. (2005). The effect of leader moral development on ethical climate and employee attitudes. *Organizational Behavior and Human Decision Processes, 97*(2), 135–151.

Schuler, R., & Jackson, S. (2001). HR issues and activities in mergers and acquisitions. *European Management Journal, 19*(3), 239–253.

Schweiger, D. M., & DeNisi, A. S. (1991). Communication with employees following a merger: A longitudinal field experiment. *Academy of Management Journal, 34*(1), 110–135.

Schweiger, D. M., & Goulet, P. K. (2000). Integrating mergers and acquisitions: An international research review. *Advances in Mergers and Acquisitions, 1*, 61–91.

Schweiger, D. M., & Goulet, P. K. (2005). Facilitating acquisition integration through deep-level cultural learning interventions: A longitudinal field experiment. *Organization Studies, 26*(10), 1477–1499.

Serrano Segura, J., & Barba Aragón, M. I. (2012). La gestión de los recursos humanos en las corporaciones locales [Human resources management in local companies]. *Cuadernos de Gestión* [*Management Notebooks*], *12*(2), 149–168.

Sielh, C., & Smith, D. (1990). Avoiding the loss of a gain: Retaining top managers in an acquisition. *Human Resource Management, 29*(2), 167–185.

Vaara, E. (2003). Post-acquisition integration as sensemaking: Glimpses of ambiguity, confusion, hypocrisy, and politicization. *Journal of Management Studies, 40*(4), 859–894.

Vosse, B. J., & Aliyu, O. A. (2018). Determinants of employee trust during organisational change in higher institutions. *Journal of Organizational Change Management, 31*(5), 1105–1118.

Weber, Y., & Tarba, S. Y. (2010). Human resource practices and performance of mergers and acquisition in Israel. *Human Resource Management Review, 20*(3), 203–211.

Wei, T., & Clegg, J. (2014). Successful integration of target firms in international acquisitions: A comparative study in the medical technology industry. *Journal of International Management, 20*(2), 237–255.

Yu, J., Wang, J., Lin, W., & Li, S. (2005). The genomes of Oryza sativa: A history of duplications. *Plos Biology, 3*(2), 266–281.

Zaheer, A., McEvily, B., & Perrone, V. (1998). Does trust matter? Exploring the effects of interorganizational and interpersonal trust on performance. *Organization Science, 9*(2), 141–159.

CHAPTER 4

CULTURE, PARADOXICAL FRAMES, AND BEHAVIORAL STRATEGY

Joshua Keller
Erica Wen Chen

ABSTRACT

We provide a theoretical exploration into how cross-cultural differences in the use of paradoxical frames may influence the behavioral strategy of a firm. We postulate that cross-cultural differences in the use of paradoxical frames establish divergent patterns in the way executives categorize issues and actions, which influences the categories of issues that firm leaders focus attention on and the categories of actions that firm leaders use in their strategic formulation process. We discuss the environmental conditions that make cultural differences in the use of paradoxical frames salient, such as environmental complexity, low munificence, and rapid change. We also discuss the strategic implications of the contrasts in the use of paradoxical frames, such as their impact on performance and innovation. Finally, we discuss how the focus on paradoxical frames integrates research on behavioral strategy with research on culture.

Cultural Values in Strategy and Organization, pages 109–132

INTRODUCTION

When South Korea's Samsung group emerged as a major global conglomerate, many features of the company's strategy appeared paradoxical. The firm combined low cost manufacturing with R&D innovation, combined specialization in core businesses with high levels of overall diversification, and combined seniority-based care with merit-based incentives (Khanna, Song, & Lee, 2011). Within East Asia, this engagement in seemingly contradictory behaviors is far from an isolated case. Networks of Japanese buyers and suppliers called *keiretsu* often cooperate in production while competing within the same markets (Dowling, Roering, Carlin, & Wisnieski, 1996; Luo, 2004). Korean manufacturers often engage in "incremental innovation," where they seek novel solutions with instant commercial viability (Lee & Kang, 2007; Viotti, 2002). And many Chinese state-owned enterprises undergo dramatic change while remaining essentially the same (Ralston, Terpstra-Tong, Terpstra, Wang, & Egri, 2006).

In this chapter, we propose that underlying this general tendency for East Asian firms to act paradoxically is a greater proclivity among East Asian firm leaders (compared to Western firm leaders) to use paradoxical frames when engaging in behavioral strategy. Paradoxical frames are mental templates that can be used to recognize and embrace contradictory elements of strategic issues and actions (Smith & Tushman, 2005). For example, a firm leader who uses paradoxical frames may conceptualize a strategic issue as both a threat and an opportunity or to consider engaging in strategic actions that are both cooperative and competitive. Paradoxical frames impact strategic actions by drawing attention to the plausibility that seemingly contradictory issues or actions can co-exist and by encouraging the embrace of their coexistence (Miron-Spektor, Gino, & Argote, 2011). This can have a profound impact on how firms behave strategically, encompassing a range of strategic issues from how firms cooperate and compete to how firms explore and exploit to how firms differentiate and reduce costs.

One of the biggest challenges in behavioral strategy research is addressing the link between micro-level cognition and macro-level culture (Gavetti, Greve, Levinthal, & Ocasio, 2012; Powell, Lovallo, & Fox, 2011). One barrier to integrating these perspectives is the emphasis on cognitive processes at the micro-level (e.g., Felin, Foss, Heimeriks, & Madsen, 2012; Foss & Lindenberg, 2013; Gavetti, 2012; Hodgkinson & Healey, 2011) and the emphasis on cognitive content at the macro-level (e.g., Kaplan, 2011; Riad & Vaara, 2011). Whereas research on the impact of micro-level cognitive processes on behavioral strategy has centered on general factors that are considered universal, such as bounded rationality (e.g., Gavetti, 2012) and motivation (e.g., Foss & Lindenberg, 2013), research on the impact of macro-level cognitive content on behavioral strategy has centered on the internalization of institutionalized logics (e.g., Jonsson & Regnér, 2009) and practices (e.g., Whittington, 2006). The way macro-level culture shapes the underlying cognitive processes that influence behavioral strategy is less explored.

Research on paradoxical framing provides a link between macro-level culture and micro-level cognition in a way that encompasses both cognitive processes and cognitive content because paradoxes are fundamental, meta-level features of organizing (Lewis & Smith, 2014; Schad, Lewis, Raisch, & Smith, 2016) and macro-level culture shapes the cognitive processes used to manage these meta-level concerns (Keller, Loewenstein, & Yan, 2017; Leung, Liou, Miron-Spektor, Chan, & Eisenberger, 2016). In this chapter, we discuss how culture shapes paradoxical framing and how cross-cultural differences in the proclivity to use paradoxical frames impact firms' strategic behavior and outcomes across a multitude of strategic issues, including competitive dynamics, strategy formulation, and corporate governance. In the process, we integrate macro and micro perspectives on behavioral strategy by connecting behavioral strategy research with research on macro-level cultural knowledge of paradoxes and the micro-level cognitive processes that shape how firm leaders manage strategic paradoxes.

In the following sections we first discuss *what* the cultural differences are in the use of paradoxical frames and their influence on firm strategic behavior in practice, using category conventions as a framework. We then discuss *when* cross-cultural differences are likely to manifest as differences in strategic behavior by discussing the relationship between categorization conventions, attention, and action formation. Finally, we discuss *how* firms leverage the strategic opportunities that arise because of culture's influence on the use of paradoxical frames by discussing the role of rationality and plasticity bounds.

BEHAVIORAL STRATEGY, PARADOXES, AND PARADOXICAL FRAMES

A central concern of behavioral strategy is the incorporation of cognitive and social perspectives in strategic management theory and practice. According to Powell and colleagues, "behavioral strategy aims to bring realistic assumptions about human cognition, emotions, and social behavior to the strategic management of organizations and, thereby, to enrich strategy theory, empirical research, and real-world practice" (Powell et al., 2011, p. 1371). The field incorporates cognitive and psychological factors through three different paradigms: reductionist, pluralist, and contextualist (Powell et al., 2011). Reductionist research focuses on strategic decision making, examining how the key decision makers that drive the strategic moves of the firm are affected by cognitive biases. Pluralist research focuses on differences in strategic perspectives within the firm and the conflicts and strategic issues that are solved through conflict resolutions. Finally, contextualist research focuses on the extent to which management perception and sensemaking are socially constructed and hence shaped by a broader macro context. Because each of these paradigms covers a different aspect of behavioral strategy, the integration of different paradigms is pivotal to understanding how individual, organizational, and macro contexts shape behavioral strategy (Bendersky & McGinn, 2010).

We contend that examining the role of paradox provides an avenue for integrating these three perspectives, as the examination of paradoxes provides a meta-level theory that connects micro and macro levels of organizational phenomena (Schad et al., 2016; Smith, 2014). We base our argument on the premise that strategic issues and actions are inherently paradoxical (Smith & Lewis, 2011). This includes issues and actions associated with cooperation and competition (Bengtsson & Kock, 2014; Raza-Ullah, Bengtsson, & Kock, 2014), exploration and exploitation (Andriopoulos & Lewis, 2009; Raisch & Birkinshaw, 2008), and stability and change (Audia, Locke, & Smith, 2000; Farjoun, 2010). Although paradoxes are inherent in many strategic issues and actions, they often remain latent, with firm leaders not even recognizing their existence (Knight & Paroutis, 2017; Sharma & Good, 2013). If firm leaders recognize paradoxes, they may try to suppress the tension that ensues by ignoring one element or switching back and forth between two elements and addressing only one at a time (Lewis, 2000; Smith & Lewis, 2011).

However, because the contradictory elements that comprise a paradox persist, ignoring one element or switching back and forth between elements can never completely resolve the tension (Smith & Lewis, 2011). The use of paradoxical frames therefore plays a critical role in firm leaders' experience with paradoxes, as they influence both the recognition and the embrace of seemingly contradictory issues and actions. For example, firm leaders who use paradoxical frames are more likely to recognize the simultaneous presence of cooperation *and* competition, exploration *and* exploitation, and stability *and* change. They are also more likely to cooperate *while* competing, explore *while* exploiting, and maintain stability *while* promoting change. This impact of using paradoxical frames on performance has been supported empirically, both qualitatively (e.g., Smith, 2014) and quantitatively (e.g., Miron-Spektor, Ingram, Keller, Smith, & Lewis, 2018).

The notion that the way leaders use paradoxical frames impacts firm strategy is both congruent and incongruent with a reductionist approach to behavioral strategy. On the one hand, research on paradoxes suggests that managers have cognitive biases because they are less able to recognize or embrace paradoxical tension. On the other hand, research on paradoxes also suggest that the underlying cognitive bias is not a deviation from rationality but an overreliance on linear, logical thinking (Smith & Lewis, 2011). One reason why leaders may lack paradoxical framing is a cognitive bias that stems from the linear, rational thinking that epitomizes Western thinking.

The assumption that logic entails an absence of contradictions is deeply rooted in Aristotelian logic. While paradoxes exist in all societies and individual firm leaders can vary in whether they use paradoxical frames (e.g., Smith, 2014), multiple scholars have noted contrasts in the traditional philosophical approaches to paradoxes between the East and the West (e.g., Chen, 2002, 2008; Eisenhardt & Westcott, 1988; Fang, 2012; Li, 2014; Li, Tung, & Ralston, 2016). Whereas the Aristotelian law of noncontradiction is a fundamental component of traditional Western philosophy, the Taoist law of contradiction is a fundamental component of traditional Eastern philosophy (Peng & Nisbett, 1999). Therefore, while the existence of paradoxes is recognized in both philosophical traditions, the two different philosophical traditions begin with a different premise. Traditional Western philosophy emphasizes the contrast, distinction, and separation of seemingly contradictory elements, whereas Eastern philosophy emphasizes the complementarity, unity, and integration of paradoxical elements (Chen, 2008; Li et al., 2016). Philosophical differences manifest as differences in the proclivity to use paradoxical frames, with Westerners more likely to frame contradictory issues and actions as "either/or" and East Asians more likely to frame contradictory issues and actions as "both/and" (Keller et al., 2017). Therefore, the inability for leaders to use paradoxical frames is both reductionist and contextualist, as the inherent biases are influenced by macro culture.

Paradoxical Frames and Categorization Conventions

To examine how macro culture shapes the use of paradoxical frames in ways that impact firm behavior, we begin with the premise that firm leaders use categories to interpret strategic issues and actions and to guide strategic behavior accordingly (Dutton & Jackson, 1987; Ocasio, 2011). Categories are comprised of sets of examples with a common label (Loewenstein, Ocasio, & Jones, 2012). They can be used to group any type of phenomena including products (Durand & Paolella, 2013), firms (e.g., Porac, Thomas, Wilson, Paton, & Kanfer, 1995; Reger & Palmer, 1996), actions (Keller & Wu, 2012), issues (Jackson & Dutton, 1988), and ideas (Loewenstein & Mueller, 2016). Culture impacts categories by creating categorization conventions, which are conventional ways of generating word-to-word and word-to-example relations that are shared across members of a cultural group (Keller & Loewenstein, 2011; Loewenstein et al., 2012).

Categorization conventions connect macro-level culture with micro-level cognition by instantiating higher-order culturally-guided logics and beliefs within specific situational contexts (Ocasio, Loewenstein, & Nigam, 2015; Thornton, Ocasio, & Lounsbury, 2012). Moreover, because individuals use categories to guide behavior (Murphy, 2002; Smith, 1989), categorization conventions do not only link culture to cognition but culture to day-to-day behavior in practice. Cross-cultural differences in the use of paradoxical frames will likely create differences in categorization conventions because categorization can involve either feature-based or rule-based processes (Chen, Ross, & Murphy, 2014; Love, 2014). Feature-based categorization processes involve comparing an issue or action to a prototype (commonly used in strategic management literature; e.g., Dutton & Jackson, 1987; Porac et al., 1995). Rules-based categorization, on the other hand, involves categorizing issues or actions based on whether the example satisfies a particular rule (Smith & Sloman, 1994). One common rule used in categorization is *antonymy* (Jones, 2002; Paradis & Willners, 2011), which stipulates that objects that are classified as members of one category should be classified as the opposite member of an antonymic category (Keller & Chen, 2017). Based on the rule of antonymy, an issue that is a threat is by rule not an opportunity, an action that is cooperative is by rule not competitive, and a project that is exploratory is by rule not exploitative.

In most cases, feature-based and antonymy-based categorization will yield the same results, as the most prototypical features of opposing categories typically indicate the opposite of the other category (Paradis & Willners, 2011; Paradis, Willners, & Jones, 2009). For example, the most prototypical features of cooperation and competition are likely to be either cooperative or competitive and not both (Keller et al., 2017). Accordingly, firm leaders are likely to categorize prototypically cooperative actions such as the sharing of information with other firms as exclusively cooperative (not competitive) and prototypically competitive actions such as the launching of a price war as exclusively competitive (and not cooperative). These prototypical actions serve as a basis for distinguishing between cooperation and competition as two antonymic categories of actions. Antonymy therefore provides an efficient rule-based categorization heuristic (Keller & Chen, 2017; Love, 2014; Smith & Sloman, 1994). Because firm leaders already assume that an issue or action that is a member of one category is *not* a member of its opposite category, firm leaders typically do not need to consider whether the features match the opposite category. Accordingly, if an issue is a threat, then it is not an opportunity. If an action is competitive, then it is not cooperative.

The strategic environment, however, is more complex than antonymic relations suggest (Pozzebon, 2004). Few antonyms are logically contradictory (e.g., life and death). Some issues and actions have features of both of two antonymic categories. For example, the arrival of a new venture into an industry can be both a threat and an opportunity because it represents both a potential competitor and a potential alliance partner. Issues or actions that are members of two antonymic categories, however, contradict antonymy-based rules of categorization and hence are likely to appear contradictory to anyone who notices common features. In order to reconcile the contradiction, firm leaders must either deny the contradiction and assume that an issue or action with shared features of antonymic categories is not plausible or accept the contradiction and consider the issue or action to be members of both categories. Therefore, categorizing an example as an indicator of two antonymic categories entails using paradoxical frames (Keller & Chen, 2017; Keller et al., 2017), as it implicitly involves the acceptance that a paradox exists.

Individual firm leaders from any cultural background have the propensity to use paradoxical frames (Smith, 2014), and thus categorize issues or actions as indicators of two antonymic categories. However, because of cultural differences in general proclivities to use paradoxical frames, categorization conventions are likely to diverge along cultural lines. Cultures encourage or discourage the use of paradoxical frames by providing narratives and artifacts that address general approaches to paradoxes (Peng, Spencer-Rodgers, & Nian, 2006). Eastern narratives and artifacts emphasize holism and change, which promotes tolerance of contradictions (Peng & Nisbett, 1999; Spencer-Rodgers, Williams, & Peng, 2010).

Cultural proclivities to use paradoxical frames do not require conscious acts of philosophizing. Chinese firm leaders, for example, do not carry a copy of Laozi's *Tao Te Ching* to the boardroom, and in fact, may never have read the book before. Instead, categorization conventions emerge during day-to-day interpretations of the environment and the communication of those day-to-day interpretations with other members of the culture (Liu, Keller, & Hong, 2015; Ocasio et al., 2015). One firm leader may use a paradoxical frame to categorize an issue in one context. For example, the firm leader may find an example of a potential threat that is also a potential opportunity. The firm leader then describes the instance with other members of the top management team or describes the instance as part of a public statement to outside stakeholders. Eventually, through recurring patterns of communication across a field, categorization conventions across an entire population of firms emerge.

Because cross-cultural differences in paradoxical framing create cross-cultural differences in the propensity to categorize issues and actions as simultaneously members of antonymic categories, we can expect divergent categorization conventions. We can expect that firm leaders from Eastern cultural backgrounds will typically take a "both/and" approach and categorize issues and actions based on their features even if that entails categorizing them as members of both of two antonymic categories. On the other hand, we can expect that firm leaders from Western cultural backgrounds will typically take an "either/or" approach and categorize issues and actions based on which category fits the features of the issues and actions and exclusively categorize the issues and actions as a member of one and not the other category.

PARADOXICAL FRAMES AND FIRM STRATEGIC BEHAVIOR

So how does the use of paradoxical frames in categorization conventions impact firms' strategic behavior? We propose that they establish cross-cultural differences in the issues that firms pay attention to and the actions that firms formulate as part of their overall strategy.

Paradoxical Frames, Categorization Conventions, and Attention to Issues

Attention within strategic management is defined as "the noticing, encoding, interpreting, and focusing of time and effort by organizational decision makers on both (a) *issues*: the available repertoire of categories for making sense of the environment... and (b) *answers*: the available repertoire of action alternatives" (Ocasio, 1997, p. 189, emphasis in original). One critical aspect of research on attention is the interplay between the focus of attention and the situated environment (Miller & Chen, 2004; Ocasio, 1997, 2011). Firm leaders use categories of issues and actions to focus attention on particular aspects of the environment while scanning the environment, making inferences about what they see in the environment (Das & Kumar, 2010), and guiding their firm's reactions accordingly (Thomas, Clark, & Gioia, 1993). For example, after airline deregulation, airline firm leaders shifted their attention from *engineering* issues to *entrepreneurial* issues, which impacted subsequent hiring decisions and strategic actions (Cho & Hambrick, 2006). Similarly, firm leaders that paid more attention to *external* issues instead of *internal* issues were more likely to pay attention to globalization and subsequently engage in more global actions (Levy, 2005).

Categorization conventions play a critical role in how attention shapes the interpretation of the environment because the specific examples that firm leaders indicate as a member of a category is influenced by categorization conventions (Loewenstein et al., 2012). Firm leaders' focus of attention is not on actual specific issues within a specific situated context, but on categories of issues (Ocasio, 1997). Therefore, whether a specific issue draws attention depends on whether the specific issue fits the overall category, as inferences about the specific issue will be made based on the category as a whole (Markman & Ross, 2003; Yamauchi & Markman, 2000). Because the categorization of a specific issue depends on categorization conventions, the inferences that each firm leader makes about a specific issue will depend on whether the specific issue is conventionally considered a member of the category. For example, within an alliance, all firm leaders may see *control* and *trust* as two important indicators of confidence in the cooperation between the two parties (Das & Teng, 1998). When paying attention to various sources of confidence, some may see control and trust as antithetical and only pay attention to whether the source indicates control or trust, whereas others may see aspects of the source that facilitates both control and trust and pay attention to both elements of the relationship while examining the source. Paradoxical framing can influence whether the issue is considered to be only one or both.

Paradoxical framing is likely to influence the attention to issues across multiple domains. Potential events can be *threats* and *opportunities* (Dutton & Jackson, 1987). Firms entering the industry can be potential *competitors* and potential *collaborative* partners (Chen, 2008). Future projects can be *exploratory* and *exploitative.* Because Western culture deemphasizes the use of paradoxical frames in categorization, categorization conventions in the West are more likely than categorization conventions in the East to involve the exclusive categorization of issues as indicators of one category and not its antonym. Any issue that is a threat is not an opportunity, regardless of whether it has features of both a threat and an opportunity. Similarly, any firm that is a potential competitor is not a potential collaborator, regardless of whether it has features of potential competitiveness and potential cooperativeness. On the other hand, because Eastern culture emphasizes the use of paradoxical frames in categorization, categorization conventions in East Asia are more likely than categorization conventions in the West to involve the categorization of issues as indicators of both of two antonymic categories. Any issue that is a threat can also be an opportunity, as long as it has features of both a threat and an opportunity. Similarly, any firm that is a potential competitor can also be a potential collaborator, as long as it has features of potential competitiveness and potential cooperativeness.

We suggest that these contrasting categorization conventions will influence attention in two critical ways. First, because Western firm leaders are more likely to focus attention on specific categories of issues, they are less likely to pay attention to issues that fall under an opposite category. For example, firm leaders often pay attention to either exploratory or exploitative aspects of ongoing projects and make investments accordingly. The projects may have features of exploration and exploitation. For instance, they may simultaneously have features that are both breaking-edge and commercially viable. However, because Western categorization conventions are more likely to involve exclusive categorization, Western firm leaders are less likely to consider a project to be exploratory if it is exploitative or vice-versa. They may use other categories such as "short-term" vs. "long-term" or "risky" vs. "safe," but the underlying heuristic will be similar—because projects are one or the other and not both, focus one aspect of a project entails not recognizing aspects of a project that also indicate the other. East Asian firm leaders, on the other hand, should be more likely to recognize projects that are both "cutting edge" and "practical," "short-term" and "long-term," and "risky" and "safe." Regardless of whether their focus is on exploration or exploitation, they will focus their attention on aspects of projects that encompass both. As a result, East Asian firm leaders should be more likely than Western firm leaders to pay attention to projects that are both exploratory and exploitative and recognize a project that has features of both when they see it.

Second, because East Asian categorization conventions are more likely to categorize specific issues as indicators of two antonymic categories of issues, they are more likely to make inferences based on both categories. For example, once Western firm leaders pay attention to exploratory aspects of a project, information about the exploratory aspects of the projects are more likely to be used as the sole base of judgment for further action. Exploitative aspects of the project are less likely to be considered because the exploitative aspects of the project are left unnoticed. East Asian firm leaders, on the other hand, are more likely to draw inferences based on both exploratory and exploitative aspects of the project and draw inferences accordingly.

Paradoxical Frames, Categorization Conventions, and Action Formulation

Categorization conventions are not only salient aspects of firm leaders' interpretation of the external environment, but also salient aspects of the ideas that firm leaders form when engaging in the strategy formulation process. One key feature of the strategy formulation process is the actions that firms choose as components of their strategic repertoire (Chen & Miller, 2012; Miller & Chen, 1996). When firms choose a set of actions, they in fact are choosing categories of actions (Ferrier, 2001; Ferrier & Lyon, 2004; Ferrier, Smith, & Grimm, 1999). These categories of actions become guides for further action. For example, once a firm decides to include operational efficiency as a competitive action, resources and attention will be devoted towards areas that the firm leaders perceive as indicators of operational efficiency. Categorization conventions are therefore likely to play a role in strategy formulation because they influence how specific actions are categorized. This in turn influences which specific actions are integrated into a firm's strategic repertoire.

Cross-cultural research has found that East Asians are more likely to generate ideas that span two antonymic categories. For example, East Asians are more likely to consider creativity to be both encompassing novelty and usefulness and therefore generate ideas that encompass both facets (Loewenstein & Mueller, 2016). We propose that because of the greater proclivity among East Asian firm leaders compared to Western firm leaders to categorize actions as members of two antonymic categories, they will more likely come up with ideas about actions that encompass both antonymic categories. As a result, their repertoire of actions should be more likely to include actions that have features of both antonymic categories. For example, East Asian firm leaders should be more likely than Western firm leaders to include actions that have features of both cooperation and competition or differentiation and cost leadership. For example, participating in an industry association has features of both cooperation and competition as it provides opportunities to coordinate collective action while also providing access to information that helps positions themselves competitively. Given the overlapping features, East Asian firm leaders should be more likely than Westerners to consider joining an association and using it as a mechanism for competing. Similarly, East Asians may be more likely than Western firm leaders to choose to develop a product that positions themselves as both differentiators and cost leaders.

In sum, cross-cultural differences in the use of paradoxical frames are likely to impact both the issues that firm leaders pay attention to and the actions that firm leaders generate.

PARADOXICAL FRAMES, CATEGORIZATION CONVENTIONS, AND ENVIRONMENTAL CONTINGENCIES

Because attention occurs within a situated context, the use of paradoxical frames will only apply to specific issues and actions within the environment that are paradoxical. Accordingly, only specific issues and actions that have features of both antonymic categories trigger the potential for cross-cultural differences in attention associated with the use of paradoxical frames. Smith and Lewis (2011) suggest that there are three aspects of an environment that are most likely to produce paradoxical elements.

The first is *plurality*, which denotes a multiplicity of ideas, beliefs, and goals within the environment. Within the strategic environment, plurality is most likely to emerge when there is institutional complexity (Ocasio & Radoynovska, 2016; Vermeulen, Zietsma, Greenwood, & Langley, 2016). When there is institutional complexity, there are more opportunities for the same specific issue to be framed differently depending on the particular logic used (Ocasio et al., 2015). As a result, there are more opportunities for specific issues to be categorized as indicators of two antonymic categories because there are more alternative features of the same specific issue. For example, an issue of how to cooperate with others from the industry (e.g., working together on a lobbying effort) may not also consider issues around competition from a market perspective but can from a status perspective (Dorobantu, Kaul, & Zelner, 2017). The pluralistic ways of conceptualizing competition and cooperation enable firm leaders to consider how issues can simultaneously consider both cooperation and competition. Cross-cultural differences in the use of paradoxical frames should therefore be more salient when the focus of attention is within an institutionally pluralistic environment. For example, the institutional complexity around guanxi provides an overlap between personal and professional spheres (Guo & Miller, 2010). This provides a salient context for Chinese firm leaders to use paradoxical framing, as they must constantly wrestle with the overlap between the personal and professional spheres.

The second is *scarcity*, which denotes a lack of resources in the environment. Within the strategic environment, scarcity is most likely to become salient when there is low environmental munificence (Dess, Ireland, & Hitt, 1990). In these cases, focusing attention on multiple issues is more necessary, as there is little slack to enable any issue to be left alone. In this case, both of two antonymic categories of issues are likely to draw attention to firm leaders. However, Western firm leaders may be more likely to perceive these categories as mutually exclusive, and hence any specific issue involves a trade-off. East Asian firm leaders, on the other hand, may be more likely to look for specific issues that encompass both. This cultural difference only becomes salient when a lack of munificence is an issue.

The third is *change*, which denotes changes in the environment. Change in the environment requires focus of attention on both old and new issues in the environment. Many old and new issues may appear contradictory (Lüscher & Lewis, 2008). As in the case of scarcity, change may force all firm leaders to consider focusing on issues that encompass both of two antonymic categories. And as in the case of scarcity, differences in categorization conventions may lead to contrasts in the inferences made, with trade-offs more likely to occur in the West. These trade-offs become more salient when Western firms are undergoing rapid change.

PARADOXICAL FRAMES, CATEGORIZATION, AND FIRM STRATEGIC OPPORTUNITIES

Although we propose that there are cross-cultural differences in strategic firm behavior associated with the use of paradoxical frames, the effect of these differences are unclear. Comparing cultural effects on overall firm performance is notoriously difficult, as many conflating socioeconomic and regulatory factors can influence how firms perform (Taras, Kirkman, & Steel, 2010). Even research at the individual-level is inconclusive. No previous study has examined the link between national-level cross-cultural differences in managing paradoxes and individual performance, and other previous research on paradoxical frames suggests mixed results. For example, Miron-Spektor and colleagues (2011) found that priming Americans with integrative paradoxical frames aided creativity. The positive effects were attributed to a sense of conflict. East Asians' greater general proclivity to use integrative paradoxical frames suggest that they should be, on average, more creative, but because they are also less likely to perceive conflict associated with paradoxes (Ng & Hynie, 2014), they are unlikely to harness the benefits of using paradoxical frames. Smith and Tushman (2005) also suggest that any benefit of using paradoxical frames requires recognition that tension between paradoxical elements exist, and hence successful efforts at managing paradoxes does not only require recognition that paradoxes exist but recognition that there is tension.

The different aspects of categorization conventions found in the East and West, however, do point to opportunities that firms can engage in that can link behavioral strategies to preferential strategic outcomes. To describe these opportunities, we conceptualize categorization conventions as *rationality* and *plasticity* bounds that present opportunities for superior performance among those who surpass the bounds (Gavetti, 2012).

Rationality Bounds and Strategic Opportunities

Rationality bounds are systematic cognitive tendencies that provide opportunities for firms to exploit. Some scholars suggest that firms' ability to exploit opportunities depends on their ability to overcome cognitive biases (Das & Teng, 1999). Others point to positive benefits of heuristics (Maitland & Sammartino, 2015). Because Western firm leaders are less likely to see issues and actions as members of two antonymic categories, categorization conventions within the West can be conceptualized as a form of cognitive bias, even though the underlying rationale for making categorical distinctions is, on the surface, rational (Keller & Chen, 2017). East Asian firm leaders are thus more likely to recognize specific issues that encompass multiple categories—even those that appear contradictory. At the same time, because East Asian firm leaders are paying attention to more issues, they may be devoting relatively more cognitive resources to issues that are less beneficial. Western firm leaders, on the other hand, may be more likely to take advantage of heuristics. Similarly, from an action generation perspective, East Asian firms may benefit from recognizing specific actions that can encompass seemingly contradictory categories. However, they may be devoting too many cognitive resources to actions that are less beneficial.

We propose, however, that from the individual firm's perspective, opportunities to exploit others' general tendencies can occur when they use an alternative paradoxical frame to those within the same culture. As discussed above, the higher propensity of East Asian firm leaders compared to Western firm leaders to use paradoxical frames will manifest as differences in categorization conventions. East Asian firm leaders should be more likely to perceive the same strategic issue as both a threat and an opportunity, an emerging firm as both cooperative and competitive and a new program as both exploratory and exploitative. They should be more likely to formulate new actions that are both cooperative and competitive, both exploratory and exploitative, and both triggers of change and maintenance of stability. Categorization conventions, however, are not monolithic (Keller & Loewenstein, 2011). Although most firm leaders are likely to follow conventions, firm leaders still have agency in how they use culture (Rindova, Dalpiaz, & Ravasi, 2011; Suddaby, 2010), and not all firm leaders learn from their own cultural environment to the same degree (Thomas, Sussman, & Henderson, 2001). As a result, not all firm leaders are expected to follow the cultural norms in whether they categorize particular issues and actions as indicators of two antonymic categories.

As in any case where there are systematic cultural biases (Rindova & Fombrun, 1999), culture-specific proclivities to use or not use paradoxical frames may provide opportunities for arbitrage. Qualitative findings do suggest that American firms whose firm leaders use paradoxical frames (a somewhat counterintuitive approach within the United States) perform better (e.g., Smith, 2014). Following this logic, the opposite should also hold true in East Asia, with firm leaders withholding the use of paradoxical frames performing better.

Plasticity Bounds and Strategic Opportunities

Plasticity bounds, which restrict actions based on normative expectations of the social appropriateness of actions, however, may provide additional opportunities for those who can exploit through counter-normative behavior (Gavetti, 2012). "Cultural arbitrage" is less likely to occur in practice simply because firm leaders think differently because they may see an upside to thinking differently but a downside to acting differently. As described earlier, categorization conventions are communicated within each culture, and a shared meaning within the culture is critical for establishing common ground (Bechky, 2003). Therefore, when there is disagreement about whether a particular issue or action is an indicator of a particular category, misinterpretations may ensue. Any perceived benefit from thinking differently may be moderated by concerns over negative social consequences.

Whether to deviate from conventionality in the use of paradoxical frames can impact multiple aspects of the strategic management process. First and foremost, firm leaders in larger firms operate within a top management team. Consequently, deviation from categorization norms will create cognitive diversity within the upper echelons of the organization. Upper echelon cognitive diversity has been found to have both positive and negative influences on the strategic management decision making process because of the positive benefit of divergent ideas countered by a negative impact of disagreement (Miller, Burke, & Glick, 1998). If some firm leaders within the top management team deviate from categorization norms, then a combined negative and positive impact of the deviation is likely to arise. For example, one American firm leader may attempt to create a new project that she believes is both exploratory and exploitative, but others may not see it as plausible and hence any benefit from the firm leader's use of an integrative paradoxical frame will be limited. Similarly, one Chinese firm leader may attempt to create a new project that she believes is only exploratory in recognition of the negative impact of exploitation on exploration, but others do not see a need to distinguish and hence any benefit from the firm leader's use of a differentiating paradoxical frame will be limited.

The same paradox associated with deviating from using paradoxical frames will apply to interfirm relations as well. For example, strategic alliances are often considered to be paradoxical because they simultaneously involve sets of cooperative and competitive actions between two firms (Bengtsson & Kock, 2014; Das & Teng, 2000; Gnyawali, He, & Madhavan, 2006, 2008). If firm leaders from one Western firm deviate from categorization norms and consider a competitive act to also be cooperative, then the firm initiating the competitive move may recognize its benefit on cooperation but misunderstandings between the two firms due to differences in perceptions of the act's cooperativeness may ensue.

PARADOXES AND PLURALISM IN STRATEGIC DECISION MAKING

Of course, many firms will not only have cognitive diversity but cultural diversity within the top-management team (Knight, Pearce, Smith, Olian,

Sims, Smith, & Flood, 1999). In particular, multinational organizations are not only going to have cultural differences within the upper echelons, but have cultural differences between headquarters and subsidiaries and between the firm and stakeholders from different cultural environments (Gomez-Mejia & Palich, 1997; Palich & Gomez-Mejia, 1999). Some of the competing effects of differences in how firm leaders use paradoxical frames in categorization will apply similarly to those from cognitive diversity within a culture. Because most firm leaders are likely to follow the conventions of one culture, demographic diversity associated with these deeper cultural differences will likely establish cognitive diversity. However, given the likelihood that misunderstandings about another culture is likely to trigger stereotyping (Nishii, Gotte, & Raver, 2007) and the stereotyping may not be directly related to different uses of paradoxical frames, the potential negative social consequences may be even higher thus further undermining firm performance. However, the underlying benefit of firm leaders incorporating both integrative and differentiating paradoxical frames in how they categorize issues and actions and their application of the categorization scheme in practice is likely to improve the overall performance of the firm. Deviance in action and diversity in the decision making process can provide opportunities for breaking plasticity bounds. Therefore, cross-cultural differences in the use of paradoxical frames also may involve pluralist approaches to behavioral strategy, as cultural differences in the use of paradoxical frames may provide sources of diversity in the strategic decision making process.

A CULTURE AND PARADOXICAL FRAME RESEARCH AGENDA

Each of the proposals we raised in this chapter have been based on general findings of cultural differences in the use of paradoxical frames in contexts outside of strategic management. It is therefore critical that future research address empirically how the use of paradoxical frames influence firm leader cognition and associated firm behavior and firm outcomes. As discussed above, the most critical component in connecting culture to practice through cognition is the identification of specific issues and actions that potentially demonstrate cultural differences. This requires an identification of prototypical features of each of two antonymic categories within specific contexts. For example, while there is evidence of cross-cultural differences in the categorization of actions as both cooperative and competitive in the intra-organizational context (Keller et al., 2017), the scope of cooperation and competition in the interfirm context is far more complex and varied (Das & Teng, 2000). For example, firms can engage in simultaneous cooperation and competition as part of a two-firm alliance, a network-based alliance, and membership in an association (Bengtsson & Kock, 2014). The extent to which actions involved in these interfirm relations can be categorized as both cooperative and competitive may depend on the level of analysis.

However, in support of the notion that there are elements of paradoxes that are consistent across its various types (Lewis & Smith, 2014), empirical research is likely to be more fruitful if it is able to uncover consistencies in patterns, regardless of whether the categorization scheme of inquiry is cooperation and competition, exploration and exploitation, or stability and change. The use of paradoxical frames in categorization is a fundamental cognitive process that is shaped differently depending on cultural background. Because of the rich philosophical tradition of addressing paradoxes found in the Ancient Chinese work of *Laozi* and *Zhuangzi*, most previous research on cross-cultural differences in the use of paradoxical frames has centered on the question of East vs. West (e.g., Chen, 2014; Chen & Miller, 2015). Future research will also be aided by the inclusion of examinations into other philosophical traditions and other cultural influences at various levels of analysis (e.g., firm-level, industry-level, and field-level).

Regardless of strategic management context or level of analysis of inquiry, the plethora of antonymic relations discussed in strategic management suggest that a closer examination into how firm leaders categorize issues and actions into either one or both of two antonymic categories and its association with firm behavior and performance is warranted. This includes further examinations into how behavioral strategies adhere to general tendencies within the West and within the East, as well as within multinational corporations and other firms that encompass more cultural diversity. By combining comparative work on different cultures and work on culturally diverse environments (e.g., multinational top management teams), research on paradoxes in strategic management can address reductionist, pluralist, and contextualist issues in behavioral strategy.

In conclusion, this chapter provides an important initial step in integrating reductionist, pluralist, and contextual approaches in the study of behavioral strategy by demonstrating the importance of paradoxes in strategic management, the impact of variance in the use of paradox frames, the role of culture in shaping variance, and the contexts where cultural differences matter. As we explained, the use of paradoxical frames provides a fundamental, meta-level way of approaching a plethora of strategic issues and actions. Contrasting uses of paradoxical frames create contrasting categorization conventions, which further create contrasting strategic opportunities for those who defy the convention. Future empirical work can address how these factors contribute to behavioral strategy across multiple domains.

ACKNOWLEDGMENT

This chapter, save some minor changes, was earlier published as Keller, J., & Chen, E. W. (2017). Culture, paradoxical frames, and behavioral strategy. In T. K. Das (Ed.), *Culture and behavioral strategy* (pp. 101–123). Charlotte, NC: Information Age.

REFERENCES

Andriopoulos, C., & Lewis, M. W. (2009). Exploitation-exploration tensions and organizational ambidexterity: Managing paradoxes of innovation. *Organization Science, 20*(4), 696–717.

Audia, P. G., Locke, E. A., & Smith, K. G. (2000). The paradox of success: An archival and a laboratory study of strategic persistence following radical environmental change. *Academy of Management Journal, 43*(5), 837–853.

Bechky, B. A. (2003). Sharing meaning across occupational communities: The transformation of understanding on a production floor. *Organization Science, 14*(3), 312–330.

Bendersky, C., & McGinn, K. L. (2010). Open to negotiation: Phenomenological assumptions and knowledge dissemination. *Organization Science, 21*(3), 781–797.

Bengtsson, M., & Kock, S. (2014). Coopetition—Quo vadis? Past accomplishments and future challenges. *Industrial Marketing Management, 43*(2), 180–188.

Chen, M.-J. (2002). Transcending paradox: The Chinese "middle way" perspective. *Asia Pacific Journal of Management, 19*, 179–199.

Chen, M.-J. (2008). Reconceptualizing the competition-cooperation relationship: A transparadox perspective. *Journal of Management Inquiry, 17*(4), 288–305.

Chen, M.-J. (2014). Presidential address—Becoming ambicultural: A personal quest, and aspiration for organizations. *Academy of Management Review, 39*(2), 119–137.

Chen, M.-J., & Miller, D. (2012). Competitive dynamics: Themes, trends, and a prospective research platform. *Academy of Management Annals, 6*(1), 135–210.

Chen, M.-J., & Miller, D. (2015). Reconceptualizing competitive dynamics: A multidimensional framework. *Strategic Management Journal, 36*, 758–775.

Chen, S. Y., Ross, B. H., & Murphy, G. L. (2014). Implicit and explicit processes in category-based induction: Is induction best when we don't think? *Journal of Experimental Psychology: General, 143*(1), 227–246.

Cho, T. S., & Hambrick, D. C. (2006). Attention as the mediator between top management team characteristics and strategic change: The case of airline deregulation. *Organization Science, 17*(4), 453–469.

Das, T. K., & Kumar, R. (2010). Interpartner sensemaking in strategic alliances: Managing cultural differences and internal tensions. *Management Decision, 48*(1), 17–36.

Das, T. K., & Teng, B. (1998). Between trust and control: Developing confidence in partner cooperation in alliances. *Academy of Management Review, 23*(3), 491–512.

Das, T. K., & Teng, B. (1999). Cognitive biases and strategic decision processes: An integrative perspective. *Journal of Management Studies, 36*(6), 757–778.

Das, T. K., & Teng, B. (2000). Instabilities of strategic alliances: An internal tensions perspective. *Organization Science, 11*(1), 77–101.

Dess, G. G., Ireland, R. D., & Hitt, M. A. (1990). Industry effects and strategic management research. *Journal of Management, 16,* 7–27.

Dorobantu, S., Kaul, A., & Zelner, B. (2017). Nonmarket strategy research through the lens of new institutional economics: An integrative review and future directions. *Strategic Management Journal, 38*(1), 114–140.

Dowling, M. J., Roering, W. D., Carlin, B. A., & Wisnieski, J. (1996). Multifaceted relationships under coopetition description and theory. *Journal of Management Inquiry, 5*(2), 155–167.

Durand, R., & Paolella, L. (2013). Category stretching: Reorienting research on categories in strategy, entrepreneurship, and organization theory. *Journal of Management Studies, 50*(6), 1100–1123.

Dutton, J. E., & Jackson, S. E. (1987). Categorizing strategic issues: Links to organizational action. *Academy of Management Review, 12*(1), 76–90.

Eisenhardt, K. M., & Westcott, B. J. (1988). Paradoxical demands and the creation of excellence: The case of just-in-time manufacturing. In R. E. Quinn & K. S. Cameron (Eds.), *Paradox and transformation: Toward a theory of change in organization and management* (pp. 169–194). Cambridge, MA: Ballinger.

Fang, T. (2012). Yin yang: A new perspective on culture. *Management and Organization Review, 8*(1), 25–50.

Farjoun, M. (2010). Beyond dualism: Stability and change as a duality. *Academy of Management Review, 35*(2), 202–225.

Felin, T., Foss, N. J., Heimeriks, K. H., & Madsen, T. L. (2012). Microfoundations of routines and capabilities: Individuals, processes, and structure. *Journal of Management Studies, 49*(8), 1351–1374.

Ferrier, W. J. (2001). Navigating the competitive landscape: The drivers and consequences of competitive aggressiveness. *Academy of Management Journal, 44*(4), 858–877.

Ferrier, W. J., & Lyon, D. W. (2004). Competitive repertoire simplicity and firm performance: The moderating role of top management team heterogeneity. *Managerial & Decision Economics, 25*(6–7), 317–327.

Ferrier, W. J., Smith, K. G., & Grimm, C. M. (1999). The role of competitive action in market share erosion and industry dethronement: A study of industry leaders and challengers. *Academy of Management Journal, 42*(4), 372–388.

Foss, N. J., & Lindenberg, S. (2013). Microfoundations for strategy: A goal-framing perspective on the drivers of value creation. *Academy of Management Perspectives, 27*(2), 85–102.

Gavetti, G. (2012). Toward a behavioral theory of strategy. *Organization Science, 23*(1), 267–285.

Gavetti, G., Greve, H. R., Levinthal, D. A., & Ocasio, W. (2012). The behavioral theory of the firm: Assessment and prospects. *Academy of Management Annals, 6*(1), 1–40.

Gnyawali, D. R., He, J., & Madhavan, R. (2006). Impact of co-opetition on firm competitive behavior: An empirical examination. *Journal of Management, 32*(4), 507–530.

Gnyawali, D., He, J., & Madhavan, R. (2008). Co-opetition: Promises and challenges. In C. Wankel (Ed.), *21st century management: A reference handbook* (pp. 386–398). London, England: SAGE.

Gomez-Mejia, L. R., & Palich, L. E. (1997). Cultural diversity and the performance of multinational firms. *Journal of International Business Studies, 28*, 309–335.

Guo, C., & Miller, J. K. (2010). Guanxi dynamics and entrepreneurial firm creation and development in China. *Management and Organization Review, 6*(2), 267–291.

Hodgkinson, G. P., & Healey, M. P. (2011). Psychological foundations of dynamic capabilities: Reflexion and reflection in strategic management. *Strategic Management Journal, 32*(13), 1500–1516.

Jackson, S. E., & Dutton, J. E. (1988). Discerning threats and opportunities. *Administrative Science Quarterly, 33*(3), 370–387.

Jones, S. (2002). *Antonymy: A corpus-based perspective.* London, England: Routledge.

Jonsson, S., & Regnér, P. (2009). Normative barriers to imitation: Social complexity of core competencies in a mutual fund industry. *Strategic Management Journal, 30*(5), 517–536.

Kaplan, S. (2011). Research in cognition and strategy: Reflections on two decades of progress and a look to the future. *Journal of Management Studies, 48*(3), 665–695.

Keller, J., & Chen, E. W. (2017). A roadmap of the paradoxical mind: Expanding cognitive theories on organizational paradox. In W. K. Smith, M. W. Lewis, P. Jarzabkowski, & A. Langley (Eds.), *Oxford handbook of organizational paradox* (pp. 66–86). Oxford, England: Oxford University Press.

Keller, J., & Loewenstein, J. (2011). The cultural category of cooperation: A cultural consensus model analysis for China and the United States. *Organization Science, 22*(2), 299–319.

Keller, J., Loewenstein, J., & Yan, J. (2017). Culture, conditions and paradoxical frames. *Organization Studies, 38*(3–4), 539–560.

Keller, J., & Wu, C. (2012). Measuring "West meets East" in strategic management research Using cultural consensus model and cultural mixture model analyses. In C. L. Wang, D. J. Ketchen, & D. D. Bergh (Eds.), *Research methodology in strategy and management, Volume 7—West meets East: Toward methodological exchange* (Vol. 7, pp. 161–181). Bingley, England: Emerald.

Khanna, T., Song, J., & Lee, K. (2011). The paradox of Samsung's rise. *Harvard Business Review, 89*(7/8), 142–147.

Knight, D., Pearce, C. L., Smith, K. G., Olian, J. D., Sims, H. P., Smith, K. A., & Flood, P. (1999). Top management team diversity, group process, and strategic consensus. *Strategic Management Journal, 20*(5), 445–465.

Knight, E., & Paroutis, S. (2017). Becoming salient: the TMT leader's role in shaping the interpretive context of paradoxical tensions. *Organization Studies, 38*(3–4), 403–432.

Lee, K., & Kang, S. M. (2007). Innovation types and productivity growth: Evidence from Korean manufacturing firms. *Global Economic Review, 36*(4), 343–359.

Leung, A. K., Liou, S., Miron-Spektor, E., Chan, D., & Eisenberger, R. (2016). *Middle ground approach to paradox: Within and cross cultural examination of the creative benefits of paradoxical frames* (Working paper). Singapore: Singapore Management University.

Levy, O. (2005). The influence of top management team attention patterns on global strategic posture of firms. *Journal of Organizational Behavior, 26*(7), 797–819.

Lewis, M. W. (2000). Exploring paradox: Toward a more comprehensive guide. *Academy of Management Review, 25*(4), 760–776.

Lewis, M. W., & Smith, W. K. (2014). Paradox as a metatheoretical perspective: Sharpening the focus and widening the scope. *Journal of Applied Behavioral Science, 50*(2), 127–149.

Li, P. P. (2014). The unique value of yin–yang balancing: A critical response. *Management and Organization Review, 10*(2), 321–332.

Li, P. P., Tung, R., & Ralston, D. (2016). Global implications of the indigenous epistemological system from the East: How to apply yin-yang balancing to paradox management. *Cross Cultural & Strategic Management, 23*(1), 42–77.

Liu, X.-x., Keller, J., & Hong, Y.-y. (2015). Hiring of personal ties: A cultural consensus analysis of China and the United States. *Management and Organization Review, 11*(1), 145–169.

Loewenstein, J., & Mueller, J. (2016). Implicit theories of creative ideas: How culture guides creativity assessments. *Academy of Management Discoveries, 2*(4), 320–348.

Loewenstein, J., Ocasio, W., & Jones, C. (2012). Vocabularies and vocabulary structure: A new approach linking categories, practices, and institutions. *Academy of Management Annals, 6*(1), 41–86.

Love, B. C. (2014). Categorization. In K. N. Ochsner & S. Kosslyn (Eds.), *Oxford handbook of cognitive neuroscience* (Vol. 2; pp. 342–358). Oxford, England: Oxford University Press.

Luo, Y. (2004). *Coopetition in international business.* Copenhagen, Denmark: Copenhagen Business School Press.

Lüscher, L. S., & Lewis, M. W. (2008). Organizational change and managerial sensemaking: Working through paradox. *Academy of Management Journal, 51*(2), 221–240.

Maitland, E., & Sammartino, A. (2015). Decision making and uncertainty: The role of heuristics and experience in assessing a politically hazardous environment. *Strategic Management Journal, 36*(10), 1554–1578.

Markman, A. B., & Ross, B. H. (2003). Category use and category learning. *Psychological Bulletin, 129*(4), 592–613.

Miller, C. C., Burke, L. M., & Glick, W. H. (1998). Cognitive diversity among upper-echelon executives: Implications for strategic decision processes. *Strategic Management Journal, 19*(1), 39–58.

Miller, D., & Chen, M.-J. (1996). The simplicity of competitive repertoires: An empirical analysis. *Strategic Management Journal, 17*(6), 419–439.

Miller, K. D., & Chen, W.-R. (2004). Variable organizational risk preferences: Tests of the March-Shapira model. *Academy of Management Journal, 47*(1), 105–115.

Miron-Spektor, E., Gino, F., & Argote, L. (2011). Paradoxical frames and creative sparks: Enhancing individual creativity through conflict and integration. *Organizational Behavior and Human Decision Processes, 116*(2), 229–240.

Miron-Spektor, E., Ingram, A., Keller, J., Smith, W., & Lewis, M. (2018). Microfoundations of organizational paradox: The problem is how we think about the problem. *Academy of Management Journal, 61*(1). 26–45.

Murphy, G. L. (2002). *The big book of concepts.* Cambridge, MA: MIT Press.

Ng, A. H., & Hynie, M. (2014). Cultural differences in indecisiveness: The role of naïve dialecticism. *Personality and Individual Differences, 70,* 45–50.

Nishii, L. H., Gotte, A., & Raver, J. L. (2007). *Upper echelon theory revisited: The relationship between upper echelon diversity, the adoption of diversity practices, and organizational performance* (Working Paper Series No. 07–04). Ithaca, NY: Center for Advanced Human Resource Studies, School of Industrial and Labor Relations, Cornell University.

Ocasio, W. (1997). Towards an attention-based view of the firm. *Strategic Management Journal, 18*(Summer Special Issue), 187–206.

Ocasio, W. (2011). Attention to attention. *Organization Science, 22*(5), 1286–1296.

Ocasio, W., Loewenstein, J., & Nigam, A. (2015). How streams of communication reproduce and change institutional logics: The role of categories. *Academy of Management Review, 40*(1), 28–48.

Ocasio, W., & Radoynovska, N. (2016). Strategy and commitments to institutional logics: Organizational heterogeneity in business models and governance. *Strategic Organization, 14*(4), 287–309.

Palich, L. E., & Gomez-Mejia, L. R. (1999). A theory of global strategy and firm efficiencies: Considering the effects of cultural diversity. *Journal of Management, 25*(4), 587–606.

Paradis, C., & Willners, C. (2011). Antonymy: From convention to meaning-making. *Review of Cognitive Linguistics, 9*(2), 367–391.

Paradis, C., Willners, C., & Jones, S. (2009). Good and bad opposites using textual and experimental techniques to measure antonym canonicity. *The Mental Lexicon, 4*(3), 380–429.

Peng, K., & Nisbett, R. E. (1999). Culture, dialectics, and reasoning about contradiction. *American Psychologist, 54*(9), 741–754.

Peng, K., Spencer-Rodgers, J., & Z. Nian. (2006). Naïve dialecticism and the Tao of Chinese thought. In U. Kim, K.-S. Yang, & K.-K. Hwang (Eds.), *Indigenous and cultural psychology: Understanding people in context* (pp. 247–262). New York, NY: Springer.

Porac, J., Thomas, H., Wilson, F., Paton, D., & Kanfer, A. (1995). Rivalry and the industry model of Scottish knitwear producers. *Administrative Science Quarterly, 40,* 203–227.

Powell, T. C., Lovallo, D., & Fox, C. R. (2011). Behavioral strategy. *Strategic Management Journal, 32,* 1369–1386.

Pozzebon, M. (2004). The influence of a structurationist view on strategic management research. *Journal of Management Studies, 41*(2), 247–272.

Raisch, S., & Birkinshaw, J. (2008). Organizational ambidexterity: Antecedents, outcomes, and moderators. *Journal of Management, 34*(3), 375–409.

Ralston, D. A., Terpstra-Tong, J., Terpstra, R. H., Wang, X., & Egri, C. (2006). Today's state-owned enterprises of China: Are they dying dinosaurs or dynamic dynamos? *Strategic Management Journal, 27*(9), 825–843.

Raza-Ullah, T., Bengtsson, M., & Kock, S. (2014). The coopetition paradox and tension in coopetition at multiple levels. *Industrial Marketing Management, 43*(2), 189–198.

Reger, R. K., & Palmer, T. B. (1996). Managerial categorization of competitors: Using old maps to navigate new environments. *Organization Science, 7*(1), 22–39.

Riad, S., & Vaara, E. (2011). Varieties of national metonymy in media accounts of international mergers and acquisitions. *Journal of Management Studies, 48*(4), 737–771.

Rindova, V., Dalpiaz, E., & Ravasi, D. (2011). A cultural quest: A study of organizational use of new cultural resources in strategy formation. *Organization Science, 22*(2), 413–431.

Rindova, V. P., & Fombrun, C. J. (1999). Constructing competitive advantage: The role of firm-constituent interactions. *Strategic Management Journal, 20*(8), 691–710.

Schad, J., Lewis, M. W., Raisch, S., & Smith, W. K. (2016). Paradox research in management science: Looking back to move forward. *Academy of Management Annals, 10*(1), 5–64.

Sharma, G., & Good, D. (2013). The work of middle managers sensemaking and sensegiving for creating positive social change. *Journal of Applied Behavioral Science, 49*(1), 95–122.

Smith, E. (1989). Concepts and induction. In M. I. Posner (Ed.), *Foundations of cognitive science* (pp. 501–526). Cambridge, MA: MIT Press.

Smith, E. E., & Sloman, S. A. (1994). Similarity- versus rule-based categorization. *Memory & Cognition, 22*(4), 377–386.

Smith, W. K. (2014). Dynamic decision making: A model of senior leaders managing strategic paradoxes. *Academy of Management Journal, 57*(6), 1592–1623.

Smith, W. K., & Lewis, M. (2011). Toward a theory of paradox: A dynamic equilibrium model of organizing. *Academy of Management Review, 36*(2), 381–403.

Smith, W. K., & Tushman, M. L. (2005). Managing strategic contradictions: A top management model for managing innovation streams. *Organization Science, 16*(5), 522–536.

Spencer-Rodgers, J., Williams, M. J., & Peng, K. (2010). Cultural differences in expectations of change and tolerance for contradiction: A decade of empirical research. *Personality & Social Psychology Review, 14*(3), 296–312.

Suddaby, R. (2010). Challenges for institutional theory. *Journal of Management Inquiry, 19*(1), 14–20.

Taras, V., Kirkman, B. L., & Steel, P. (2010). Examining the impact of *Culture's consequences*: A three-decade, multilevel, meta-analytic review of Hofstede's cultural value dimensions. *Journal of Applied Psychology, 95*(3), 405–439.

Thomas, J. B., Clark, S. M., & Gioia, D. A. (1993). Strategic sensemaking and organizational performance: Linkages among scanning, interpretation, action, and outcomes. *Academy of Management Journal, 36*(2), 239–270.

Thomas, J. B., Sussman, S. W., & Henderson, J. C. (2001). Understanding "strategic learning": Linking organizational learning, knowledge management, and sensemaking. *Organization Science, 12*(3), 331–345.

Thornton, P. H., Ocasio, W., & Lounsbury, M. (2012). *The institutional logics perspective: Foundations, research, and theoretical elaboration.* Oxford, England: Oxford University Press.

Vermeulen, P., Zietsma, C., Greenwood, R., & Langley, A. (2016). Strategic responses to institutional complexity. *Strategic Organization, 14*(4), 277–286.

Viotti, E. B. (2002). National learning systems: A new approach on technological change in late industrializing economies and evidences from the cases of Brazil and South Korea. *Technological Forecasting and Social Change, 69*(7), 653–680.

Whittington, R. (2006). Completing the practice turn in strategy research. *Organization Studies, 27*(5), 613–634.

Yamauchi, T., & Markman, A. B. (2000). Inference using categories. *Journal of Experimental Psychology: Learning, Memory, and Cognition, 26*(3), 776–795.

CHAPTER 5

CULTURAL VALUES IN THE FAIR-TRADE MARKET

Examining Producers' Organizations

Mantiaba Coulibaly-Ballet
Zorana Jerinic
Djamila Elidrissi

ABSTRACT

Considered as systems of symbols or as a collective mental programming that gives identity to a group of individuals, culture is represented by the cultural values that constitute its central part. These values are considered as standards that guide the individual's functioning because their affective and behavioral dimensions participate in defining their goals. At the organizational level, an adaptation of individual values to the organizational ones is necessary to avoid conflicts. Moreover, this adaptation should allow for learning and knowledge management in order to contribute to a better performance of the organization. The objective of this chapter is to understand how the application of cultural values can lead to the effectiveness of organizations, and more precisely, of producers' organizations certified fair trade. Thus, through our case study based on producers' organizations we seek to identify critical cultural values related to the fair-trade label, as the latter is based on social,

Cultural Values in Strategy and Organization, pages 133–149

environmental, and economic principles that all the actors of the organization should respect. The results of our study indicate that there is a link between the values of the fair-trade label and the involvement of the producers in this market.

INTRODUCTION

Confronted with concerns related to sustainable development, companies question cultural values and their impact on organizational efficiency. The production of wealth must be done without annihilating that of future generations. This injunction is accompanied by a reflection on the responsibility of individuals in relation to their consumption patterns. Thus, the culture has its real significance through exchanges, since whatever the chosen orientation is (Coulibaly, Elidrissi, & Jerinic, 2017), the culture derives from a behavior and from the social environment of the individual. Culture is represented by "the basic beliefs, values, and norms regarding the why and how of knowledge generation, sharing, and utilization in an organization" (Zheng, Yang, & McLean, 2010, p. 769). It refers also to "shared motives, values, beliefs, identities, and interpretations or meanings of significant events that result from common experiences of members of collectives and are transmitted across age generations" (Mangaliso & Ndanga, 2017, p. 16). Culture can be thought as "systems of symbols" (Infield, 2001, p. 801), and capable to strengthen relationships between members of an organization and to encourage innovation (Herbi & Dunphy, 1998).

It can have several values according to the norms, the institutions, and the rites in a society. Culture is defined as a system of norms and values shared by a group of individuals and as a way of life for the group. These values describe how to do, say, and think within the organization (Schein, 2010). According to Hofstede (1980), culture is intrinsically collective mental programming; it is the average of the beliefs and values around which are individuals that inhabit a country. It determines the identity of a group. Thereby, different perceptions exist according to the application of cultural values in organizations. As cultural theory assumes the presence of culture conflict (Sellin, 1938), in this case an individual can violate some of their norms by upholding others. Tensions may arise, causing conflicts in cultural values. Culture conflict theory presupposes prior conformity in order to account for deviance. In culture conflict theory, as in cultural theory more generally, deviance remains but as the residual consequence of conformity (Rosenfeld, 1989, p. 456). For cultural and social learning theories, deviant behavior is learned, and it is learned under the same conditions as conforming behavior (Rosenfeld, 1989). According to Hayton, George, and Zahra (2002, p. 37), "It is generally assumed that a complex relationship exists among cultural values, social institutions, industry characteristics, and behavioral outcomes such as entrepreneurship" (Arora, 2017, p. 76). Furthermore, culture affects the pattern, the timeliness, and the evaluation of information (Das & Kumar, 2017, p. 232). So, it is important to consider cultural expectations which affect knowledge sharing practices and take attention to "what knowledge should be shared with the organization and what should be hoarded by individuals" (Zheng et al., 2010, p. 764). It is profitable to set up an organizational culture that is conducive to learning and knowledge management (Zheng et al., 2010, p. 769). Cultural values and norms must be integrated in strategic priorities of the company and the ones of its partners by considering the specificity of the industry or market.

We are interested in the fair-trade label used by actors in the fair-trade market. The latter is based on economic, social, and environmental principles that all of the actors should respect (Castaldo, Perrini, Misani, & Tencati, 2009). It is a market that deals with international rules and norms related to the fair-trade label. The relationships between actors of the market are subject to these rules. There are several labels in the fair-trade market among which fair trade is more used by producers' organizations. We want to understand: "How can the application of cultural values lead to the effectiveness of producers' organizations certified Fairtrade?" We seek to identify critical cultural values related to the Fairtrade label. These values must be profitable for producers' organizations and help them achieve their development objective. We will analyze cultural values around the fair-trade label that are shared by the members of producers' organizations and with their partners.

To answer our question, we will study the literature about cultural values approaches. Then, we will use a qualitative approach to analyze cultural values in the fair-trade market. We conducted interviews with producers' organizations certified fair trade and their partners in Africa. The first results of our study show a link between the mains values of the fair-trade label and the commitment of the producers' organizations in this market. Collective learning and knowledge sharing processes also exist between the members of producers' organizations and other organizations in the fair-trade market.

CULTURAL VALUES APPROACHES

Cultural Values: Definitions and Characteristics

Culture is a complex phenomenon (Fey & Denison, 2003). It is represented by "the basic beliefs, values, and norms regarding the why and how of knowledge generation, sharing, and utilization in an organization"

(Zheng et al., 2010, p. 769). As stated by Schneider, Ehrhart, and Macey (2013), most definitions of culture include the idea that it is shared: Culture refers to the shared values, beliefs, identities of members of collectives, and to the shared meanings of some events coming from their common experiences (Mangaliso & Ndanga, 2017, p. 16). Thought as "systems of symbols" (Infield, 2001, p. 801), culture can also strengthen relationships between members of the organization and encourage innovation (Herbi & Dunphy, 1998). According to Deal and Kennedy (1982), the concept of culture consists of four elements: the values that are the very foundation of culture, the heroes who embody these values, the rites that are the concrete expression of culture, and the cultural network which represents an informal organizational mode for disseminating and communicating cultural values. Culture determines the identity of a human group. These authors characterized the corporate culture, on one hand, in terms of attitudes towards taking risks in decisions, and on the other hand, in terms of the speed of reactions. Hofstede (1980, 2001) states that culture is expressed through the following notions: symbols, heroes, rituals, and values. Gradually, symbols are the visible, superficial part of culture. They are represented by words, verbal expressions, attitudes, meaningful patterns of belonging, of rallying, and they carry an identification shared by those who have this common culture. Heroes and rites are intermediate-level demonstrations, a little less visible: Heroes are real or imaginary people, living or dead, who have cultural behaviors to imitate; rites are collective activities that have a strong impact on socialization. According to Hofstede (2001), the three elements can be grouped under the term cultural practices because they are visible from the outside, but their cultural meaning can only be understood by connoisseurs.

On the other hand, values are less visible, they are more in depth, and are at the heart of the culture. Values refer to a latent construct, considering how individuals evaluate activities or outcomes. Expressed through motivations, emotions and taboos (Hofstede, Hofstede, & Minkov, 2010), they will have an indirect influence through attitudes and goals and will be sustained over time through the practices of regular activities and the influence of the environment. The concept of value brings together several approaches. According to Kluckhohn (1951), "A value is a conception, explicit or implicit, distinctive of an individual or characteristic of a group, of the desirable which influences the selection of available mode, means and ends of actions" (p. 395). Rokeach (1973) defines value as "an enduring belief that a specific mode of conduct or in-state of existence is personally orally preferable to an opposite mode of conduct or end-state of existence" (p. 5). Similarly, Hofstede (1980, 2001) states that value is a tendency to prefer one state of affairs to another, where the expression of the preference implies a positive or negative feeling.

The literature teaches us that the concept of value is heterogeneous both in terms of interpretation and expression (Abreu & Camarinha-Matos, 2008; De Mooij, 1998), but also in terms of its structure and content (Schwartz, 1992). It can be understood at different levels as a tool and purpose (Rokeach, 1973); individual or organizational (Schmidt & Posner, 1982); professional, organizational, or national (Hofstede, 1989); real or diffuse. Defined as what individuals believe are standards that guide their functioning (Brown, 2002), values have affective and behavioral dimensions, and play an important role in determining individuals' personal goals. These individual values must adapt to organizational values to avoid potential tensions and conflicts. Each individual and each organization has its own system of values or hierarchies (Méle, 2012; Schwartz, 2012; Woodward & Shaffakat, 2014). Some values, such as guiding principles, standards or quality, are shared. They are part of the organization and are often understood by everyone. For some, they are expressed in the hierarchy of values (Feather, 1995; Rokeach, 1973; Schwartz, 1992) and will have an impact on the behavior of individuals or organizations (Bardi, Lee, Hofmann-Towfigh, & Soutar, 2009; Feather, 1995). According to Schwartz (2012), features common to different approaches to value exist. These are beliefs, norms, guiding principles that have an impact on behavior and are influenced by the external environment. We can retain the typology proposed by De Mooij (1998) according to three axes: (a) the central values which are the values essential to the individual; (b) the values relating to a specific domain; and (c) product-specific values used to evaluate product attributes. These values are therefore implicit and can be individual or collective.

Cultural values, more precisely, represent implicitly or explicitly shared abstract ideas about what is good or bad. As such, they are defined as the specific norms that can tell people what is right or appropriate in a given situation (Schwartz, 1999). Individual's values system include cultural values, and some of these remain strong even after acculturation, as they are guiding principles in their life (Schwartz & Sagiv, 2000). In his theory of cultural values, Schwartz (1999) identified seven types of cultural values: (a) conservatism or embeddedness (values reflected in collective orientation, respect for tradition, maintaining the social order, etc.); (b) intellectual autonomy; (c) affective autonomy (stimulation and hedonism, and pursuing personal interest); (d) hierarchy (accepting the differences in statuses and in resource distribution); (e) egalitarianism (desire to contribute to others' wellbeing and to equal status relationships); (f) mastery (individual's need to control the social environment by pursuing his goals); and (g) harmony (values emphasizing the symbiosis with nature; Leong & Ward, 2006).

Apart from individual cultural values, the latter can be identified at the organizational level, as stated earlier. For instance, innovation, attention to detail, and outcome orientation, as explained by Miron, Erez, and Naveh

(2004), can be considered as cultural values of an organization. Their presence confirms that an organization valorizes the performance outcomes associated with these values. Moreover, some behaviors, such as teamwork, leadership, participation, have the same meaning in different cultural contexts (Segall & Georgas, 1998). According to Schein (2010), there are three levels of organizational culture: (a) artifacts, easily accessible to outsiders but with an underlying meaning (language, rituals, myths, dress code, and organization of space); (b) espoused values or the core values of the organization; and (c) underlying assumptions of organization life that can be explained through in-depth interviewing, as they are ingrained (e.g., the day-to-day life of the employees; Schneider et al., 2013). Therefore, an organization's cultural values are shaped, on the one hand, by the cultural values of the society the organization is part of, and on the other hand, by the goals that organization's members are encouraged to pursue (Sagiv & Schwartz, 2007).

Application of Cultural Values in Organizations

As stated by Denison (1984), the most important asset of an organization is its culture that stimulates the participation and the involvement of its members. Moreover, this organizational culture is the differentiating factor in productivity of companies, as culture affects the pattern, the timeliness, and the evaluation of information (Das & Kumar, 2017, p. 232). Several studies have shown, even though it is difficult because of the possible indirect influence of the culture, the relationship between an organization's effectiveness and its culture (Siehl & Martin, 1990). The theoretical basis of the explanations that help show this relationship is the relationship between organizational culture and the behavior of organizational members (Gregory, Harris, Armenakis, & Shook, 2009). As a matter of fact, as Zheng et al. (2010) explained, organizational culture shapes the behavior of its members and thus influences organizational effectiveness. Defined as "a complex set of values, beliefs, assumptions, and symbols that define the way in which a firm conducts its business" (Barney, 1986, p. 657), organizational culture defines, among others, the interaction with organization's employees and affects organizational effectiveness. Nevertheless, Barney (1986) states that, for this, culture must be valuable (add financial value to the organization), rare (not present in many other organizations), and imperfectly imitable (disabling other firms to acquire the same resources or culture).

The literature teaches us that an organization's culture can, among others, stimulate a knowledge sharing culture. Knowledge management refers to the way external and internal information are integrated into the organization. It is a way in which the members of the organization give meanings to these information and share them, and this process is conditioned by the culture of the organization (De Long & Fahey, 2000; Zheng et al., 2010). This type of organizational culture, that manages, shares, and employs knowledge, increases an organization's ability to attain the pursued objectives (Taylor, 2013). It is important to consider cultural expectations which affect knowledge sharing practices and take attention to "what knowledge should be shared with the organization and what should be hoarded by individuals" (Zheng et al., 2010, p. 764). As a matter of fact, cultural values and norms must be integrated into strategic priorities of the company and the ones of the members of its partners by considering the specificity of the industry or market. It is thus profitable for an organization to set up an organizational culture that is conducive to learning and knowledge management, since a well-managed knowledge contributes to organizational effectiveness (Zheng et al., 2010, p 769). According to some authors (Denison, 1990; Denison & Mishra, 1995; Fey & Denison, 2003), four dimensions of organizational culture can be conducive to organizational effectiveness: (a) adaptability, that refers to the degree to which an organization can change behavior, structures, and systems to survive in the wake of environmental change; (b) consistency, that refers to the extent to which beliefs, values, and expectations are held consistently by members; (c) level of participation, related to the participation of members of an organization in decision-making; and (d) mission, or the existence of a common definition of organization's purpose (Zheng et al., 2010, p. 765). In a similar way, Denison, Janovics, Young, and Cho (2006) put forward that these dimensions, namely adaptability, consistency, involvement, and mission, affect organizational performance. Moreover, the author helps us understand how these can be measured. Involvement, that refers to the commitment of organization's members, is measured, more precisely, with three indexes: empowerment, team orientation, and capability development. Consistency has "an internal system of governance based on consensual support" (Denison et al., 2006, p. 7), and is measured by core values, agreement, and coordination and integration. Creating change, customer focus and organizational learning help measure adaptability of an organization, that is, its capacity to make internal changes in response to external conditions. Finally, a mission that gives purpose and is defined as a long-term vision of the actions to be undertaken for the organization and its members, is measured by strategic intention and intent, goals and objectives, and vision. The four cultural traits of this model are interrelated, create an organization's culture and are closely related to its performance (Denison et al., 2015). In other words, an organization is considered effective if it is scoring highly in one of the presented cultural traits.

Cultural theory, according to Meek (1988), suggests that an effective organizational culture can supplant an ineffective one. However, this process requires changing people's attitudes and values, and the latter are often the main item under dispute (Gregory, 1983). Organizational culture is thus conducive to conflicts, as individuals have to "adjust" to the effective, "healthy" culture (Meek, 1988). As part of the cultural theory (Sellin, 1938), culture conflict theory states that an individual can violate some of their norms by upholding others. However, in order to account for deviance, culture conflict theory presupposes prior conformity. In this vein, deviance is seen as the residual consequence of conformity (Rosenfeld, 1989, p. 456) and for cultural and social learning theories, deviant behavior is learned under the same conditions as conforming behavior (Rosenfeld, 1989). According to Hayton et al. (2002, p. 37), "It is generally assumed that a complex relationship exists among cultural values, social institutions, industry characteristics and behavioral outcomes such as entrepreneurship" (Arora, 2017, p. 76).

APPLICATION OF CULTURAL VALUES IN THE FAIR-TRADE MARKET: THE CASE OF PRODUCERS' ORGANIZATIONS

Our research focuses on producers' organizations in the fair-trade market. To carry out our work, we have used a qualitative approach to collect data and analyze cultural values in the fair-trade market. First, we present the methodology, then our results.

Methodology

We used a qualitative approach (Yin, 2014) to analyze cultural values related to the fair-trade label. This label is more used by actors in the fair-trade market. We are interested in producers' organizations and want to understand: "How can the application of cultural values lead to the effectiveness of producers' organizations certified fair trade?" We aim to identify cultural values related to the fair-trade label, that are shared by members of producers' organizations and with some partners.

Fair trade comes from a collective and militant approach. It is a model of ethical and responsible economy, based on modes of production, marketing, and consumption that contribute to sustainable development through: better remuneration for producing farmers, respect for the fundamental rights of producers and workers, and the preservation of the environment. This trade is an alternative to the "globalized trade that creates increasingly strong inequalities and contributes to destroying our planet. Small producers and salaried workers are the first links in the chain and suffer multiple forms of exploitation and human rights violations" (Max Havelaar, 2019). So, fair trade is perceived as a trade sector that incorporates social and environmental criteria that are different to those found in traditional trade (Coulibaly & Blanchot, 2015; Gould 2003). Its evolution is linked to the creation of labels whose objective is to inform consumers about the criteria of the fair trade. This "fair" labeling covers both production and product exchanges.

To collect data, we conducted 15 interviews with producers' organizations certified fair trade and their partners in Africa, completed by telephone interviews. We prepared an interview guide (see Table 5.1) based on literature review about cultural values. The main themes that were treated are the following:

- values shared in the organization and with partners;
- expectations of the organization in the fair-trade market;
- obligations and norms around the fair-trade label (economic, social and environmental principles, mission of each producer organization);
- the four dimensions of organizational culture: adaptability (linked to behavior and environmental change), consistency (linked to beliefs, values, and expectations), involvement (participation to the decisions), and mission; and
- the presence of conflicts.

TABLE 5.1 Interview Guide
1. Presentation of the interviewee
• Profession and position in the firm
2. Presentation of the organization and their position in the fair-trade market
• What are the objectives of the organization?
• Can you present the activities of your organization in the fair-trade market (relations, actions with partners, etc.)?
3. Cultural values
• What are the main values shared in the organization and with partners?
• What are the main expectations of the organization in the fair-trade market?
• What are the regulations (obligations) and norms around the fair-trade label (economic, social and environmental principles, mission of each producer organization)?
• Are there some problems to apply the fair-trade principles?
• Do you change some of your objectives and behavior in this market?
• How do the organization (and people) adapt to the environment (sustainability development, climate change)?
• Do you participate to the main decisions in the market (with partners)?
• Do you improve your profit in the fair-trade market (why)?

We carried out the interviews from June 2018 to June 2019. They were recorded and transcribed.

Face-to-face interviews were conducted with producers' organizations and supplemented by telephone and remote interviews. The interviews lasted between 30 minutes and 1 hour. Observations on the plantations were also conducted. The organizations studied are involved in the fair-trade label. They work with Fairtrade Africa, a member of Fairtrade International. Fairtrade Africa is spread over four regions: Eastern Africa, Southern Africa, West Africa, and North Africa. It aims to ensure better positioning for workers and farmers, and to support them in sustainable development in Africa. This organization has more than 300 African producers' organizations that meet fair-trade international criteria. These are small producers' organizations (SPOs) and plantations. Among the products grown by its members there is coffee, cocoa, tea, cut flowers, bananas, pineapples, mangos, shea butter, rooibos red tea, vegetables, fresh and dried fruits, and honey (Fairtrade Africa, 2019). In our study, we worked with the West Africa (Ivory Coast) branch of Fairtrade Africa. We were in contact with four organizations: a banana plantation, an organization producing and exporting coffee and cocoa; a producers' organization of cocoa and coffee; a honey producing organization (a group of producers that extends from the center to the north of Ivory Coast). Thus, we made trips to the banana plantation, cocoa, coffee and cashew fields, and hives.

The main people interviewed are Fairtrade Africa officials; assistant of the head of the Fairtrade Premium Management Committee in charge of the quality of hygiene and the environment; human resources manager; management committee manager of a banana cooperative; sustainable development and supply manager in charge of the management of cocoa-coffee producer organizations; an export assistant and a producer member of a cocoa-coffee cooperative; producer and customer relations assistant and beekeeper (member of a honey producing organization). These interviews were completed by internal documents provided by producers' organizations and the information on the Fairtrade International website.

RESULTS

In this section, we present our main results. Firstly, our analysis allows us to identify the main dominant values of fair trade that appear within the studied producers' organizations. Secondly, we determine some dimensions of the organizational culture that have a growing influence on the organizations.

Main Principles and Values Shared in the Fair Trade

The fundamental principles of the fair-trade lead market players to share a certain number of values related to the respect of economic, social, and environmental rules in carrying out their activities. To meet legal obligations, producers and producers' organizations are accompanied by Fairtrade Africa in the certification process for the fair-trade label: "We provide support to organizations to help them maintain their certification and prepare them for audit."; "There are also agents of the state who provide freight forwarders, and who are responsible for applying regulatory provisions and compliance with phytosanitary rules for all the products in general, beyond fair trade, before issuing the certificate" (Fairtrade Africa representative, November 2018).

Within producers' organizations, an accompaniment is also provided for compliance with environmental and social standards: "As for the standards, trainers are on the field to train producers and help them. For organic, no pesticides, whereas we use the fair trade but not the products that are on the blacklist" (Sustainable development and supply manager in charge of the management of cocoa-coffee producers' organizations, January 2019).

The assistant in charge of the producers-customers relations and a beekeeper (January 2019) explained: "We say to producers not to use pesticides because it is a risk for the end product but also for the bee, and it is also protecting the environment."; "We say to put the hives near the fields because it facilitates the work of the bees. When the fields are closer, they produce more. . . ." He also added: "Child labor is forbidden. Parents are encouraged to send children to school. We check if it's a financial problem, to help them. . . ."

Organizational Culture Conducive to Producers' Organizations Effectiveness

As part of our work, we were able to identify elements related to organizational culture, that is, dimensions within producers' organizations: adaptability, consistency, level of participation, mission. These elements facilitate compliance with the principles of fair trade and the application of the values that govern this market.

Adaptability

Organizations that are already certified fair trade are working to bring other producers' organizations or associations to join fair trade: "Work is ongoing with other associations, that are not yet fair trade, to get them adhere later" (Assistant in charge of the producers-customers relations and a beekeeper, January 2019).

There is some flexibility regarding the time that is given to producers to accept certification rules: "As for the certification rules, sometimes there are producers who refuse it.... It can happen. But with explanations, sensitization, they understand. The difficulty is to make the producer understand what must be done to always sell his cocoa..." (Export assistant of a cocoa-coffee cooperative).

Consistency

Producers are reminded of the fair-trade principles by the organizations that show the benefits of good production techniques: "We explain to producers their well-being and the possibility for a better life. We explain what the bee produces; the techniques to let the bees work to increase their production. We are in discussions" (Assistant in charge of the producers-customers relations and a beekeeper, January 2019).

In order to encourage other organizations or producers to join the fair-trade label, the fallout and benefits of fair trade are often mentioned: "We encourage other cooperatives to say that it works, we have the social impact of fair trade. We make producers understand the return in relation to the premium" (Treasurer of a cocoa-coffee cooperative).

Level of Participation

Each producer has decision-making power within producers' organizations: "The union brings together all the cooperatives. We are a cooperative that belongs to the producers, but we are not an association, there is a board of directors. Each producer pays his share in the cooperative..." (Sustainable development and supply manager in charge of the management of cocoa-coffee producers' organizations, January 2019).

The interviewee also explained that collaborative work is done with each producers' organization (or cooperatives): "I work with cooperatives for certification. I monitor in close collaboration with the technical teams. Trainings with the producers are also carried out."

In addition, all members of producers' organizations are involved in the negotiations as part of the decision-making process: "There are sometimes negotiations to see what the priorities are. Everything is decided in general assembly, there is what is called the general assemblies of the sections, and then there is the general assembly of all the delegates. It is like in the national assembly, all the delegates come to approve the development plan" (Export assistant of a cocoa-coffee cooperative).

Mission

Producers' organizations sometimes engage with producers to achieve common goals: "Concessions are made with stakeholders. First, we respect the rules, we consider the context to carry out the commitment of the producers, then discussions take place..." (Assistant of the head of Fairtrade Premium Management Committee in charge of the quality of hygiene and the environment, Banana Planting, January 2019).

As part of a better use of the development premium, exchanges also take place between producers and producers' organizations by justifying the common goal around the fair-trade label:

> As Fairtrade recommends, the use of the premium should be done as part of a development plan. The development plan is established according to the needs of the populations, of the producers. Precisely because at the GA (the general assembly), they are the ones who are the supreme organ of decision, the office provides indications to say: "Here is the list of the real needs," and the various producers approve that. I take the example: if there are 5 villages that need a maternity, we will prioritize to see what village needs it most. It is precisely the equity side of sharing. (Export assistant of a cocoa-coffee cooperative)

CONCLUSION

The objective of this chapter was to understand the application of cultural values in organizations, and more precisely, how this application can lead to the effectiveness of producers' organizations. We were interested in the organizations certified Fairtrade, based on the respect of economic, social, and environmental rules that lead market players to share the values in relation to these rules. In the sense of Hayton et al. (2002), a relationship exists among cultural values, social institutions, industry characteristics, and behavioral outcomes. As an invisible part of organizational culture, values have an indirect influence through attitudes and goals. According to the literature review that we have conducted, involvement, adaptability, consistency, and mission are four dimensions of organizational culture that affect organizational effectiveness. These elements were identified in our study. We have combined several methods of collecting data, such as interviews, observations, secondary data, and were able to show through our study that a link exists between the main values of the fair trade-label and the commitment of the producers' organizations in the fair-trade market. Moreover, our study showed that collective learning and knowledge sharing processes exist between members of producers' organizations and other organizations in the fair-trade market. A conclusion can be drawn that involvement, consistency, adaptability, and mission are cultural traits that are interrelated (Denison et al., 2015) and profitable for producers' organizations, as they help them achieve their development objective. In the sense of Schwartz (1999), three cultural values can be associated to organizations of West Africa (Ivory Coast) branch of Fairtrade Africa: conservatism or embeddedness, as we could identify in the interviews the dimensions of collective orientation and maintaining the social order; egalitarianism or a desire to contribute to the wellbeing of others in order to attain an equal status relationship; harmony, that reflects the symbiosis with nature. As such, they help individuals determine what is right or wrong in a given situation.

However, our study has some limitations. It is a single case study that could be, among others, enriched with a greater number of interviews. A comparison with other producers' organizations would have been beneficial for a better understanding of our case study and the studied phenomenon, namely the cultural values in organizations. These limitations could therefore be overcome in future studies in the domain.

REFERENCES

Abreu, A., & Camarinha-Matos, L. (2008). On the role of value systems to promote the sustainability of collaborative environments. *International Journal of Production Research, 46*(5), 1207–1229.

Arora, P. (2017). Entrepreneurial breakthroughs theory: A holistic framework for studying business model innovations. In T. K. Das (Ed.), *Culture and behavioral strategy* (pp. 73–100). Charlotte, NC: Information Age.

Bardi, A., Lee, J. L, Hofman-Towfigh, N., & Soutar, G. (2009). The structure of intraindividual value change. *Journal of Personality and Social Psychology, 97*(5), 913–929.

Barney, J. B., (1986). Organizational culture: Can it be a source of sustained competitive advantage? *Academy of Management Review, 11*(3), 656–665.

Brown, D. (2002). The role of work and cultural values in occupational choice, satisfaction and success: A theoretical statement. *Journal of Counseling & Development, 80*(1), 48–56.

Castaldo, S., Perrini, F., Misani, N., & Tencati, A. (2009). Missing link between corporate social responsibility and consumer trust: The case of fair trade products. *Journal of Business Ethics, 84*(1), 1–15.

Coulibaly, M., & Blanchot, F. (2015). Selecting a certification body in the fair trade market: The importance of strategic capabilities and cooperative behavior. In T. K. Das (Ed.), *The practice of behavioral strategy* (pp. 145–168). Charlotte, NC: Information Age.

Coulibaly, M., Elidrissi, D., & Jerinic, Z. (2017). Effects of culture on behavioral strategies: The case of SMEs in the health and food sectors. In T. K. Das (Ed.), *Culture and behavioral strategy* (pp. 211–226). Charlotte, NC: Information Age.

Das, T. K., & Kumar, R. (2017). Interpretive schemes in cross-national alliances. In T. K. Das (Ed.), *Culture and behavioral strategy* (pp. 227–246). Charlotte, NC: Information Age.

De Long, D. W., & Fahey, L. (2000). Diagnosing cultural barriers to knowledge management. *Academy of Management Perspectives, 14*(4), 113–127.

De Mooij, M. K. (1998). *Global marketing and advertising: Understanding cultural paradoxes,* Thousand Oaks, CA: SAGE.

Deal, T. E., & Kennedy, A. A. (1982). *Corporate cultures: The rites and rituals of corporate life.* Boston, MA: Addison-Wesley.

Denison, D. R. (1984). Bringing corporate culture to the bottom line. *Organizational Dynamics, 13*(2), 5–22.

Denison, D. R. (1990). *Corporate culture and organizational effectiveness.* Oxford, England: Wiley.

Denison, D., Janovics, J., Young, J., & Cho, H. J. (2006). *Diagnosing organizational cultures: Validating a model and method* (Working Paper). Ann Arbor, MI: Denison Consulting Group.

Denison, D. R., & Mishra, A. K. (1995). Toward a theory of organizational culture and effectiveness. *Organization Science, 6*(2), 204–223.

Fairtrade Africa. (2019). "Product profile," [online], https://fairtradeafrica.net/product-profile/ (accessed April 4, 2021)

Feather, N. T. (1995). Values, valences, and choice: The influences of values on the perceived attractiveness and choice of alternatives. *Journal of Personality and Social Psychology, 68*(6), 1135–1151.

Fey, C. F., & Denison, D. R. (2003). Organizational culture and effectiveness: Can American theory be applied in Russia? *Organization Science, 14*(6), 686–706.

Gould, N. J. (2003). Fair trade and the consumer interest: A personal account. *International Journal of Consumer Studies, 27*(4), 341–345.

Gregory, B. T., Harris, S. G., Armenakis, A. A., & Shook, C. L. (2009). Organizational culture and effectiveness: A study of values, attitudes, and organizational outcomes. *Journal of Business Research, 62*(7), 673–679.

Gregory, K. L. (1983). Native-view paradigms: Multiple Cultures and culture conflicts in organization. *Administrative Sciences Quarterly, 28*(3), 359–376.

Hayton, J., George, G., & Zahra, S. (2002). National culture and entrepreneurship: A review of behavioral research. *Entrepreneurship: Theory and Practice, 26*(4), 33–52.

Herbig, P., & Dunphy, S. (1998). Culture and innovation. *Cross Cultural Management: An International Journal, 5*(4), 13–21.

Hosfede, G. (1980). *Culture's consequences: International differences in work-related values.* Beverly Hills, CA: SAGE.

Hofstede, G. (2001). *Culture's consequences: Comparing values, behaviors, institutions and organizations across nations* (2nd ed.). London, England: SAGE.

Hosfede, G., Hosfede, G. J., & Minkov, M. (2010). *Culture and organizations: Software of the mind* (3rd ed.). New York, NY: McGraw-Hill.

Infield, M. (2001). Cultural values: A forgotten strategy for building community support for protected areas in Africa. *Conservation Biology, 15*(3), 800–802.

Kluckhohn, C. K. (1951). Values and value orientations in the theory of action. In T. Parsons & E. A. Shils (Eds.), *Toward a general theory of action* (pp. 388–433). Cambridge, MA: Harvard University Press.

Leong, C. H., & Ward, C. (2006). Cultural values and attitudes toward immigrants and multiculturalism: The case of the Eurobarometer survey on racism and xenophobia. *International Journal of Intercultural Relations, 30*(6), 799–810.

Mangaliso, M. P., & Ndanga, L. Z. B. (2017). Cultural diversity and strategic choice: The role of the repatriated executive. In T. K. Das (Ed.), *Culture and behavioral strategy* (pp. 1–30). Charlotte, NC: Information Age.

Max Havelaar. (2019). Qu'est-ce que le commerce équitable? [What is fair trade?]. Retrieved from https://maxhavelaarfrance.org/le-commerce-equitable/quest-ce-que-le-commerce-equitable/

Meek, V. L. (1988). Organizational culture: Origins and weaknesses. *Organization Studies, 9*(4), 453–473.

Méle, D. (2012). *Management ethics: Placing ethics at the core of good management.* New York, NY: Palgrave MacMillan.

Miron, E., Erez, M., & Naveh, E. (2004). Do personal characteristics and cultural values that promote innovation, quality, and efficiency compete or complement each other? *Journal of Organizational Behavior, 25*(2), 175–199.

Rokeach, M. (1973). *The nature of human values.* New York, NY: Free Press.

Rosenfeld, R. (1989). Robert Merton's contributions to the sociology of deviance. *Sociological Inquiry, 59*(4), 453–466.

Sagiv, L., & Schwartz, S. H. (2007). Cultural values in organizations: Insights for Europe. *European Journal of International Management, 1*(3), 176–190.

Schein, E. H. (2010). *Organizational culture and leadership.* 4th ed. San Francisco, CA: Jossey-Bass.

Schmidt, W. H., & Posner, B. Z. (1982). *Managerial values and expectations: The silent power in personal and organizational life.* New York, NY: American Management Association.

Schneider, B., Ehrhart, M. G., & Macey, W. H. (2013). Organizational climate and culture. *Annual Review of Psychology, 64*(1), 361–388.

Schwartz, S. H. (1992). Universal in the content and structure of values: Theoretical advances and empirical test in 20 countries. *Advances in Experimental Social Psychology, 25,* 1–65.

Schwartz, S. H. (1999). A theory of cultural values and some implications for work. *Applied Psychology, 48*(1), 23–47.

Schwartz, S. H. (2012). An overview of the Schwartz theory of basic values. *Online Readings in Psychology and Culture, 2*(1), 11.

Schwartz, S. H., & Sagiv, G. (2000). Value consensus and importance: A cross-national study. *Journal of Cross-Cultural Psychology, 31*(4), 465–497.

Segall, M. H., & Georgas, J. (1998). International Association for Cross-Cultural Psychology. *European Psychologist, 3*(1), 76–77.

Sellin, T. (1938). *Culture conflict and crime.* New York, NY: Social Science Research Council.

Siehl, C., & Martin, J. (1990). Organizational culture: A key to financial performance? In B. Schneider (Ed.), *Organizational climate and culture* (pp. 241–281). San Francisco, CA: Jossey-Bass.

Taylor, G. (2013). Implementing and maintaining a knowledge sharing culture via knowledge management teams: A shared leadership approach. *Journal of Organizational Culture, Communications & Conflict, 17*(1), 69–91.

Woodward, I. C., & Shaffakat, S. (2014). *Understanding values of insightfully aware leadership* (Working Paper 2014/46/OBH). Retrieved from https://papers.ssrn.com/sol3/papers.cfm?abstract_id=2471492

Yin, R. K. (2014). *Case study research design and methods* (5th ed.). Thousand Oaks, CA: SAGE.

Zheng, W., Yang, B., & McLean, G. N. (2010). Linking organizational culture, structure, strategy, and organizational effectiveness: Mediating role of knowledge management. *Journal of Business Research, 63*(7), 763–771.

CHAPTER 6

NATIONAL CULTURE AND LEGITIMACY IN INTERNATIONAL ALLIANCES

Rajesh Kumar
T. K. Das

ABSTRACT

In this chapter we explore the interrelationship between national cultural values and the dynamics of legitimacy management in international alliances. Alliances are prone to instability and international alliances may suffer the additional problem of a cultural gap that may further enhance such instability. The idea that interpartner legitimacy is crucial in shaping alliance success is now being increasingly recognized in the literature but there is as yet little systematic work that demonstrates the linkages between national culture and legitimacy management in international alliances. The chapter discusses how national cultural values may impact different types of legitimacy (pragmatic, moral, cognitive) in an international alliance. The concept of national culture has been operationalized in many ways but for the purposes of this chapter we draw upon the construct of individualism-collectivism that has

Cultural Values in Strategy and Organization, pages 151–169

garnered much attention in the literature. Individualistic and collectivistic cultures are known to differ on a number of dimensions and these differences have significant implications for legitimacy management in alliances. These differences have an impact on the process by which legitimacy is attained, the relative importance of different types of legitimacy, and the issue of legitimacy repair. We also discuss the legitimacy dynamics at the different stages of alliance development. A number of propositions are derived for each of these alliance development stages to facilitate empirical testing. We conclude by discussing the key managerial implications of the framework proposed in the chapter regarding the interrelationship between national cultural values and the dynamics of legitimacy management.

INTRODUCTION

The growing popularity of strategic alliances is often accompanied by heightened instability. Scholars have begun to explain this puzzle drawing upon a variety of theoretical perspectives that seek to understand the roles of opportunism (Das & Rahman, 2010), internal tensions (Das & Teng, 2000), bargaining power (Inkpen & Beamish, 1997), learning asymmetry (Hamel, 1991), a perceived lack of fairness (Luo, 2008), and cultural differences (Kumar & Nti, 2004).

Implicit in all these perspectives on alliance instability is the argument that alliances fail either because of poor governance arrangements or clashing expectations, the origins of which could be many. We recognize that these theoretical perspectives have gone some way in advancing our knowledge of alliances but we would also have to make the broader argument that, with few exceptions, these perspectives have failed to adequately consider the micro dynamics of alliance management. It may be argued that micro dynamics are irrelevant to understanding alliances, as they do not provide a parsimonious explanation of alliance failure. We suggest, by contrast, that micro behavioral dynamics are critical in explaining alliance performance because without an understanding of this one would be hard pressed to appreciate how alliances work in practice.

A micro behavioral perspective sensitizes us to the fact that managerial perceptions, cognitions, and behavior are crucial in understanding how alliances evolve over time. A wide body of literature in strategic management and organizational behavior has reinforced the importance of managerial perceptions and cognitions in influencing decision making (e.g., Das, 1986, 2003; Das & Teng, 1999), and this is indeed beginning to be recognized in the field of strategic alliances (e.g., Das & Kumar, 2007, 2010a, 2010b; Kumar & Das, 2010a). In general, as many scholars have noted, understanding alliance practice remains an under-researched area in the alliance literature.

The micro behavioral perspective looks at the dynamics of interorganizational interaction, using as its building block the impact of different variables such as emotions, culture, and regulatory focus on how the relationship between the partners evolves over time. Alliance managers are confronted with the necessity of making decisions and this by definition implicates the relevance of the human agency (Kumar & Das, 2010a). It is for this reason that variables that impact managerial decision making are crucial in understanding how alliances develop over time. For example, the presence of negative emotions such as frustration or anger has the potential of undermining trust and creating a negative vicious circle (Kumar, 1997, 2008). In a similar vein, differences in national culture may also give rise to misunderstandings, distrust, and prevent the partners from effectively dealing with the problems at hand (Kumar & Nti, 2004; Pak, Ra, & Park, 2009). Recent work (Das & Kumar, 2011) has also highlighted how differences in alliancing firm's regulatory focus may both condition their willingness to commit opportunistic acts as well as their willingness to tolerate opportunistic actions of their partner. This stream of research has been very useful in providing a useful corrective to the more macro perspectives that remain dominant in the study of alliances, but it does remain the case that the existing micro behavioral work still remains somewhat partial, and has not been developed to its maximal potential.

How do we address this limitation in the extant alliance literature? We propose that the concept of interpartner legitimacy as recently articulated by Kumar and Das (2007) may play an influential role in this regards. The concept refers to how the partner firms evaluate each other with the implicit recognition that the attainment of interpartner legitimacy "can facilitate cooperation, lower transaction costs, and enhance the reputational capital of the partners" (Kumar & Das, 2007, p. 2). A recent study by Gulati, Lavie, and Singh (2009) notes that alliancing firms learn more from "partner specific experience" as opposed to a "general partnering experience." We would suppose and draw the conclusion that partner specific experiences are more enriching as opposed to a general partnering experience because they permit the alliancing firms to establish legitimacy. This is not to say that such legitimacy will always be created; it is only to make the argument that partner specific experiences provide the apposite context for the creation of such legitimacy. It is therefore not surprising that 'partner specific experiences' are more enriching from the standpoint of learning.

We would suppose that interpartner legitimacy is a concept that is macro level in character but has micro level foundations. It is a macro level concept in that it exists at a firm level, but the roots of it lie in the interpersonal interactions that occur among alliance managers. As such, this concept can be quite useful in integrating both the micro and the macro perspectives in the study of alliance evolution. The starting point of our analysis is the recognition that while all alliancing firms are faced with the strategic imperative of attaining legitimacy, their ability to do so and their ability in sustaining it might be crucially dependent on the national culture that they emanate from (Kumar & Das, 2010a). Although this insight has been recognized earlier, it has not been fully developed, and it is this imbalance that we are seeking to redress in this chapter. The chapter begins by sketching out first of all the notion of culture. We then outline the concept of legitimacy and demonstrate the linkages between culture and legitimacy. The chapter concludes by outlining future directions for research and discussing managerial implications.

CONCEPT OF NATIONAL CULTURE

In a globalizing world, national culture has come to play an important role. International alliances bring together managers socialized in different cultures. A wide body of work most clearly suggests that national cultural differences can impede cross-border cooperation (e.g., Gibson, 1999; Hofstede, 1980; Kumar & Nti, 2004). National cultural differences among other things impede effective communication (Hall, 1959) and exacerbate the difficulties of successfully concluding a negotiation agreement (Graham & Lam, 2003; Kumar 1999a, 1999b) and resolving conflicts (Kozan, 1997). This is by no means an exhaustive list of all of the ways in which national cultural differences can affect cross-border cooperation but it is clearly suggestive of the kinds of difficulties alliance managers must be prepared to deal with. Most importantly, these differences cannot only be distracting but may also have the potential of creating a poisonous atmosphere among the alliance partners.

National culture refers to the dominant values and beliefs that exist in a given society. It is to be noted, however, that no culture is completely consistent in regard to any particular set of values and beliefs. That said, there are clusters of values and beliefs that are more dominant in one culture as opposed to another culture. North American and European cultures are primarily individualistic, while Confucian-based cultures of East Asia are primarily collectivistic. It is also to be noted that national cultures are often dynamic and not static (Leung, Bhagat, Buchan, Erez, & Gibson 2005). A dynamic conception of national culture presumes that changes in values and beliefs may be more commonplace than what has assumed to be the case so far.

A number of cultural typologies have appeared in the literature (e.g., Hofstede, 1980; House, Hanges, Javidan, Dorfman, & Gupta, 2004; Schwartz, 1994). One of the most influential of these typologies is that developed by the Dutch social psychologist Geert Hofstede. Based on an empirical study of IBM employees, Hofstede (1980) identified four fundamental dimensions along which cultures vary. The dimensions are individualism-collectivism, power distance, uncertainty avoidance, and masculinity-femininity. The dimension of individualism-collectivism refers to the degree to which individuals give priority to their own goals as opposed to the larger collective. The dimension of power distance refers to the degree to which power is distributed unequally in a society. Uncertainty avoidance refers to the degree to which people are troubled by ambiguity. Masculinity-femininity refers to the degree to which the dominant values in the society are masculine or feminine. The fifth dimension (Confucian dynamism) was added later to the list. Although Hofstede's work has been influential, it has had its share of criticism (e.g., McSweeney, 2002).

Notwithstanding this controversy, it does remain the case that Hofstede's work has been very influential both among scholars and practitioners (Ailon, 2008). We suspect that many, if not all, of Hofstede's dimensions have an intuitive appeal and are empirically well-supported in the literature. This remains particularly true for the construct of individualism-collectivism, which has been extensively relied upon by cross-cultural researchers (Brewer & Chen, 2007). We will therefore be relying primarily upon the construct of individualism-collectivism to demonstrate the linkage between culture and legitimacy management in international alliances.

The dimension of individualism-collectivism is particularly germane to understanding legitimacy management in international alliances for a wide range of reasons. It has direct implications both for the kinds of goals that alliancing firms seek to pursue, and also for the best way they might pursue these goals (Kumar & Das, 2010a). In turn, the nature of the goals as well as the means by which they are attained have direct implications for the partner firms' ability in both attaining and maintaining legitimacy. Secondly, the construct of individualism and collectivism has direct implications for how alliancing firms embedded in these different cultures view the concept of partnering. Although partnering has become a popular concept, it remains the case that, for individualistically oriented firms, it may not be as natural or commonplace a phenomenon as it is for a more collectivistically oriented firm. This is so for the fundamental reason that in individualistic cultures individual interests take priority over group interests. This may have implications also for how the partnering firms seek to manage legitimacy, and how successful they are likely to be. Finally, a firm in an individualistically oriented culture, as opposed to a collectivistically oriented culture, may be less adept in dealing with ambiguity with corresponding implications for legitimacy management. Individualistic cultures are often less tolerant of ambiguity compared to their collectivistic counterparts (Kumar & Worm, 2004). Scholars note that alliances are often characterized by ambiguity and the effective management of ambiguity therefore becomes a salient issue (Walter, Lechner, & Kellermanns, 2008).

CONCEPT OF INTERPARTNER LEGITIMACY

The concept of legitimacy is intrinsic in much of social science theorizing. It has more recently been imported into organizational studies, with Suchman's (1995) article being an influential contribution. Suchman (1995) defines legitimacy as "a generalized perception or assumption that the actions of an entity are desirable, proper, or appropriate within some socially constructed system of norms, values, beliefs, and definitions" (p. 574). Legitimacy judgments, as Kumar and Das (2007) note, are "made by the constituents or the societal groups to which the organization must be responsive" (p. 1427). Legitimacy evaluation is a subjective process in which the actions of the focal entity are evaluated within the context of the existing dominant set of values.

Kumar and Das (2007) build upon the work of Suchman and suggest that alliancing firms are faced with the necessity of evaluating the actions of their partners. The product of this evaluation is either the attainment or non-attainment of interpartner legitimacy. Interpartner legitimacy is defined as "the mutual acknowledgement by the alliance partners that their actions are proper in the developmental processes of the alliance" (Kumar & Das, 2007, p. 1430). If the alliancing firms are able to attain and maintain interpartner legitimacy they are likely to effectively deal with both internal and external challenges that they may be confronted with. By contrast, where interpartner legitimacy is lacking, the alliance is likely to be much less successful and may not be able to prosper or thrive over time.

Suchman (1995) also draws a distinction between three alternative types of legitimacies that he labels as pragmatic, moral, and cognitive. Pragmatic legitimacy has the derivative implication that the alliancing firms see their involvement in the alliance as beneficial. The evaluation of moral legitimacy is predicated on how the alliancing firms view the actions of their partner. If their partner is seen to behave in an appropriate way, the alliance is seen to be exhibiting moral legitimacy. If, by contrast, an alliance firm acts in an opportunistic way or is insensitive to its partner's concerns the alliance will lack moral legitimacy. Finally, cognitive legitimacy, as Suchman (1995) notes, is probably the highest level of legitimacy and is indicative of a situation where the alliancing firms do not question the wisdom of entering into an alliance. This judgment overrides the judgment that may be based on pragmatic or moral legitimacy concerns.

In their conceptualization, Kumar and Das (2007) have shown that different types of legitimacy are relevant at different phases of alliance development. Scholars note that alliances evolve through the stages of formation, operation, and outcome (Das & Teng, 2002). At the formation stage pragmatic legitimacy takes center stage. If the alliance partners cannot at this stage see any tangible benefit from the alliance they will refrain from entering it. At the operation stage, moral legitimacy becomes vitally important. The behavior of the partner firms is crucial. If, for example, a firm reneges on its commitment, or is unwilling to share information, it will have acted in ways that may have compromised the moral legitimacy of the alliance. Cognitive legitimacy takes on major significance at the outcome or evaluation stage of the alliance. It is at this stage that the alliancing firms will make the decision if alliancing is indeed the way to go for them. Their article explores the determinants of pragmatic, moral, and cognitive legitimacies at different stages of alliance development. These authors also note that moral legitimacy has the greatest salience for joint ventures and a minimal salience for minority equity and non-equity alliances. The argument is also made that joint ventures require the greatest amount of effort to attain pragmatic and cognitive legitimacies while non-equity alliances require the least amount of effort.

INDIVIDUALISM VERSUS COLLECTIVISM

Scholars have theorized about the distinction between the two constructs of individualism and collectivism on the basis of four key dimensions (e.g., Chen, Chen, & Meindl, 1998; Triandis, 1995). The four dimensions are (a) nature of the self, (b) goal orientation, (c) relative importance of attitudes/norms, and (d) relational orientation. Individualists are known to possess an independent self whereas the collectivists possess an interdependent self (Markus & Kitayama, 1991). Individuals with an independent self make decisions on the basis of their own self-interests and needs whereas individuals with an interdependent self are bound to explore the consequences of whatever decisions they make on other individuals who are part of their group. Individualists are solely preoccupied with achieving their own goals while collectivists give greater weightage to group goals over their own goals. Collectivists' behavior may be heavily constricted by attitudes and norms whereas the behavior of individualists is subject to few constraints of this kind. Finally, individualists emphasize goal attainment over relationships, while the collectivists prioritize relationships over goal attainment.

In a more recent conceptualization, Brewer and Chen (2007) differentiate between individualism and collectivism on the basis of three dimensions, namely, the locus of identity, the locus of agency, and the locus of obligations. The identity dimension focuses on the uniqueness of the self. This uniqueness could either be in relation to others, or in relation to the group as a whole. From this perspective, individualism is related to the uniqueness of the self, whereas collectivism is related to relationships with significant others. The agency dimension relates to the locus of responsibility for generating any outcome. The individualists assume that outcomes are a product of individual action whereas collectivists believe that outcomes are a consequence of group effort. The obligations dimension defines whether individuals are acting to achieve their own goals or whether their effort and actions are constrained by the need to conform to group norms. As is to be expected, individualists are primarily motivated to attain their own goals while collectivists have the motivation to conform to the group norms. A key insight from Brewer and Chen's work is that researchers have to be sensitive both to the fundamental distinction between relational and group collectivism as also to the aspect of individualism-collectivism (self-representation, agency, values) that may be most relevant to explaining behavior.

INDIVIDUALISM-COLLECTIVISM AND LEGITIMACY DYNAMICS IN INTERNATIONAL ALLIANCES

Alliances evolve through the stages of formation, operation, and outcome (Das & Teng, 2002). At the formation stage the alliance partners are tasked with assessing their partner and concluding a negotiated agreement. The operation stage of the alliance begins when the partners put into practice the commitments and the agreements that they had agreed to at the negotiation stage. Finally, at the outcome stage, the alliance partners evaluate the performance of the alliance to date and come to a judgment as to whether or not they wish to persist with the alliance. We will discuss how national culture as operationalized in terms of individualism-collectivism plays an important role at all three stages of alliance development.

Formation Stage

At the formation stage it is critical that the alliance partners be successful in establishing interpartner legitimacy. If such legitimacy is not attained, the alliance may not even come into existence. A successful negotiation between the alliance partners implies that pragmatic legitimacy has been attained. Attaining negotiation success is not easy, however, for several reasons (see Kumar & Das, 2010b, for a comprehensive discussion of interpartner negotiations in alliances). First of all, the partners are tasked with the need to forge an agreement in a mixed-motive situation. This makes negotiation difficult because it induces uncertainty about how their potential partner might behave over time. As Kumar and Das (2007) note, "The mixed-motive character of the interaction makes it difficult for the top management in either firm to persuade its alliance managers about the motives of the top management of its partner firm" (p. 1436). The problem is no doubt compounded by cultural differences, because in addition to the uncertainty about partner's motives and behavior, there is the added problem that the process of negotiation varies across individualistic and collectivistic cultures (Kumar 1999a). Individualists, as opposed to the collectivists, are contract-focused, do not care much about building relationships, and are very sensitive to time. If investing in a particular partnership is time-consuming and the results uncertain they may withdraw. They may also tend to be direct, aggressive, and less consensually inclined in their decision making process. This is very much at variance with the collectivistic spirit. Collectivists are relationship-oriented, seek to build consensus, and are wary of committing themselves to the other party, unless they are able to establish affective trust (Chen, Chen, & Meindl, 1998).

Differences in negotiation styles are therefore likely to lead to script incongruence (Kumar, 1999b). Script incongruence refers to the expectational inconsistency among the alliance partners as to how the negotiation is going to unfold. Script incongruence generates negative emotions, and prevents the emergence of trust (Kumar, 1999b). It may also generate frequent interruptions as each partner acting on the basis of its norms and values violates the expectations of its partner. Negotiators embedded in individualistic cultures are likely to experience dejection-related emotions while negotiators embedded in collectivistic cultures are likely to experience agitation-related emotions (Kumar, 1999b). Dejection related emotions are indicative of an absence of a positive outcome while agitation-related emotions signify the potential presence of a negative outcome. It has been maintained that dejection-related emotions will foster aggressive behavior on part of the individualists, while agitation-related emotions will lead the collectivists to withdraw (Kumar, 1999a). This may intensify the frustration of the individualists who may begin to wonder if they can conclude the agreement. A vicious circle is likely to develop, and the alliance partners, instead of coming together, are likely to drift further apart, and this makes it even less likely that the negotiations will be successful. Impasses may be frequent and not easily bridged, absent a trusted third party.

Secondly, even in the circumstance that negotiation style differences do not generate excessive negative emotions, the alliance partners will nevertheless face a protracted negotiation process due not only to differences in negotiation styles but also for the extra time and effort required to bridge the differences. Finally, given the differences between the individualistic and the collectivistic cultural orientations, it is by no means clear that, even if the actors perceive to have successfully established pragmatic legitimacy, they will necessarily have complete clarity about what they have negotiated. Cultural differences may be bridged successfully but this does not necessarily imply that complete clarity has been attained. Notwithstanding the intentions of either party, this may be impeded by contractual incompleteness, time constraints, and conflicting cognitions. In other words, cultural bridging while essential for the attainment of interpartner legitimacy, does not necessarily imply an accurate understanding as to what the alliance entails. This will be particularly true if the alliancing firms are both new to alliances as also to cross cultural interactions. Most often, it is only at the implementation stage that the alliance partners begin to determine the veracity of their assumptions. This leads us to the following propositions:

> **Proposition 1(a):** *Alliancing partners embedded in differing cultures, individualistic and collectivistic, will encounter frequent interruptions as they negotiate to establish interpartner legitimacy.*

> **Proposition 1(b):** *Alliancing partners embedded in individualistic cultures will seek to speedily establish interpartner legitimacy, relative to their collectivistic counterparts; the slowness of the negotiation process in collectivistic cultures will only fuel frustration among their individualistic counterparts.*

> **Proposition 1(c):** *In the event that the partners are able to bridge their differences, interpartner pragmatic legitimacy will no doubt be established, but nonetheless it may still remain unclear as to whether the partners have a good and accurate understanding of their agreement.*

Operation Stage

At the operation stage the alliance partners start making the alliance a concrete reality. A new entity is established, employees seconded to the venture from the partners, new hires brought in from the outside. It is conceivable that everything proceeds smoothly. If so, then there are no issues for the alliance partners to address. In actual fact such a condition may often be a rarity for several reasons. First of all, as Luo (2002) suggests, "Alliances vary in the levels of engaged risk and interdependence" (p. 690). The higher the risk and interdependence between the partners, the greater the task difficulty confronting them. Cultural distance will not only aggravate this problem, it may create problems of its own. The partners may experience communicative difficulties and this may prevent trust from being strengthened. The decision styles of the partners may also be variable, and this too may create additional problems. Consensus decision making is the norm in collectivistic cultures whereas in individualistic cultures this is not the dominant practice. Then too, the alliance partners may differ in the types of attributions that they make about any deviation from the expected performance (Kumar & Nti, 2004). Attributional reasoning refers to the rationale for a given outcome. If, for example, an alliance has fared poorly, an internal attribution would suggest that it is either one's own fault or the fault of one's partner. A situational attribution, by contrast, would suggest that perhaps external forces may account for the alliance's poor results. Scholars note that collectivists (e.g., East Asians) are often prone to making situational attributions whereas the individualists (Europeans, North Americans) tend to make internal attributions (Nisbett, Peng, Choi, & Norenzayan, 2001). This may give rise to an "attributional conflict" (e.g., Kumar & Nti, 2004).

Whatever be the specific nature of the problem, associated with each of these problems is likely to be an unfavorable process or outcome discrepancy (Kumar & Nti, 1998). An unfavorable process discrepancy means that the partners are dissatisfied with the manner they are interacting with each other. An unfavorable outcome discrepancy means that the alliance has been ineffective in attaining its goals over a period of time. The existence of unfavorable process and outcome discrepancies poses a grave challenge to both moral and pragmatic legitimacy of the alliance. Moral legitimacy comes into play because the existence of process discrepancies suggests that the partners have not behaved in the manner that they ought to. Of course, this judgment is being made from the cultural standpoint of the partner concerned. Pragmatic legitimacy comes into play because an unfavorable outcome discrepancy suggests that the alliance has not been able to attain its goal.

Alliance management becomes challenging if both pragmatic and moral legitimacies come to be challenged during the operation of the alliance. The necessity of dealing with both types of legitimacy simultaneously may result in an excessive amount of managerial burden. The process becomes even more challenging because both types of legitimacy may not have the same resonance in individualistic and collectivistic cultures. It has been maintained that moral legitimacy is more important in a collectivistic culture while pragmatic legitimacy is more important in an individualistic culture (Kumar & Das, 2010a). A key reason for this differential importance is the difference in the locus of obligations in an individualistic as opposed to a collectivistic culture (Brewer & Chen, 2007). In a collectivistic culture it is incumbent upon the participants to act in ways that will maximize group welfare, whereas in an individualistic culture the pursuit of self-interest is dominant. A key implication of this is that when the alliance is not doing well the collectivistic partner will expect that its counterpart subordinate its self-interest to that of the larger alliance. The individualistic partner, by contrast, will have the obligation to pursue its interest in an untrammeled way. Thus, not only do we have the fact that the alliance has a problem, but the situation is made worse by the fact that the partners may not even agree as to what is the dominant problem in the alliance. It may also be worth noting that in an individualistic culture there may be less of a consensus about the need to attain moral legitimacy, and even in the case where such a need is acknowledged, there may be less of a consensus as to whether such legitimacy exists at any given point in time. This too stands in sharp opposition to the scenario in a collectivistic culture, where not only is there likely to be a strong consensus about the need for moral legitimacy, but there will also be a strong consensus as to the existence or the non existence of moral legitimacy.

A related problem revolves around the fact that when legitimacy is violated, the repair of legitimacy is far from a straightforward process. This is so for several reasons. First is the issue of responsibility: Who is to blame? Second is the issue of determining what actions needed to be taken, the scope of the actions, and how they should be implemented in resolving the impasse. This is not an easy issue, given especially the large cultural distance between the parties. The problem is aggravated by the fact that in all alliances there is an inherent tension between value creation and value appropriation, and this may simultaneously create a tension between and within the partners as they seek to balance the use of integrative with the use of distributive strategies (Ness, 2009). Finally, and perhaps most crucially, the collectivistic cultures differ from individualistic cultures in the steps that they require for the reestablishment of moral legitimacy. Face plays a key role in collectivistic cultures (Chen, Chen, & Meindl, 1998; Earley, 1997) and when moral legitimacy is lost, then so is face. Moral legitimacy implies that the partners have behaved inappropriately. The non-fulfillment of obligations or adopting inappropriate behaviors may reflect negatively on an individual's character. This requires face repair strategies from the individualistically oriented firm, and apart from the fact that they may not know how to repair face, they may also question the wisdom of doing so, as this practice is likely to be culturally alien to them. It is also a process that takes time, and the individualists are unlikely to be pleased by this. This only exacerbates the problem. The challenge facing the collectivistically-oriented firm is altogether different. It will need to cater to the demands of its individualistic counterpart who is, above all, interested in pragmatic legitimacy. This collectivistic firm must be swift in its response so as to cater to the heightened time sensitivity that is a characteristic feature of individualistic cultures. It must also be proactive and convince its individualistic counterpart that it is undertaking actions which will help to rectify the problem.

Another issue has to do with the managerial levels that might be involved in the management of legitimacies. We would surmise that in individualistically oriented cultures legitimacy management will be largely dependent on the discretion of the alliance managers. By contrast, in collectivistic cultures, legitimacy management is likely to be a top–down process. Hofstede's work shows that collectivism by and large goes hand in hand with a high power distance. This raises the problem that in collectivistically oriented cultures legitimacy management may be a drawn-out process, given the fact that the top management is likely to be intimately involved. At the same time it raises the other problem, namely, that there might be a conflict between the managerial levels involved in legitimacy management, and this internal conflict may further aggravate the problem.

It is also conceivable that the methods used by the alliancing firms to resolve unfavorable pragmatic legitimacy may further exacerbate the crisis. As we mentioned earlier, firms embedded in an individualistic societal context are more sensitive to the presence or absence of pragmatic legitimacy. When they find that such legitimacy has been eroded, they will undertake a variety of actions to reverse this condition. They may influence their partner, put pressure on it, use threats, and in the ultimate instance may withdraw from the venture. These are face-threatening actions and will not go down well with their collectivistic counterparts for whom process may be even more important than the final outcome. The collectivistic firm is likely to react negatively to this and may feel that its trust in its partner has been misplaced. This can only accelerate the demise of the venture. This leads us to the following propositions:

Proposition 2(a): *Pragmatic legitimacy will be more valued by a partner embedded in an individualistic culture whereas moral legitimacy will be more valued by a partner embedded in a collectivistic culture.*

Proposition 2(b): *In alliancing firms from individualistic cultures, as opposed to collectivistic cultures, there will be less of a consensus about the presence or absence of moral legitimacy.*

Proposition 2(c): *In repairing moral legitimacy with their collectivistically oriented partner, the individualistically oriented alliancing firm will have to engage in face management strategies.*

Proposition 2(d): *In repairing pragmatic legitimacy with their individualistically oriented alliance partner, the collectivistically oriented firm will need to be proactive and flexible.*

Proposition 2(e): *An alliancing firm embedded in an individualistically oriented culture will find that repairing legitimacy with a collectivistically oriented partner will be a drawn-out process.*

Proposition 2(f): *An alliancing firm embedded in a time-sensitive individualistically oriented culture may employ strategies to reestablish legitimacy that may ironically further undermine the legitimacy.*

Outcome Stage

At a certain point in time alliance partners are faced with the necessity of evaluating alliance performance. Is the performance satisfactory or is it unsatisfactory? Should they persist with or, alternatively, withdraw from the alliance? These are important questions that may have a significant impact on how the alliance evolves over time. The constructs of individualism and collectivism have an important bearing at the outcome stage in a variety of ways. First, the individualists, as opposed to the collectivists, are likely to be much more hard-nosed about the evaluation. In other words, if the alliance does not deliver the expected results, they will be among the first both to note this possibility and to communicate it to their partner. They will also not be reluctant to pull the plug on the venture if, in their judgment, there do not exist realistic alternatives for enhancing alliance performance. Given their focus on attaining and maintaining pragmatic legitimacy, these conclusions should by no means surprise us.

The individualists, as opposed to the collectivists, will also differ in the metrics that they use for assessing alliance performance. For the individualists, the metrics will have to be tangible, be it the development of new technology, the attainment of certain profitability levels, and so on. Tangible metrics are useful because they provide a clear-cut benchmark for evaluating pragmatic legitimacy. The collectivists, while not necessarily opposed to financial metrics, will also make an assessment of the nature of their relationship with their alliancing partner. Is the relationship developing in the right direction? Is an appropriate level of trust being established? The focus on the relational dimension and on whether they are developing the partnership with the right kind of partner highlights the importance of moral legitimacy to them. Put differently, the collectivists will use multidimensional measures, as opposed to unidimensional measures in assessing alliance performance. Again, this is not surprising, given the relational orientation and the focus on moral legitimacy that is so often a characteristic feature of collectivistic societies.

If the alliance has succeeded in attaining moral legitimacy, then the collectivists, as opposed to the individualists, are more likely to transfer that legitimacy to other alliances involving the same partner. We would suppose that this is so for the fundamental reason that the establishment of moral legitimacy implies that the partners have come to trust each other. If, on the other hand, the alliancing partners do not have any other alliance in which they are connected before hand, they may well seek to initiate new ventures with their existing partner. This leads to the following propositions:

Proposition 3(a): *Alliancing firms embedded in individualistic, as opposed to collectivistic, cultures will be faster in assessing pragmatic legitimacy, and* *as a consequence thereof, will be more expeditious in deciding whether to persist with or withdraw from the venture.*

Proposition 3(b): *Alliancing firms embedded in individualistic, as opposed to collectivistic, cultures will be more prone to using financial metrics in assessing whether an alliance has succeeded in attaining pragmatic legitimacy.*

Proposition 3(b): *If the alliance has succeeded in attaining moral legitimacy, the collectivists, as opposed to the individualists, will be much more inclined in transferring this legitimacy to other alliances involving the same partner.*

CONCLUSION

In this chapter we have attempted to highlight the impact of national culture on legitimacy management in international alliances. The issue of interpartner legitimacy and that of the impact of national culture remains an under-researched area in the alliance literature. This is a surprising omission given that many alliances cross national boundaries, and while doing that, they must also motivate their partner to act in ways that facilitate interpartner legitimacy. This is by no means an easy undertaking but at the same time it is vital if the alliance is to survive and prosper.

The framework articulated in this chapter has important theoretical as well as managerial implications. It first of all extends the existing literature on interpartner legitimacy by showing how national cultural differences can impact legitimacy dynamics in international alliances. Secondly, it bridges the national culture and legitimacy literatures that have to this date remained distinct and disparate. This is surprising inasmuch as that at the root of the national culture construct is the notion of legitimacy. National cultures determine through their own prisms of values and beliefs what is legitimate and what is not. Third, the chapter articulates a series of propositions that link national culture (individualism-collectivism) to the different facets of legitimacy management. These propositions can be empirically tested either through case studies, survey based investigations, or some combination thereof. To our knowledge, there is no study as yet that has explicitly made the attempt to link national culture with legitimacy management in alliances. We would suggest that this is long overdue and our chapter hopefully provides some impetus for further work in this area. At a broader level the chapter contributes to extending the micro behavioral paradigm for studying alliances by linking the concepts of national culture and legitimacy.

The framework outlined here has important managerial implications. Alliancing firms need to be well aware of the cultural assumptions on which they operate as well as the cultural assumptions of their partner, and especially so because of the fact that these assumptions do not operate in any overt or concrete manner. Although this is not a novel insight and the point has been made before, it has not been previously linked to the legitimacy literatures (for an exception, see Kumar & Das, 2010a). This is vital to effectively bridging the culture gap between the parties. It needs to be noted of course that while the culture gap can be bridged it cannot be eliminated altogether. Alliancing firms must recognize this because, in its absence, unrealistic expectations may prove to be another potent source of problems. They must also recognize that, notwithstanding good intentions, problems are still likely to arise and till the time they are able to develop information about the intentions of their partner, they must not overreact even if they remain unhappy with the actions of their partner. The issue of finding the right balance between temperance and action is essential for effective alliance management. The framework also suggests the need for cultural training for managers at all levels of the organization. This may not be easy or cheap, but is nonetheless essential. Alliances have become commonplace but, as the literature suggests, they have often been far from successful. It is our hope that the arguments set forth in this chapter will prove useful both for extending the literature and providing useful managerial guidance.

ACKNOWLEDGMENT

This chapter, save some minor changes, was earlier published as Kumar, R., & Das, T. K. (2011). National culture and legitimacy in international alliances. In T. K. Das (Ed.), *Strategic alliances in a globalizing world* (pp. 243–261). Charlotte, NC: Information Age.

REFERENCES

Ailon, G. (2008). Mirror, mirror on the wall: Culture's consequence in a value test of its own design. *Academy of Management Review, 33*(4), 885–904.

Brewer, M. B., & Chen, Y.-R. (2007). Where (who) are collectives in collectivism? Toward conceptual clarification of individualism and collectivism. *Psychological Review, 114*(1), 133–151.

Chen, C. C., Chen, X. P., & Meindl, J. R. (1998). How can cooperation be fostered? The cultural effects of individualism-collectivism. *Academy of Management Review, 23*(2), 285–304.

Das, T. K. (1986). *The subjective side of strategy making: Future orientations and perceptions of executives.* New York, NY: Praeger.

Das, T. K. (2003). Managerial perceptions and the essence of the managerial world: What is an interloper business executive to make of the academic-researcher perceptions of managers? *British Journal of Management, 14*(1), 23–32.

Das, T. K., & Kumar, R. (2007). Learning dynamics in the alliance development process. *Management Decision, 45*(4), 684–707.

Das, T. K., & Kumar, R. (2010a). Interpartner sensemaking in strategic alliances: Managing cultural differences and internal tensions. *Management Decision, 48*(1), 17–36.

Das, T. K, & Kumar, R. (2010b). Interpretive schemes in cross-national alliances: Managing conflicts and discrepancies. *Cross Cultural Management: An International Journal, 17*(2), 154–169.

Das, T. K., & Kumar, R. (2011). Regulatory focus and opportunism in the alliance development process. *Journal of Management, 37*(3), 682–708.

Das, T. K., & Rahman, N. (2010). Determinants of partner opportunism in strategic alliances: A conceptual framework. *Journal of Business and Psychology, 25*(1), 55–74.

Das, T. K., & Teng, B. (1999). Cognitive biases and strategic decision processes: An integrative perspective. *Journal of Management Studies, 36*(6), 757–778.

Das, T. K., & Teng, B. (2000). Instabilities of strategic alliances: An internal tensions perspective. *Organization Science, 11*(1), 77–101.

Das, T. K., & Teng, B. (2002). The dynamics of alliance conditions in the alliance development process. *Journal of Management Studies, 39*(5), 725–746.

Earley, P. C. (1997). *Face, harmony, and social structure: An analysis of organizational behavior across cultures.* New York, NY: Oxford University Press.

Gibson, C. B. (1999). Do they do what they believe they can? Group efficacy and group effectiveness across tasks and cultures. *Academy of Management Journal, 42*(2), 138–152.

Graham, J. L., & Lam, N. M. (2003). The Chinese negotiation. *Harvard Business Review, 81*(10), 82–91.

Gulati, R., Lavie, D., & Singh, H. (2009). The nature of partnering experience and the gains from alliances. *Strategic Management Journal, 30*(11), 1213–1233.

Hall, E. T. (1959). *The silent language.* New York, NY: Doubleday.

Hamel, G. (1991). Competition for competence and interpartner learning within international strategic alliances. *Strategic Management Journal, 12*(Summer Special Issue), 83–103.

Hofstede, G. (1980). *Culture's consequences: International differences in work related values.* Newbury Park, CA: SAGE.

House, R. J., Hanges, P. J., Javidan, M., Dorfman, P. W., & Gupta, V. (2004). *Culture, leadership, and organizations: The GLOBE study of 62 societies.* Newbury Park, CA: SAGE.

Inkpen, A., & Beamish, P. W. (1997). Knowledge, bargaining power, and international joint venture instability. *Academy of Management Review, 22*(1), 177–202.

Kozan, M. K. (1997). Culture and conflict management: A theoretical framework. *International Journal of Conflict Management, 8*(4), 338–360.

Kumar, R. (1997). The role of affect in negotiations: An integrative overview. *Journal of Applied Behavioral Science, 33*(1), 84–100.

Kumar, R. (1999a). A script theoretical analysis of international negotiating behavior. *Research on Negotiation in Organizations, 7,* 285–311.

Kumar, R. (1999b). Communicative conflict in intercultural negotiations: The case of American and Japanese business negotiations. *International Negotiation, 4,* 63–78.

Kumar, R. (2008). Contested meanings and emotional dynamics in strategic alliances. In N. Ashkanasy & C. Cooper (Eds.), *Research companion to emotion in organizations* (pp. 561–574). London, England: Edward Elgar.

Kumar, R., & Das, T. K. (2007). Interpartner legitimacy in the alliance development process. *Journal of Management Studies, 44*(8), 1425–1453.

Kumar, R., & Das, T. K. (2010a). Strategic alliances and culture in a globalizing world. In J. Ulijn, G. Duysters, & E. Meijer (Eds.), *Strategic alliances, mergers and acquisitions: The influence of culture on successful cooperation* (pp. 13–29). London, England: Edward Elgar.

Kumar, R., & Das, T. K. (2010b). Interpartner negotiations in the alliance development process. In T. K. Das (Ed.), *Researching strategic alliances: Emerging perspectives* (pp. 207–257). Charlotte, NC: Information Age.

Kumar, R., & Nti, K. O. (1998). Differential learning and interaction in alliance dynamics: A process and outcome discrepancy model. *Organization Science, 9*(3), 356–367.

Kumar, R., & Nti, K. O. (2004). National cultural values and the evolution of process and outcome discrepancies in international strategic alliances. *Journal of Applied Behavioral Science, 40*(3), 344–361.

Kumar, R., & Worm, V. (2004). Institutional dynamics and the negotiation process: Comparing India and China. *International Journal of Conflict Management, 15*(3), 304–334.

Leung, K., Bhagat, R. S., Buchan, N. R., Erez, M., & Gibson, C. B. (2005). Culture and international business: Recent advances and their implications for future research. *Journal of International Business Studies, 36,* 357–378.

Luo, Y. (2002). Building trust in cross-cultural collaborations: Toward a contingency perspective. *Journal of Management, 28*(5), 669–694.

Luo, Y. (2008). Procedural fairness and interfirm cooperation in strategic alliances. *Strategic Management Journal, 29*(1), 27–46.

Markus, H. R., & Kitayama, S. (1991). Culture and self: Implications for cognition, emotion, and motivation. *Psychological Review, 98*(2), 224–253.

McSweeney, B. (2002). Hofstede's model of national cultural differences and their consequences: A triumph of faith—A failure of analysis. *Human Relations, 55*(1), 89–118.

Ness, H. (2009). Governance, negotiations, and alliance dynamics: Explaining the evolution of relational practice. *Journal of Management Studies, 46*(3), 451–480.

Nisbett, R. E., Peng, K., Choi, I., & Norenzayan, A. (2001). Culture and systems of thought: Holistic vs analytic cognition. *Psychological Review, 108*(2), 291–310.

Pak, Y. S., Ra, W., & Park, Y-R. (2009). Understanding IJV performance in a learning and a conflict mediated context. *International Business Review, 18*(5), 470–480.

Schwartz, S. H. (1994). Beyond individualism/collectivism: New cultural dimensions of values. In U. Kim, H. C. Triandis, C. Kagitcibasi, S. C. Choi., & G.

Yoon (Eds.), *Individualism and collectivism: Theory, methods, and applications* (pp. 85–119). Newbury Park, CA: SAGE.

Suchman, M. C. (1995). Managing legitimacy: Strategic and institutional approaches. *Academy of Management Review, 20*(3), 571–610.

Triandis, H. C. (1995). *Individualism and collectivism.* Boulder, CO: Westview.

Walter, J., Lechner, C., & Kellermanns, F. W. (2008). Disentangling alliance management processes: Decision making, politicality, and alliance performance. *Journal of Management Studies, 45*(3), 530–560.

CHAPTER 7

ARE FAMILY BUSINESSES VALUES-DRIVEN ORGANIZATIONS?

An Exploratory Research

Angela Dettori
Michela Floris

ABSTRACT

This chapter investigates how values become strong identity elements in family businesses. The aim is to identify the peculiarities inherent to this kind of business to address other business models and to better understand and follow the principles that shape family businesses. The research was conducted using the NVivo 12 software for a sample of three family businesses. Findings challenge the existing literature and offer direction for future scholarly research. Evidence from this study suggests that family values are the heart of the family business culture and are based on the figure of the "father." A family guards this type of firm by protecting, developing, and transmitting the firm to its successors, thus creating a link between the old and new generations to conserve and preserve the values, and spread them with the territory where the family firm is embedded.

Cultural Values in Strategy and Organization, pages 171–186

INTRODUCTION

Scholars argue that family businesses possess a conglomerate of values that strongly characterizes them (Binz Astrachan & Botero, 2018) and acts as a support and stimulus especially during periods of change or particular challenges, when family businesses draws their vital nourishment from their shared and transmitted values. These are sometimes defined as "lived" values and sometimes as "married" values, which may not survive changes or challenges (Gatrell, Jenkins, & Tucker, 2001). Aronoff and Ward (2001), describing the power of family business values emphasize that they represent the foundation of corporate culture and provide a model for decision making processes. Moreover, family business values are a determining element in the recruitment and motivation phase of employees and often contribute to providing meaning to the work; they can also encourage solidarity, commitment, and enthusiasm among shareholders (Aronoff & Ward, 2011).

However, even if the attention of scholars is clear, researches remain often at a conceptual level. This situation emphasizes that there are very few empirical analyses. In this scenario, the aim of this chapter is to contribute in filling this need in order to analyze which are the main family business values that contribute to define these as values-driven, assuring the continuity and success across generations.

The chapter is organized into three sections: literature background, methodology, and conclusion. Literature background defines the concept of "value," firstly in a general view and secondly, focusing on family business scholars' perspectives, in order to investigate the main studies and frame the system of values that family businesses possess. The methodology section explains the research design, the qualitative methods used, and finally, focuses on the data analysis and findings. The concluding section depicts how and why family businesses base their behavior and strategies on specific values that are able to determine their success and survival. Implications and limitations are then discussed.

THEORETICAL BACKGROUND

The Concept of Value

The term value in everyday language refers to desirability, importance, usefulness, and monetary worth; in a plural form, the term values can also mean moral principles, ethical standards, or behavioral norms (Koiranen, 2002).

Several authors have provided more than one definition of value. Kluckhohn (1958) defines value as a concept, either implicit or explicit, of the desire that influences the selection of available ways, means, and aims of an action. Guth and Tagiuri (1965) describe values as desirable end-states, Rokeach (1973) argues that values are generalized, enduring beliefs regarding the personal and social desirability of different means of contact or end-states of existence, whereas Connor and Becker (1975) underline the attitudinal and behavioral processes.

Values represent the bedrock of any corporate culture (Deal & Kennedy, 1983), identify influences that affect each aspect of social life, stimulating individuals to act and to pursue objectives (Dumas & Blodgett, 1999), and it refer to an individual's reasons for acting and their judgments regarding such reasons (Özar, 1997). Other scholars (e.g., Aronoff & Ward, 2011) affirm that values represent the cornerstones of human effort, achievement, solidarity, enthusiasm, and commitment, which encourage shareholders to face difficulties. Values are relatively stable across time and situations, which differentiates them from other more contextual constructs such as attitudes. Psychologists have agreed that values are abstract psychological concepts that lie at the foundation of more concrete psychological constructs, such as interests, preferences, attitudes, and these are strongly linked to the individual's or organization's identity (Rokeach, 1973). Accordingly, they transcend specific situations and are applied more generally to guide organizational behavior and decision making (Schwartz & Bilsky, 1987). Values are considered as normative rather than positive states; they guide stakeholders to what ought to be rather than what is (Rokeach, 1973). In other words, "Values specify an individual's personal beliefs about how he or she 'should' or 'ought' to 'behave'" (Meglino & Ravlin, 1998, p. 354).

It is widely accepted that values can be classified and hierarchically ordered (Lyons, Higgins, & Duxbury, 2010). For example, according to Meglino and Ravlin (1998), there are three kinds of values: values referred to as objects or outcomes (e.g., the value an employee places on quality or excellence), terminal values (e.g., self-sufficient end-states a person is willing to achieve, such as happiness or success), and instrumental or behavioral values (e.g., the behaviors that facilitate the attainment of terminal values, such as altruism or optimism). Moreover, there is a distinction between explicitly stated values and implicit values. For instance, Osborne (1991) explains the use of corporate value statements and the term espoused values, which indicates the materialization of values (Thornbury, 2003).

In sum, it can be affirmed that values have become an important management tool in the postindustrial economy (Anderson, 1997; Pruzan, 1998); therefore, organizations require values-based management that inspires employees, while also serving as a source of identity and pride for the organization's members.

Toward a Definition of Family Business and of Family Business Values

The concept of the family business warrants particular interest from scholars given the presence and diffusion of these entities around the globe, explained as the firms' ubiquity (Poza, 2013). Though family businesses represent more than 90% of all businesses worldwide (IFERA, 2003), theoretical research frameworks continue to be fragmented, and no common definition of a family business exists.

This field of study is relatively new, with the first publication on family business appearing in the 1970s. Since then, family business studies have gradually increased (Dyer, 1986; Ward, 1997). In the early 1990s, scholars attempted to cluster family firms based on distinctive features. These studies produced numerous definitions of family business based on the distinguishing factors present in this form of entrepreneurship.

Litz (1995) identified a family firm by the extent to which its ownership and management are concentrated within a family unit and by the extent to which its members strive to achieve and/or maintain intra-organizational family-based relatedness.

Astrachan and Shanker (2003) studied the objective and subjective aspects identifying three definitions of a family business. These definitions depend on the degree of family involvement as follows: broad, in which the family has effective control over the strategic direction and the business is intended to remain in the family; middle, which adds to the broad concept through the involvement of the founder or descendant who runs the company; and narrow, which in addition to the former criteria, involves multiple generations with direct family involvement in the daily operations and more than one family member with significant management responsibilities.

Chua, Chrisman, and Sharma (1999) define a family firm as a firm governed and/or managed with the intention of shaping the firm and pursuing a vision held by a dominant coalition controlled by members of the same family or a small number of families in a manner that is potentially sustainable across generations of the family or families.

Other scholars have contributed to the debate by delving into the elements that, more than others, characterize the family business, such as property (Barnes & Hershon, 1976; Barry, 1975; Diaz-Moriana, Clinton, Kammerlander, Lumpkin, & Craig, 2018; Lansberg, Perrow, & Rogolsky, 1988; Muñoz-Bullón & Sanchez-Bueno, 2011; Stanley, Hernández-Linares, López-Fernández, & Kellermanns, 2019); family involvement (Astrachan, Klein, & Smyrnios, 2002; Astrachan & Shanker, 2003); family control and management and the intention to transfer the business to subsequent generations (Astrachan & Shanker, 2003; Handler, 1989; Litz, 1995); culture

(Litz, 1995); family attachment (Aldrich & Cliff, 2003; Chrisman, Chua, & Steier, 2005; Zahra, Hayton, & Salvato, 2004); power and experience (Astrachan et al., 2002); and the values of the founder and the attention of the family towards the preservation of the socio-emotional heritage, that is, all that determines the attachment and commitment to the firm by family members and determines their unity, solidity, and serenity in their relationships (Arregle, Naldi, Nordqvist, & Hitt, 2012; Barnett, Long, & Marler, 2012; Cennamo, Berrone, Cruz, & Gomez-Mejia, 2012; García-Álvarez & López-Sintas, 2001; Habbershon, Williams, & MacMillan, 2003).

When an owning of family values forms the basis of a business culture, vital synergies can arise. Indeed, "shared values" (Aronoff & Ward, 2001) allow family members to derive satisfaction and meaning by supporting relationships between different generations, always reaching out for the organization's goals. A constant commitment to values is the greatest strength that the family can bring to the firm. According to Aronoff and Ward (2000), the power of values in family businesses is linked to several factors: It lays the foundation for business culture, provides a model for decision making processes, supports a long-term vision, enhances the territory to which it belongs, challenges conventional thinking, adapts to change and the market, improves strategic planning, creates new strategic alliances, serves to recruit and retain employees, and finally gives meaning to "hard work."

Scholars (Tàpies & Ward, 2008), regarding the fact that values constitute a great resource for companies, states that recent studies have provided significant evidence that family businesses have a special competitive advantage as *values-driven*, driven by values. In this sense, values pervade every aspect of the family business. Aronoff (2004) underlines the importance of values as pillars of the culture of the family business and that these elements, strong culture and unique values, allow family businesses to differentiate themselves from other types of companies, therefore they can rightly constitute an advantage irreplaceable competition.

Family business values can be defined as explicit or implicit conceptions of what is desirable in both the family and business life. Given that conflicts of interest often arise between the two dimensions (business and family goals), family business values should be defined and shared so as to create a common ground for a durable value system that benefits both dimensions (Aronoff & Ward, 2001).

Family values stabilize the three dimensions of the family business system: family, firm, and ownership (Neubauer & Lank, 2016). In this sense, as Collins and Porras (1996) argue, the core values and beliefs represent the glue that holds the family, the hard work and the firm together, specifically when conflicts of interests are present within the firm.

Among the various lists of values followed by the various scholars, Cappuyns (1998) identifies five values that could contribute to the success of the family business, summarized with the acronym ELISA (excellence, laboriousness, initiative, simplicity, and austerity), while Aronoff and Ward (2011) identify a list of corporate values specific to family businesses: responsibility, value added, collective good, training, ethical behavior, concentration on values, fun, justice, meritocracy, opening, pragmatism, initiative, confidence, leadership, social purpose, entrepreneurial spirit, input enhancement, attention, and interaction with stakeholders.

Values are one of the key factors that constitute "the family effect" (Dyer, 2006) or the impact of the family on the performance of the company. Solid and clear values can contribute to defining a business in which each member shares a sense of pride in belonging to that specific organization, which promotes not only economic efficiency, but also the well-being of the community in which it operates (Ceja, Agulles, & Tàpies, 2010). In other words, values represent the essence of the spirit of the family business and guide all the actions of the company itself.

METHODOLOGY

Research Design and Setting

With the aim of investigating values in small family firms, by understanding whether these organizations are value-driven, this research engages in a qualitative study, particularly appropriate for family business studies (McCollom, 1990) to penetrate the veil of the family and avoid gathering data that is not useful (Litz, 1997).

Specifically, this work is based on a cross-case analysis, a suitable method that facilitates the comparison of commonalities and differences among case studies (Miles & Huberman, 1994) to produce a synthesized outcome (Khan & VanWynsberghe, 2008), organizing data from the cases in tables and graphs. In addition, case studies are able to answer "how" and "why" questions, providing explanation of events, exploring causality, and generating theory (Eisenhardt, 1989a; Yin, 2008, 2011).

The chosen methodology comprised a structured approach where theoretical contents were identified first from the literature and then, through an iterative process, were refined with the collection and analysis of data come from the cases and finally, were returned to earlier literature (Miles & Huberman, 1994; Wolcott, 1994). Selected case studies showed the ability in exploring meanings and processes (Van Maanen, 1983) and in understanding individual behaviors without being influenced by researcher's views (Finch, 1988), that is particularly relevant to investigate the effects of culture (Howorth & Ali, 2001) and, conversely, context.

In line with other scholars (Miles & Huberman, 1994), the choice of the cases was purposeful. Moreover, this agreed also with Patton's suggestions (1990, 2002):

> The logic and power of purposeful sampling lie in selecting information-rich cases for study in depth. Information-rich cases are those from which one can learn a great deal about issues of central importance to the purpose of the inquiry, thus the term purposeful sampling. Studying information-rich cases yields insights and in-depth understanding rather than empirical generalizations. (Patton, 2002, p. 230)

Specifically, we built on a sample of three meaningful firms, with the family business owner–manager as our unit of analysis. These small family firms are able to generate innovation and are representative as described by Howorth, Rose, and Hamilton (2006). Their owners can be labeled as "heroes" (Welter, Baker, Audretsch, & Gartner, 2017) as they manage "everyday entrepreneurships," characterized by a blooming heterogeneity, and they operate under resource constraints and condition of adversity (Bradley, 2015; Powell & Baker, 2014).

Data Gathering

As regard to data collection, we gathered data from multiple sources: (a) in depth semi-structured interviews with the family owner managers (to understand the firm history, strategy, and behavior, and above all, the main family business values); (b) archival data (business reports, press articles, firm materials); and (c) informal follow-ups by phone.

Specifically, in the third quarter of 2018, we conducted in-depth interviews with the family owners of the three small family firms sampled. After a prior understanding of the demographical data of each firm, the interviews were planned with each family owner and were conducted in person using an interview protocol. The interviews (average duration 70 minutes) consisted of unstructured and semi structured questions to gain an understanding of the firm's history, the family owner's feelings, the implemented strategies, and the conglomerate of values that the sampled firms was aware to possess and spread. Each conversation was recorded for a total of 210 minutes of interviews and transcribed verbatim shortly after the interview. We then transcribed 30 pages of interview transcripts, and, when information was missed, we engaged in informal follow-up phone calls. Therefore, we gathered further secondary information, consisting of 10 business reports, three journal articles, and the official Internet pages of the firms.

Data Analysis

To analyze our qualitative data, we applied a three-step process (Mayring, 2010). In the first step, we created a chronological structured description of each firm with all the relevant demographic information of the family and the firm. These documents comprised three to 10 pages per firm. All sampled firms were small- and medium-sized businesses that involved 10–100 employees. Table 7.1 shows the main demographic characteristics of each firm.

In the second step, we engaged in a cross-case analysis (Eisenhardt, 1989b; Patton, 1990) to identify common patterns across the sample (Eisenhardt & Graebner, 2007). To do this, after having read each the primary and the secondary data, we used Nvivo 12's word count feature to calculate the most frequently occurring words within the in-depth interviews. The words used most often were viewed as a proxy that represented participants' perspectives. Supporting this approach was the assumption that important and significant words would be used more frequently (Carley, 1993; see Table 7.2 and Figure 7.1).

In the third step, three subsequent levels of coding were done. In the first, each author independently proposed a list of codes, derived from the

TABLE 7.1 Firm Characteristics

Firm	Generation	Sector	Employees	Interviewee
A	III	Winery	20–70	Junior
B	II	Bread and bakery	10–20	Junior
C	II	Tourism sector	30–100	Junior

TABLE 7.2 Using NVivo Queries to Identify the Most Frequently Used Words in the Data

Words	Length	Number of Uses	Weighted Percentage (%)
Father	5	106	0.54
We	7	105	0.53
Firm	7	95	0.48
Our	6	53	0.32
Family	8	43	0.22
Passage	9	34	0.17
Hardwork	6	32	0.16
Market	7	31	0.16
Territory	8	30	0.15
Generation	11	24	0.12

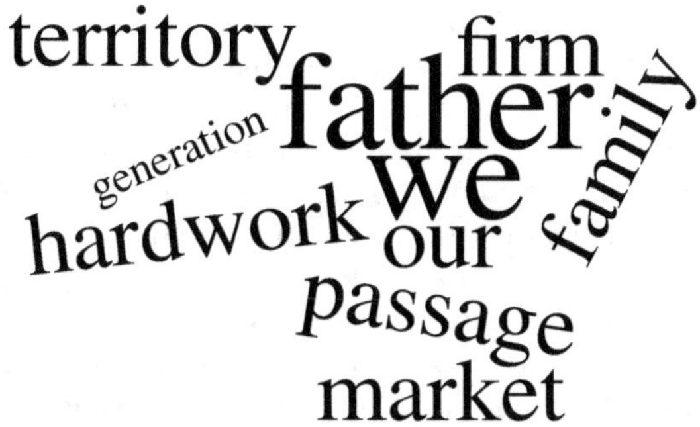

Figure 7.1 Wordcloud.

most frequently occurring words in the interviews (Miles & Huberman, 1994). In the second, the authors compared their own codes with those of the other and, together, determined the finals (Krippendorff, 2004). In the third, the data were analyzed switching the original transcripts with the coded data (Strauss & Corbin, 1998).

FINDINGS AND DISCUSSION

The analysis revealed that the sampled family firms were grounded on a conglomeration of values that catch on the figure of the father as the most influential family firm member able to impress his footprint within the firm and trace how family firm relates with the territory, spreading and developing his values. In fact, as an interviewee from Firm A states:

> My father has transmitted us the passion, the spirit of sacrifices, and hard work. He shared with us his knowledge and his care for the territory in which we are embedded. Thanks to him, we started since our infancy to consider the firm as our treasure to preserve across generations.... He [the father] created a strong relationship with our territory, developing and spreading trust, respect, and green policies.

The father is considered as "the most influential person within our family firm, able to motivate employees, to create a positive organizational climate, to sustain our family especially in difficult periods and to promote and activate positive values with the local community" (Firm B). Thanks to this charismatic attitude, the father is depicted as able to develop the sense of "we" and "our," meaningful for building the sense of community and mutual aids within the firms. This emerges not only for what concerns the family but also with reference to the employees. In fact, "our father has established very special relations with our employees. He considers them as part of our family and tries to guarantee them and their families, satisfaction and happiness" (Firm C). In addition, the father is seen as the "truth voice" (Firm A), particularly attentive towards the generational passage and the responsibility of the incoming generation. In other words, "Every day our father remembers us that we have to assume the responsibility to guarantee family firm survival for posterities" (Firm B).

In sum, the father centrality includes the ability that the father had in sharing the sense of "we" and "our," developing the concept of community, the sense of firm belonging, and the feelings of psychological possession and the long-term vision, based on the willingness towards the firm survival across the future generations.

These kinds of values are transmitted in the family and lived in the firm, as a result of the sense of community that the father has created with family and non-family members. "Our father has based his relationship with us on reliability, accuracy, trust, and unity, also when we conflict... He continuously tells us that we have to create the same relationship with our employees, with our customers, with our suppliers" (Firm A). In addition, "Our father transmitted us the pride for the hard work and the high commitment and the proclivity toward the increasing efforts and sacrifices. Our firm is part of our life" (Firm B). Moreover, "We started in our firm very early and thanks to our father's teachings, we know all aspects of the firm, particularly the dynamic and peculiarities of our difficult market" (Firm C).

What briefly underlined allows interpreting that from the father's centrality derives an inherited strong attachment to the firm, in terms of commitment, hard work, and market awareness. This means that the fathers' values are transmitted inside the firm and represent the driver to manage the family business. The father's ability to transfer values within the family firm continues his virtuous circle by producing positive effects to the territory in which the firm is embedded. In other words,

> Our father has always demonstrated his special care for our region, Sardinia, and for our territory in particular. Now, we are actively engaged in many green initiatives to reduce the impact of our business activity... the investments, in this sense, preserve the natural environment and increase in value our territory, by emphasizing its unpolluted nature. (Firm A)

Moreover,

> He [the father] has taught us how to meet tradition and innovation, by reinterpreting the Sardinian culture in innovative ways, valorizing our isle and our local specificities. He sustains that we have a twofold responsibility: one is

> related to internal firm aspects and dynamics, the other refers to the relation with our territory, that has to be based on trust. (Firm B)

Finally,

> Our product has excellent quality, which depends not only on our work but also on our territory. What we live in our home and our company, we live in our territory. And not only for the natural environment but also for civic communities. (Firm C)

The exemplary quotes show that the father's centrality plays an important role, also for what concerns the relations between family firms and the territory. The attachment for Sardinia and the care for the local areas in which family firms are embedded permits to transform the system of internal family business values into a system of lived and experienced local values.

The expressed concepts are synthesized in Figure 7.2, which frames the dynamic values creation and diffusion in the context of family firms. The pivotal role of the father activates the sharing of a conglomerate of family business values that are restored to the territory, by concurring in developing values.

The proposed dynamic model underlines the role that the father has in creating, sharing, and developing values inside and outside his family firms.

CONCLUSION

This chapter aimed to contribute to the debate around the topic of values by focusing on a specific kind of firm: the small family firm. Scholars have underlined that family businesses possess a conglomerate of values that concur to differentiate them from the others. However, a large amount of studies

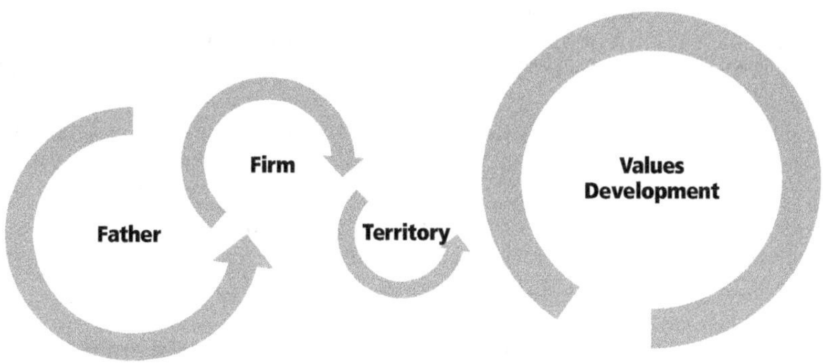

Figure 7.2 The dynamic model to develop values.

has remained at a conceptual level. This study is challenging this topic, by proposing a qualitative empirical analysis carried out through the deep analysis of what happens in three exemplary small family businesses. Thanks to the content analysis of the unstructured and semi-structured interviews with the family owners, what has emerged is the father centrality as the cornerstone from which values are created, shared and diffused inside and outside the family firm. A dynamic model has been conceived as a useful tool to immediately understand the role of the father in this virtuous mechanism.

Findings contribute to the literature on values, by focusing on small family businesses as one of the most diffused form of businesses in the world that possess specific values that take form from the family and, specifically, from the father centrality. In addition, the dynamic model contributes to the literature on family business values, challenging and extending previous studies, by proposing an empirical evidence of what is the real contribution of small family firms in the development of values. Further research can be addressed to enlarge the sample and, by conducting a content analysis of narratives and interviews, understand whether the proposed model fits also in other settings and samples.

This study shows interesting insights for practitioners. Identifying how, why, and which of the father's values affect the family firm and, thus, the territory, could generate a set of best practices that can be followed also by other firms, contributing to a more widespread of values, firstly in a local perspective and secondly, in a more ample vision.

REFERENCES

Aldrich, H. E., & Cliff, J. E. (2003). The pervasive effects of family on entrepreneurship: Toward a family embeddedness perspective. *Journal of Business Venturing, 18*(5), 573–596.

Anderson, H. (1997). *Conversation, language, and possibilities: A postmodern approach to therapy.* New York, NY: Basic Books.

Aronoff, C. (2004). Self-perpetuation family organization built on values: Necessary condition for long-term family business survival. *Family Business Review, 17*(1), 55–59.

Aronoff, C., & Ward, J. (2000). *Family business values: How to assure a legacy of continuity and success* (Family Business Leadership Series). Marietta, GA: Business Owner Resources.

Aronoff, C., & Ward, J. (2001). *Family business values: How to assure a legacy of continuity and success.* Marinetta, GA: Family Enterprise.

Aronoff, C., & Ward, J. (2011). *Family business values: How to assure a legacy of continuity and success.* New York, NY: Palgrave MacMillan.

Arregle, J. L., Naldi, L., Nordqvist, M., & Hitt, M. A. (2012). Internationalization of family-controlled firms: A study of the effects of external involvement in governance. *Entrepreneurship Theory and Practice, 36*(6), 1115–1143.

Astrachan, J. H., & Shanker, M. C. (2003). Family businesses' contribution to the U.S. economy: A closer look. *Family Business Review, 16*(3), 211–219.

Astrachan, J. H., Klein, S. B., & Smyrnios, K. X. (2002). The F-PEC scale of family influence: A proposal for solving the family business definition problem. *Family Business Review, 15*(1), 45–58.

Barnes, L. B., & Hershon, S. A. (1976). Transferring power in family business. *Harvard Business Review, 54*(4), 105–114.

Barnett, T., Long, R. G., & Marler, L. E. (2012). Vision and exchange in intra-family succession: Effects on procedural justice climate among nonfamily managers. *Entrepreneurship Theory and Practice, 36*(6), 1207–1225.

Barry, B. (1975). Development of organization structure in family firm. *Journal of General Management, 3*(1), 42–60.

Binz Astrachan, C., & Botero, I. C. (2018). "We are a family firm" an exploration of the motives for communicating the family business brand. *Journal of Family Business Management, 8*(1), 2–21.

Bradley, S. W. (2015). Entrepreneurial resourcefulness. In C. L. Cooper, M. H. Morris, & D. F. Kuratko (Eds.), *Wiley encyclopedia of management* (pp. 1–3). New York, NY: Wiley.

Cappuyns, K. (1998, July). *Reasons for success of successful family businesses.* Paper presented at the FBN 9th Annual World Conference Proceedings, Paris, France.

Carley, K. (1993). Coding choices for textual analysis: A comparison of content analysis and map analysis. *Sociological Methodology, 23*, 75–126.

Ceja, L., Agulles, R., & Tàpies, J. (2010). *The importance of values in family-owned firms* (Working paper No. 875). Barcelona, Spain: IESE BusinessSchool, University of Navarra.

Cennamo, C., Berrone, P., Cruz, C., & Gomez-Mejia, L. R. (2012). Socioemotional wealth and proactive stakeholder engagement: Why family-controlled firms care more about their stakeholders. *Entrepreneurship Theory and Practice, 36*(6), 1153–1173.

Chrisman, J. J., Chua, J. H., & Steier, L. P. (2005). Sources and consequences of distinctive familiness: An introduction. *Entrepreneurship Theory and Practice, 29*(3), 237–247.

Chua, J. H., Chrisman, J. J., & Sharma, P. (1999). Defining the family business by behavior. *Entrepreneurship Theory and Practice, 23*(4), 19–39.

Collins, J. C., & Porras, J. I. (1996). Building your company's vision. *Harvard Business Review, 74*(5), 65–77.

Connor, P. E., & Becker, B. W. (1975). Values and the organization: Suggestions for research. *Academy of Management Journal, 18*(3), 550–561.

Deal, T. E., & Kennedy, A. A. (1983). Culture: A new look through old lenses. *Journal of Applied Behavioral Science, 19*(4), 498–505.

Diaz-Moriana, V., Clinton, E., Kammerlander, N., Lumpkin, G., & Craig, J. B. (2018). Innovation motives in family firms: A transgenerational view. *Entrepreneurship Theory and Practice, 44*(2), 256–287. https://doi.org/10.1177/1042258718803051

Dumas, C., & Blodgett, M. (1999). Articulating values to inform decision making: Lessons from family firms around the world. *International Journal of Value-Based Management, 12*(3), 209–221.

Dyer, W. G. (1986). *Cultural change in family firms.* San Francisco, CA: Jossey-Bass.

Dyer, W. G. (2006). Examining the "family effect" on firm performance. *Family Business Review, 19*(4), 253–273.

Eisenhardt, K. M. (1989a). Agency theory: An assessment and review. *Academy of Management Review, 14*(1), 57–74.

Eisenhardt, K. M. (1989b). Building theories from case study research. *Academy of Management Review, 14*(4), 532–550.

Eisenhardt, K. M., & Graebner, M. E. (2007). Theory building from cases: Opportunities and challenges. *Academy of Management Journal, 50*(1), 25–32.

Finch, J. (1988). *Research and policy: The uses of qualitative methods in social and educational research.* London, England: Falmer Press.

García-Álvarez, E., & López-Sintas, J. (2001). A taxonomy of founders based on values: The root of family business heterogeneity. *Family Business Review, 14*(3), 209–230.

Gatrell, J., Jenkins, H., & Tucker, J. (2001, September). *Family values in family business.* Paper presented at the 12th Annual FBN World Conference, Roma, Milano.

Guth, W. T., & Tagiuri, R. (1965). Personal values and corporate strategies. *Harvard Business Review, 43*(5), 123–132.

Habbershon, T. G., Williams, M. L., & MacMillan, I. C. (2003). A unified systems theory of family firm performance. *Journal of Business Research, 18*(4), 451–465.

Handler, W. C. (1989). *Managing the family firm succession process: The next-generation family member's experience* (Unpublished PhD dissertation). Boston University, Boston, MA.

Howorth, C., & Ali, Z. A. (2001). Family business succession in Portugal: An examination of case studies in the furniture industry. *Family Business Review, 14*(3), 231–244.

Howorth, C., Rose, M., & Hamilton, E. (2006). Definitions, diversity, and development: Key debates in family business research. In M. Casson (Ed.), *The Oxford handbook of entrepreneurship* (pp. 225–247). Oxford, England: Oxford University Press.

IFERA. (2003). Family businesses dominate. *Family Business Review, 16*(4), 23–5240.

Khan, S., & VanWynsberghe, R. (2008). Cultivating the under-mined: Cross-case analysis as knowledge mobilization. *Forum: Qualitative Research, 9*(1), 1–26.

Kluckhohn, C. (1958). The scientific study of values and contemporary civilization. *Proceedings of the American Philosophical Society, 102*(5), 469–476.

Koiranen, M. (2002). Over 100 years of age but still entrepreneurially active in business: Exploring the values and family characteristics of old Finnish family firms. *Family Business Review, 15*(3), 175–187.

Krippendorff, K. (2004). *Content analysis: An introduction to its methodology.* Thousand Oaks, CA: SAGE.

Lansberg, I. S., Perrow, E. L., & Rogolsky, S. (1988). Family business as an emerging field. *Family Business Review, 1*(1), 1–8.

Litz, R. A. (1995). The family business: Toward definitional clarity. *Family Business Review, 8*(2), 71–81.

Litz, R. A. (1997). The family firm's exclusion from business school research: Explaining the void; addressing the opportunity. *Entrepreneurship Theory and Practice, 21*(3), 55–71.

Lyons, S. T., Higgins, C. A., & Duxbury, L. (2010). Work values: Development of a new three-dimensional structure based on confirmatory smallest space analysis. *Journal of Organizational Behavior, 31*(7), 969–1002.

Mayring, P. (2010). *Qualitative Inhaltsanalyse: Grundlagen und Technik* [Qualitative content analysis: Basics and technology]. Beltz, Ukraine: Weinheim und Basel.

McCollom, M. (1990). Problems and prospects in clinical research on family firms. *Family Business Review, 3*(3), 245–262.

Meglino, B. M., & Ravlin, E. C. (1998). Individual values in organizations: Concepts, controversies, and research. *Journal of Management, 24*(3), 351–389.

Miles, M., & Huberman, M. (1994). *Qualitative data analysis.* Thousand Oaks, CA: SAGE.

Muñoz-Bullón, F., & Sanchez-Bueno, M. J. (2011). The impact of family involvement on the R&D intensity of publicly traded firms. *Family Business Review, 24*(1), 62–70.

Neubauer, F., & Lank, A. G. (2016). *The family business: Its governance for sustainability:* New York, NY: Springer Nature.

Osborne, R. L. (1991). Second-generation entrepreneurs: Passing the baton in the privately held company. *Management Decision, 29*(1), 42–46. https://doi.org/10.1108/00251749110141185

Özar, Ö. (1997). Economic co-operation organization: A promising future. *Perceptions: Journal of International Affairs, 2*(1). Retrieved from https://dergipark.org.tr/en/pub/perception/issue/49042/625621

Patton, M. Q. (1990). *Qualitative evaluation and research methods.* Newbury Park, CA: SAGE.

Patton, M. Q. (2002). Two decades of developments in qualitative inquiry: A personal, experiential perspective. *Qualitative Social Work, 1*(3), 261–283.

Powell, E. E., & Baker, T. (2014). It's what you make of it: Founder identity and enacting strategic responses to adversity. *Academy of Management Journal, 57*(5), 1406–1433.

Poza, E. J. (2013). *Family business.* Boston, MA: Cengage Learning.

Pruzan, P. (1998). From control to values-based management and accountability. *Journal of Business Ethics, 17*(13), 1379–1394.

Rokeach, M. (1973). *The nature of human values* (Vol. 438). New York, NY: Free Press.

Schwartz, S. H., & Bilsky, W. (1987). Toward a universal psychological structure of human values. *Journal of personality and social psychology, 53*(3), 550.

Stanley, L. J., Hernández-Linares, R., López-Fernández, M. C., & Kellermanns, F. W. (2019). A typology of family firms: An investigation of entrepreneurial orientation and performance. *Family Business Review, 32*(2), 174–194. https://doi.org/10.1177%2F0894486519838120

Strauss, A. L., & Corbin, J. M. (1998). *Basics of qualitative research* (2nd ed.). Thousand Oaks, CA: SAGE.

Tàpies, J., & Ward, J. (2008). *Family values and value creation: The fostering of enduring values within family-owned businesses.* Basingstone, England: Palgrave MacMillan.

Thornbury, J. (2003). Creating a living culture: The challenges for business leaders. *Corporate Governance: The International Journal of Business in Society, 3*(2), 68–79.

Van Maanen, J. (1983). *Qualitative methodology.* Beverly Hills, CA: SAGE.

Ward, J. L. (1997). Growing the family business: Special challenges and best practices. *Family Business Review, 10*(4), 323–337.

Welter, F., Baker, T., Audretsch, D. B., & Gartner, W. B. (2017). *Everyday entrepreneurship—A call for entrepreneurship research to embrace entrepreneurial diversity.* Los Angeles, CA: SAGE.

Wolcott, H. F. (1994). *Transforming qualitative data: Description, analysis, and interpretation*: Thousand Oaks, CA: SAGE.

Yin, R. K. (2008). *Case study research* (4th ed.). Thousand Oaks, CA: SAGE.

Yin, R. K. (2011). *Applications of case study research*: Thousand Oaks, CA: SAGE.

Zahra, S. A., Hayton, J. C., & Salvato, C. (2004). Entrepreneurship in family vs. non-family firms: A resource-based analysis of the effect of organizational culture. *Entrepreneurship Theory and Practice, 28*(4), 363–381.

CHAPTER 8

THE CASE OF EXECUTIVES' CULTURAL INTELLIGENCE IN BEHAVIORAL STRATEGY

An Introductory Essay and a Research Agenda

Arash Najmaei

ABSTRACT

The field of behavioral strategy incorporates psychological factors in the theory and practice of strategic management. The rapid pace of globalization, the increasing internationalization of small and large organizations, and the accelerating rate of international business transactions have made executive cultural intelligence (CQ), defined as an executive's ability to act effectively in culturally diverse settings, a key strategic competency which is missing from the behavioral strategy literature. This chapter shows that incorporating executive CQ into behavioral strategy will give it more theoretical substance and open up new opportunities to explore and investigate its potential. Drawing on this reasoning, I will discuss how studying executive cultural intelligence informs the theory and practice of behavioral strategy. I will also highlight

Cultural Values in Strategy and Organization, pages 187–228

several implications of this perspective for management education and finish the chapter with an agenda for future research in this area.

INTRODUCTION

We may have different religions, different languages, different colored skin, but we all belong to one human race.

—Kofi Annan[1]

No culture can live if it attempts to be exclusive.

—Mahatma Gandhi[2]

These quotes from Kofi Annan, the 7th UN Secretary-General, and 2001 Nobel Peace Prize Winner, and Mahatma Gandhi, the leader of Indian independence, highlight the importance of acknowledging cultural differences and the rising importance of cultural diversity in today's life. Cultural diversity is, in fact, ubiquitous in the business world, and has occupied a central place in the management literature (Brislin & Kim, 2003; Cox & Blake, 1991; Groves & Feyerherm, 2011). Today's managers are increasingly facing the challenge of dealing with cultural diversity, both inside and outside their organizations. There is no doubt that the failure of managers to embrace these internal and external diversities affects their strategic behavior and consequently jeopardizes the performance of their firms. The question is how the strategy literature can address this issue.

According to Nag, Hambrick, and Chen (2007) the field of strategy "deals with the major intended and emergent initiatives taken by general managers on behalf of owners, involving utilization of resources, to enhance the performance of firms in their external environments" (p. 944). Strategy therefore "rests on the assumption that the thoughts, feelings, and social relations of general managers influence the activities and performance of firms" (Powell, 2011, p. 1485). Given this realization, not only does manager behavior in culturally diverse contexts matter in strategy but such manager behavior has also become more prominent than ever before in today's diverse business landscape. As students of strategy what we need to determine is thus not whether cultural differences matter to companies and managers, but rather what strategy theory can do to better understand this challenge and incorporate it into the theory and practice of strategic management.

Towards this end, I borrow the concept of cultural intelligence (CQ; Earley & Ang, 2003; Earley & Mosakowski, 2004). CQ has been defined as "an outsider's seemingly natural ability to interpret someone's unfamiliar and ambiguous gestures the way that person's compatriots would" (Earley & Mosakowski, 2004, p. 140) from the organizational and social psychology literature, and situate it in the socio-cognitive texture of strategic management theory known as the behavioral strategy (behavioral strategy; Powell, Lovallo, & Fox, 2011; Schrager & Madansky, 2013). Evidence of the performance impact of CQ is accumulating across disciplines, such as cross-cultural management (Earley & Ang, 2003; Presbitero, 2016; Wood & St Peters, 2014), management education (Oliver, de Botton, Soler, & Merrill, 2011; Rosenblatt, Worthley, & MacNab, 2013), and the leadership literature (Elenkov & Manev, 2009; Kim & Van Dyne, 2012; Maldonado & Vera, 2014), but surprisingly it has yet to break into mainstream research on behavioral strategy.

The purpose of this chapter, therefore, is to introduce CQ to the behavioral strategy community and to provide an outline for future research. Toward these goals, I provide a synthesized review of the field of behavioral strategy and argue for the important yet missing notion of CQ in debates about behavioral strategy. I discuss the origin, drivers, and potential benefits of CQ, and suggest several ways it can be incorporated into the behavioral strategy literature. The chapter concludes with a suggestive list of research directions which can help researchers enrich and advance the applications of CQ in behavioral strategy.

BEHAVIORAL STRATEGY: AN OVERVIEW

Background of Behavioral Strategy

Strategy is about winning the competition. To win the competition, firms need strategies or sets of activities that differentiate their behaviors in the marketplace (Porter, 1979, 1980). The primary role and function of executives or strategists at the helm of a firm has always been to formulate and execute these activities (Barnard, 1938). The firm and its strategies are therefore reflections of the way executives think, behave, and act (Hambrick & Mason, 1984). Early views of strategy did not consider the importance of executive behaviors, and assumed that executives behaved predictably and similarly under competitive conditions (Porter, 1980, 1985). As succinctly explained by Cyert and Wlliams (1993):

> The early assumptions of neoclassical economic theory essentially eliminate the concept of strategy. Where the firm is in a competitive market and cannot influence price, and where the conditions for all firms are assumed to be the same, there is no room for strategy of any kind on the part of decision makers. (p. 5)

This view is the precursor of contemporary strategic management theory. Accordingly, the notion of strategy is predominantly based on the three economic pillars of industry structure and analysis (Bain, 1949; Porter, 1980, 1985), resources of the firm (Penrose, 1959; Wernerfelt, 1984), and technological innovation (Schumpeter, 1934; Teece, 1986). These three pillars, although interesting and insightful, are surprisingly parochial (Powell et al., 2011) and would offer only an incomplete picture of strategy because they overlook the role of manager behaviors and actions in the craft of strategy making (Mintzberg, 1988). As argued by Powell et al. (2011), the field of strategy thus "needs a robust subfield of behavioral strategy to serve as the fourth pillar of strategic management theory" (p. 1370). In comparison with other pillars which are concerned with industries and firms, behavioral strategy is predominantly about the behaviors of managers. The emerging domain of behavioral strategy "merges cognitive and social psychology with strategic management theory and practice" (Powell et al., 2011, p. 1371) in order to bring realistic assumptions about human cognition, emotions, and social behavior to the strategic management of organizations.

The Theoretical Domain of Behavioral Strategy

The field of behavioral strategy is expanding in at least six theoretical domains: (a) the behavioral theory of the firm (Cyert & March, 1963; Gavetti, Greve, Levinthal, & Ocasio, 2012); (b) the strategic leadership and top management team theory (Hambrick, 1989, 2007; Hambrick & Mason, 1984); (c) the strategic cognition view (Das & Kumar, 2010a, 2010b; Das & Teng, 1999; Narayanan, Zane, & Kemmerer, 2011); (d) managerial psychology (Carmeli, 2003; Das, 1986; Das & Teng, 1999; Hodgkinson & Healey, 2011); (e) the neuroscience of strategy, also known as neuro-strategy (Powell, 2011); and (f) the strategy-as-practice view (Das, 2015; Whittington, 1996). Table 8.1 offers a summary of these six domains.

What is evident from Table 8.1 is that behavioral strategy is not a single theory, but rather an amalgamation of ideas, perspectives, and theoretical models which shape a new paradigm, or as Powell et al. (2011) put it, a new "pillar" in the field of strategic management. All these strands share a common assumption: Strategy is created by executives and thus behavioral factors shape the process of strategy making.

Each strand of behavioral strategy aspires to paint one side of the strategy picture and to obtain a complete picture of strategy making and a comprehensive understanding of how and why strategies look and are shaped the way they are; we need to have contributions from different perspectives. As noted earlier, one psychological factor which relates to all strands is the executive ability to take an appropriate course of action when facing multiple cultures. This ability is called *cultural intelligence* (CQ). In order to understand how executive cultural intelligence relates to the different

TABLE 8.1 Theoretical Domains of Behavioral Strategy

Theoretical Domain	Key Premises	Contribution to Behavioral Strategy	Representative Work
Behavioral theory of the firm (BTF)	Organizing is about decision making. Decision making is interwoven with psychology. Managers as decision makers are boundedly rational. They satisfice; adopt quasi resolutions to conflict; search for limited alternatives; avoid uncertainty; and navigate their firm through phases of learning and unlearning where rules, standards, and goals are constantly adapted.	Serves as the foundation of research on cognition, rationality, executive's behavior, attention, and many other neighboring domains.	Cyert & March (1963); Gavetti et al. (2012)
TMT and strategic leadership	Based on BTF. Suggests that behaviors of an organization are reflections of the behaviors of its executives. Behaviors of executives are, in turn, reflections of their psychological makeup.	Laid the foundation of research on top management team diversity, team dynamics, team decision making, interactions between CEOs, and other team members.	Cannella & Pettigrew (2001); Hambrick & Mason (1984)
Strategic cognition	Focuses on cognitive factors mainly heuristics, biases, mental models, schemas and cognitive styles which affect dynamics and outcomes of strategic choices made by executives.	Gave identity to research on cognitive factors which underpin competitive behaviors of executives such as micro-foundations of resource acquisition, allocation, configurations, bundling, strategic group membership, and strategic issue analysis.	Kahneman & Tversky (1979); Narayanan et al. (2011)
Psychology of strategy	Psychology of executives, affect, passion, emotions, attention, leadership style, sensemaking, and attention matter as much as their cognitive schemas and other behavioral factors in shaping the strategic directions of the firm.	Closely related to strategic cognition but extends it into cognitive-psychology of executives.	Carmeli, (2003); Hodgkinson & Healey (2011)
Neuro-strategy	Study of the brain of executives via methods such as fMRI opens up new doors to underlying factors that define strategies behaviors of the executives and by implication firms they lead.	Not only does it complement research on strategic cognition and cognitive psychology but also opens new avenues for research on behavioral micro-foundation of strategy.	Hodgkinson, Sadler-Smith, Burke, Claxton, & Sparrow (2009); Powell (2011)
Strategy as practice	Study of tools and techniques which are used and activities which are involved in shaping the practice of strategy making and execution by executives.	Complements the cognitive and psychological views by relating them to practices, activity systems, and actions of executives.	Jarzabkowski (2004); Whittington (1996)

theoretical domains of behavioral strategy, we need to know the theoretical boundaries and core premises of each domain. The following is a synopsis of each domain.

1. The behavioral theory of the firm (BTF), developed by Cyert and March (1963), opens the black box of the firm as a productive unit and suggests that a business firm is a social organization in which individuals with conflicting goals and interests are coordinated, and that quasi-resolutions of conflict drive the firm toward its goals. Manager rationality is limited, as is their ability to search for information, understand business surroundings, and resolve conflicts. Managers set goals and aspire to achieving them. When aspiration levels are met, higher aspirations are set. When aspirations are not met, a search for problems and feedback leads to adjustments to organizational goals. Managers form a dominant coalition in order to make decisions. The dynamics of this coalition is determined by the political skills of members, negotiations, and manager personas, which collectively create a complex setting for making and executing strategic decisions (Gavetti et al., 2012).
2. The top management team (TMT), also known as the strategic leadership theory was developed by Hambrick and Mason (1984) as an extension of BTF. It suggests that the composition and dynamics of a firm's top management team (i.e., dominant coalition or strategic leaders) shapes its strategic posture. A TMT is composed of managers with different tangible and intangible characteristics, such as age, gender, education, exercise, tenure, skills, personality, and so on. Diversity in teams, in terms of these factors and the way members work together as a team, shapes the behavior of the firm. Research into TMT can be grouped in four areas: (a) the role of an executive's tangible (e.g., age, gender, etc.) and intangible (e.g., psychology and personality) characteristics in their behaviors and the subsequent performance of their firms (Hambrick, 2007); (b) the diversity in TMTs, types, and consequences (Nielsen, 2010); (c) the drivers and outcomes of different team mechanisms such as communication, knowledge sharing, conflict resolution, and behavioral integration, among other areas (Carmeli, Schaubroeck, & Tishler, 2011); and (d) types, drivers, and consequences of interactions between the CEO as the most powerful member of the TMT and other members (Cao, Simsek, & Zhang, 2010).
3. Strategic cognition departs from strategic leadership by specifically seeking to identify and study the cognitive factors that underpin the strategic behaviors of executives (Das, 1986; Kaplan, 2011; Najmaei, Rhodes, & Lok, 2015; Najmaei & Sadeghinejad, 2016). Research has

examined factors as diverse as cognitive biases and heuristics in executive decision making (Barnes, 1984; Das, 2016; Das & Teng, 1999), intuition (Khatri & Ng, 2000), shared cognition among executives (Prahalad & Bettis, 1986), cognitive schemas and mental models (Das & Kumar, 2010a, 2010b; Nadkarni & Narayanan, 2007), cognitive styles (Gallén, 2006), and the cognitive diversity of top management teams (Olson, Parayitam & Yongjian, 2007), among others.

4. The psychology of strategy making is closely related to the domain of strategic cognition. Its point of difference is its focus on a broader range of psychological factors, such as the psychological well-being of managers (Uy, Foo, & Song, 2012), manager emotions (Huy, 2012), executive hubris (Tang, Qian, Chen, & Shen, 2015), narcissism (Chatterjee & Hambrick, 2007), the leadership style of executives (Anderson & Sun, 2017), and social and emotional intelligences (Antonakis, Ashkanasy & Dasborough, 2009).
5. Neuro-strategy takes advantage of recent advances in neuro-system and brain scanning in order to study the neuro-system of executives when they make risky, intuitive decisions for taking strategic actions (Powell, 2011). Neuro-strategy uses techniques such as field-magnetic resonance imaging (FMRI) to study the areas of brains that are activated under different conditions and how they relate to each other (Hodgkinson et al., 2009). Neuro-strategy is an extension of the cognitive and psychological strands of behavioral strategy and gives behavioral strategy a more medical flavor. As Powell (2011) argues, neuro-strategy may not be very appealing to students and practitioners of behavioral strategy, but it has the potential to take behavioral strategy to the next level by enriching our understanding of how brains actually work when strategic actions are taken and strategic behaviors are planned and formed.
6. The strategy as practice view (S-as-P) suggests that strategy is something that executives do in a context characterized by social and organizational norms (Jarzabkowski, 2004). To understand strategy, we therefore need to understand the actions, activities, and practices involved in creating strategy (Whittington, 1996). S-as-P therefore acknowledges the cognitive and psychological underpinnings of strategy (Das, 1986), and complements them by taking a practice perspective in order to provide interesting insights into "the tools and methods of strategy-making (practices), how strategy work takes place (praxis), and the role and identity of the actors involved (practitioners)" (Vaara & Whittington, 2012, p. 285).

Figure 8.1 shows a holistic view of the field of behavioral strategy and its theoretical domains.

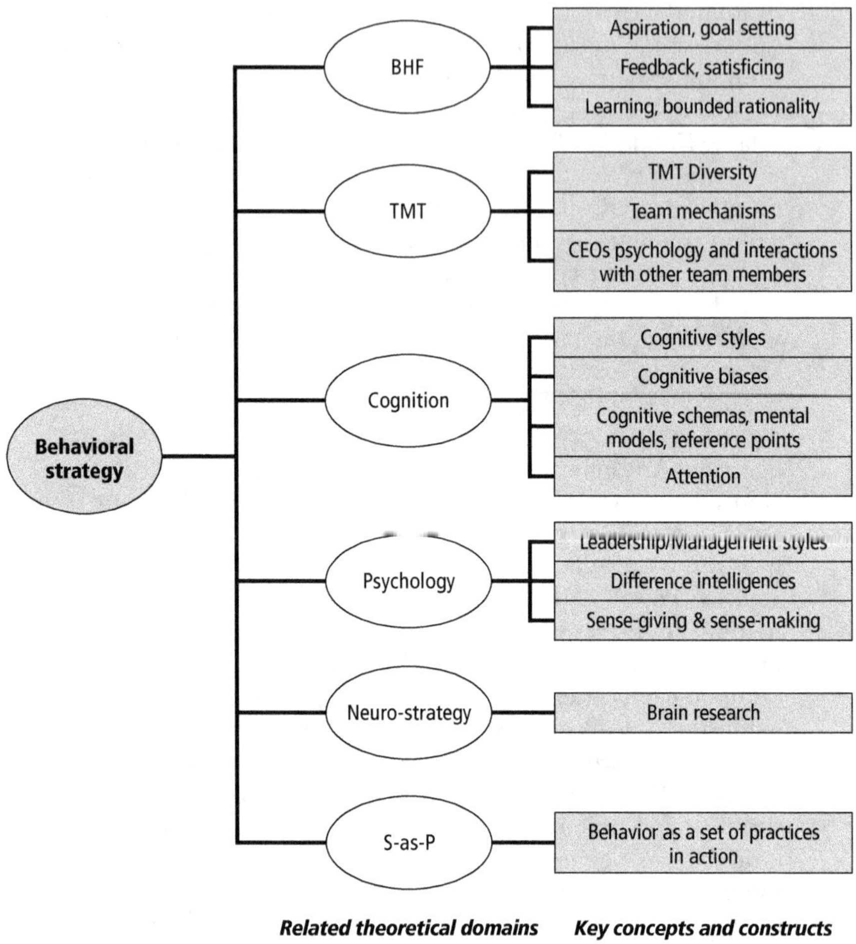

Figure 8.1 Theoretical domains of behavioral strategy.

Powell et al. (2011) identify three philosophical schools which underpin behavioral strategy, the reductionist, the pluralist, and the conceptualist schools. The reductionist school is concerned with individual decision making, intragroup decision making, and individual executive personality, cognition, and behaviors. The pluralist school addresses teams, groups, and social behaviors. It therefore guides research on intergroup bargaining, problem-solving, politics, conflict resolution, organizational learning, resource allocation by teams, and social identities and actions. Finally, the conceptualist school shapes the foundation of research into subjects including perceptions, sensemaking, cognitive schemas and rationality. It is important to note that "the three paradigms are not incompatible and that research in behavioral strategy can combine a wide field of vision with a capacity for disciplinary integration" (Powell et al., 2011, p. 1380). Table 8.2 offers a summary of these three paradigms.

On the grounds that the anatomy of behavioral strategy and its three underlying philosophical schools is clear, we can discuss the notion of executive cultural intelligence and how it fits into the field of behavioral strategy.

TABLE 8.2 Philosophical Schools in Behavioral Strategy

	Reductionist	Pluralist	Conceptualist
Core process	Individual decision-making, intragroup decision-making	Intergroup bargaining, problem solving, politics, conflict resolution, organizational learning, resource allocation	Sensemaking, perception, enactment, action generation
Key psychological	Bounded rationality, prospect theory, heuristics and biases, dynamic inconsistency	Reference groups, social cognition, social identity theory	Cognitive schema, language, meaning, signs, ideology, action rationality, culture
Methodology	Hypothesis testing, decision experiments, simulation, mathematical and computational modeling, neural methods	Field studies, event studies, multivariate statistics, cases, mixed methods	Interpretive histories, ethnography, grounded theorizing, hermeneutics, textual analysis, discourse analysis, semiotics, cases
Assumption about firm	Firms' decisions are made by top executives, entrepreneurs, and top management teams; decisions are subject to cognitive biases	Firms consist of subgroups with conflicting goals and perspectives; firms resolve strategy problems via conflict resolution and intergroup bargaining	Firms and environments are socially constructed; firms are ideological; decisions and actions are decoupled; actions are emergent, externally influenced
Contribution to strategic management	Cognitive biases in strategic decisions (e.g., competitive blind spots, competition neglect, winner's curse, hubris, escalation of commitment); dynamic inconsistency	Behavioral theory of the firm, group identification, aspirations, maladaptive learning, organizational neuroses	Action rationality, cognitive schema, cognitive maps, cognitive rivalry, dominant logic, sensemaking, misperception, enactment, mindfulness, critical theory

What Is Cultural Intelligence?

Individual abilities in intercultural effectiveness have long been an interesting topic in behavioral sciences. Based on the general concept of intelligence, defined as "the ability to grasp and reason correctly with abstractions (concepts) and solve problems" (Schmidt & Hunter, 2000, p. 3), and the realization that there are different foci of intelligence within a person (Sternberg, 1986), Earley and Ang (2003) adopted the concept of cultural intelligence defined as "the capability to function effectively in culturally diverse settings" (Ang et al., 2007, p. 336) to capture differences in cross-cultural capabilities among individuals. Cultural intelligence is a multidimensional construct aimed at situations involving cross-cultural interactions arising from differences in race, ethnicity, and nationality (Ang et al., 2007), which directly affect cross-cultural teams and international business transactions (Chen & Lin, 2013; Crotty & Brett, 2012; Groves & Feyerherm, 2011; Janssens & Brett, 2006; Zander, et al. 2012).

There are two conceptualizations of CQ in the business literature. The first was developed by Earley and Mosakowski (2004), where CQ consists of three components: the cognitive, the physical, and the emotional/motivational. The cognitive component is concerned with learning about the beliefs, norms, values customs, and taboos of other cultures. The physical component aligns behaviors actions and demeanor with new cultures because "by adopting people's habits and mannerisms, you eventually come to understand in the most elemental way what it is like to be them. They, in tum, become more trusting and open" (p. 141).

Finally, the motivational component creates self-confidence and self-belief in understanding and leading new cultures. This is essential because "adapting to a new culture involves overcoming obstacles and setbacks. People can do that only if they believe in their own efficacy" (Earley & Mosakowski, 2004, p. 142). Earley and Mosakowski (2004) add that "cultural intelligence resides in the body and the heart, as well as the head. Although most managers are not equally strong in all three areas, each faculty is seriously hampered without the other two" (p. 141).

Earley and Mosakowski (2004) identify six profiles of cultural intelligence based on the composition of its three components: (a) the provincial can be quite effective when working with people of similar background, but runs into trouble when venturing farther afield; (b) the analyst methodically deciphers a foreign culture's rules and expectations by resorting to a variety of elaborate learning strategies; (c) the natural relies entirely on their intuition rather than on a systematic learning style; (d) the ambassador, like many political appointees, may not know much about the culture they have just entered, but they convincingly communicate their certainty that they belong there; (e) the mimic has a high degree of control over their actions and behavior, if not a great deal of insight into the significance of the cultural cues they pick up (mimicry definitely puts hosts and guests at ease, facilitates communication, and builds trust); and (f) the chameleon possesses high levels of all three CQ components and is a very uncommon managerial type (they may even be mistaken for a native of the country). More importantly, chameleons don't generate any of the ripples that unassimilated foreigners inevitably do. Some are able to achieve results that natives cannot, due to their insider skills and outsider perspective.

The second conceptualization of CQ was proposed by Earley and Ang (2003) and further validated by Ang et al. (2007). According to Early and Ang (2003), CQ encompasses four sets of abilities: metacognitive, cognitive, motivational (mental capabilities), and behavioral, which are about actions (Ang et al., 2007). Ang et al. (2007) define these four as follows. Metacognitive CQ reflects the mental processes that individuals use to acquire and understand cultural knowledge, including knowledge of and control over individual thought processes relating to cultures. Therefore, "those with high metacognitive CQ are consciously aware of others' cultural preferences before and during interactions and question cultural assumptions and adjust their mental models during and after cross-cultural interactions" (p. 338). Cognitive CQ reflects knowledge of the norms, practices and conventions of different cultures, acquired from education and personal experiences. Cognitive CQ includes knowledge of the economic, legal, and social systems of different cultures and subcultures, and knowledge of the basic frameworks of cultural values, and therefore, "those with high cognitive CQ understand similarities and differences across cultures" (p. 338). Motivational CQ drives adaptive behaviors and actions. It reflects the ability to direct attention and energy toward learning about and functioning in situations characterized by cultural differences, and therefore, "those with high motivational CQ direct attention and energy toward cross-cultural situations based on intrinsic interest and confidence in their cross-cultural effectiveness" (p. 338). Lastly, behavioral CQ is the manifestation of appropriate behaviors in culturally diverse settings. It reflects the ability to use appropriate verbal and nonverbal actions when interacting with people from different cultures, and therefore, "those with high behavioral CQ exhibit situationally appropriate behaviors based on their broad range of verbal and nonverbal capabilities, such as exhibiting culturally appropriate words, tone, gestures and facial expressions" (p. 338).

The main difference between this four-factor conceptualization and the former three-factor one is that the four-factor conceptualization breaks down the cognitive part (i.e., the mind) into cognitive and metacognitive in order to more explicitly emphasize the adaptive nature of CQ. Both models show that CQ is not a personality or value, but rather a repertoire of behaviors and skills (Ng, Van Dyne, & Ang, 2012). In a culturally diverse setting, a person with high cultural intelligence can understand and interpret a person's or group's behavior as to those features that would be true of all people and all groups, those peculiar to this person or this group, and those that are neither universal nor idiosyncratic (Earley & Mosakowski, 2004). CQ is, therefore, a basis for explaining the vast variety of inter-individual differences regarding understanding and behaving in new cultural settings (Ward, Fischer, Zaid Lam, & Hall, 2008).

Research Into Cultural Intelligence

Research into cultural intelligence can be classified into three streams: (a) the antecedents or enablers of CQ, (b) the psychological correlates of cultural intelligence, and (c) the benefits or outcomes of cultural intelligence. I systematically reviewed and selected a list of 58 studies that represent these three streams. Table 8.3 offers a summary of studies in this representative list. The list is not exhaustive but offers a reflective overview of what has already been done, and is known about, where cultural intelligence comes from, how it interacts with other psychological factors, and what benefits it brings to organizations.

TABLE 8.3 An Overview of Prior Research on Antecedents and Consequences of CQ

Study	Type	Summary
Herrmann, Call, Hernandez-Lloreda, Hare, & Tomasello (2007)	A	CQ is an evolutionary species-specific set of social-cognitive skills, emerging early in ontogeny, for participating and exchanging knowledge in cultural groups. CQ is missing in two of humans' closest primate relatives—chimpanzees and orangutans.
Erez et al. (2013)	C	Sample of 1,221 graduate management students, 312 virtual multicultural teams were examined and it was found that cultural intelligence and global identity are correlated.
Gilbert & Cartwright (2008)	C	Six case studies of western management development programs in Russia revealed that cultural intelligence is essential for adoption and diffusion of management development programs in non-Westerns societies and business schools.
Ming Li, Mobley, & Kelly (2013)	A	Analyses of data collected from 294 international executives and graduate business students in China and Ireland indicated that the positive relationship between the length of overseas experience and cultural intelligence is strengthened when global executives have a divergent learning style, not when they have an assimilative, convergent, or accommodative learning style.

(continued)

TABLE 8.3 An Overview of Prior Research on Antecedents and Consequences of CQ (continued)

Study	Type	Summary
Mor, Morris, & Joh (2013)	C	Five studies using both quasi-field and experimental approaches of MBA students indicate that cultural perspective taking facilitates intercultural coordination and cooperation, and that a manipulation that boosts cultural perspective taking would be especially beneficial for individuals who score low in dispositional cultural metacognition.
Ng, Van Dyne, & Ang (2009a)	C	Cultural intelligence acts as a moderator that enhances the likelihood that individuals on international assignments will actively engage in the four stages of experiential learning (experience, reflect, conceptualize, experiment), which in turn leads to global leadership self-efficacy, ethnorelative attitudes toward other cultures, accurate mental models of leadership across cultures, and flexibility of leadership styles.
Pless, Maak, & Stahl (2011)	A	Sensing students of management to work in NGOs in developing countries and content analyses of interviews with them. The study revealed this experiment positively affects responsible mind-set, ethical literacy, cultural intelligence, global mind-set, self-development, and community building.
Reichard et al. (2015)	A	A thematic analysis of 85 U.S. undergraduate students working and studying abroad showed an increase in cultural intelligence and a decrease in ethnocentrism following training on a series of cross-cultural trigger events replicating those experienced during international work assignments.
Taras et al. (2013)	A	Data from over 6,000 students from nearly 80 universities in 43 countries worked in global virtual teams for 2 months showed that working in global virtual teams enhance development of CQ.
Varela & Gatlin-Watts (2014)	A	Data from 84 business students who completed academic coursework abroad indicated that studying abroad acts differently on CQ. While participants exhibited development of the cognitive-based components of the competence, studying abroad was innocuous in advancing participants' motivational and behavioral cultural intelligence.
Johnston (2014)	A	Interviews with 16 global supply chain leaders indicate that short-term business travel provides the context for participant reflection on their CQ development as global leaders.
Li (2009)	A	The impact of experiential learning theory on the development of cultural intelligence in global leaders. It proposes a model that addresses the relationship between four modes of experiential learning and four facets of cultural intelligence; and hypothesizes that learning styles exercise a moderating effect on the relationship between international experience and cultural intelligence.

(continued)

TABLE 8.3 An Overview of Prior Research on Antecedents and Consequences of CQ (continued)

Study	Type	Summary
Ng, Van Dyne, & Ang (2009b)	C	Proposing that cultural intelligence (CQ) is an essential learning capability that leaders can use to translate their international experiences into effective experiential learning in culturally diverse contexts.
Gerrard (2011)	C	Proposing three principles for directing global assignment strategies: First, effective global assignments are powerful sources of leader development. Second, assignments differ in their developmental value with some assignments providing significantly more value than others. Third, individuals differ in their ability to perform on assignment based on their CQ.
Leung, Ang, & Tan (2014)	A, C	Intercultural competencies can be classified based on traits, attitudes and worldviews, capabilities, or a combination of these dimensions.
Kim & Van Dyne (2012)	A, C	Results of two samples of working adults showed that intercultural contact has mediated effects on international leadership potential via cultural intelligence. Further, moderated mediation analyses demonstrate that cultural intelligence mediates the relationship between prior intercultural contact and international leadership potential for majorities, but not for minorities.
Crowne (2008)	A	140 surveys indicate that certain types of exposures to other cultures (such as education abroad and employment abroad) and the level of exposure from these experiences increases cultural intelligence.
Deng & Gibson (2009)	C	Semi-structured, in-depth interviews were conducted with 32 Western expatriate managers and 19 local Chinese managers working in Australian businesses operating in Shanghai and Beijing revealed a core series of cross-cultural leadership competencies that call upon all three factors of transformational leadership, emotional intelligence, and cultural intelligence.
Jyoti & Kour (2015)	C	Organizations in India are multicultural in nature. In this context, cultural intelligence is a tool, which can increase an individual's ability to interact with people outside his/her culture. Data from the 225 managers working in nationalized banks in Jammu province (J & K, India) reveals that cultural intelligence significantly contributes toward task performance. The findings further reveal full mediation of cultural adjustment between cultural intelligence and task performance.
Yunlu & Clapp-Smith (2014)	A, C	Cultural psychological capital has a positive relationship with motivational cultural intelligence, which in turn relates to metacognitive awareness, and perspective taking does not moderate the relationship between motivational cultural intelligence and metacognition.

(continued)

TABLE 8.3 An Overview of Prior Research on Antecedents and Consequences of CQ (continued)

Study	Type	Summary
Kaplan (2014)	A	Review of the history of management in European business schools reveals that BSs in Europe should focus on cross-cultural courses to develop students' CQ for working in diverse business context of Europe.
Groves & Feyerherm (2011)	C	Data from 99 culturally diverse organizational leaders and 321 of their followers demonstrated that leader CQ predicted follower perceptions of leader performance and team performance in contexts where work teams were characterized by significant ethnic and nationality diversity. Furthermore, leaders' CQ predicted follower perceptions of leader performance and team performance on culturally diverse work teams beyond the effects of leader emotional intelligence and other leadership competencies.
Moon (2010b)	A	Cultural intelligence (CQ) can exist at the organizational level. Drawing on the individual level of CQ conceptualization and the dynamic capability framework, the proposed organizational CQ theory suggests how micro theories of cultural intelligence can be relevant to the macro theories of organizational CQ.
Moon (2010a)	A, C	Data from 381 students in Korea support discriminant validity of the four factor model of cultural intelligence scale (CQS) in relation to the emotional intelligence (EQ) construct. This study also demonstrates that the EQ factors related to social competence (social awareness and relationship management) explain CQ over and beyond the EQ factors related to self-competence.
Moon (2013)	C	Data from 73 project groups comprising 327 members demonstrated that the degree of cultural diversity on multi-cultural teams influences team performance over time, and that those teams with higher levels of CQ tend to gradually exhibit higher rates of performance improvement. In addition, the results indicate that CQ moderates the relationship between cultural diversity and team performance.
Triandis (2006)	C	CQ enhances suspending judgment until enough information about the other person becomes available; paying attention to the situation; cross-cultural training that increases isomorphic attributions, appropriate affect, and appropriate behaviors.
Zhang (2013)	C	CQ enhances expatriates' cross-cultural adjustment in multinational corporations and cross-border organizations.
Chen & Lin (2013)	C	CQ is a key driver of knowledge sharing among culturally diverse teams. Knowledge sharing is directly influenced by metacognitive, cognitive, and motivational cultural intelligence. At the same time, knowledge sharing is indirectly impacted by metacognitive and behavioral cultural intelligence through the mediation of perceived team efficacy.

(continued)

TABLE 8.3 An Overview of Prior Research on Antecedents and Consequences of CQ (continued)

Study	Type	Summary
Story, Barbuto, Luthans, & Bovaird (2014)	A, C	Leaders' global mindset is made up of one's cultural intelligence and global business orientation. Utilizing a diverse sample ($N = 136$) of global leaders of a well-known multinational, we found that personal, psychological, and role complexity antecedents were related to the participants' level of global mindset.
Gregory, Prifling, & Beck (2009)	C	Project members' cultural intelligence enables the emergence of negotiated culture in IT offshore projects. Interpretive, in-depth single-case study based on 31 qualitative interviews show that the cultural intelligence framework serves as a "sensitizing device" to develop a model of cross-cultural interaction in IT offshore outsourcing projects. Also, cultural intelligence is found to be an important driver for the development of a negotiated culture, characterized by trust-based interpersonal relationships, shared understanding, and the effective resolution of conflicts in IT offshore outsourcing projects.
Dollwet & Reichard (2014)	A, C	A new measure of cross-cultural psychological capital (PsyCap) was validated and related to cultural intelligence, openness to experience, ethnocentrism, and cross-cultural adjustment.
Remhof, Gunkel, & Schlaegel (2014)	C	Cognitions including CQ specified by the theory of planned behavior (TPB) were examined as mediators of the relationship between individuals' personality traits and the intention to work abroad. A sample of 518 German business students suggests that CQ fully mediates the relationships between the personality traits of openness to experience and extraversions and the intention to work abroad.
Gudmundsdottir (2015)	C	The sample consists of 178 Nordic (Danish, Finnish, Icelandic, Norwegian, and Swedish) expatriates working and living in the United States reveal that cultural intelligence facilitates cross-cultural adjustment for Nordic expatriates. Also, the results indicate that a greater general adjustment is related to greater meta-cognitive and motivational cultural intelligence.
Lin, Chen, & Song (2012)	C	Data from 295 international college students who studied for a degree or were interested in learning Chinese as a second language in Taiwan used to test the effect of CQ on cross-cultural adjustment, and the moderating effect of EQ on the relationship between CQ and cross-cultural adjustment. The results showed that CQ had a positive effect on cross-cultural adjustment and that EQ positively moderated the relationship between CQ and cross-cultural adjustment.

(continued)

TABLE 8.3 An Overview of Prior Research on Antecedents and Consequences of CQ (continued)

Study	Type	Summary
Tuan (2016)	C	Found the positive effect of all four dimensions of CQ (metacognitive, cognitive, motivational, and behavioral) on ethical and legal CSR, as well as knowledge-based and identity-based trust, which leverage supply chain performance. The connectivity between supply chain performance and CQ was also established.
Felicio, Duarte, & Rodrigues (2016)	C	Found that CQ of managers in 51 Portuguese SMEs relate to global mindset (IGM) and SMEs' internationalization behavior.
Adair, Hideg, & Spence (2013)	C	The cultural heterogeneity of work teams moderates the way in which team cultural intelligence (CQ) affects the development of team shared values. Results show that behavioral and metacognitive CQ had a positive effect on shared values in culturally heterogeneous teams; however, motivational and metacognitive CQ had a negative effect on shared values in culturally homogeneous teams.
Klafehn, Li, & Chiu (2013)	A	Results indicated that self-reported metacognition (as measured by the CQS) is distinct from personality, but highly correlated with the other sub-facets of self-reported cultural intelligence. In addition, it explored the criterion-related validity of the Metacognitive subscale of the CQS, in particular, demonstrated that self-reported metacognition did not predict international students' adaptation.
Johnson, Lenartowicz, & Apud (2006)	C	CQ enhances managers' cultural competency but it is contingent on environmental and contextual factors.
Reichard, Dollwet, & Louw-Potgieter (2014);	A	Positive psychological capital (hope, efficacy, resilience, and optimism) resulted in significant gains in cross-cultural psychological capital, cultural intelligence, and positive emotions as well as decreases in ethnocentrism.
Bucker & Poutsma (2010);	C	The global mindset, cross-cultural competence, intercultural sensitivity, and cultural intelligence all related to global management competencies of executives.
Morley & Cerdin (2010);	C	CQ facilitates intercultural competence in the international business arena
Rockstuhl, Seiler, Ang, Van Dyne, & Annen (2011)	C	A sample of 126 Swiss military officers with both domestic and cross-border leadership responsibilities shows that (a) general intelligence predicted both domestic and cross-border leadership effectiveness; (b) emotional intelligence was a stronger predictor of domestic leadership effectiveness, and (c) cultural intelligence was a stronger predictor of cross-border leadership effectiveness.

(continued)

TABLE 8.3 An Overview of Prior Research on Antecedents and Consequences of CQ (continued)

Study	Type	Summary
Elenkov & Manev (2009)	C	Data from 153 senior expatriate managers and 695 subordinates from companies in all 27 countries of the European Union show that senior expatriates' visionary-transformational leadership influences the rate of innovation adoption in the organizations or units they head, but cultural intelligence moderates this relationship. Also, cultural intelligence moderates the effect of senior expatriates' leadership on organizational innovation, but not on product-market innovation.
Lisak & Erez (2015)	C	Emergent leaders in multicultural teams score higher than non-leaders in terms of the three global characteristics, of cultural intelligence, global identity, and openness to cultural diversity.
Zander, Mockaitis, & Butler (2012)	C	Emergent concepts of biculturalism, global mindset, and cultural intelligence with respect to team leaders are emerging themes in the effectiveness of global teams.
Crotty & Brett (2012)	C	Data were from 246 members of 37 multicultural teams indicates that across teams, when team members were more highly culturally metacognitive, fusion teamwork and creativity were more likely.
Maldonado & Vera (2014)	C	It associates different degrees of leaders' cultural intelligence (CQ), improvisation—the ability to act spontaneously and creatively to executives' ability to deal with international crisis.
Mirvis, Hurley, & MacArthur (2014);	C	CQ enhances leaders' diplomatic skills and capabilities to deal with multi-stakeholder, multisector challenges.
Chipulu et al. (2016)	A	Specific national cultural dimensions—"Collectivism," "Uncertainty Avoidance," and to a lesser extent, "Power Distance"—are the most salient cultural denominators for advertised international project management positions. So these are dimensions that can be better understood by CQ of projects managers and help organizations become more culturally intelligent.
Yitmen (2013)	C	Cultural intelligence (CQ) on the organizational level is an organization's capacity to reconfigure its capability to function and manage effectively in culturally diverse environments and to gain and sustain its competitive advantages via effective strategies such as alliance and contracting.
Gertsen & Soderberg (2010)	A	Narrations stimulate cultural learning processes, thereby enhancing cultural intelligence both at the organizational and at the individual level.

(continued)

TABLE 8.3 An Overview of Prior Research on Antecedents and Consequences of CQ (continued)

Study	Type	Summary
Earley & Mosakowski (2004)	Both	Leaders CQ is essential for effective team works, people who are detached from their culture can more easily adopt new ones. CQ is a total of cognitive, physical, and emotional or motivational components.
Kaufman & Hwang (2015)	A	Mindfulness (empathy, open-mindedness, and using all senses) is an important building block of CQ. A case study of two French banking institutions operating in the United States showed similar emphasis on cross-cultural knowledge but differences in cross-cultural behavioral ability due to differences in mindfulness components of empathy, open-mindedness, and using all senses.
Charoensukmongkol (2015)	C	Data from 129 surveys revealed a positive association between the CQ of entrepreneurs and the quality of the relationships that small and medium enterprises (SMEs) had with foreign customers, foreign suppliers, and foreign competitors. The quality of the relationships was also associated positively with export performance.
Magnusson, Schuster, & Taras (2014)	C	The team members' motivational cultural intelligence is a moderating factor between expectation of challenges as well as the level of team effort attainment.
Froese, Kim, & Eng (2016)	C	Survey responses from 148 inpatriates in Korea-based MNCs showed that greater levels of English use as a common corporate language in the HQ and perceived organizational-level motivational cultural intelligence (MCQ) were negatively related to inpatriate turnover intention. Furthermore, the negative relationships were attenuated by inpatriates' host country language proficiency and individual-level of MCQ.
Mosakowski, Calic, & Earley (2013)	A	A moderate level of cultural distance, a tight culture, low context, and high moral desirability in cross-cultural boot camps increases cultural intelligence of students and make them more willing to choose entrepreneurship and self-employment.

Note: "A" denotes antecedents or enablers; "C" denotes consequences or outcomes

As shown in Figure 8.2, cultural intelligence can be enabled in several different ways. Herrmann et al. (2007) found that CQ is an evolutionary species-specific set of social-cognitive skills that emerge via intercultural interactions. Several studies have found evidence for this assertion. For instance, Crowne (2008) realized that exposure to other cultures (such as education abroad and employment abroad), and the level of that exposure, shapes the cultural intelligence of employees. Extending this view, Pless et al. (2011) found that working at NGOs in developing countries helps managers develop cultural sensitivity and intelligence. Mosakowski et al. (2013) show that a moderate level of cultural distance, a tight culture, low context, and high moral desirability between a home culture and other host cultures enhances the cultural intelligence of expatriates. Similarly, Li, Mobley, and Kelly (2013) observed that the length of overseas experience facilitates executive cultural intelligence, and divergent learning style strengthens this association. Johnston (2014) observed that short-term business travel helps managers better reflect on their CQ. Reichard et al. (2015) studied business students and found that studying abroad helped them develop higher levels of cultural intelligence and reduce ethnocentrism. Finally, Kaufman and Hwang (2015) argue that mindfulness (empathy, open-mindedness, and using all senses) is an important building block of CQ. All in all, a host of factors including openness to other cultures, mindfulness, and cultural exposure via teaching, travel, training, and short and long term experiences, help an individual develop their CQ.

Research paints a clear picture of the psychological correlators of CQ. CQ is different from emotional and social intelligences, and correlates strongly with several types of personality. Deng and Gibson (2009) studied 32 Western expatriate managers and 19 local Chinese managers working in Australian businesses operating in Shanghai and Beijing, and found that transformational leadership, emotional intelligence, and cultural intelligence complement each other in enabling managers to succeed in culturally diverse contexts. Moon (2010a) studied a sample of Korean students studying abroad and noted that cultural intelligence was related to social competence (social awareness and relationship management) and that these effects did not hold for emotional intelligence, which explained student competence. Groves and Feyerherm (2011) focused on the interactions between leaders and their followers in culturally diverse teams and observed that leader CQ predicted follower perceptions of leader performance and team performance, and these effects went beyond the effects of a leader's emotional intelligence and other leadership competencies. In more controlled and parsimonious research, Rockstuhl et al. (2011) studied a sample of 126 Swiss military officers with both domestic and cross-border leadership responsibilities, and reported the following findings: (a) general intelligence predicted both domestic and cross-border leadership effectiveness; (b) emotional intelligence was a stronger predictor of domestic leadership effectiveness; and (c) cultural intelligence was a stronger predictor of cross-border leadership effectiveness. Overall, the most important point that can be clearly deduced from the literature in this regard is that cultural (CQ), emotional (EQ), social (SQ), and general intelligence (GQ) are distinct forms of intelligence and none are superior or inferior to another. These intelligences complement each other in various ways and their complementary associations can explain different aspects of behavioral strategy.

The third strand of research on CQ pertains to its benefits or consequences. This strand is perhaps the most prolific and active area of research on CQ. Research lists a host of empirically proven benefits of CQ. Most notable are an enhanced "cultural adjustment" and an advanced "cross-cultural competence" for networking and cross-cultural task performance. For instance, Zhang (2013) found that CQ enhances the cross-cultural adjustment of expatriates in multinational corporations and cross-border organizations. Jyoti and Kour (2015) reported that CQ contributes significantly toward the task performance of bank managers in India by facilitating their cultural adjustment. Dollwet and Reichard (2014) observed that CQ not only enhances cultural adjustment but also improves openness to cultural experience. In addition, many studies, including Johnson et al. (2006), Bucker and Poutsma (2010), and Morley and Cerdin (2010) have found positive associations between manager CQ and their cross-cultural competencies. Another factor which has been argued as enhanced by CQ is the development of cross-cultural relationships or cross-cultural networking. Gregory et al. (2009) studied IT offshore projects and found that cultural intelligence not only acts a "sensitizing device" to develop a model of cross-cultural interaction in IT offshore outsourcing projects, but also facilitates the development of a negotiated culture, characterized by trust-based interpersonal relationships, shared understanding, and the effective resolution of conflicts in IT offshore outsourcing projects. Remhof et al. (2014) found that an individual's CQ improves their intention to work abroad and facilitates their socialization by increasing their openness to experience. In another study, Charoensukmongkol (2015) showed that the CQ of entrepreneurs significantly explains the quality of the relationships that small and medium enterprises (SMEs) have with foreign customers, foreign suppliers, and foreign competitors.

Other benefits of CQ include the executive adoption of a global mindset, executive ability to respond to international crises, and executive ability to develop an atmosphere of knowledge and value sharing in multicultural organizations. Story et al. (2014) argued that a leader's global mindset is made up of their cultural intelligence and global business orientation. They then tested and found empirical support for this assumption. In a similar and more recent study, Felicio et al. (2016) found that manager CQ is directly related to their global mindset and through that to the internationalization behavior of their firms. Finally, with respect to international crisis management, Maldonado and Vera (2014) showed that a leader's CQ interacts with their improvisation—the ability to act spontaneously and creatively—to shape an executive's ability to deal with international crises. Finally, research has documented positive associations between an

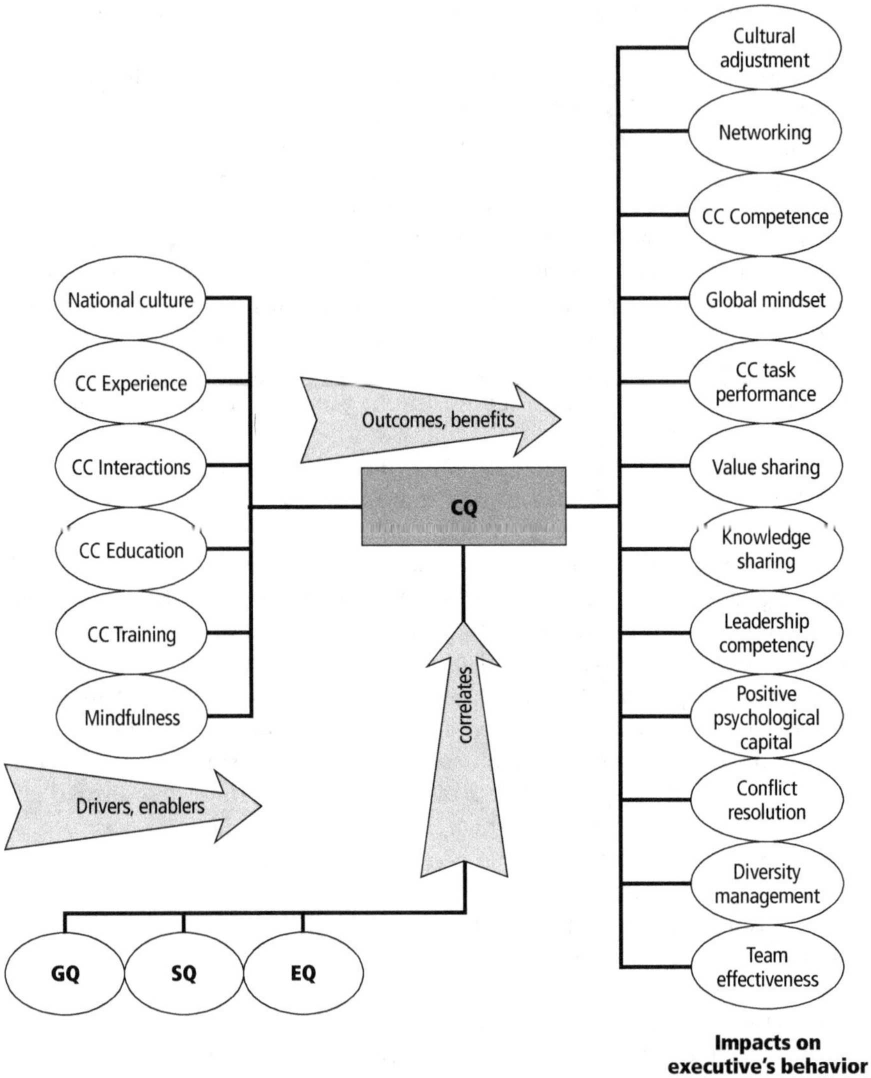

Figure 8.2 Antecedents, correlates, and outcomes of CQ.

individual's CQ and their tendency to share knowledge and value in multicultural teams. For instance, Gregory et al. (2009) show that offshore project manager CQ enhances their ability to negotiate and share value and information with other project managers from different cultures. Adair et al. (2013) observed different mechanisms through which team CQ affects the development of shared team values. Their study showed that behavioral and metacognitive CQ positively, and motivational and metacognitive CQ negatively, affected shared values in culturally homogeneous teams. Lastly, Chen and Lin (2013) showed that CQ is a key driver of knowledge sharing among culturally diverse teams. They further found that knowledge sharing is directly affected by metacognitive, cognitive, and motivational cultural intelligence. At the same time, knowledge sharing is indirectly impacted by metacognitive and behavioral cultural intelligence through the mediation of perceived team efficacy. Figure 8.2 depicts a conceptual framework summarizing the research on CQ.

In light of the above, the next section incorporates cultural intelligence as a powerful psychological factor in the domain of behavioral strategy.

Incorporating CQ Into the Domain of Behavioral Strategy

Executive CQ becomes meaningful when their task environment becomes culturally diverse. This could take place in two ways, as schematically illustrated in Figure 8.3 when the internal environment of an organization contains multicultural teams, divisions, and units; and when the external environment encompasses multicultural players such as suppliers, financers, distributors, consultants, and partners, primarily in cross-border international business activities. Assuming that CQ is only to enrich the international business and global strategy literature is myopic and incomplete, because executive CQ matters as much in managing international strategic affairs as it does in managing domestic strategic activities involving employees from various cultural backgrounds. It is obvious, however, that when a manager's internal and external task environments are both culturally diverse, their CQ becomes even more essential in facilitating their success.

Behavioral strategy, as discussed, is concerned with the general behavior of executives and does not distinguish different psychological aspects of strategic behavior, nor does it explicitly address the way executive cultural intelligence relates to other theoretical strands, as previously discussed. The following two points can be made when we embed executive CQ in behavioral strategy to fill these voids:

1. The cultural intelligence of executives is expected to enhance various aspects of their internal performance. For example, culturally intelligent executives are expected to perform better than less culturally intelligent ones when leading and managing multicultural top teams. In addition, culturally intelligent executives are expect-

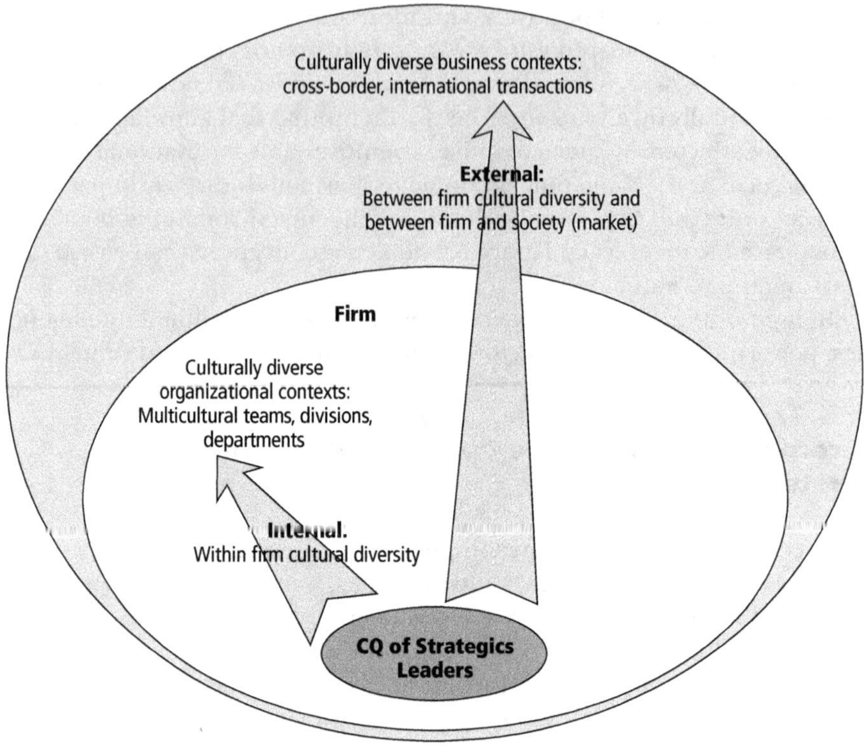

Figure 8.3 Internal and external domains of executives' CQ.

ed to more efficiently develop organizational capabilities involving multicultural employees.

2. The cultural intelligence of executives is expected to enhance various aspects of their external performance. For instance, culturally intelligent executives are expected to more efficiently develop and manage international strategies involving partnership or integration with firms from different cultures and respond more quickly to opportunities and threats emerging in the international markets where the firm operates or intends to operate.

The purpose of this chapter is not to discuss all the internal and external benefits of executive CQ, but to highlight its potential and stimulate cumulative research into these issues. Toward this end, the next section offers some general directions to guide future research on executive CQ within the paradigm of behavioral strategy and its theoretical domains.

A SUGGESTED RESEARCH AGENDA

Powell et al. (2011) suggest that "behavioral strategy should strive for growth, dynamism, and creative leadership in defining new research problems and methods. Many changes are happening even now—the shift from decisions to complex judgments; from individual biases to choice architecture; from introspection to cognitive neuroscience" (p. 1381). In response to this call for research on new problems, we believe that executive behaviors in cross-cultural and diverse contexts represent a set of problems that deserves more attention. Incorporating executive cultural intelligence into behavioral strategy is a promising approach that could fuel the growth and drive the leadership of behavioral strategy for years to come. I propose six research directions (RDs) to stimulate research in this domain. These six directions pave the way for accumulative knowledge creation on the benefits and potential of executive cultural intelligence for the field of strategic management in general and behavioral strategy in particular. Figure 8.4 illustrates what I have in mind.

The first promising research direction is to explore and examine how behavioral theory of the firm (BTF) embraces executive cultural intelligence. As previously noted, BTF has a clear behavioral agenda for how a business firm works. This agenda is comprised of cognitive and relational concepts that form the fabric of executive behavior in the firm. Concepts such as satisficing, limited rationality, limited scope of search, expectations and aspirations, quasi-resolution of conflict, problematic search, and uncertainty avoidance shape the theoretical landscape of BTF (Gavetti et al., 2012). Because CQ affects the way executives think, react, and behave in diverse contexts, it is important to address questions such as: "How does executive cultural intelligence affect their aspirations, search, coalition building and political behaviors?" and "Are culturally intelligent executives better able to resolve intra- and inter-firm conflicts when their task environments are culturally diverse?" following the typology of philosophical schools proposed by Powell et al. (2011). This direction seems to subscribe to both pluralist and conceptualist views because it involves teams and social behaviors as well as perceptions, schemas and the mental models of executives. Research in this direction can use a variety of methods such as the survey of executives at team level, interviews, grounded theories, hermeneutics, and semiotics to generate new insights into the effects of CQ on a repertoire of mechanisms discussed in the behavioral theory of the firm.

The second research direction stems from the top management team (TMT) and strategic leadership literature. The central foci of TMT literature are the profit impacts of various aspects of executive psychology, diversity of TMT, team mechanisms, and intra-team interactions (Hambrick

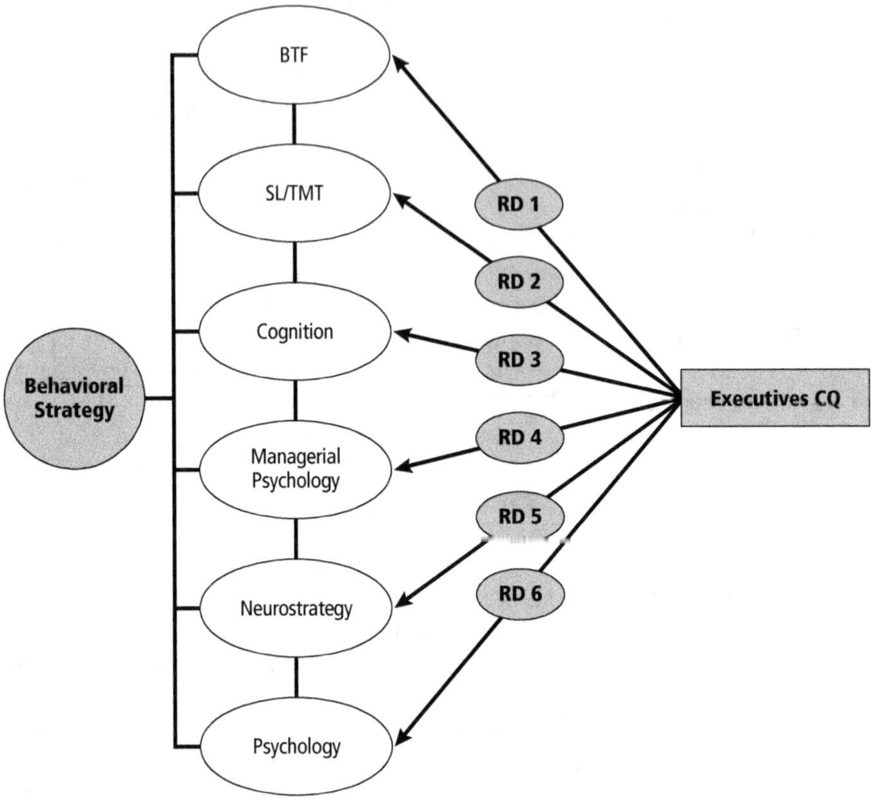

Figure 8.4 Research directions to incorporate executives CQ into behavioral strategy.

2007). In so far as CQ in general is concerned, we can argue that an executive's CQ affects their interactions, and by implications team processes, in culturally diverse teams. It is also very possible that executives in a team have different levels of CQ. This diversity would affect the behaviors and performance of TMTs, and by implications their firms, significantly. Surprisingly, however, there has been no explicit attempt to study such phenomena. A plethora of research questions should thus be addressed here. For instance, "How can we best measure and capture top team diversity in cultural intelligence?"; "How does cultural intelligence affect a CEO's interactions with team members in diverse TMTs?"; and "How does executive cultural intelligence affect team mechanisms such as information sharing, the speed of decision making, conflict resolution, and behavioral integration in TMTs?" Addressing these questions necessitates methodological and philosophical pluralism because it requires focus on individual executives, executives in teams and team level diversity. Different philosophical viewpoints, ranging from reductionist to pluralist and even conceptualist, can thus be adopted in this line of research. Methodological and philosophical pluralism enables multimethod research. Methods as diverse as multivariate modeling at individual level, team-level modeling, and interviews with executives can be used to advance our understanding of different facets of executive CQ in the context of top management teams.

The next research direction pertains to the cognitive side of CQ. The cognitive view of executives entails concepts such as the cognitive styles of executives, defined as the stylistic, intuitive, and analytic ways in which executives think, behave, and act (e.g., Gallen, 2006), and the cognitive biases and heuristics which affect executive decision making (e.g., Barnes 1984; Das & Teng, 1999). Since executive CQ directly affects their cross-cultural perceptions, thinking process, and behavioral responses, there is theoretical ground to argue that CQ could interact not only with executive cognitive styles but also with the scope, range, and scale of the heuristics they use when making decisions in culturally diverse settings. The extant literature on CQ has not addressed these issues, leaving a gap in our understanding of the role and position of CQ in the literature on strategic cognition. Seeking to address simple questions such as "What is the relationship between cultural intelligence and cognitive styles of executives?"; "How does executive cultural intelligence affect their strategic schemas, dominant logic, mental models, and perception of strategic issues in diverse context?"; and "What is the relationship between cultural intelligence and cognitive biases or heuristics that executives use when making decisions in culturally diverse situations?" could be the starting point for a fruitful line of research in this direction.

As previously noted, the psychology of creating strategy extends the cognitive side of strategy by incorporating concepts such as emotions, hubris, leadership styles, and narcissism in the nomenclature of behavioral strategy. Research into cultural intelligence has not examined whether and how executive CQ relates to their leadership styles, hubris, narcissism, and other psychological factors. There are interesting questions at this intersection that need to be addressed if we want a more complete understanding of executive behaviors in culturally diverse contexts. For instance, "How does the cultural intelligence of executives affect their leadership style when working in diverse settings?"; "Is there any relationship between CQ and transactional or transformational styles?"; "To what extent does CQ affect executive ability to incorporate positive or negative emotions when making sense of issues in diverse contexts?"; or "How do more culturally intelligent leaders distribute their attention, make sense of strategic issues, and deal with positive and negative emotions which emerge then dealing with complex issues?" We can adopt either a reductionist or a conceptualist approach to addressing these questions. Using the reductionist approach, executives can be surveyed or interviewed in order to examine or explore the relationships and mechanisms which govern the relationships between CQ and executive psychological factors. There are many test inventories which help researchers parse the interactions between styles and intelligences. From a conceptualist perspective, interviews and field observations can be undertaken to explore the hidden facets of executive CQ and their relationships with their emotional management, coping mechanisms, attention distribution, and leading styles in action. Caution should be applied, however, with regard to more sensitive concepts such as hubris and narcissism, when designing research, as data and findings can be easily invalidated if the context, approach, or analysis is subject to bias. Research into the psychology of executives offers important guidelines in this regard (e.g., Chatterjee & Hambrick, 2007; Hiller & Hambrick, 2005) which need to be extended and validated for multicultural and cross-cultural settings.

The next direction for future research relates to the emerging domain of neuro-strategy. As briefly discussed, neuro-strategy is the application of neuro-science in strategy (Powell 2011). Research has, for instance, examined how intuitive and rational decision making activate different parts of executive brains and how brain scanning advances our understanding of strategic thinking and decision making (Treffers & Fehse, 2016). Continuing this line of research, future studies can also focus on the different components of cultural intelligence, namely the metacognitive, cognitive, affective, and conative in controlled experiments to see how the neuro-systems of highly culturally intelligent executives differ from their less culturally intelligent counterparts, and how cross-cultural exposure, training, education, interactions, and experiences affect the texture and fabric of executive neuro-system. Some questions to guide future research in this direction are: "Does cultural intelligence have a distinctive spot in the brain of executives?"; "What regions of the brain are affected when cultural intelligence is developed?"; and "What is the difference in the level and scope of activities in the central neuro-systems of highly culturally intelligent executives versus less culturally intelligent ones?" The reductionist school seems to be the most appropriate here because it focuses on individual executives and allows the application of laboratory tools such as FGMI in controlled experimental environments (Powell et al., 2011).

The last direction for future research aims to stimulate research into the actions, practices, and activities of executives working in culturally diverse settings. The S-as-P domain takes the lead when executive practices and activities are concerned (Vaara & Whittington, 2012). The central tenet of S-as-P is that strategy work is affected by roles and identity of executives as well as tools and methods they use (Vaara & Whittington, 2012). The extant body of S-as-P research, however, has overlooked the role of cultural diversity in this context and seems to have assumed that cultural factors and executive CQ do not affect strategy work. This chapter showed that this is not the case. In fact, the CQ of executives can affect their strategy work, identity, role, and use of tools and techniques in meaningful, predictable, and considerable ways when practitioners (i.e., strategy workers or executives) are placed in culturally diverse settings. S-as-P in culturally diverse settings is therefore a less-developed side of S-as-P, which can be advanced through the lens of executive CQ. There are many research questions in this context, two of which, for instance, are "How do the strategic practices of culturally intelligent executives differ from their counterparts when working in diverse contexts?" and "What tools and techniques do culturally intelligent executives use to make better decisions in diverse contexts?" Because the focus here seems to be more on the actions, activities, and practices of single strategy practitioners, the reductionist and conceptualist schools are more appropriate for guiding research designs in this line.

Table 8.4 presents a summary of these six research directions.

DISCUSSION AND IMPLICATIONS

The question that motivated this chapter was whether the converging body of literature on behavioral strategy is able to address executive behavioral differences in culturally diverse environments. I argued that the current repertoire of constructs in the behavioral strategy literature is insufficient to address this issue. Cultural intelligence as a construct that is specifically designed to capture the essence of such phenomena should be added to the portfolio of topics in mainstream behavioral strategy research. I will briefly discuss the implications of this approach for the theory, practice, and education of behavioral strategy.

Implications for the Theory of Behavioral Strategy

Theoretical contributions to the field of behavioral strategy originate primarily from exploring new research frontiers at the intersection of strategy and psychology (Powell et al., 2011). This chapter addresses one of these frontiers; namely, executive CQ. As far as executive CQ in behavioral strategy is concerned, research has been ignorant or at best taken an overly simplistic position, assuming that executives behave equally under various cultural conditions. In fact, it takes executive abilities to interpret information coming from various cultural settings for granted. This does not take the notion of CQ into account in socially embedded and culturally bound mechanisms such as information sharing and networking. As a result, assumptions of behavioral strategy in culturally diverse contexts

TABLE 8.4 Research Directions at the Intersection of Behavioral Strategy and CQ

CQ in Behavioral Strategy	Research Direction (RD)	Suggestive Research Questions	Behavioral Strategy Paradigm	Suggested Research Design and Approach
CQ in BTF	RD 1	• How does executive cultural intelligence affect their coalition building and political behavior? • Are culturally intelligent executives better capable of dealing with resolving intra and inter firm conflicts? • How does cultural intelligence of executives affect leader's capacity to initiate and lead organizational learning procedures? • How do more culturally intelligent leaders differ from less culturally intelligent ones in selling aspirations in diverse settings and respond to performance feedback?	Pluralist and conceptualist	Survey at team level for multi-variate models, experimentations at team level, interviews with executives for grounded theories hermeneutics, semiotics
CQ in SL	RD 2	• How can we best measure and capture top team diversity in cultural intelligence? • How does cultural intelligence affect CEO's interactions with team members in diverse TMTs? • How does executives' cultural intelligence affect team mechanism such as information sharing, speed of decision making, conflict resolution, and behavioral integration in TMTs?	Reduction, pluralist, and conceptualists	Multivariate modeling, team level modeling, interviews with executives
SQ and SC	RD 3	• What is the relationship between cultural intelligence and cognitive styles of executives? • How does executives' cultural intelligence affect their strategic schemas, dominant logic, mental models, and perception of strategic issues in diverse contexts? • What is the relationship between cultural intelligence and cognitive biases or heuristics that executives use when making decisions in culturally diverse situations?	Reductionist and conceptualist	Survey at individual level for multivariate modeling, experimentation, interviews with executives for grounded theory, hermeneutics

(continued)

TABLE 8.4 Research Directions at the Intersection of Behavioral Strategy and CQ (continued)

CQ in Behavioral Strategy	Research Direction (RD)	Suggestive Research Questions	Behavioral Strategy Paradigm	Suggested Research Design and Approach
CQ in MP	RD 4	• How does cultural intelligence of executives affect their leadership style when working in diverse settings? • How do more culturally intelligent leaders distribute their attention, make sense of strategic issues, and deal with positive and negative emotions which emerge when dealing with complex issues? • What is the relationship between cultural intelligence of leaders and their self-efficacy, hubris, and other intelligences specifically in diverse contexts?	Reductionist and conceptualist	Surveys for multivariate modeling, interviews and qualitative inductive research methods such as grounded theories
CQ in NS	RD 5	• Does cultural intelligence have a distinctive spot in the brain of executives? • What regions of brains are affected when cultural intelligence is developed? • What is the difference in the level and scope of activities in the central neuro system of highly culturally intelligent executives versus less culturally intelligent ones?	Reductionist	Laboratory research using methods such as fMRI
CQ in SaP	RD 6	• How strategic practices of culturally intelligent executives differ from their counterparts when working in diverse contexts? • What tools and techniques culturally intelligent executives use to make better decisions in diverse contexts?	Reductionist	Field observations, interviews, case studies and grounded theories

are incomplete and misleading unless they incorporate executive cultural intelligence into the drivers and consequences of choices and actions. This logic led us to argue that executive CQ is a potential yet missing factor in the burgeoning literature on behavioral strategy and micro-foundations of firm strategic behaviors. We have built on this realization, and showed that CQ can advance the theory of behavioral strategy by adding to the six domains of research on behavioral theory; namely, the behavioral theory of firms, top management teams and strategic cognition, managerial psychology, neuro-strategy, and strategy-as-practice.

Implications for Behavioral Strategy Practice

Strategizing is something managers do (Jarzabkowski, 2004). This makes behavioral strategy a very practical field. The effectiveness of strategies is, therefore, subject to factors which underpin the behaviors of strategy makers. This chapter illuminates one of those factors, executive cultural intelligence. As a factor which manifests itself only in specific conditions, namely culturally diverse settings, the drivers, consequences, and mechanisms through which cultural intelligence functions have significant implications for the practice of strategy. The publication of a report on the importance of cultural intelligence in organizations (Earley & Mosakowski, 2004) in the *Harvard Business Review*, a leading practitioner-oriented journal, clearly testifies to this fact.

This chapter showed that cultural intelligence can be improved via exposure to new cultures, training in new cultures, and gaining cross-cultural experience. The practical side of behavioral strategy can focus on the methods, tools and techniques which help executives plan and execute such activities. There is already ample evidence in the corporate world showing how different organizations are embracing cultural diversity and preparing their executives to function effectively in culturally diverse settings. For example, in an interview with the British Broadcasting Corporation (BBC), Jayne Hrdlicka, the CEO of Jetstar, an Australian airline, talked about how her culturally diverse team practices cross-cultural learning via a nationality swap—"where for one day Australian staff pretended to be Japanese and the Japanese staff pretended to be Australian" (Hope, 2016). Hrdlicka further explains:

> "While an exercise like this could seem superficial, we were able to appreciate the different ways of working, and the importance of building on the best of all those different ways of working rather than trying to force one over another," she says. In the end, though, she says embracing a more diverse workforce requires a broad shift in how those at the top think about things,

> meaning that it's time that will make the biggest difference. "It's the right thing to do, but it's a smart thing to do. You get the best outcomes for your shareholders and you get the best outcomes for all the stakeholders involved in your business when you really do create an environment that brings the best out of everyone."

These sorts of activities enable managers to learn new cultures and become familiar with the similarities, commonalities, and differences between cultures. Even though the interview above was about how Jetstar embraces cultural diversity in its top team rather than executive CQ, it clearly described practices which could improve executive CQ. Studying and identifying such practices helps us advance the practical side of behavioral strategy and improve our understanding of practices, which make strategy creation more effective under various, previously unstudied, conditions.

Implications for Strategic Management Education

Almost 60 years ago, Herbert Simon pointed to the importance of the current curriculum in business school when he argued that "the tasks of a business school are to train men for the practice of management (or some special branch of management) as a profession, and to develop new knowledge that may be relevant to improving the operation of business" (Simon, 1967, p. 1). When Simon identified practical relevance as a key aspect of management education the world was not as internationally open as it is now. Current curriculums should recognize these changes. To stay relevant, business schools must adjust their curriculum to embrace the increasing role of cultural diversity in global business affairs. One way to achieve this goal is to incorporate CQ into the strategic management curriculum. Behavioral strategy has only recently started to be explicitly discussed in business schools, and as this chapter shows, CQ is a crucial aspect of the strategic behavior of executives when business settings are multicultural and diverse. Top business schools are all culturally heterogeneous organizations. They recruit teaching and research staff from different backgrounds and harbor students from different corners of the world, all to train managers with a global mindset. This chapter shows the potential of CQ as a key factor in helping business schools achieve these goals. The premise is simple. If a strategic management curriculum is to embrace behavioral strategy as a new pillar (Powell et al., 2011), then executive cultural intelligence will be the lens through which students can see and tease out behavioral strategy in international and culturally diverse contexts.

CONCLUSION

The central thesis of this chapter is simple. As students and practitioners of strategy, "we need models that solve the problems faced by thinking and feeling human beings, and this requires a robust and dynamic field of behavioral strategy" (Powell et al., 2011, p. 1382). Behavioral strategy, in all its glory, rests on behavioral assumptions, and is confined to behavioral limits; one of which is the ability to behave appropriately in culturally diverse settings. This chapter was motivated by the recognition that we need to address this issue in a more explicit and straightforward fashion. It, thus, brought the concept of CQ to the forefront of behavioral strategy and discussed the conceptual meaning, anatomy and structure of executive cultural intelligence. A set of directions for future research on this subject was then proposed to help researchers advance the cultural side of behavioral strategy within reductionist, pluralist, and conceptualist paradigms. This chapter is a first step toward enhancing the theoretical precision, methodological rigor, and practical relevance of behavioral strategy in international and cross-cultural contexts. I hope that it allows new insight into the behavioral sides of strategy creation in today's global and "not-so-flat" world, and stimulates more focused research into why, when, and how the strategic behavior of executives differs in different cultural contexts.

NOTES

1. Quote from Kofi Annan is taken from https://www.values.com/inspirational-quotes/7498-we-may-have-different-religions-different
1. Quote from Mahatma Gandhi is taken from https://www.brainyquote.com/quotes/quotes/m/mahatmagan165367.html

ACKNOWLEDGMENT

This chapter, save some minor changes, was earlier published as Najmaei, A. (2017). The case of executives' cultural intelligence in behavioral strategy: An introductory essay and a research agenda. In T. K. Das (Ed.), *Culture and behavioral strategy* (pp. 31–72). Charlotte, NC: Information Age.

REFERENCES

Adair, W. L., Hideg, I., & Spence, J. R. (2013). The culturally intelligent team: The impact of team cultural intelligence and cultural heterogeneity on team shared values. *Journal of Cross-Cultural Psychology, 44*(6), 941–962.

Anderson, M. H., & Sun, P. Y. T. (2017). Reviewing leadership styles: Overlaps and the need for a new "full-range" theory. *International Journal of Management Reviews, 19*(1), 76–96.

Ang, S., Van Dyne, L., Koh, C., Ng, K. Y., Templer, K. J., Tay, C., & Chandrasekar, N. A. (2007). Cultural intelligence: Its measurement and effects on cultural judgment and decision making, cultural adaptation and task performance. *Management and Organization Review, 3*(3), 335–371.

Antonakis, J., Ashkanasy, N. M., & Dasborough, M. T. (2009). Does leadership need emotional intelligence? *Leadership Quarterly, 20*(2), 247–261.

Bain, J. S. (1949). A note on pricing in monopoly and oligopoly. *American Economic Review, 39*(2), 448–464.

Barnard, C. I. (1938). *The functions of the executive.* Cambridge, MA: Harvard University Press.

Barnes, J. H., Jr. (1984). Cognitive biases and their impact on strategic planning. *Strategic Management Journal, 5*(2), 129–137.

Brislin, R. W., & Kim, E. S. (2003). Cultural diversity in people's understanding and uses of time. *Applied Psychology, 52*(3), 363–382.

Bucker, J., & Poutsma, E. (2010). Global management competencies: A theoretical foundation. *Journal of Managerial Psychology, 25*(8), 829–844.

Cannella, A. A., & Pettigrew, A. (2001). Upper echelons: Donald Hambrick on executives and strategy. *Academy of Management Executive, 15*(3), 36–42.

Cao, Q., Simsek, Z., & Zhang, H. (2010). Modelling the joint impact of the CEO and the TMT on organizational ambidexterity. *Journal of Management Studies, 47*(7), 1272–1296.

Carmeli, A. (2003). The relationship between emotional intelligence and work attitudes, behavior and outcomes: An examination among senior managers. *Journal of Managerial Psychology, 18*(8), 788–813.

Carmeli, A., Schaubroeck, J., & Tishler, A. (2011). How CEO empowering leadership shapes top management team processes: Implications for firm performance. *Leadership Quarterly, 22*(2), 399–411.

Charoensukmongkol, P. (2015). Cultural intelligence of entrepreneurs and international network ties the case of small and medium manufacturing firms in thailand. *Management Research Review, 38*(4), 421–436.

Chatterjee, A., & Hambrick, D. C. (2007). It's all about me: Narcissistic chief executive officers and their effects on company strategy and performance. *Administrative Science Quarterly, 52*(3), 351–386.

Chen, M.-L., & Lin, C.-P. (2013). Assessing the effects of cultural intelligence on team knowledge sharing from a socio-cognitive perspective. *Human Resource Management, 52*(5), 675–695.

Chipulu, M., Ojiako, U., Marshall, A., Williams, T., Neoh, J. G., Mota, C., & Shou, Y. Y. (2016). Building cultural intelligence: Insights from project management job advertisements. *Production Planning & Control, 27*(3), 133–147.

Cox, T. H., & Blake, S. (1991). Managing cultural diversity: Implications for organizational competitiveness. *The Executive, 5*(3), 45–56.

Crotty, S. K., & Brett, J. M. (2012). Fusing creativity: Cultural metacognition and teamwork in multicultural teams. *Negotiation and Conflict Management Research, 5*(2), 210–234.

Crowne, K. A. (2008). What leads to cultural intelligence? *Business Horizons, 51*(5), 391–399.

Cyert, R. M., & March, J. G. (1963). *A behavioral theory of the firm.* Englewood Cliffs, NJ: Prentice-Hall.

Cyert, R. M., & Williams, J. R. (1993). Organizations, decision making and strategy: Overview and comment. *Strategic Management Journal, 14,* 5–10.

Das, T. K. (1986). *The subjective side of strategy making: Future orientations and perceptions of executives.* New York, NY: Praeger.

Das, T. K. (Ed.). (2015). *The practice of behavioral strategy.* Charlotte, NC: Information Age.

Das, T. K. (Ed.). (2016). *Decision making in behavioral strategy.* Charlotte, NC: Information Age.

Das, T. K., & Kumar, R. (2010a). Interpartner sensemaking in strategic alliances: Managing cultural differences and internal tensions. *Management Decision, 48*(1), 17–36.

Das, T. K., & Kumar, R. (2010b). Interpretive schemes in cross-national alliances: managing conflicts and discrepancies. *Cross Cultural Management: An International Journal, 17*(2), 154–169.

Das, T. K., & Teng, B. (1999). Cognitive biases and strategic decision processes: An integrative perspective. *Journal of Management Studies, 36*(6), 757–778.

Deng, L., & Gibson, P. (2009). Mapping and modeling the capacities that underlie effective cross-cultural leadership: An interpretive study with practical outcomes. *Cross Cultural Management: An International Journal, 16*(4), 347–366.

Dollwet, M., & Reichard, R. (2014). Assessing cross-cultural skills: Validation of a new measure of cross-cultural psychological capital. *International Journal of Human Resource Management, 25*(12), 1669–1696.

Earley, P. C., & Ang, S. (2003). *Cultural intelligence: Individual interactions across cultures.* Stanford, CA: Stanford University Press.

Earley, P. C., & Mosakowski, E. (2004). Cultural intelligence. *Harvard Business Review, 82*(10), 139–146.

Elenkov, D. S., & Manev, I. M. (2009). Senior expatriate leadership's effects on innovation and the role of cultural intelligence. *Journal of World Business, 44*(4), 357–369.

Erez, M., Lisak, A., Harush, R., Glikson, E., Nouri, R., & Shokef, E. (2013). Going global: Developing management students' cultural intelligence and global identity in culturally diverse virtual teams. *Academy of Management Learning & Education, 12*(3), 16–41.

Felicio, J. A., Duarte, M., & Rodrigues, R. (2016). Global mindset and SME internationalization: A fuzzy–set QCA approach. *Journal of Business Research, 69*(4), 1372–1378.

Froese, F. J., Kim, K., & Eng, A. (2016). Language, cultural intelligence, and inpatriate turnover intentions: Leveraging values in multinational corporations through inpatriates. *Management International Review, 56*(2), 283–301.

Gallén, T. (2006). Managers and strategic decisions: Does the cognitive style matter? *Journal of Management Development, 25*(2), 118–133.

Gavetti, G., Greve, H. R., Levinthal, D. A., & Ocasio, W. (2012). The behavioral theory of the firm: Assessment and prospects. *Academy of Management Annals, 6*(1), 1–40.

Gerrard, M. M. (2011). Global assignment effectiveness and leader development. In W. H. Mobley, M. Li, & Y. Wang (Eds.), *Advances in global leadership* (Vol. 6; pp. 243–266). Bingley, England: Emerald Group.

Gertsen, M. C., & Soderberg, A. M. (2010). Expatriate stories about cultural encounters—A narrative approach to cultural learning processes in multinational companies. *Scandinavian Journal of Management, 26*(3), 248–257.

Gilbert, K., & Cartwright, S. (2008). Cross-cultural consultancy initiatives to develop Russian managers: An analysis of five Western aid-funded programs. *Academy of Management Learning & Education, 7*(4), 504–518.

Gregory, R., Prifling, M., & Beck, R. (2009). The role of cultural intelligence for the emergence of negotiated culture in its offshore outsourcing projects. *Information Technology & People, 22*(3), 223–241.

Groves, K. S., & Feyerherm, A. E. (2011). Leader cultural intelligence in context: Testing the moderating effects of team cultural diversity on leader and team performance. *Group & Organization Management, 36*(5), 535–566.

Gudmundsdottir, S. (2015). Nordic expatriates in the US: The relationship between cultural intelligence and adjustment. *International Journal of Intercultural Relations, 47*, 175–186.

Hambrick, D. C. (1989). Putting top managers back in the strategy picture. *Strategic Management Journal, 10*(Special Issue), 5–15.

Hambrick, D. C. (2007). Upper echelons theory: An update. *Academy of Management Review, 32*(2), 334–343.

Hambrick, D. C., & Mason, P. A. (1984). Upper echelons: The organization as a reflection of its top managers. *Academy of Management Review, 9*, 193–206.

Herrmann, E., Call, J., Hernandez-Lloreda, M. V., Hare, B., & Tomasello, M. (2007). Humans have evolved specialized skills of social cognition: The cultural intelligence hypothesis. *Science, 317*(5843), 1360–1366.

Hiller, N. J., & Hambrick, D. C. (2005). Conceptualizing executive hubris: The role of (hyper-)core self-evaluations in strategic decision-making. *Strategic Management Journal, 26*(4), 297–319.

Hodgkinson, G. P., & Healey, M. P. (2011). Psychological foundations of dynamic capabilities: Reflexion and reflection in strategic management. *Strategic Management Journal, 32*(13), 1500–1516.

Hodgkinson, G. P., Sadler-Smith, E., Burke, L. A., Claxton, G., & Sparrow, P. R. (2009). Intuition in organizations: Implications for strategic management. *Long Range Planning, 42*, 277–297.

Hope, K. (2016, June 21). Why it's important to be yourself at work. *BBC News.* Retrieved from http://www.bbc.com/news/business-36574837

Huy, Q. N. (2012). Emotions in strategic organization: Opportunities for impactful research. *Strategic Organization, 10*, 240–247.

Janssens, M., & Brett, J. M. (2006). Cultural intelligence in global teams—A fusion model of collaboration. *Group & Organization Management, 31*(1), 124–153.

Jarzabkowski, P. (2004). Strategy as practice: Recursiveness, adaptation, and practices-in-use. *Organization Studies, 25*(4), 529–560.

Johnson, J. P., Lenartowicz, T., & Apud, S. (2006). Cross-cultural competence in international business: Toward a definition and a model. *Journal of International Business Studies, 37*, 525–543.

Johnston, A. M. (2014). Short-term business travel and development of executive leader global mindset. In J. S. Osland, M. Li, & Y. Wang (Eds.), *Advances in global leadership* (Vol. 8; pp. 293–316). Bingley, England: Emerald Group.

Jyoti, J., & Kour, S. (2015). Assessing the cultural intelligence and task performance equation mediating role of cultural adjustment. *Cross Cultural Management: An International Journal, 22*(2), 236–258.

Kahneman, D., & Tversky, A. (1979). Prospect theory: An analysis of decision under risk. *Econometrica, 47*(2), 263–291.

Kaplan, A. (2014). European management and European business schools: Insights from the history of business schools. *European Management Journal, 32*(4), 529–534.

Kaplan, S. (2011). Research in cognition and strategy: Reflections on two decades of progress and a look to the future. *Journal of Management Studies, 48*(3), 665–695.

Kaufman, S. R., & Hwang, A. (2015). Cultural intelligence and mindfulness in two French banks operating in the US environment. *Management Research Review, 38*(9), 930–951.

Khatri, N., & Ng, H. A. (2000). The role of intuition in strategic decision making. *Human Relations, 53*(1), 57–86.

Kim, Y. J., & Van Dyne, L. (2012). Cultural intelligence and international leadership potential: The importance of contact for members of the majority. *Applied Psychology: An International Review, 61*(2), 272–294.

Klafehn, J., Li, C. C., & Chiu, C. Y. (2013). To know or not to know, is that the question? Exploring the role and assessment of metacognition in cross-cultural contexts. *Journal of Cross-Cultural Psychology, 44*, 963–991.

Leung, K., Ang, S., & Tan, M. L. (2014). Intercultural competence. In F. P. Morgeson (Ed.), *Annual review of organizational psychology and organizational behavior* (Vol. 1; pp. 489–519). Palo Alto, CA: Annual Reviews.

Li, M. (2009). An examination of the role of experiential learning in the development of cultural intelligence in global leaders. In W. M. Mobley, Y. Wang, & M. Li (Eds.), *Advances in global leadership* (Vol. 5; pp. 251–271). Bingley, England: Emerald Group.

Li, M., Mobley, W. H., & Kelly, A. (2013). When do global leaders learn best to develop cultural intelligence? An investigation of the moderating role of experiential learning style. *Academy of Management Learning & Education, 12*(1), 32–50.

Lin, Y. C., Chen, A. S. Y., & Song, Y. C. (2012). Does your intelligence help to survive in a foreign jungle? The effects of cultural intelligence and emotional intelligence on cross-cultural adjustment. *International Journal of Intercultural Relations, 36*(4), 541–552.

Lisak, A., & Erez, M. (2015). Leadership emergence in multicultural teams: The power of global characteristics. *Journal of World Business, 50*(1), 3–14.

Magnusson, P., Schuster, A., & Taras, V. (2014). A process-based explanation of the psychic distance paradox: Evidence from global virtual teams. *Management International Review, 54*(3), 283–306.

Maldonado, T., & Vera, D. (2014). Leadership skills for international crises: The role of cultural intelligence and improvisation. *Organizational Dynamics, 43*(4), 257–265.

Mintzberg, H. (1988). The craft of strategy. *McKinsey Quarterly, 3,* 71–90.

Mirvis, P. H., Hurley, S. T., & MacArthur, A. (2014). Transforming executives into corporate diplomats: The power of global pro bono service. *Organizational Dynamics, 43*(3), 235–245.

Moon, T. (2010a). Emotional intelligence correlates of the four-factor model of cultural intelligence. *Journal of Managerial Psychology, 25*(8), 876–898.

Moon, T. (2010b). Organizational cultural intelligence: Dynamic capability perspective. *Group & Organization Management, 35*(4), 456–493.

Moon, T. (2013). The effects of cultural intelligence on performance in multicultural teams. *Journal of Applied Social Psychology, 43*(12), 2414–2425.

Mor, S., Morris, M., & Joh, J. (2013). Identifying and training adaptive cross-cultural management skills: The crucial role of cultural metacognition. *Academy of Management Learning & Education, 12*(3), 139–161.

Morley, M. J., & Cerdin, J. L. (2010). Intercultural competence in the international business arena. *Journal of Managerial Psychology, 25*(8), 805–809.

Mosakowski, E., Calic, G., & Earley, P. C. (2013). Cultures as learning laboratories: What makes some more effective than others? *Academy of Management Learning & Education, 12*(3), 198–212.

Nadkarni, S., & Narayanan, V. K. (2007). Strategic schemas, strategic flexibility, and firm performance: The moderating role of industry clockspeed. *Strategic Management Journal, 28*(3), 243–270.

Nag, R., Hambrick, D. C., & Chen, M.-J. (2007). What is strategic management, really? Inductive derivation of a consensus definition of the field. *Strategic Management Journal, 28,* 935–955.

Najmaei, A., Rhodes, J., & Lok, P. (2015). A practice-based view of business modeling: Cognition and knowledge in action. In T. K. Das (Ed.), *The practice of behavioral strategy* (pp. 77–104). Charlotte, NC: Information Age.

Najmaei, A., & Sadeghinejad, Z. (2016). Metacognition in strategic decision making: An integrative review and a research agenda. In T. K. Das (Ed.), *Decision making in behavioral strategy* (pp. 49–81). Charlotte, NC: Information Age.

Narayanan, V. K., Zane, L. J., & Kemmerer, B. (2011). The cognitive perspective in strategy: An integrative review. *Journal of Management, 37*(1), 305–351.

Ng, K. Y., Van Dyne, L., & Ang, S. (2009a). Developing global leaders: The role of international experience and cultural intelligence. In W. M. Mobley, Y. Wang, & M. Li (Eds.), *Advances in global leadership* (Vol. 5; pp. 225–250). Bingley, England: Emerald Group.

Ng, K. Y., Van Dyne, L., & Ang, S. (2009b). From experience to experiential learning: Cultural intelligence as a learning capability for global leader development. *Academy of Management Learning and Education, 8*(4), 511–526.

Ng, K. Y., Van Dyne, L., & Ang, S. (2012). Cultural intelligence: A review, reflections, and recommendations for future research. In A. M. Ryan, F. T. L. Leong, & F. L. Oswald (Eds.), *Conducting multinational research: applying organizational psychology in the workplace* (pp. 29–58). Washington, DC: American Psychological Association.

Nielsen, S. (2010). Top management team diversity: A review of theories and methodologies. *International Journal of Management Reviews, 12*(3), 301–316.

Oliver, E., de Botton, L., Soler, M., & Merrill, B. (2011). Cultural Intelligence to overcome educational exclusion. *Qualitative Inquiry, 17*(3), 267–276.

Olson, B. J., Parayitam, S., & Yongjian, B. (2007). Strategic decision making: The effects of cognitive diversity, conflict, and trust on decision outcomes. *Journal of Management, 33*(2), 196–222.

Penrose, E. (1959). *The theory of the growth of the firm.* New York, NY: Oxford University Press.

Pless, N. M., Maak, T., & Stahl, G. K. (2011). Developing responsible global leaders through international service-learning programs: The Ulysses experience. *Academy of Management Learning & Education, 10,* 237–260.

Porter, M. E. (1979). How competitive forces shape strategy. *Harvard Business Review, 57*(2), 137–145.

Porter, M. E. (1980). *Competitive strategy: Techniques for analyzing industries and competitors.* New York, NY: Free Press.

Porter, M. E. (1985). *Competitive advantage.* New York, NY: Free Press.

Powell, T. C. (2011). Neurostrategy. *Strategic Management Journal, 32,* 1484–1499.

Powell, T. C., Lovallo, D., & Fox, C. R. (2011). Behavioral strategy. *Strategic Management Journal, 32,* 1369–1386.

Prahalad, C. K., & Bettis, R. A. (1986). The dominant logic: A new linkage between diversity and performance. *Strategic Management Journal, 7*(6), 485–501.

Presbitero, A. (2016). Cultural intelligence (CQ) in virtual, cross-cultural interactions: Generalizability of measure and links to personality dimensions and task performance. *International Journal of Intercultural Relations, 50*(1), 29–38.

Reichard, R. J., Dollwet, M., & Louw-Potgieter, J. (2014). Development of cross-cultural psychological capital and its relationship with cultural intelligence and ethnocentrism. *Journal of Leadership & Organizational Studies, 21*(2), 150–164.

Reichard, R. J., Serrano, S. A., Condren, M., Wilder, N., Dollwet, M., & Wang, W. (2015). Engagement in cultural trigger events in the development of cultural competence. *Academy of Management Learning & Education, 14*(4), 461–481.

Remhof, S., Gunkel, M., & Schlaegel, C. (2014). Goodbye Germany! The influence of personality and cognitive factors on the intention to work abroad. *International Journal of Human Resource Management, 25*(16), 2319–2343.

Rockstuhl, T., Seiler, S., Ang, S., Van Dyne, L., & Annen, H. (2011). Beyond general intelligence (IQ) and emotional intelligence (EQ): The role of cultural intelligence (CQ) on cross-border leadership effectiveness in a globalized world. *Journal of Social Issues, 67,* 825–840.

Rosenblatt, V., Worthley, R., & MacNab, B. (2013). From contact to development in experiential cultural intelligence education: The mediating influence of expectancy disconfirmation. *Academy of Management Learning & Education, 12*(3), 42–65.

Schmidt, F. L., & Hunter, J. E. (2000). Select on intelligence. In E. A. Locke (Ed.), *The Blackwell handbook of organizational principles* (pp. 3–14). Oxford, England: Blackwell.

Schrager, J. E., & Madansky, A. (2013). Behavioral strategy: A foundational view. *Journal of Strategy and Management, 6*(1), 81–95.

Schumpeter, J. (1934). *The theory of economic development.* Cambridge, MA: Harvard University Press.

Simon, H. (1967). The business school: A problem in organizational design. *Journal of Management Studies, 4*(1), 1–16.

Sternberg, R. J. (1986). A framework for understanding conceptions of intelligence. In R. J. Sternberg & D. K. Detterman (Eds.), *What is intelligence? Contemporary viewpoints on its nature and definition* (pp. 3–15). Norwood, NJ: Ablex.

Story, J. S. P., Barbuto, J. E., Luthans, F., & Bovaird, J. A. (2014). Meeting the challenges of effective international HRM: Analysis of the antecedents of global mindset. *Human Resource Management, 53*(1), 131–155.

Tang, Y., Qian, C., Chen, G., & Shen, R. (2015). How CEO hubris affects corporate social (ir)responsibility. *Strategic Management Journal, 36*(9), 1338–1357.

Taras, V., Bryla, P., Caprar, D. V., Ordenana, X., Rottig, D., Bode, A., . . . Huang, V. Z. Y. (2013). A global classroom? Evaluating the effectiveness of global virtual collaboration as a teaching tool in management education. *Academy of Management Learning & Education, 12*(3), 100–121.

Teece, D. J. (1986). Profiting from technological innovation: Implications for integration, collaboration, licensing and public policy. *Research Policy, 15*(6), 285–305.

Treffers, T., & Fehse, K. (2016). The neural correlates of emotion and overconfidence in strategic decision making. In T. K. Das (Ed.), *Decision making in behavioral strategy* (pp. 83–98). Charlotte, NC: Information Age.

Triandis, H. C. (2006). Cultural intelligence in organizations. *Group & Organization Management, 31*(1), 20–26.

Tuan, L. T. (2016). From cultural intelligence to supply chain performance. *International Journal of Logistics Management, 27*(1), 95–121.

Uy, M. A., Foo, M.-D., & Song, Z. (2012). Joint effects of prior start-up experience and coping strategies on entrepreneurs' psychological well-being. *Journal of Business Venturing, 28*(5), 583–597.

Vaara, E., & Whittington, R. (2012). Strategy-as-practice: Taking social practices seriously. *Academy of Management Annals, 6*(1), 285–336.

Varela, O. E., & Gatlin-Watts, R. (2014). The development of the global manager: An empirical study on the role of academic international sojourns. *Academy of Management Learning & Education, 13*(2), 187–207.

Ward, C., Fischer, R., Zaid Lam, F. S., & Hall, L. (2008). The convergent, discriminant, and incremental validity of scores on a self-report measure of cultural intelligence. *Educational and Psychological Measurement, 69*(1), 85–105.

Wernerfelt, B. (1984). A resource-based view of the firm. *Strategic Management Journal, 5*, 171–180.

Whittington, R. (1996). Strategy as practice. *Long Range Planning, 29*, 731–735.

Wood, E. D., & St. Peters, H. Y. Z. (2014). Short-term cross-cultural study tours: Impact on cultural intelligence. *International Journal of Human Resource Management, 25*(4), 558–570.

Yitmen, I. (2013). Organizational cultural intelligence: A competitive capability for strategic alliances in the international construction industry. *Project Management Journal, 44*(4), 5–25.

Yunlu, D. G., & Clapp-Smith, R. (2014). Metacognition, cultural psychological capital and motivational cultural intelligence. *Cross Cultural Management: An International Journal, 21*(4), 386–399.

Zander, L., Mockaitis, A. I., & Butler, C. L. (2012). Leading global teams. *Journal of World Business, 47*(4), 592–603.

Zhang, Y. (2013). Expatriate development for cross-cultural adjustment: Effects of cultural distance and cultural intelligence. *Human Resource Development Review, 12*(2), 177–199.

CHAPTER 9

BUILDING AN ALLIANCE CULTURE

Lessons From Quintiles

Dave Luvison
Ard-Pieter De Man
Jack Pearson

ABSTRACT

Scholars have framed an organization's ability to successfully manage its strategic alliances in terms of the firm's experience, its alliance management practices, and the extent to which these capabilities have been institutionalized. The alliance literature has also hinted that a behavioral construct known as an "alliance culture" or "alliance mindset" is a likewise necessary aspect of alliance capability. Based on an in-depth case study of Quintiles, a global biopharmaceutical services company, we document the evolution of Quintiles' alliance culture, its origins, characteristics, and the factors that affected its development.

Cultural Values in Strategy and Organization, pages 229–258

INTRODUCTION: THE IMPORTANCE OF DEFINING AN ALLIANCE CULTURE

The alliance capability literature indicates that companies having implemented specific alliance management processes are more effective in creating and sustaining alliances (Draulans, de Man, & Volberda, 2003; Heimeriks & Duysters, 2007; Kale, Dyer, & Singh, 2002). It has also noted that, next to formal management processes, behavioral aspects are an element of alliance capability as well (de Man, Duysters, & Saebi, 2010). Alliance cultures or alliance mindsets that are geared towards collaboration ensure that staff members exhibit behavior that promotes alliance performance (Bamford, Gomes-Casseres, & Robinson, 2003; Spekman, Isabella, & MacAvoy, 2000). Even though the conceptual literature has identified alliance culture as a relevant antecedent of alliance success, empirical work researching alliance culture is scarce. Research has focused almost exclusively on the tangible aspects of alliance management, such as the tools and management processes in place.

This study contributes to the alliance literature in two ways. First, it helps to fill the empirical gap in our knowledge of alliance capability by highlighting the relational aspects found in a company's alliance culture through an in-depth case study. This is a step towards further operationalization of the alliance culture concept. Second, this study takes a longitudinal perspective and describes the origin, emergence, and development of alliance culture. Most work in alliance capability is of a cross-sectional nature. An understanding of how alliance cultures are built up over time may ultimately shed light on why performance differences found in cross-sectional research have arisen in the first place. Cultures evolve, rather than change overnight, so it is worthwhile to study the evolution of a company towards new alliance behaviors over time. This may help to clarify the mechanisms that promote and limit the development of an alliance culture.

The core of our investigation is a case study of a successful alliance company, Quintiles, that has gone through several phases in developing its alliance culture. Operating as a clinical development and commercialization services provider to the biopharmaceutical industry, it faces a rapidly changing business environment that, on the one hand, forced it to enter into alliances, but, on the other hand, opened up opportunities to gain a competitive advantage through alliances. More specifically, our case study aims to shed light on four questions regarding the development of an alliance culture:

- Do "hard" structural elements of alliance management develop simultaneously with "soft" cultural elements, or does one precede the other?

- How does alliance experience affect cultural change?
- Is there an order in which alliance culture develops, that is, do some elements develop earlier than others? If so, why?
- What internal and external factors drive changes in alliance culture?

This chapter starts by defining alliance culture in such a way that the concept can be operationalized. Next we present our case study methodology, followed by the case study of Quintiles where the different phases it went through in developing its alliance culture are described. Finally, the discussion section presents the answers to the four questions raised above as well as highlighting elements that are relevant for further research and practice.

THEORETICAL BACKGROUND AND OPERATIONALIZATION OF THE ALLIANCE CULTURE CONSTRUCT

Although there has been minimal study of alliance culture to the extent that it will be examined in this analysis, scholars have discussed discrete components of this construct. These investigations have focused on behavioral dimensions such as trustworthiness (Gulati, 1995; Krishnan, Martin, & Noorderhaven, 2006), bonding (Schreiner, Kale, & Corsten, 2009), and commitment (Das & Kumar, 2009; Kauser & Shaw, 2004) but they have not considered how these dimensions combine and interact in the broader context of an organization's overall culture. Furthermore, when studies have discussed more deep-seated elements such as the values and norms that might underpin a culture (Schein, 1985, 1990) they have largely been conceptual (de Man et al., 2010).

Culture is traditionally viewed as a multidimensional concept (Casey, 1996; Hatch, 1993; Schein, 1985), and we follow Clegg and colleagues (Clegg, Pitsis, Rura-Polley, & Marosszeky, 2002) in defining an alliance culture as a construct having multiple elements. In their in-depth case study of a construction industry alliance, they identify four elements of culture that are related to alliances: values and norms, partner focused processes[1] language, and public displays.

Alliance values shape the norms of a firm's employees for dealing with its partners. Alliance values consequently form the foundation for the relational view of alliances (Dyer & Singh, 1998; Liu, Ghauri, & Sinkovics, 2010), and the resultant norms have been discussed in areas such as marketing relationships (e.g., Heide & John, 1992) and interorganizational contracting (e.g., Cannon, Achrol, & Gundlach, 2000). Scholars have researched a number of relational aspects that are a part of values, such as trustworthiness (Ariño, de la Torre, & Ring, 2005; Das & Teng, 2001b; Gulati, 1995;

Krishnan et al., 2006), commitment (Das & Kumar, 2009; Kauser & Shaw, 2004; Wu & Cavusgil, 2006), flexibility (Das & Teng, 2000; de Ridder & Rusinowska, 2008), and conflict mitigation (Gibler, 2008; Kale, Singh, & Perlmutter, 2000; Robson, Skarmeas, & Spyropoulou, 2006; Yi, Lee, & Dubinsky, 2010). However, it is important to note that these studies have considered the interfirm relationship between partners, not the internal culture of companies. In this case study we are focused on the manner in which alliance values are manifest within firms.

Partner focus, a second element of alliance culture, describes the extent to which intra-organizational processes facilitate coordination. Examples of these can include communication and decision making processes that simplify interaction with a partner. There has been a substantial amount of research into the various processes that make up this element since they can lower the coordination cost of alliances (Gulati & Singh, 1998). For example, the literature investigating the role of a firm's alliance management function has outlined a number of related processes (Ethiraj, Kale, Krishnan, & Singh, 2005; Kale, Dyer, & Singh, 2001; Kale et al., 2002; Schreiner et al., 2009).

Language and public displays make up the remaining elements of alliance culture. Language reflects the stories and terminology surrounding alliances that occur in the organization. From a cultural standpoint an organization's consistent alliance vocabulary, frequency of communication about partners, and model behaviors portrayed through alliance success stories all serve to reinforce desired behaviors (Boyce, 1996) and assist the process of organizational change (Casey, 1996) that can promote a stronger alliance culture. Public displays represent the symbols and artifacts associated with alliances and hence constitute the visible components of the firm's alliance culture. Therefore, the presence of alliance logos and trademarks signal that alliances are an important activity for the firm. Such symbols have long been recognized as an important manifestation of organizational culture (Casey, 1996; Galaskiewicz, 1985; Schein, 1990).

As noted above, an organization's alliance culture represents the synthesis of a number of areas of alliance behaviors. However, it is important to note that the value of understanding, and ultimately measuring, a firm's alliance culture comes from the belief that it plays a significant role in determining the strategic choices that a firm makes in its alliances, the manner in which it adapts to the requirements for interfirm coordination and the efforts it makes to encourage the appropriate levels of collaborative behaviors across its organization. In the following section we describe the methodology used to investigate the emergence and manifestations of alliance culture at Quintiles.

OVERVIEW OF THE RESEARCH SETTING AND METHODOLOGY

As was noted above, there has been minimal empirical research into the makeup of an organization's alliance culture. For that reason this analysis has been conducted as a single case study. Single case studies are considered appropriate when seeking to answer questions of "why" and "how," when it is necessary to observe an otherwise inaccessible phenomenon, and when we wish to observe changes over time (Yin, 2003). Moreover, case studies permit the researcher to understand the dynamics that occur within individual settings (Eisenhardt, 1989).

Quintiles was chosen as the subject of this case study because it offered a number of important attributes by which to analyze alliance culture. First of all, the company operates in the pharmaceutical industry, which features a high level of alliance intensity (Ahn, Meeks, Davenport, & Bednarek, 2009). As such Quintiles has been operating in a dynamic alliance environment. Second, Quintiles has been forming alliances for a number of years and has, over that time, entered into a variety of research and marketing relationships. This has served to increase the range of market challenges it has had to understand and address. Hence, we may expect its alliance culture to have evolved through various parts of the organization. Third, as the company's alliance experience has increased it has similarly evolved the manner in which it administers its relationships. Consequently, the company has experimented with a number of structural and procedural approaches to manage its alliances and change its partner focus. Finally, Quintiles' rationale for and approach to alliances has also evolved over time. With that has come some notoriety for its proficiency: the company received an award from the Association of Strategic Alliance Professionals for excellence in alliance management, and one of its alliances was profiled in the *Harvard Business Review* (Kaplan, Norton, & Rugelsjoen, 2010). As a result, the company provides the opportunity to assess how changes in strategy and culture have co-evolved.

Data Collection and Analysis

Data was collected for this case study using two primary sources. First of all interviews were conducted with eight members of Quintiles' top management team. In addition, we interviewed an executive from one of the company's larger alliances to gain an understanding how its partners viewed the company's efforts. These interviews were semi-structured, allowing for consistency across the executives interviewed while at the same time providing the opportunity to investigate new, relevant areas when they were raised during these discussions. The interviews were transcribed and subsequently coded to enable insights to be summarized and organized for interpretation (Miles & Huberman, 1994). Second, archival data consisting of company documents and magazine articles about Quintiles' were reviewed. (Some of this archival information was provided by two of the authors, based on consulting or employee experience with the company.) Finally, our analyses were provided to the company in order for them to check facts for accuracy.

Since an objective of this study was to understand how Quintiles' alliance culture evolved over time, the data collected were used to assemble a qualitative event history. As suggested above, case studies are a valuable tool for understanding the influence of events on subsequent actions of the firm (Yin, 2003). For this study we compared chronological events with the behavioral outcomes that produced or intensified specific elements of alliance culture. Consequently, we were able to assess the evolution of Quintiles' alliance culture over time and as it was influenced by critical events

CASE STUDY OF THE DEVELOPMENT OF ALLIANCE CULTURE AT QUINTILES

Quintiles is a fully integrated biopharmaceutical services company offering clinical, commercial, consulting, and capital solutions. It operates in 60 countries with a staff of approximately 22,000 employees. The company's primary areas of operation are contract research (CRO) and contract sales (CSO) services that facilitate the development and delivery of therapeutic products. Quintiles has been associated with bringing each of the top 30 best-selling drugs to market (Anonymous, n.d.b) and in both 2009 and 2010 was named "Contract Research Organization of the Year" by the SCRIP Awards (Anonymous, 2009, 2010). Based on independent surveys of the biopharma industry, the company has been identified as one of the most favored research organizations, being ranked number one across a range of service, and reputation attributes ranging from breadth of service through to therapeutic expertise (Anonymous, n.d.a). Information about the company is summarized in Table 9.1.

Founded in January 1974 by Dennis Gillings, a professor at the University of North Carolina, the organization provided statistical and data management consulting for pharmaceutical clients until its incorporation in 1982. In April of 1994 it completed an initial public offering of its stock and thereafter expanded through a combination of organic growth and acquisitions. It operated as a public company until September 2003, at which time it converted back to a private company, remaining so since that time.

TABLE 9.1 Details About Quintiles

Net Revenue (2009)	$3.0 billion (Quintiles is a private company; revenues are approximate)
Number of Employees	22,000
Geographic Locations	60 countries
Operating Groups:	
Clinical Development Services	Aimed at regulatory approval and post-launch research about product safety and value.
Commercial Solutions	Help customers identify optimal value of drug/biologic products, launch and promote treatments, and demonstrate value over time by engaging with patients and driving adherence.
Consulting	Help customers maximize potential and minimize risk from discovery through development and commercialization.
Capital Solutions	Help customers achieve strategic goals through custom-tailored risk-based alliances that address their complex strategic and financial needs.

Quintiles has been involved in various partnership activities since the late 1980s. The rest of this section discusses the evolution of these relationships, breaking them into five time periods characterizing steps in the evolution of the organization's alliance culture. The first period discusses early relationships occurring from the late 1980s through the late 1990s. The second covers the late 1990s through 2000 as alliances developed into a formal business model. The third period, occurring from 2001 through the middle of the first decade of the 21st century, discusses alliances with Solvay Pharmaceuticals and Eli Lilly and Company that were instrumental in defining the company's alliance strategy, while the fourth is characterized by the company's efforts to formalize its alliance management focus and function. The final phase covers 2008 through the present, reflecting Quintiles' efforts to expand its alliance culture into the broader organization.

Phase 1: Early Strategic Relationships

Quintiles began forming alliance-like relationships in the mid-1980s. Since a major strategic focus of the company during this period was growth through acquisition, alliance activity was minimal, however. These early partnerships initially focused on the execution of clinical trials[2] for pharmaceutical companies. They later expanded to include commercial relationships aimed at co-marketing new products using their commercial operation Innovex Ltd., a U.K-based contract pharma company specialized in delivering sales and marketing services that was acquired in 1996. In addition, the organization began to focus on longer-term client relationships, which caused it to begin to place individuals in account management roles.

These early partnerships provided formative lessons for Quintiles, such as the importance of interfirm relationship building, and they became the stimulus for Quintiles to create a number of functional procedures and roles that facilitated this. The program manager position was instituted to oversee the actions of multiple project managers associated with a given client or program initiative. Such functionality was subsequently formalized as the program management and planning (PM&P) group. Rather than merely provide improved coordination, PM&P allowed Quintiles to better facilitate interaction across multiple internal groups and discrete projects with the partner. Similarly, the position of global account executive was created to formally manage key client accounts so that they were treated as relationships rather than transactions. Both roles were formed as a result of Quintiles' recognition that partnerships depended upon the ability of Quintiles to foster effective relationships through improved coordination and communication processes. In so doing, they allowed the company to cut red tape, improve the level of integration with the partner companies and increase the speediness of its response to the partner.

Phase 2: Alliances as a Formal Business Strategy

Between the late 1990s and 2000, alliances had evolved to become an important component of Quintiles' business model. Market conditions had changed such that the pharmaceutical industry was increasingly looking to smaller, biotechnology companies to provide avenues for innovative therapeutic products. While this provided expanded opportunity for these biotechs, it also meant that they needed financial capital to enable them to ramp up their development efforts more quickly. Quintiles entered this field through a program of financial investment alliances with these biotech companies. Under this model, Quintiles provided investment capital to these companies to support the development of their prospective therapies. These alliances were termed "at risk" alliances by the company since they involved equity investment which would be lost if the biotech companies foundered. Because Quintiles' interests at this stage were primarily financial, there was minimal attention paid to developing strong relationships; the company's focus was on looking after these relationships as investments.

However, it soon became evident that these partnerships also provided an opportunity to incorporate Quintiles' service offerings into these alliances. Thus, Quintiles began to also structure contract research or clinical trial management services into its agreements. The company began to note that its approach to working with these alliances needed to go beyond contractual, financial arrangements. It was at this point that management recognized that a different manner of operating relationship was necessary. In the words of one executive:

> The real tipping point was when the second or third true deal didn't successfully align the services with the investment. Operationally these relationships were failing and the services group was criticized for it. On the other hand, they were hitting their financial returns. However, what really occurred was the disconnect between the contract and what was required for the business... We realized that we needed to also offer services and this caused us to work toward a position that builds the relationship as well as ways of navigating the clinical and commercial process. We found we needed to start providing "consultative oversight."

Such involvement hence raised the importance that Quintiles began to place on these partners and induced it to find better ways of sharing information with the partner and solving problems jointly.

To address these concerns Quintiles began to designate specialized individuals within its organization to oversee these relationships. Initially these individuals operated as part of what was named the PharmaBio Group, but they were subsequently incorporated into the company's corporate development organization.

Phase 3: Key Alliances Help Define the Alliance Model

In 2001 Quintiles entered into an alliance relationship with Solvay Pharmaceutical, a Belgian company specializing in cardiovascular, neuroscience and gastroenterology (Solvay was later acquired by Abbot in 2009). Under the initial agreement the companies formed a number of joint clinical teams to manage clinical trial and procurement processes and align procedures. While Quintiles offered its services to Solvay for reduced fees, the alliance was still fundamentally operating as a fee-for-service relationship. However, in 2006 it was decided that the two companies would enhance their relationship to one involving mutually shared risk and gains. Under this new relationship, Quintiles took on a greater role in developing Solvay's products by contributing to development costs; both companies stood to gain from improvements in productivity, efficiency, and development speed. In return for Quintiles' investment Solvay agreed to accept less control over projects (Kaplan et al., 2010).

A second defining alliance began in 2002 between Quintiles and Eli Lilly and Company. This alliance was formed to expand the commercial push of Lilly's antidepressant and pain reliever product Cymbalta. Rather than operate merely under a CSO outsourcing agreement, Quintiles and Lilly structured an alliance based on shared risk and shared return principles similar to those of the Solvay relationship. For Cymbalta, Quintiles coordinated data management services and a variety of advisory tasks during the preapproval program, invested in marketing programs and provided 500 sales representatives to supplement the Lilly sales force. In total, Quintiles' capital commitment to Cymbalta's commercialization was more than $400 million by 2007. In return for this financial commitment Quintiles would receive royalties based on Lilly's net U.S. sales of Cymbalta (Perkins, 2007).

Both alliances increased Quintiles' level of obligation and commitment beyond that of its traditional service business. In so doing, it reinforced the importance of managing the alliance as an ongoing relationship since financial success was contingent on long-term program success. Because Quintiles elected to share risk as well as returns in these two alliances, it marked the emergence of values that emphasized mutuality, solidarity and trustworthy behavior. Additionally, it called upon both companies in the alliance to share a similar strategic outlook since ultimate returns were tied to the successful completion of joint goals. One of Quintiles' partners discussed this value change in these terms:

> There is a trust model in the alliance with Quintiles. This makes it possible to experiment with new models. The behavior of people is important; they should not try to transfer risk to another and they should not make profit at the expense of the partner.

Although Quintiles had already been using designated alliance managers to oversee key at risk relationships, these two alliances highlighted the importance of creating a more formalized alliance management function within the company which served to increase Quintiles' partner focus. As one executive phrased it:

> As a result of this investment, there was a concern whether project managers on the ground could manage the investment and implement right governance, etc., and the answer was "No" in that they couldn't necessarily deliver the alliance management process. The alliance management group was created to quarterback those investments... Alliance management comes with skills, background and a code of conduct to form the relationship and governance vehicle with customers. Clearly they see the end goal better than "tightening the screws" as a project manager would tend to see it.

The Cymbalta relationship created an opportunity for Quintiles to learn from many of the alliance management practices that Eli Lilly had previously developed. Moreover, the importance of these two relationships meant that there was increased executive management involvement in these alliances, and the alliance management group was now briefing the top management team quarterly of these and other key partnerships. Hence, the increase in frequency of communication about alliances began to stimulate increased mention of specific alliance related stories. Similarly, the operationalization of partner relationships was expanded at Quintiles, such that relationships were now being built with partners at multiple levels in each organization. This created new requirements for communication, decision making and trust-building across Quintiles' organization. One Quintiles executive involved with the Cymbalta relationship described this dynamic in the following way:

> You start to get calls back from your partner's CEO, senior management, or other groups that you wouldn't normally get. Having such a large sales force deployed in support of Cymbalta's launch helped, but Lilly was hearing such good things about the alliance that many people at Lilly wanted to talk about how they could work with Quintiles. Instead of being an afterthought Quintiles became the first choice for additional business.

Phase 4: Raising Alliances to a Professional Discipline

The Solvay and Lilly alliances, as well as a number of other relationships that Quintiles formed between 2001 and 2007, highlighted the need to improve the level of alliance management capability in the company. During this period a number of initiatives were undertaken by the alliance management group to further develop its skills, procedures, and tools. Although the Quintiles alliance managers were experienced senior level managers with extensive pharmaceutical industry expertise, the company created a 2-year MBA-style credentialing program designed to ensure consistent, core alliance management practices across all the members of the group. This was augmented by a mentoring program in which new members of the group were paired with experienced alliance managers to ensure effective knowledge transfer (Love, 2007). Additionally, the group formulated a number of tools designed to foster improved relationships across and within organizational boundaries, such as an alliance team charter. It adapted the balanced scorecard model to ensure that the governance structure in its alliances encompassed both operational and relational elements so that emerging relational and cultural issues were addressed in a proactive manner. All of these initiatives served to improve the level of integration with partners and increase responsiveness. The group's efforts were being recognized outside of the organization as well. In 2006 Quintiles won an award from the Association of Strategic Alliance Professionals in recognition of its efforts to develop its alliance capability.

Quintiles signaled its growing commitment to alliances in 2006 with the launch of NovaQuest. This represented an expansion of Quintiles' strategic partnering group (i.e., the PharmaBio group) in order for it to better support co-development and co-promotion alliances. NovaQuest, supported by a non-exclusive alliance with TPG-Axon Capital, provided a more comprehensive platform for Quintiles to structure relationships since it could now offer expanded financial resources in conjunction with its service and alliance management expertise. The relationship with the investment fund now permitted Quintiles to invest in large partnerships (Dubin, 2007).

The alliance management function was incorporated into NovaQuest, permitting Quintiles to offer a consistent approach to managing its relationships. A dedicated alliance manager was assigned to each NovaQuest relationship; that manager was to remain with the relationship over its entire lifecycle. The consistent presence of this individual provided for a continued relationship and augmented the governance structure that oversaw administration of clear goals, responsibilities and performance metrics. It should be noted that the alliance management group's presence highlighted the importance of having a strong set of relational criteria at work in these alliances. However, it also pointed out a potential issue, namely that there was a gap in relational capability between the alliance managers and the broader population of Quintiles employees. As one executive noted, "It's been difficult to transition both the internal and external (i.e., customer) elements over to our partnering mentality." Although the company had developed effective routines to foster strong relationships, it had not yet managed to transfer such behaviors throughout the organization.

Phase 5: Expansion of the Alliance Management Culture

A number of conditions occurring since NovaQuest was formed in 2006 have combined to stimulate Quintiles to make alliance relationship building more of an organization-wide behavior. Most notably, the pharmaceutical industry is undergoing changes that are calling upon CRO/CSOs such as Quintiles to redefine their role. A number of major pharmaceutical companies are facing the prospect of major products falling off patent protection within the next few years. This is occurring against the backdrop of escalating drug development costs and increased risks of developing successful new therapies: For every 5,000 compounds discovered only one reaches the market and fewer than a third of those recoup their research and development costs (Saftlas, 2008). Consequently, these companies need to improve innovation and operational efficiency.

Quintiles' executives maintain that responsive service companies committed to a philosophy of partnerships among equals will provide the means for pharmaceutical companies to better meet those objectives, as is shown in the following statement:

> In our business you can't get away from the risks of the science, but our challenge is to make that the only thing that can possibly cause an alliance to fail. In fact, we want to get to those failure points sooner. Unfortunately, all too often failure comes from management and governance breakdowns. That's why I'm a believer that professional partnering is a value creator for the organization; it can eliminate those non-science based things that are a risk to success. It also allows firms to draw on their unique strengths more effectively than is the case of acquisitions, which are plagued by integration issues.

As a result, there has been an increased appreciation within Quintiles for the potential offered by a more relational model. For example, business conducted with Eli Lilly increased 25 times from where it was before the Cymbalta relationship, partially due to the new opportunities that emerged as a result of the relationship. As one executive indicated: "It went from a customer/vendor relationship to a non-procurement based relationship." However, becoming more of an equal partner for service oriented companies presents a number of difficulties, most notably getting away from falling into the traditional role of providing services requested by the client rather than striving for more say in the process. One executive phrased it this way:

> Traditionally a pharma company incubates an idea for a protocol for 9-12 months, puts out an RFP (Request for Proposal) and requests a turnaround in a week to 10 days. This puts the CRO in a very awkward position and reflects a poor partnership dynamic. Now we incubate a joint team six months before, even to the point of working through the specifications with them to create a plan...We have to remind our employees to make recommendations rather than offer alternatives that the client can select... It takes a huge cultural shift to act like a customer, which you do when you are more aligned with them.

Although Quintiles has committed itself to this newer model, there are still a number of challenges. One Quintiles executive reflected on this challenge by noting that proper alliance management is "a cultural requirement of partnerships" and that "there is an awareness at senior levels of its importance, but it still needs to trickle down to the rest of the company." Figure 9.1 is evidence of such unevenness across the company. In 2010 Quintiles took part in an independent study that investigated the level of alliance culture across its internal departments. The figure points out that there are small variances across the various departments in terms of partner focus, but larger differences in the area of language and public displays. Individuals in policy-setting positions tended to have a higher overall culture than did those in customer and product/service focused groups. Additionally, the absolute scores suggest that there is less visibility of alliances (i.e., public displays) in relation to language, norms, or partner focus. This

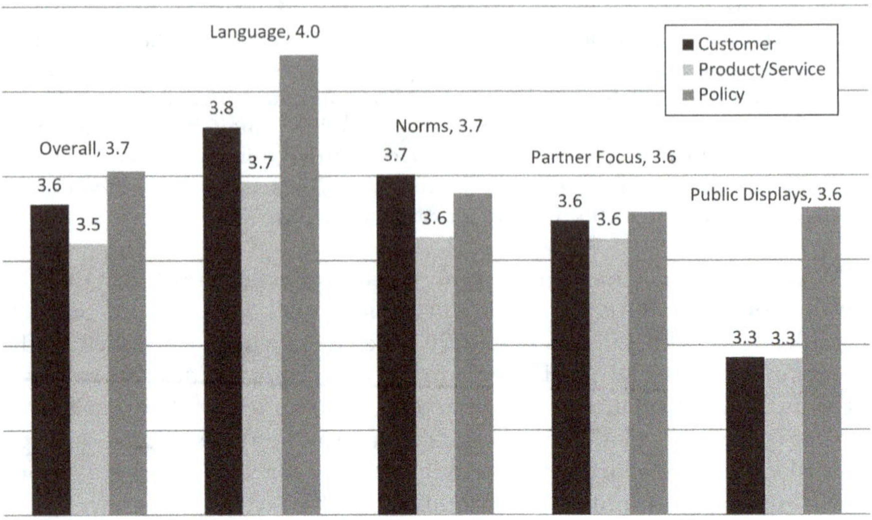

Figure 9.1 Comparison of alliance culture categories across departments.

study provided information for Quintiles' management to consider where to apply culture-enhancing efforts.

While still in their initial stages, efforts to "trickle down" this alliance mindset have consisted of a number of approaches. One aspect of this cultural change involves extending the role of Quintiles' alliance management group to facilitate what one interviewee termed the "cultural adoption of alliance practices." For example, the group implemented a core-agent model whereby the centralized "core" of alliance management expertise and tools residing in the alliance management group is disseminated to designated "agents" operating in business units who are then responsible for learning and applying these resources within their groups. This not only increases the frequency and importance of discussions on alliance management, but it also improves alliance management visibility and branding across the company. Similarly, there has been more deliberate use of language and symbolic actions to reinforce this change. One is the effort to drop the "billable/non-billable" categorization used for service oriented employees. As one executive explained:

> As you know, for a service business this is the traditional measure of the state of the business and the key motivator for how services firms are organized. Now we're realizing that we need people to do more in the way of alliance management and that this may not be billable in the traditional sense. Similarly, a large part of our budget is aimed at developing our professional partnering capabilities throughout the organization.

Most significantly, Quintiles has revised its positioning to emphasize its belief in the importance of partnering, which in turn raises the importance of strong alliance values. In 2010 the NovaQuest brand was discontinued even though the functions it provided continue to exist. Not only was this a symbolic act, but it was also done to address the perception that an alliance mindset should operate only in specific sectors of the company. As one executive framed it: "Our marketing approach is now to 'institutionalize partnerships' and the first thing we now talk about is our alliance management framework. This is very much a direction of the company; our CEO holds that partnering is our way forward."

DISCUSSION

Table 9.2 summarizes the evolution of the various elements of Quintiles' alliance culture across the five time periods identified above. This table shows that in the first phase the company initially tended to develop the partner focused aspects of its culture that would enable it to better achieve its alliance objectives. This cultural area was expanded over subsequent phases through the formation of an alliance management function, development of standardized tools and procedures, and, ultimately, implementation of a model by which these processes might be utilized by the rest of the organization. Public displays tended to appear in the second phase, as did early recognition that values had to change from short term financial to longer-term relational success. By the third phase greater use of alliance related language emerged across the company and the fee-for-services model began to change toward one based on risk-sharing values. As Quintiles entered the fourth and fifth phases both public displays and language became more prominent through the creation of NovaQuest and greater promotion of its alliance capability. Similarly, alliance values continued to become more critical as the organization looked to expand the behavioral aspects of alliance management throughout the organization.

As was indicated above, there were four research questions that we set out to investigate through this case study. In the following sections we consider how Quintiles' evolution informs those points, beginning with the question of whether alliance culture develops in conjunction with the structural aspects of alliance management.

Simultaneity of Structural and Cultural Elements

The details of this case suggest that Quintiles first created "hard" structural elements for alliance management in order to better coordinate and

TABLE 9.2 Summary of Alliance Culture Development by Phase

	Early Relationships	Formal Business	Alliances Define Model	Alliances as Professional Discipline	Expansion of Alliance Management Culture
Alliance Language			• Executive briefings create opportunity for increased dialogue about alliances within Quintiles • Increased executive-to-executive meetings increase frequency and importance of alliance language	• Credentialing program creates standardized language around alliances • NovaQuest launch causes partnering concepts to be more widely discussed across the organization	• Term "deals" now replaced with "relationships" • "Billable/non-billable" terminology deemphasized
Alliance Values		• Alliance model adapts to biotech industry requirements • Initially viewed as financial transactions, alliances now seen as requiring an operational component that "goes beyond the contract"	• Shared risk/return focus emerges	• NovaQuest creates broader partnering philosophy within the firm	• Partnering seen as the appropriate industry model • Management expresses commitment to expansion of partnering capabilities throughout the organization

(continued)

TABLE 9.2 Summary of Alliance Culture Development by Phase (continued)

	Early Relationships	Formal Business	Alliances Define Model	Alliances as Professional Discipline	Expansion of Alliance Management Culture
Public Displays		• Creation of partnering identity through formation of PharmaBio group	• Alliance Management Group presents quarterly executive briefings, raising the visibility of alliances to senior management and within organization	• Implemented credentialing program for alliance managers • Recognized with ASAP award and print articles • NovaQuest launch heightens partnering identity	• Core-agent model raises identity of alliance management throughout organization
Partner Focus	• Developed formal project management processes • Organization structure begins to adapt to relational requirements	• Developed processes to oversee "at risk" alliances	• Formed Alliance Management Group	• Standardized tools and procedures used by Alliance Management Group	• Core-agent model implemented to disseminate Alliance Management Group's procedures

Source: "Alliance Culture at Quintiles Transnational," Internal report prepared by Dave Luvison and Ard-Pieter de Man.

manage its relationships before it developed the "soft" behavioral attributes that formed its culture. For example, operational demands early in the company's partnering efforts fostered the need for improved relationship management processes; these subsequently evolved into a more comprehensive partner focus. The creation of the program management and planning group was intended to provide a better means of coordination across multiple projects with a customer. Similarly, Quintiles created the global account executive position to better manage the needs of large customers. Finally, the company assigned managers to its "at risk" alliances in order to oversee Quintiles' financial interests. Although these functions clearly met Quintiles' objective to better manage these alliances, it was quickly evident that a stronger behavioral emphasis was necessary to enable these relationships to be more open, better integrated, and less bureaucratic. As a result, the roles of functions such as alliance management were expanded.

Similarly, as its alliances became more important to the company, quarterly executive reporting was instituted. However, with the increase in reporting came the recognition of the need for higher levels of involvement by senior leadership. This was instrumental in opening channels of communication across multiple hierarchical levels at both Quintiles and the partners. As a result, the increased frequency and importance of communication helped enhance the language aspect of its alliance culture. Similarly, the decision to share alliance management tools and procedures across the company led to an expanded role for the alliance management group that had two effects. First, it further increased the use of alliance language across the company. Second, the designation of the alliance management group as a center of relationship knowledge resulted in the development of public displays that enhanced the visibility and branding of that group.

Quintiles' strategic decision to differentiate itself from competing CRO/CSOs by pushing toward a shared risk/return partnering model led it to develop and implement new types of alliance relationships and ultimately create its NovaQuest unit. These decisions created new requirements for governance, investment, and consultative selling procedures. As these were implemented it was recognized that changes in Quintiles' value system had to occur so that members across the company operated more proactively, exhibited greater flexibility, and worked toward long-term relationships. One executive phrased it as follows: "Alliance management (the group) has worked to respond to the need to add value, but more recognition is needed that we don't necessarily need an alliance management professional so much as operational experts who understand alliance management."

The trend of events at Quintiles suggests that its alliance culture developed in response to structural elements of alliances rather than vice versa. However, it should be noted that cultural growth often occurred relatively quickly after structural aspects were created. For example, the expanded incidence of alliance communication and codification of alliance language across the company followed directly on the heels of the expanded executive briefings. Similarly, the evolution of some aspects of the partner focus dimension, such as cutting red tape and more openly sharing information and recommendations, followed from the implementation and expansion of the various relationship management roles. Based on the findings of this case it appears evident that a firm's alliance culture tends to develop because of the structural components it puts in place to address business requirements. This appears consistent with extant studies finding that changes in processes influence culture changes (e.g., Casey, 1996; Clegg et al., 2002).

On a broader level, these influence effects suggest that various forms of experience play a key role in the development of a firm's alliance culture. This leads to a discussion of our second research question: the effect of experience on alliance culture formation.

The Effect of Experience on Alliance Culture Development

Many scholars have studied the role of prior experience on alliance performance, though the findings have been mixed. One stream of research (e.g., Anand & Khanna, 2000) has found a direct relationship between experience and alliance success. A second stream has found that experience gained with a particular partner can lead to future success with that partner, but that general experience does not appear to affect performance of a firm's alliances (e.g., Gulati, Lavie, & Singh, 2009). While the various findings of these streams fail to show that all experience leads to increased performance in all cases, the implication of these findings is that experience does have an effect on alliance behaviors and relationship quality (Ariño & de la Torre, 1998). We maintain that this influence of experience on behaviors also results in changes in alliance culture.

In the Quintiles case study, we can take a fine-grained look at the role of alliance experience in developing culture. Specifically, we see that experience appears to stimulate the development of different cultural elements depending upon its entry point and form. As was noted above, the inability to create long term alliances led to the formation of an alliance management group which subsequently became a center of excellence for the company as the number of organizational relationships expanded. Consequently, Quintiles' behavioral response to its experience was to form more partner-conducive processes that enabled it to more consistently coordinate with its partners. However, we see other experiences that acted on different cultural dimensions and which produced different sets of behaviors.

Most notably, the experience gained from dealing with the Pharma-Bio alliances initially and the Solvay and Lilly relationships down the road caused Quintiles to evolve from an operationally oriented, fee-for-service approach to a strategically oriented, shared risk approach in its alliances. While this approach could better differentiate it from its competitors, it would also require the company to foster a more behaviorally oriented set of alliance values. It was the experiences demonstrating the potential for shared opportunities that led to a change in approach that predicated the need to also address its alliance value system. It appears that the specific nature of a firm's experience will dictate which cultural dimension is affected and that the evolution of individual cultural dimensions is not necessarily correlated with one another. This is an interesting finding; alliance experience has always been thought of in quantitative terms whereas our findings indicate that the qualitative aspect may matter as well. In other words, the type of partner or partnership that creates the experience is relevant.

It therefore becomes evident from this case that the effects of experience tend to be transferred through each of the alliance culture dimensions in a different manner and at different times. This observation leads us to consider our third research question, namely whether behaviors representing alliance culture occur in a predictable sequence.

Sequence of Alliance Culture Development

There has been minimal inquiry into the sequence of conditions that cause an organization's alliance culture to evolve. While the literature investigating the alliance management function has discussed the importance of that function in transferring learning through the organization (e.g., Kale & Singh, 2007), there has been no consideration of how the various categories of culture interact and influence one another. However, it is possible to build off the extant literature on culture. For instance, behavioral scholars have found that the use of language and symbols will influence the development of an organization's culture (e.g., Casey, 1996).

Taking this as a starting point, this case study highlights three findings that add to our understanding of alliance culture development. The first finding is that partner focus appears to be the initial element of alliance culture to emerge. This is due to the need to develop processes that allow the firm to adapt to alliance counterparts. As has been discussed above, Quintiles progressively recognized that it had to change its way of operating to produce long-term business with its partners. Such partner focus was formalized in the tools and procedures developed and administered by the alliance management group, but over time these processes were shared throughout the organization.

Second, the emergence of alliance language and public displays appears to follow the formation of partner focus. At Quintiles, visibility for alliances began to grow with the naming of the alliance centric PharmaBio group, the identification of the alliance management function and the initiation of formal, quarterly reviews for senior management. This became even more overt through the formation of its NovaQuest group and validation of its alliance capability internally through its credentialing initiative. This ultimately led to the promotion of its alliances in industry trade articles and recognition of excellence by the Association of Strategic Alliance Professionals. It is important to note that such use of language and symbols directly followed from Quintiles' development of its alliance management processes. In fact, without the ability to effectively manage its relationships due to improved partner focus it would not have been able to successfully raise its level of visibility.

This finding appears to differ from that of other studies (e.g., Casey, 1996), which suggest language and symbols tend to be the starting point for the development of other cultural elements. While we accept that the emergence of language and public displays precede the formation of deeper-level values, as discussed below, we suggest that the procedural changes that alliances require of a firm appear to be the initiating mechanism of cultural development. A number of scholars have commented on the complexity of alliances as manifest by failure rates as high as 70% (Royer & Simons, 2009) as well as hurdles posed by the challenges inherent in interfirm coordination and trust building (Krishnan et al., 2006; Schreiner et al., 2009). Based on this case study it appears that it will be difficult to create positive language and displays around alliances until the firm has seen that they can be effectively managed.

The third finding in the area of the sequencing of alliance culture is that alliance values are likely to be the last element to evolve within the firm. This is not surprising since values are typically viewed as a deeper level of organizational culture that is more difficult to affect (Schein, 1985, 1990). Nevertheless, the details of this case study suggest that the development of process capability alone may not necessarily encourage the formation of alliance values. Instead, Quintiles' refinement of its alliance value system appears to have been most influenced by the need to adapt to market changes. We contend that had Quintiles continued to approach its alliances as a traditional CRO/CSO it would have been less likely to push so aggressively to evolve its alliance values. The level of organizational commitment to this culture change is predicated by the belief that Quintiles must adopt a different business model to sustain its competitive advantage. As one executive notes:

> Perhaps the biggest change is the mindset of (pharma) customers as partners. Quintiles has been successful in the past by being responsive to what the cus-

> tomer asks, but recently we have realized that pharma firms need more. To that extent Quintiles has been a victim of its prior success by being somewhat locked into traditional roles. However, we are trying to reposition ourselves as a partner that can help pharmas manage their risk and reduce their variability. It's a tough sale, but the traditional pharma-CRO model is not viable in the future.

While it's clear that Quintiles has used language and public displays to help drive the conversion of alliance values, it does not appear that in and of themselves they would have encouraged the change in alliance values as quickly without such external pressure.

This case study suggests that alliance culture tends to form in the organization through a process that starts with the development of procedures that create partner focus, and that once these have been judged to be effective the categories of alliance language and public displays become more developed. Alliance values appear to be the last dimension to change, though the speed of such change is likely to be influenced by the urgency of strategic adaptation the firm faces. This last point transitions us to a discussion of the final research question: What internal and external factors are most likely to drive changes in alliance culture?

Factors Driving Changes in Alliance Culture

As has already been noted above, the evolution of Quintiles' alliance culture has been influenced by both internal and external conditions. Partner demands for better relational management caused Quintiles to work to rethink its partner focus. Alliances are subject to high coordination costs since tasks must be decomposed in a manner to allow them to be allocated and managed by multiple parties (Gulati & Singh, 1998). Firms that do not participate in alliances will have no need to exert the effort necessary to manage such activities. As the Quintiles case demonstrates, many of the company's functions (e.g., PM&P, Global Account Executives, the alliance management group) arose from the need to provide a higher level of partner-friendliness. Based on the manner in which Quintiles progressively recognized the relational requirements of alliances, these functions developed as a response to coordination challenges posed by the alliances. Hence, the maturation of the organization's partner focus occurred because Quintiles began to adapt its routines and procedures to external conditions created by its alliances.

Quintiles' development in the area of alliance values was similarly caused by external conditions. The rising cost of pharmaceutical drug development, coupled with the increasing difficulty in synthesizing efficacious compounds (Saftlas, 2008) created the need for different economic models, which in turn has led to the increasing importance of alliances in the industry. As pharma companies look to reduce their risk, it has become evident that service providers such as Quintiles needed to alter their business models. However, making the change from a fee-for-service provider to an equal partner has required Quintiles, as well as its partners, to embrace a different set of values. One Quintiles executive narrated a situation in which he startled his partner when he asked for their future plans in a given product area. The partner at first declined to provide this information, indicating that this wasn't something that they shared with other companies. However, the Quintiles executive made the case that their alliance was a partnership rather than a vendor relationship and that he needed to ensure that all parties' interests were going to be met in the future. The partner subsequently understood this difference and complied with the request. Had it been operating in accordance with its traditional values, Quintiles personnel would not have felt comfortable taking this tack.

Internal conditions, on the other hand, appear to have been instrumental in the development of Quintiles, language and public display cultural dimensions. As the frequency of communication associated with alliances increased, it served to enhance the importance of creating a stronger identity for alliance management in general and the alliance management group in particular. Efforts to create the recognition that alliance management is a professional discipline provided the symbols that improved its visibility within the company. Most recently, the decision to retire terms such as "billable/non-billable" have helped send the internal message that behaviors need to change to become more relationship based. Of course, the use of language and symbols has also augmented Quintiles' external alliance branding efforts; being able to claim a high level of alliance proficiency satisfies an important criterion of potential alliance partners (Futrell, Slugay, & Stephens, 2001). However, the details of this case suggest that internal factors have largely driven the development of alliance language and public displays at Quintiles.

Therefore, this case suggests that development of cultural dimensions in the areas of partner focus and alliance values is most directly influenced by external conditions, whereas the development of cultural dimensions of language and public displays is more subject to internal factors, save where it might be used to promote future alliances.

Opportunities for Future Research

Our case study identifies some new avenues for research. A first set of questions pertains to alliance culture in relation to the structural elements of alliance capability. A relevant question is how structural and cultural elements interact. The findings of this case study, showing that they do affect each other, need to be tested empirically on a larger scale. This may also help to answer the question whether alliance culture explains more of the variance in alliance performance between companies than structural elements of alliance management. In addition the question whether culture and structure are complementary (which our case study seems to indicate) or whether they are substitutes awaits further large-scale empirical testing. Finally, the sequencing in which cultural categories develop requires further empirical validation. Whether the sequence found in Quintiles is representative of what happens in other companies needs to be explored. The answers to these questions call for cross-sectional research as well as further longitudinal case studies.

A second set of research implications relates to possible industry differences. Quintiles operates in a dynamic industry that partners extensively. While there are other industries that feature similar levels of alliance intensity, such as high technology, there are also industries for which partnering is less prominent (Hagedoorn, 1993). It is important to investigate a broad cross-section of industries in order to determine whether the patterns observed in this case operate independently of sector differences. The drivers behind alliance formation may differ across industries leading companies to emphasize other elements of alliance culture. For example, the specific problems of the pharmaceutical industry do not exist in other industries. Client demand may therefore be less important as a driver for building an alliance culture. Additionally, in Quintiles the changes in the structure of their alliance management were rapid and frequent due to the fast changing business environment in which the company operates. This may influence the sequencing of alliance culture development. In a slow moving industry the development of norms and values may run more parallel with developing the other three categories of alliance culture.

Next, it is interesting to research the implications of alliance culture on other elements of alliance behavior. It is likely that as a firm's alliance culture—and particularly its level of alliance values—strengthens, it may engage differently in various aspects of negotiation and governance (Barney & Hansen, 1994). Companies with a well-developed alliance culture may be more inclined to avoid zero sum bargaining and to instead emphasize increasing value to both partners when they negotiate alliance deals. There may also be an effect on the speed of negotiations, with negotiations involving more aspects of relationship building. In addition, companies with a high level of alliance culture may opt for governance models with lower levels of control (Das & Teng, 2001a), specifically when their counterpart has a well-developed alliance culture as well. In short, alliance culture may have an effect on alliance behavior in a number of different ways that are worth exploring.

The interviews with Quintiles management suggest that as its culture improved its performance did likewise. Whether the relationship between alliance culture and alliance success is that straightforward needs to be established in large scale research. Mediating and moderating relationships are worth exploring here. For example, alliance culture may be a moderator between alliance experience and alliance success. Experience may lead companies to adapt their partner focus and alliance values, which in turn increases performance. Alternatively, experience may have a direct effect on success, with alliance culture acting as a mediator. Finally, different elements of alliance culture may affect success differently. Values or partner focus may have a more enduring or deeper impact on alliance success than public displays. The former are harder to implement, but once in existence they are also harder to undo. Companies with well-developed alliance values and a high degree of partner focus may therefore be more successful with alliances over the long-term than companies that are high only in public display elements.

Implications for Management

Quintiles' executives note that its alliances have been successful and that they have become an important component of its business strategy. As a result, there are valuable lessons for managers to consider for their own alliances. Foremost is the need to appreciate that an alliance culture is developed across four categories: alliance values, language, partner focus, and public displays. This study shows that the development of tools and procedures is instrumental to improving the ability of the firm to interact and coordinate with a partner. As a result, attention should be given to operationalizing mechanisms that encourage transparency, cut red tape, and improve the ability to respond to alliance needs. However, this case study suggests that Quintiles' success would not have been as assured had it only worked to improve partner focused processes.

The findings of the case also suggest that a critical aspect of alliance culture development comes through more ostensible use of alliance language and symbols. Other case studies have noted the influence of language and symbols on behavioral change within an organization (e.g., Casey, 1996; Clegg, et al., 2002). As a result, it becomes incumbent on managers to find ways to increase the frequency of communication about alliances, develop a vocabulary that can be utilized across the organization, and to create visible symbols and rituals that highlight the significance of these relationships to the organization.

Of the three categories of alliance culture, the development of alliance values may be the most difficult because it operates at a lower level of organizational identity than observable artifacts such as language, public displays, and processes (Schein, 1990). In essence, instilling values that emphasize the importance of restraint, openness, conflict harmonization and flexibility toward partners in an environment where they do not currently exist will become an exercise in organizational change. Models for change (e.g., Kotter, 1995, 1996) suggest that it occurs in an organization when there is a compelling event and when it is championed from top management down. Key details from the Quintiles case suggest that these factors were operant here. There were, for example, a number of conditions which created compelling reasons for change. The company's early experience with alliances showed it that it was generating financial success but not long-term operational value from its relationships. Industry changes were creating pressures on both biopharmaceutical companies and contract organizations to become more collaborative. Financially, the success of Quintiles' more relationally driven model has reinforced the benefits of a different perspective on partnering. Likewise, there has been a strong level of senior management advocacy to raise its level of alliance culture. Nevertheless, as one Quintiles executive noted, "This is a top–down strategy and we're still years away from having it fully pervade our organization and our customers and partners."

Consequently, developing an alliance culture calls for a high level of commitment on the part of management. The fact that it is difficult to "pervade" an organization suggests that managers looking to enhance their alliance culture need to visibly espouse and reinforce the values and focus that define an alliance culture. Similarly, they need to facilitate the dispersion of learning that comes through their alliances by encouraging mechanisms that spread effective alliance practices across the organization. The core-agent model may be an example firms can use.

Limitations

There are limitations to this study that need to be acknowledged. First of all, this is a single case study so it is not possible to broadly generalize these findings to the universe of all firms. However, scholars have noted that the use of extreme settings for case studies, such as organizations that are successful, can provide useful insights (Eisenhardt, 1989). Moreover, the ability to study the evolution of a phenomenon in association with its holistic setting over time (Yin, 2003) enables us to better understand conditions that were instrumental in creating alliance culture. Nevertheless, we acknowledge that multiple cases or broad-based empirical analysis is necessary to more comfortably extrapolate the findings of this study to the behaviors of firms in alliances.

A second limitation lies in the fact that Quintiles and its alliances occur in the pharmaceutical industry. The dynamics of this industry lend themselves to greater use of alliances, if only to ensure access to promising therapeutic science being developed by biotech companies and in university laboratories. As a result, the high level of alliance intensity across the industry may result in timelines and experience effects that might not be replicable by companies in other industries.

CONCLUSION

While it's clear from this study that a firm's experiences and strategic choices are instrumental in forming its alliance culture, it is also important to recognize that a firm's level of alliance culture appears to be a useful measure of its overall alliance capability. We suggest that it is now time to begin to understand how a firm's behaviors, as reflected by its alliance culture, influence its ability to successfully partner.

NOTES

1. In their study, Clegg et al. (2002) used the term "customer focus" to describe these processes. However, they defined that to mean "where employees and other significant stakeholders in the project are considered as end-users and not just the customer" (p. 324). Because we are concerned with how an organization's culture works with partners we are using the term "partner focused" instead.
2. Clinical trials refer to the process of testing new drugs on human beings. These trials are complex and expensive, which leads pharma companies to collaborate with organizations such as Quintiles that have specialized expertise to coordinate and manage the testing process.

ACKNOWLEDGMENT

This chapter, save some minor changes, was earlier published as Luvison, D., De Man, A.-P., & Pearson, J. (2011). Building an alliance culture: Lessons from Quintiles. In T. K. Das (Ed.), *Behavioral perspectives on strategic alliances* (pp. 51–81). Charlotte, NC: Information Age.

REFERENCES

Ahn, M. J., Meeks, M., Davenport, S., & Bednarek, R. (2009). Exploring technology agglomeration patterns for multinational pharmaceutical and biotechnology firms. *Journal of Commercial Biotechnology, 16*(1), 17–32.

Anand, B. N., & Khanna, T. (2000). Do firms learn to create value? The case of alliances. *Strategic Management Journal, 21*(3), 295–315.

Anonymous. (2009). The SCRIP Awards 2009. In A. Shimmings (Ed.), *SCRIP* (pp. 1–24). London, England: Informa Healthcare.

Anonymous. (2010). The SCRIP Awards 2010. In M. Ward (Ed.), *SCRIP* (pp. 1–28). London, England: Informa Healthcare.

Anonymous. (n.d.a). *Corporate milestones 2006–present.* Retrieved from http://www.quintiles.com/about-us/company-milestones/

Anonymous. (n.d.b). *Working with Quintiles.* Retrieved from http://www.quintiles.com/about-us/working-with-quintiles/

Arino, A., & de la Torre, J. (1998). Learning from failure: Towards an evolutionary model of collaborative ventures. *Organization Science, 9*(3), 306–325.

Ariño, A., de la Torre, J., & Ring, P. S. (2005). Relational quality and inter-personal trust in strategic alliances. *European Management Review, 2*(1), 15–27.

Bamford, J. D., Gomes-Casseres, B., & Robinson, M. S. (2003). *Mastering alliance strategy: A comprehensive guide to design, management, and organization.* San Francisco, CA: Wiley.

Barney, J. B., & Hansen, M. H. (1994). Trustworthiness as a source of competitive advantage. *Strategic Management Journal, 15*(Special Issue), 175–190.

Boyce, M. E. (1996). Organizational story and storytelling: A critical review. *Journal of Organizational Change Management, 9*(5), 5–26.

Cannon, J. P., Achrol, R. S., & Gundlach, G. T. (2000). Contracts, norms, and plural form governance. *Academy of Marketing Science Journal, 28*(2), 180–194.

Casey, C. (1996). Corporate transformations: Designer culture, designer employees and 'post-occupational' solidarity. *Organization, 3*(3), 317–339.

Clegg, S. R., Pitsis, T. S., Rura-Polley, T., & Marosszeky, M. (2002). Governmentality matters: Designing an alliance culture of inter-organizational collaboration for managing projects. *Organization Studies, 23*(3), 317–337.

Das, T. K., & Kumar, R. (2009). Interpartner harmony in strategic alliances: Managing commitment and forbearance. *International Journal of Strategic Business Alliances, 1*(1), 24–52.

Das, T. K., & Teng, B.-S. (2000). Instabilities of strategic alliances: An internal tensions perspective. *Organization Science, 11*(1), 77–101.

Das, T. K., & Teng, B.-S. (2001a). A risk perception model of alliance structuring. *Journal of International Management, 7*(1), 1–29.

Das, T. K., & Teng, B.-S. (2001b). Trust, control, and risk in strategic alliances: An integrated framework. *Organization Studies, 22*(2), 251–283.

de Man, A.-P., Duysters, G. M., & Saebi, T. (2010). Alliance capability as an emerging theme: Past, present, future. In T. K. Das (Ed.), *Researching strategic alliances: Emerging perspectives* (pp. 57–76). Charlotte, NC: Information Age.

de Ridder, A., & Rusinowska, A. (2008). On some procedures of forming a multi-partner alliance. *Journal of Economics & Management Strategy, 17*(2), 443–487.

Draulans, J., de Man, A.-P., & Volberda, H. W. (2003). Building alliance capability: Management techniques for superior alliance performance. *Long Range Planning, 36*(2), 151–166.

Dubin, C. H. (2007). NovaQuest: Strategic partnering to optimize portfolio value, growth & profits. *Specialty Pharma, 7*(6), 84–88.

Dyer, J. H., & Singh, H. (1998). The relational view: Cooperative strategy and sources of interorganizational competitive advantage. *Academy of Management Review, 23*(4), 660–679.

Eisenhardt, K. M. (1989). Building theories from case study research. *Academy of Management Review, 14*(4), 532–550.

Ethiraj, S. K., Kale, P., Krishnan, M. S., & Singh, J. (2005). Where do capabilities come from and how do they matter? A study in the software services industry. *Strategic Management Journal, 26*(1), 25–45.

Futrell, D., Slugay, M., & Stephens, C. H. (2001). Becoming a premier partner: Measuring, managing and changing partnering capabilities at Eli Lilly and Company. *Journal of Commercial Biotechnology, 8*(1), 5–13.

Galaskiewicz, J. (1985). Interorganizational relations. *Annual Review of Psychology, 11*(1), 281–304.

Gibler, D. M. (2008). The costs of reneging: Reputation and alliance formation. *Journal of Conflict Resolution, 52*(3), 426–454.

Gulati, R. (1995). Does familiarity breed trust? The implications of repeated ties for contractual choice in alliances. *Academy of Management Journal, 38*(1), 85–112.

Gulati, R., Lavie, D., & Singh, H. (2009). The nature of partnering experience and the gains from alliances. *Strategic Management Journal, 30*(11), 1213–1233.

Gulati, R., & Singh, H. (1998). The architecture of cooperation: Managing coordination costs and appropriation concerns in strategic alliances. *Administrative Science Quarterly, 43*(4), 781–814.

Hagedoorn, J. (1993). Understanding the rationale of strategic technology partnering: Interorganizational modes of cooperation and sectoral differences. *Strategic Management Journal, 14*(5), 371–385.

Hatch, M. J. (1993). The dynamics of organizational culture. *Academy of Management Review, 18*(4), 657–693.

Heide, J. B., & John, G. (1992). Do norms matter in marketing relationships? *Journal of Marketing, 56*(2), 32–44.

Heimeriks, K. H., & Duysters, G. (2007). Alliance capability as a mediator between experience and alliance performance: An empirical investigation into the alliance capability development process. *Journal of Management Studies, 44*(1), 25–49.

Kale, P., Dyer, J. H., & Singh, H. (2001). Value creation and success in strategic alliances: Alliancing skills and the role of alliance structure and systems. *European Management Journal, 19*(5), 463–471.

Kale, P., Dyer, J. H., & Singh, H. (2002). Alliance capability, stock market response, and long-term alliance success: The role of the alliance function. *Strategic Management Journal, 23*(8), 747–767.

Kale, P., & Singh, H. (2007). Building firm capabilities through learning: The role of the alliance learning process in alliance capability and firm-level alliance success. *Strategic Management Journal, 28*(10), 981–1000.

Kale, P., Singh, H., & Perlmutter, H. (2000). Learning and protection of proprietary assets in strategic alliances: Building relational capital. *Strategic Management Journal, 21*(3), 217–237.

Kaplan, R. S., Norton, D. P., & Rugelsjoen, B. (2010). Managing alliances with the Balanced Scorecard. *Harvard Business Review, 88*(1), 114–120.

Kauser, S., & Shaw, V. (2004). The influence of behavioral and organizational characteristics on the success of international strategic alliances. *International Marketing Review, 21*(1), 17–52.

Kotter, J. P. (1995). Leading change: Why transformation efforts fail. *Harvard Business Review, 73*(2), 59–67.

Kotter, J. P. (1996). *Leading change.* Boston, MA: Harvard Business School Press.

Krishnan, R., Martin, X., & Noorderhaven, N. G. (2006). When does trust matter to alliance performance? *Academy of Management Journal, 49*(5), 894–917.

Liu, C.-L. E., Ghauri, P., & Sinkovics, R. R. (2010). Understanding the impact of relational capital and organizational learning on alliance outcomes. *Journal of World Business, 45*(3), 237–249.

Love, C. (2007). *A strategic approach to alliance management* (pp. 1–4). Cary, NC: Quintiles.

Miles, M. B., & Huberman, A. M. (1994). *Qualitative data analysis: An expanded sourcebook* (2nd ed.). Thousand Oaks, CA: SAGE.

Perkins, T. (2007, November). The new deal. *Pharmaceutical Executive, Inside Outsourcing Special Insert.*

Robson, M. J., Skarmeas, D., & Spyropoulou, S. (2006). Behavioral attributes and performance in international strategic alliances. *International Marketing Review, 23*(6), 585–609.

Royer, S., & Simons, R. (2009). Evolution of cooperation and dynamics of expectations–implications for strategic alliances. *International Journal of Strategic Business Alliances, 1,* 73–88.

Saftlas, H. (2008). Healthcare: Pharmaceuticals industry survey. In E. M. Bossong-Martines & D. Cappadona (Eds.), *Standard & Poor's industry surveys.* New York, NY: Standard & Poor's.

Schein, E. H. (1985). *Organizational culture and leadership.* San Francisco, CA: Jossey-Bass.

Schein, E. H. (1990). Organizational culture. *American Psychologist, 45*(2), 109–119.

Schreiner, M., Kale, P., & Corsten, D. (2009). What really is alliance management capability and how does it impact alliance outcomes and success? *Strategic Management Journal, 30*(13), 1395–1419.

Spekman, R. E., Isabella, L. A., & MacAvoy, T. C. (2000). *Alliance competence: Maximizing the value of your partnerships.* New York, NY: Wiley.

Wu, F., & Cavusgil, S. T. (2006). Organizational learning, commitment, and joint value creation in interfirm relationships. *Journal of Business Research, 59*(1), 81–89.

Yi, H. T., Lee, J., & Dubinsky, A. J. (2010). An empirical investigation of relational conflicts in comMarketing alliances. *Journal of Business to Business Marketing, 17,* 249–278.

Yin, R. K. (2003). *Case study research: Design and methods* (3rd ed.). Thousand Oaks, CA: SAGE.

CHAPTER 10

PERSONAL VALUES OF CIVIL ENGINEERS AND ARCHITECTS IN THE STRATEGIC DECISIONS OF CONSTRUCTION COMPANIES

Atilla Damci
David Arditi
Gul Polat
Harun Turkoglu

ABSTRACT

Civil engineers and architects are often involved in strategic decisions in their company. Because professionals' personal values affect their decisions, the question of whether there is a difference between the personal values of civil engineers and architects should be of interest to construction companies. Construction companies can be in a better position to improve their strategic decision making processes if they have access to this information. Although the personal values of individuals have been explored by several researchers, studies that explore the personal values of civil engineers and architects are limited, particularly in association with strategy-making. This study attempts

Cultural Values in Strategy and Organization, pages 259–277

to fill the gap. The objectives of the study are (a) to understand which personal values are considered to be important by civil engineers and architects, (b) to explore the existence of significant differences between civil engineers' and architects' personal values, and (c) how the differences/similarities affect strategic decision making in construction companies. The most cited personal values in the literature were identified and a questionnaire survey was administered to civil engineers and architects to seek information about their personal values. The Mann-Whitney U test was performed on the collected data to verify whether a significant statistical relationship exists between civil engineers and architects' personal values. The results suggest that some of the personal values of civil engineers are statistically different from the personal values of architects, but some are not.

INTRODUCTION

Over the years, professionals and researchers have investigated various aspects of how personal values affect professionals' decisions. Understanding the effect of personal values on individuals' decisions is difficult in the absence of a clear definition of values. The literature provides several definitions of values (e.g., Braithwaite & Blamey, 1988; Guth & Tagiuri 1965; Kluckhohn, 1951; Rokeach, 1973; Schwartz, 1992). For example, Rokeach (1973), who is the author of one of the most cited studies focused on personal values, defines value as "an enduring belief that a specific mode of conduct or end-state of existence is personally or socially preferable to an opposite or converse mode of conduct or end-state of existence" (p. 5). According to Schwartz (1992) value is "desirable states, objects, goals, or behaviors, transcending special situations and applied as normative standards to judge and to choose among alternative modes of behavior" (p. 2). These definitions make it clear that values have an influence on individuals' decisions. Indeed, there are studies asserting that personal values are one of the key factors that significantly affect how individuals perceive something and how they decide. For example, Elizur and Sagie (1999) pointed out that the values emphasized in the private lives of individuals cover the values that they emphasize in their organizations. In another study by Suar and Khuntia (2010), it is argued that personal values are related to individuals' professional preferences.

Moreover, researchers (e.g, Kilby, 1992; McCuen, 1998; Rokeach, 1973) commonly agree that individuals are often influenced by their personal values when they are making decisions. It is therefore important that managers be interested in identifying which personal values are the more important for their subordinates since these personal values are important in making strategic decisions which are crucial for a company's success. Indeed, there is a strong desire to understand personal values because managers want to know how to improve their subordinates' performance in making strategic decisions (e.g., Elizur & Sagie, 1999; Suar & Khuntia, 2010). Despite this strong desire in different fields, little research has been carried out about the personal values of construction professionals (e.g., civil engineers, architects), particularly in association with strategy-making. This study attempts to fill this gap. Construction professionals, namely architects and civil engineers, are often involved in strategic decisions in their organizations. Therefore, their performance not only on technical decisions, but also on strategic decisions may have severe consequences on the success of construction projects. For example, McCuen (1998) states that individuals may attach importance to different personal values at different levels and that their decisions may change accordingly. Since individuals' personal values affect their decisions, it is important to determine the personal values that construction professionals consider important in making strategic decisions. However, identifying the most important personal values for civil engineers and architects is only the first step of understanding the perception of personal values by civil engineers and architects. Therefore, the question of whether there is a statistically significant difference in the perception of personal values by civil engineers and architects should also be of interest to project team leaders responsible for assigning team members to positions which involve making strategic decisions. Differences in personal values may call for differences in making strategic decisions. Hence, the personal values emphasized in the personal lives of professionals should fit the personal values desired in positions earmarked for making strategic decisions by civil engineers and architects. Construction companies can be in a better position to improve their strategic decision making processes if they have access to this information. Therefore, the purpose of this study is to understand which personal values are considered to be important by civil engineers and architects and explore the existence of statistically significant differences in the perception of personal values by civil engineers and architects. If there is a significant difference in the perception of civil engineers and architects' personal values, then it can be presumed that this will be a useful tool in project team building. The objectives of the study are (a) to understand which personal values are considered to be important by civil engineers and architects, (b) to explore the existence of statistically significant differences in the perception of civil engineers and architects' personal values, and (c) how the differences/similarities affect strategic decision making in construction companies. A questionnaire was designed on the basis of an in-depth review of literature to understand which personal values are considered to be important by civil engineers and architects. The Mann-Whitney U test was performed on the collected data to verify whether significant statistical relationships exist between civil engineers and architects' personal values.

The chapter is structured as follows. The introduction starts out by stating that the personal values of professionals are important in making strategic decisions. It then sets up the hypothesis that there may be a significant difference between civil engineers and architects' personal values. The next section consists of a discussion of how personal values may affect the judgement of these professionals when they make strategic decisions. The methodology used in the study is then described, including the questionnaire survey and the non-parametric statistical analyses used to interpret the data collected. This is followed by a section that discusses the findings in the study and identifies the differences and similarities between civil engineers' and architects' personal values, with specific recommendations about how to use these differences and similarities in making strategic decisions in construction companies. Finally, the chapter concludes with a statement to the effect that even though personal values may not be the only factor that affects the judgement of civil engineers and architects, they may rank personal values in a different order of importance when they are involved in making strategic decisions in their organizations.

THEORETICAL BACKGROUND AND LITERATURE REVIEW

The roles of construction professionals in a project team may require attaching more importance to some values which should reflect the values that are important for them not only in their professional lives but also in their personal lives. For example, if an individual places great emphasis on personal values such as "imaginative" and "intellectual," while the project's characteristics require being self-controlled and logical, the decisions made by that individual may end up in failure. Therefore, being aware that individuals may attach different levels of importance to different personal values can be an advantage for project team leaders or managers of construction companies as they can assess their subordinates' decisions with the knowledge that these decisions are made under the influence of their subordinates' personal values (McCuen, 1998).

The findings of the studies conducted by Biber et al. (2008), Lan et al. (2013), and Sverdlik (2012) reveal that individuals put personal values such as "broadminded," "logical," "forgiving," "responsible," "helpful," and "honest" among the most important personal values because they give higher priority to appreciation, protection, and enhancement of the welfare of not only all people but also people in everyday interaction. On the other hand, Biber et al. (2008) assert that individuals placing emphasis on the aforementioned personal values attach less importance to personal values like "ambitious" and "capable." According to Lan et al. (2013) and Steenhaut and Van Kenhove (2006), individuals who attach greater importance to personal values such as "broadminded," "logical," "forgiving," "responsible," "helpful," and "honest," also attach greater importance to ethical behavior, greater job satisfaction, and greater social responsibility in their professional lives. The findings of the studies conducted by Schmidt and Posner (1982) and Posner and Schmidt (1992) reveal that individuals who are responsible for making strategic decisions for their organizations place personal values such as "honesty," "broadmindedness," and "responsibility" among the most important personal values. Since construction professionals, namely civil engineers and architects, are also responsible for making strategic decisions, these personal values might be of importance to them, too.

Dubinsky et al. (1997) claimed that achievement is driven by self-direction. In addition, according to Rice (2006), self-direction also promotes creativity. Rokeach (1973) stated that self-direction is expressed by personal values like "imaginative," "intellectual," and "independent." Actually, according to the findings of a number of studies (e.g., Lan et al., 2008; Sverdlik, 2012), individuals place these personal values among the most important personal values. However, Steenhaut and Van Kenhove's (2006) assertion is that the more an individual attaches importance to these personal values when compared to other personal values, the more likely this individual is to behave unethically.

Even though the findings of the aforementioned studies lead to a relationship between creativity and behaving unethically, Stouffer et al. (2004) state that "the next generation of engineers will require a creative outlook to approach technical problems in new ways" (p. 10), which is consistent with Richards's (1998) assertion that creativity is an integral part in engineering design. According to a task committee study published by the Structural Engineering Institute and the American Society of Civil Engineers (2013), self-direction is considered to be one of the soft skills that future structural engineers will need. Hence, personal values categorized under self-direction such as "independent," "imaginative," and "intellectual" may be important for architects and civil engineers who are responsible for solving design problems that require creativity.

Rice (2006) asserts that individuals' creativity is negatively affected by personal values such as "responsible," "self-controlled," "politeness," "obedience," and "neat and tidy" because these personal values intend to keep actions or impulses that are likely to upset or harm others under control. In addition, the findings of the studies conducted by Biber et al. (2008) and Sverdlik (2012) suggest that if an individual attaches great importance to personal values such as "obedience" and "politeness," then he/she pays less attention to personal values such as "imaginative," "ambitious," "independent," "capable," and "courageous." On the other hand, according to the findings of the study conducted by Steenhaut and Van Kenhove (2006), an individual who considers the personal values "obedience" and "politeness" as important, is expected to be more idealistic and ethical. In addition to this contention, Steenhaut and Van Kenhove (2006) also claim that an individual may hold an unethical disposition when he/she attaches importance to personal values such as "loving" and "cheerful" which are related to pleasure and enjoyment of life. Civil engineers and architects who deal with strategic decisions must pay serious attention to professional ethics, because participants of the construction industry witness unethical behavior very often (Survey of Construction Industry Ethical Practices, 2004). Besides, ethical problems may have a negative impact on the success of a construction project.

Individuals may perform well in their organization by demonstrating competence according to social standards. In other words, personal success is related to personal values such as "capable" and "ambitious" (Adkins & Naumann, 2016; Dubinsky et al., 1997; Parks & Guay, 2012). According to Sousa et al. (2012), being more confident in executing a job well depends on the level of importance that individuals attach to these personal values. Indeed, studies exist in the literature (e.g., Lan et al., 2008; Sverdlik, 2012) revealing that most employers put these personal values among the most important personal values. Moreover, these studies assert that if an individual pays greater attention to these personal values rather than others, the performance of that individual may improve.

Although there are many studies that focus on the personal values of individuals in the relevant literature (e.g., Karacaer et al., 2009; Lan et al., 2008, 2013; Lee & Trail, 2011), there are only a few studies investigating the personal values of construction professionals, namely civil engineers and architects (e.g., Johnson & Singh, 1998; McCuen, 1998; McCuen & Pritchard, 1983). The existence of significant differences in the perception of personal values by civil engineers and architects has never been explored, especially from the strategic decision making perspective. This study attempts to fill this gap. This study explored not only the personal values that civil engineers and architects find important, but also the relationship between the level of importance they attach to these personal values.

There is a reason for performing the study in Turkey. According to Schwartz (2009), an individual's life experience has a profound effect on the level of importance that an individual attaches to personal values. From this point of view, personal values are likely to be different for individuals with different life experiences or in different countries with different cultures. For this reason, construction professionals' personal values are, by definition, local. In other words, a study examining personal values cannot be carried out on a global level. Therefore, a non-trivial location has to be selected to conduct such a study. In this study, the case of Turkey is examined by surveying civil engineers and architects working in Turkish construction/consulting companies, because Turkish contractors are among the leading international contractors according to Engineering News-Record (Engineering News-Record, 2018).

RESEARCH METHODOLOGY

Based on the information obtained in the literature review, a questionnaire was designed to understand which personal values are considered to be important by civil engineers and architects. The survey was administered to Turkish architects and civil engineers via e-mail. In this research, the target population was established as members of the Istanbul Chamber of Turkish Civil Engineers and the Istanbul Chamber of Turkish Architects, which are the main professional bodies of civil engineers and architects in Turkey.

There are a number of powerful tests to identify individuals' personalities and personal values in the literature. For example, a commonly used test called Myers-Briggs Type Indicator employs 16 personality types to identify individuals' personality characteristics. In this test, researchers, who intend to use this test in their studies, can categorize personality traits in terms of four scales; namely, extraversion–introversion, sensation–intuition, thinking–feeling, judgment–perception (Carlyn, 1977; Jung, 1923/1971; McCrae & Costa, 1989; Quenk, 2009). One of the other well-known tests is Big Five Personality Traits (aka, Five Factor Model). This test is based on a framework that identifies personality traits according to five factors (e.g., agreeableness, extraversion, neuroticism, openness to experience, and conscientiousness; Barrick & Mount, 1991; McCrae & Allik, 2002). Another behavioral test called Belbin Self-Perception Inventory identifies and measures an individual's team roles (e.g., coordinator, resource investigator, monitor evaluator, completer-finisher, teamworker; Belbin, 2010; Senior & Swailes, 1998). Even though the Belbin Self-Perception Inventory is a commonly used test, Furnham et al. (1993) questioned its statistical validity and reliability.

After reviewing the relevant literature about tools developed to identify individuals' personal values, only 18 "instrumental values" defined by Rokeach (1973) were selected in this study. Rokeach (1973) also defined "terminal values" to identify individuals' personal values, but these values were not used in this study because they do not suit the needs of this study. Instrumental values refer to modes of behavior, while terminal values refer to end-state of existence that does not reflect the personalities of civil engineers and architects. Moreover, the instrumental values of Rokeach (1973) were the most cited in the literature (e.g., Karacaer et al., 2009; Lan et al., 2008; Lan et al., 2013; Lee & Trail, 2011). These 18 personal values are presented in the first column of Table 10.1. In the questionnaire, the respondents were asked to rate the level of importance of these 18 personal values on a Likert-like scale of 1–5 where 1 represents *not important* and 5 *very important.*

There are several techniques used to verify the reliability of the scale used in a study. Cronbach's Alpha (α) is the most widely used technique to

TABLE 10.1 Rank, "Cronbach's Alpha if Item Deleted" and Mann-Whitney U Test Sig. Values for Personal Values

Personal Values	Severity Index		Cronbach's Alpha		Mann-Whitney U Test Sig.
	CE	ARCH	CE	ARCH	
Ambitious	.687	.714	.829	.846	.155
Broadminded	.862	.892	.827	.839	.026*
Capable	.833	.824	.823	.834	.363
Cheerful	.804	.837	.821	.831	.066
Neat and tidy	.802	.784	.827	.837	.210
Courageous	.757	.769	.824	.835	.502
Forgiving	.855	.854	.825	.833	.492
Helpful	.844	.838	.822	.829	.714
Honest	.953	.939	.832	.831	.039*
Imaginative	.731	.799	.827	.833	.000*
Independent	.762	.807	.825	.832	.006*
Intellectual	.693	.746	.829	.837	.003*
Logical	.893	.861	.830	.833	.014*
Loving	.739	.785	.818	.832	.019*
Obedient	.868	.859	.826	.832	.423
Polite	.768	.808	.819	.824	.017*
Responsible	.926	.921	.829	.833	.355
Self-controlled	.847	.852	.829	.831	.910

* Statistically significant at 95%

Note: CE: Civil Engineer, ARCH: Architect

determine the internal consistency of a questionnaire when using a Likert scale (Oyedele, 2013). This technique estimates the reliability of a specified set (Gliem & Gliem, 2003; Santos, 1999). In this study, the reliability analysis was carried out using the statistical package for social sciences (IBM SPSS 25). The standardized Cronbach's alpha value can be calculated using the formula in Equation 10.1.

$$\alpha = \frac{N}{(N-1)} x \left(\frac{\sigma_x^2 - \sum_{i=1}^{N} \sigma_{yi}^2}{\sigma_x^2} \right) \tag{10.1}$$

where N is the number of items on the test, σ_x^2 is the variance of the observed item scores, and σ_{yi}^2 is the sum of all i item variances.

Cronbach's alpha can take values between 0 and 1. If it is closer to 1, it indicates that the scale used is highly reliable (Field, 2013). However, having a Cronbach's alpha value that is equal to or greater than 0.60 means that the reliability of the scale is satisfactory (Gliem & Gliem, 2003; Santos, 1999). "Cronbach's alpha if item deleted" values have also been calculated to assess how well each individual personal value contributes to this internal consistency. A "Cronbach's alpha if item deleted" value greater than the overall Cronbach's alpha value implies that if the criterion is removed, the overall Cronbach's alpha value would be greater (Field, 2013).

It is commonly claimed that using a severity index (a non-parametric ranking analysis procedure) rather than arithmetic mean scores (parametric statistics) to rank data would yield more significant outcomes. The formula used to determine the severity index is given below (Chen et al., 2010; Idrus & Newman, 2002):

$$\text{Severity Index} = \sum_{i=1}^{5}\left(\frac{w_i \times f_i}{n \times a}\right) \tag{10.2}$$

where i is the point given to each personal value by the respondent (ranging from 1 to 5); w_i is the weight for each point (where 1 represents *not important* and 5 represents *very important*); f_i is the frequency of the point i by all respondents; n is the total number of responses; and a is the highest weight (in this study $a = 5$).

Carifio and Perla (2008) and Jamieson (2004) recommend that non-parametric tests should be used to analyze Likert-like data. Therefore, after computing Cronbach's alpha values and severity indices, Mann-Whitney U tests were performed on the collected data to explore the existence of significant differences between civil engineers' and architects' personal values.

FINDINGS AND DISCUSSION

A total of 179 members of the Istanbul Chamber of Turkish Architects and a total of 394 members of the Istanbul Chamber of Turkish Civil Engineers returned duly completed questionnaires. Cronbach's alpha values are computed via IBM SPSS 25 to check the internal consistency of the scale used in the questionnaire. The overall Cronbach's alpha values are 0.834 and 0.850 for the data collected from Turkish civil engineers and architects, respectively. Since the Cronbach's alpha value of each group is higher than 0.60, that is, the minimum value recommended by George and Mallery (2003), it can be concluded that the internal consistency of the scale used in the questionnaire is satisfactory. None of the "Cronbach's alpha if item deleted" values presented in Table 10.1 are greater than the overall Cronbach's alpha values. Therefore, none of the personal values need to be deleted.

The rankings of Turkish civil engineers' and architects' personal values and the relationship between civil engineers' and architects' perception of personal values are discussed in the succeeding sections.

Civil Engineers' and Architects' Personal Values

Civil engineers and architects were asked to rate themselves with respect to 18 personal values; namely: "ambitious," "broadminded," "capable," "cheerful," "clean," "courageous," "forgiving," "helpful," "honest," "imaginative," "independent," "intellectual," "logical," "loving," "obedient," "polite," "responsible," and "self-controlled." The ranking of the personal values shown in Table 10.1 is based on the magnitude of the severity indices. The findings of the study reveal that respondent civil engineers and architects put "honest" and "responsible" among the most important personal values (Figures 10.1 and 10.2). High scores on "honest" and "responsible" are consistent with the findings of studies carried out in various countries and industries (e.g., Karacaer et al., 2009; Kotey & Meredith, 1997; Lan et

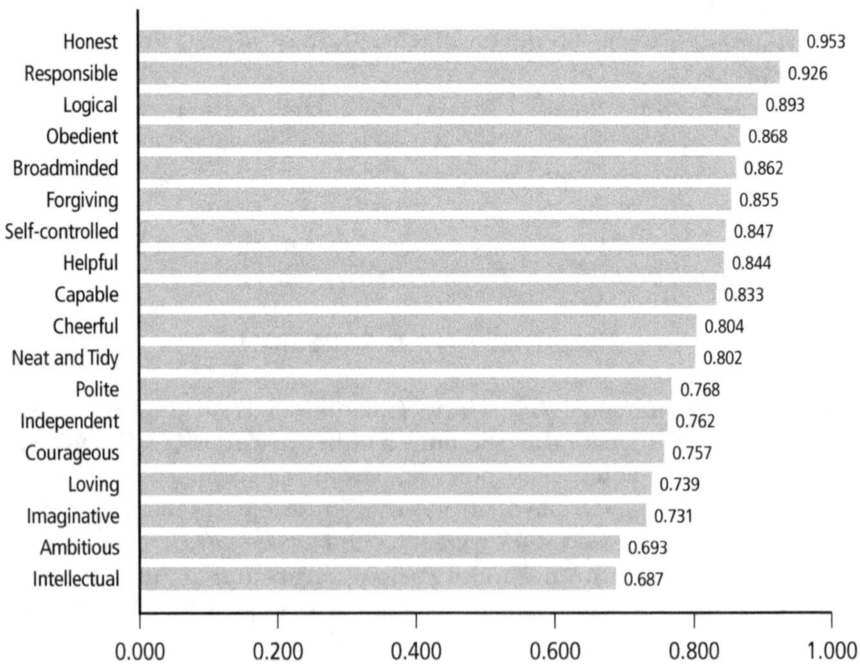

Figure 10.1 Severity Index for personal values of civil engineers.

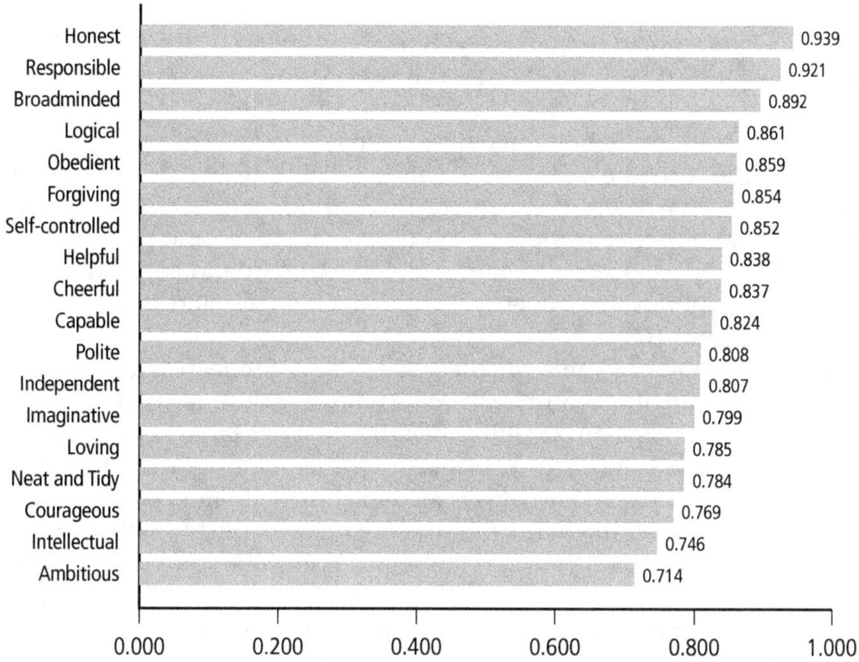

Figure 10.2 Severity Index for personal values of architects.

al., 2008, 2013; Lee & Trail, 2011; Posner & Schmidt, 1992; Rassin, 2008; Schmidt & Posner, 1982; Stackman et al., 2005). From the perspective of cultural values in strategic decision making, these values have a significant impact on individuals' behavior in decision making, because earning loyalty, trust, and honor is highly relevant to the personal values "honest" and "responsible" (Fritzsche, 1995). Moreover, individuals who attach greater importance to these personal values, also give higher priority to ethical behavior and greater social responsibility in their professional lives (Lan et al. 2013; Steenhaut & Van Kenhove, 2006). It is clear that civil engineers and architects who responded to this survey have a grave concern about ethical behavior. This finding can be explained by the fact that civil engineers and architects make strategic decisions related to activities in the design and construction phases of a project and that their job description includes the pursuit of ethical conduct. Placing a high level of importance on being "honest" and "responsible" is not only related to the moral code of a society but also to professional ethics. Moreover, Schmidt and Posner (1982) and Posner and Schmidt (1992) also pointed out that responsibility and honesty are of great importance to managers who make strategic decisions for their organizations. The personal values "honest," "responsible," and "logical" are also found to be the most important personal values for individuals in studies conducted by Biber et al. (2008), Lan et al. (2013), and Sverdlik (2012). Even though the first two most important personal values are the same for both civil engineers and architects (see Figures 10.1 and 10.2), the third highest ranked personal value was "logical" for civil engineers while "broadminded" for architects. This is not surprising because Biber et al. (2008) found in their study that individuals who attach the highest level of importance to "logical" and "broadminded" also place the lowest level of importance on "ambitious." Indeed, "ambitious" is one of the least important personal values for both civil engineers and architects (see Figures 10.1 and 10.2).

Having "ambitious" and "intellectual" among the least important personal values of engineers and architects is a positive finding because according to Steenhaut and Van Kenhove (2006), the lesser importance individuals place on these values, the more likely it is that they will behave ethically. Obviously, engineers and architects are concerned about professional ethics. Moreover, according to the findings of Lan et al. (2013) and Steenhaut and Van Kenhove (2006), having "ambitious" and "intellectual" as the least important personal values supports the finding that "honest" and "responsible" are among architects' and engineers' most important personal values (see Figures 10.1 and 10.2). In Karacaer et al.'s (2009) and Rassin's (2008) studies, the very same set of personal values are listed among the least important personal values even though Karacaer et al.'s (2009) and Rassin's (2008) studies focus on the personal values of professionals working in accounting and nursing professions, respectively.

According to the findings related to the most and least important personal values, civil engineers and architects are in general agreement in their perceptions of personal values except for the other most and least important personal values. This result can be explained by the fact that both civil engineers and architects are employed in the construction industry. In addition, both civil engineers and architects are involved in making strategic decisions related to design and construction. It is most likely that being involved in these strategic decisions lead them to place the very same personal values among the most and least important personal values. On the other hand, Schwartz's (2009) study supports the argument that personal values are not a one-size-fits-all concept, and points out that individuals' priorities on personal values depend on different life experiences. It is possible that the most and least important personal values can be found to be different in other studies. This explains the finding that civil engineers and architects attach different levels of importance to some personal values despite the fact that these professions go hand-in-hand in the same industry. It is, therefore, possible that individuals can rank personal values in a different order of importance whether they are employed in the same or different industries or they hold the same or different nationalities (Damci et al., 2017; Wang et al., 2016).

Another study conducted by McCuen (1998) states that personal values cannot be classified as good or bad even though individuals attach different levels of importance to them. For example, in professional life, one of the important personal values to which an employee should attach great importance is being "responsible." If a professional has information that one of his/her team members falsified some important documents to gain personal benefit, this professional may act publicly on the information because this individual attaches great importance to being responsible. However, an individual who places a greater importance to being "loyal" to his/her project team rather than being "responsible," may prefer optimizing his/her career expectations by deciding not to act on the information.

Relationship Between Civil Engineers' and Architects' Personal Values

One of the objectives of this study is to explore the similarity or difference in civil engineers and architects' perceptions of personal values. Therefore, the Mann-Whitney U test was used to test for the significance of the differences in the perception of personal values reported by civil engineers and architects. The null hypothesis is that there are no differences in the mean scores. However, if the null hypothesis is rejected, it means that the difference between the mean scores of the personal values are statistically significant at $p = 0.05$, indicated by an asterisk (*) in Table 10.1. A statistically significant difference ($p < 0.05$) is observed in the perception of 8 out of the 18 personal values reported by civil engineers and architects (see Table 10.1).

- Both civil engineers and architects ranked "honest" and "responsible" as the first and second most important personal values, respectively. This finding is understandable as these personal values are important for technical/functional-anchored individuals such as civil engineers and architects, because they have to consider professional ethics while performing their jobs. Even though "honest" is the most important personal value for both civil engineers and architects, it was observed that there is a statistically significant difference between engineers and architects in the perception of "honest" and "logical." This finding reveals that even two professions that collaborate quite closely in practice may attach different levels of importance to personal values. Some researchers claim that the possible reasons for this difference may be individuals' demographics or different personal life experiences. For example, according to Damci (2016) and Damci et al. (2017), the significant difference in civil engineers' perceptions of personal values and motivators is caused by civil engineers' demographics.

- There is a statistically significant difference in the perceptions of personal values "broadminded," "imaginative," "independent," and "intellectual." Architects attach more importance to these personal values than civil engineers. This result is understandable since architects do mostly design work. An architect's performance has an impact on the success/failure of a construction project. Having personal values such as "broadminded," "intellectual," "independent," and "imaginative" should be important for an architect who deals with design problems that require not only a good solution but also creativity. In other words, an architect's broad-mindedness and independency in making strategic-decisions related to design, an architect's intellect used in imagining extraordinary design solutions determine the level of the architect's performance. According to the findings of the study conducted by Rice (2006), the personal values "broadminded," "intellectual," "independent," and "imaginative" advance creativity.

  Construction companies should review the strategic decisions of architects carefully, because Steenhaut and Van Kenhove (2006) found that attaching great importance to the personal values "broadminded," "intellectual," "independent," and "imaginative" may lead to unethical behaviors. On the other hand, civil engineers attach less importance to these personal values than architects. Nevertheless, Richards (1998) and Stouffer et al. (2004) claim that creativity is a key factor in finding a good solution not only for architectural design problems but also for engineering/construction problems. It is not surprising that architects attach more importance than civil engineers to the personal values "broadminded," "imaginative," "independent," "intellectual," "loving," and "polite," because of the skills required for their profession.
- There is a statistically significant difference between civil engineers and architects' perceptions of personal values "loving" and "polite." This finding can be explained by the working environment rather than by the individuals' personal lives. Architects mostly work in design offices where they have an intimate working environment defined by close proximity to their colleagues and superiors. On the other hand, civil engineers commonly work on large construction projects which is one of the factors that has a negative impact on having a close relationship with their colleagues and superiors.

> Therefore, it makes sense that civil engineers and architects perceive these personal values in a different way.

In sum, the findings of this study contribute to a better understanding of civil engineers' and architects' perceptions of personal values. It was found that they perceive some personal values differently even though they collaborate closely in the construction industry. Having this information can assist construction companies and design firms to hire civil engineers and architects so that their personal values fit with the values required of their position. The strategic decisions made by properly selected professionals may ensure the successful completion of the design and construction. It should be noted however that there may also be other factors that may have an impact on individuals' personal values, such as demographics or life experiences.

CONCLUSION

Construction professionals make not only technical decisions but also strategic decisions in their professional life. Since professionals' personal values affect their decisions, it is important to know which personal values they consider important. The question of whether there is a significant difference in the perception of engineers and architects' personal values should be of interest to project team leaders and managers who are responsible for assigning team members or employees to positions that require making strategic decisions. Companies in the construction industry can be in a better position to improve their strategic decision making processes if they have access to this information. The literature review revealed that studies that explore the personal values of civil engineers and architects are limited, especially in connection with making strategic decisions. This study aims to fill this gap.

The objectives of the study include understanding which personal values are considered important by civil engineers and architects, exploring the existence of significant differences between civil engineers and architects' personal values, and determining how the differences/similarities affect strategic decision making in design/construction companies. The most cited personal values in the literature were identified and a questionnaire was designed to understand which personal values are considered to be important by civil engineers and architects. The questionnaire survey was administered to Turkish civil engineers and architects and the collected data were analyzed using a severity index and Mann-Whitney U tests to compare the respondents' perceptions of their personal values. The analysis of the data indicates that the perceptions of civil engineers and architects relative to eight of the 18 personal values are statistically different, which supports the main hypothesis of this study. Knowing the personal values that are considered most important or perceived differently by civil engineers and architects can assist companies in the construction industry in hiring/appointing professionals by making sure that the professionals' personal values fit the personal values desired in positions earmarked for making strategic decisions. The only limitation of this study is that personal values may be affected by individuals' demographics and life experiences. This issue should be investigated in future research.

ACKNOWLEDGMENTS

This research was supported by a grant from The Scientific and Technological Research Council of Turkey (TUBITAK). The authors gratefully acknowledge this support.

REFERENCES

Adkins, C. L., & Naumann, S. E. (2016). The value of achievement and responses to the work environment. *Journal of Behavioral and Applied Management, 3*(2), 993.

Barrick, M. R., & Mount, M. K. (1991). The big five personality dimensions and job performance: A meta-analysis. *Personnel Psychology, 44*(1), 1–26.

Belbin, M. (2010). *Management teams: Why they succeed or fail* (3rd ed.). Oxford, England: Elsevier.

Biber, P., Hupfeld, J., & Meier, L. L. (2008). Personal values and relational models. *European Journal of Personality, 22*(7), 609–628.

Braithwaite, V. A., & Blamey, R. (1998). Consensus, stability and meaning in abstract social values. *Australian Journal of Political Science, 33*(3), 363–380.

Carifio, J., & Perla, R. (2008). Resolving the 50-year debate around using and misusing Likert scales. *Medical Education, 42*(12), 1150–1152.

Carlyn, M. (1977). An assessment of the Myers-Briggs type indicator. *Journal of Personality Assessment, 41*(5), 461–473.

Chen, Y., Okudan, G. E., & Riley, D. R. (2010). Sustainable performance criteria for construction method selection in concrete buildings. *Automation in Construction, 19*(2), 235–244.

Damci, A., (2016). Impact of personal demographics on civil engineers' motivators—Case study of Turkey. *Journal of Management in Engineering, 32*(2), 05015006.

Damci, A., Arditi, D., & Polat, G. (2017). Civil engineers' personal values/demographics linkage in project team building. *Engineering, Construction and Architectural Management, 24*(6), 1337–1349.

Dubinsky, A. J., Kotabe, M., Lim, C. U., & Wagner, W. (1997). The impact of values on salespeople's job responses: A cross-national investigation. *Journal of Business Research, 39*(3), 195–208.

Elizur, D., & Sagie, A. (1999). Facets of personal values: A structural analysis of life and work values. *Applied Psychology, 48*(1), 73–87.

Engineering News-Record. (2018). *ENR top 250 international contractors.* Retrieved from https://www.enr.com/toplists/2018-Top-250-International-Contractors-1

Field, A. (2013). *Discovering statistics Using IBM SPSS Statistics.* London, England: SAGE.

Fritzsche, D. J. (1995). Personal values: Potential keys to ethical decision making. *Journal of Business Ethics, 14*(11), 909–922.

Fumham, A., Steele, H., & Pendleton, D. (1993). A psychometric assessment of the Belbin team-role self-perception inventory. *Journal of Occupational and Organizational Psychology, 66*(3), 245–257.

George, D., & Mallery, P. (2003). *SPSS for Windows step by step: A simple guide and reference, 11.0 Update* (4th ed.). Boston, MA: Allyn & Bacon.

Gliem, J. A., & Gliem, R. R. (2003, October). *Calculating, interpreting, and reporting Cronbach's alpha reliability coefficient for Likert-type scales.* Paper presentation at the Midwest Research-to-Practice Conference in Adult, Continuing, and Community Education, Ohio State University, Columbus, OH.

Guth, W. D., & Tagiuri, R. (1965). Personal values and corporate strategy. *Harvard Business Review, 43*(5), 123–132.

Idrus, A. B., & Newman, J. B. (2002). Construction related factors influencing the choice of concrete floor systems. *Construction Management and Economics, 20*(1), 13–19.

Jamieson, S. (2004). Likert scales: How to (ab)use them. *Medical Education, 38*(12), 1217–1218.

Johnson, H. M., & Singh, A. (1998). The personality of civil engineers. *Journal of Management in Engineering, 14*(4), 45–56.

Jung, C.G. (1971). *Psychological types* (translated and revised by H. G. Baynes and R. F. C. Hull). Princeton, NJ: Princeton University Press. (Original work published 1923)

Karacaer, S., Gohar, R., Aygün, M., & Sayin, C. (2009). Effects of personal values on auditor's ethical decisions: A comparison of Pakistani and Turkish professional auditors. *Journal of Business Ethics, 88*(1), 53–64.

Kilby, R. W. (1992). *The study of human values.* Lanham, MD: University Press of America.

Kluckhohn, C. (1951). Values and value-orientations in the theory of action. In T. Parsons & E. A. Shils (Eds.), *Toward a general theory of action* (pp. 388–433). Cambridge, MA: Harvard University Press.

Kotey, B., & Meredith, G. G. (1997). Relationships among owner/manager personal values, business strategies, and enterprise performance. *Journal of Small Business Management, 35,* 37–64.

Lan, G., Gowing, M., McMahon, S., Rieger, F., & King, N. (2008). A study of the relationship between personal values and moral reasoning of undergraduate business students. *Journal of Business Ethics, 78*(1/2), 121–139.

Lan, G., Okechuku, C., Zhang, H., & Cao, J. (2013). Impact of job satisfaction and personal values on the work orientation of Chinese accounting practitioners. *Journal of Business Ethics, 112*(4), 627–640.

Lee, D., & Trail, G. (2011). The influence of personal values and goals on cognitive and behavioral involvement in sport. *Journal of Sport Management, 25*(6), 593–605.

McCuen, R. H. (1998). Balancing corporate and personal values. *Journal of Management in Engineering, 14*(2), 40–44.

McCuen, R. H., & Pritchard, M. S. (1983). Association between personal and professional values. *Journal of Professional Issues in Engineering, 109*(1), 1–9.

McCrae, R. R., & Allik, J. (2002). *The five-factor model of personality across culture.* New York, NY: Springer Science Business Media.

McCrae, R.R., & Costa, P.T. (1989). Reinterpreting the Myers-Briggs type indicator from the perspective of the five-factor model of personality. *Journal of Personality, 57*(1), 17–40.

Oyedele, L. O. (2013). Analysis of architects' demotivating factors in design firms. *International Journal of Project Management, 31*(3), 342–354.

Parks, L., & Guay, R. P. (2012). Can personal values predict performance? Evidence in an academic setting. *Applied Psychology, 61*(1), 149–173.

Posner, B. Z., & Schmidt, W. H. (1992). Values and the American manager: An update updated. *California Management Review, 34*(3), 80–94.

Quenk, N. (2009). *Essentials of Myers-Briggs Type Indicator assessment* (2nd ed. Hoboken, NJ: Wiley.

Rassin, M. (2008). Nurses' professional and personal values. *Nursing Ethics, 15*(5), 614–630.

Rice, G. (2006). Individual values, organizational context, and self-perceptions of employee creativity: Evidence from Egyptian organizations. *Journal of Business Research, 59*(2), 233–241.

Richards, L. G. (1998). Stimulating creativity: Teaching engineers to be innovators. In *Proceedings of 1998 IEEE Frontiers in Education Conference* (Vol. 3; pp. 1034–1039). New York, NY: IEEE.

Rokeach, M. (1973). *The nature of human values.* New York, NY: Free Press.

Santos, J. R. A. (1999). Cronbach's alpha: A tool for assessing the reliability of scales. *Journal of Extension, 37*(2), 1–5.

Schmidt, W. H., & Posner, B. Z. (1982). *Managerial values and expectations: The silent power in personal and organizational life.* New York, NY: American Management Association.

Schwartz, S. H. (1992). Universals in the content and structure of values: Theoretical advances and empirical tests in 20 countries. *Advances in Experimental Social Psychology, 25*(1), 1–65.

Schwartz, S. H. (2009, June). *Basic human values.* Paper presentation at the Cross-national Comparison Seminar on the Quality and Comparability of Measures for Constructs in Comparative Research: Methods and Applications, Bolzano (Bozen), Italy.

Senior, B., & Swailes, S. (1998). A comparison of the Belbin self perception inventory and observer's assessment sheet as measures of an individual's team roles. *International Journal of Selection and Assessment, 6*(1), 1–8.

Stackman, R. W., Connor, P. E., & Becker, B. W. (2005). Sectoral ethos: An investigation of the personal values systems of female and male managers in the public and private sectors. *Journal of Public Administration Research and Theory, 16*(4), 577–597.

Steenhaut, S., & Van Kenhove, P. (2006). An empirical investigation of the relationships among a consumer's personal values, ethical ideology and ethical beliefs. *Journal of Business Ethics, 64*(2), 137–155.

Structural Engineering Institute (SEI), & American Society of Civil Engineers. (2013). *A vision for the future of structural engineering and structural engineers: A case for change* (A Board of Governors Task Committee Paper). Retrieved from https://www.asce.org/uploadedFiles/visionforthefuture.pdf

Sousa, C. M., Coelho, F., & Guillamon-Saorin, E. (2012). Personal values, autonomy, and self-efficacy: Evidence from frontline service employees. *International Journal of Selection and Assessment, 20*(2), 159–170.

Stouffer, W. B., Russell, J. S., & Oliva, M. G. (2004, June). *Making the strange familiar: Creativity and the future of engineering education.* Paper presentation at the 2004 American Society for Engineering Education Annual Conference and Exposition, Salt Lake City, UT.

Suar, D., & Khuntia, R. (2010). Influence of personal values and value congruence on unethical practices and work behavior. *Journal of Business Ethics, 97*(3), 443–460.

Survey of Construction Industry Ethical Practices. (2004). *FMI/CMAA survey of construction industry ethical practices* (pp. 1–18). Raleigh, NC: FMI Management Consultant for the Construction Industry and Construction Management Association of America.

Sverdlik, N. (2012). The content of internal conflicts: A personal values perspective. *European Journal of Personality, 26*(1), 30–44.

Wang, D., Arditi, D., & Damci, A. (2016). Construction project managers' motivators and human values. *Journal of Construction Engineering and Management, 143*(4), 04016115.

CHAPTER 11

CULTURAL CHARACTERISTICS OF CHILEAN AND BRAZILIAN WORKFORCES AND STRATEGIC HUMAN RESOURCE MANAGEMENT

An Integrative Literature Review

Francisca Álvarez-Figueroa

ABSTRACT

Latin American countries have experienced an increase in the number of international organizations, especially Chile and Brazil. However, frequently, the specialized literature analyzes the Latin American cluster comprising all its countries as an undifferentiated entity, without acknowledging the particular local characteristics or exceptional cases of development, such as Chile and Brazil. Thus, based on the GLOBE (global leadership and organizational behavior effectiveness) cultural dimensions, this chapter aims to provide a revised perspective regarding the principal cultural characteristics of these countries, as well as the management strategies they have developed. The

Cultural Values in Strategy and Organization, pages 279–325

methodology adopted in our study is a review of the literature published in the *Web of Science* and *Scopus*. Content analysis is developed after an inclusion/exclusion process. Among the findings, both these countries evidence significant cultural differences. Brazil is characterized by hierarchical relationships where workers are loyal and trust their leaders; the *Jeitinho* is a trait that affects transversally in all the aspects of their lives and relates to an easy-going and non-confrontational behavior that allows them to obtain what they desire. In Chile, a paternalistic and hierarchical style shapes passive relationships characterized by the fear to confront and question authority. *Compadrazgo* is a mechanism to establish beneficial relationships and contacts. Also, the Chilean culture is pessimistic and fatalistic about its future. Among the management strategies, research in Brazil has shown a significant development in comparison to the Chilean, evidencing pending challenges. Finally, we expected to contribute to the literature by providing knowledge about the cultural particularities of two countries under-researched by the literature on strategic management and culture.

INTRODUCTION

Globalization has influenced the significant interdependence between nations. Indeed, the international trade rose over 400% (US$18 trillion annually) in the last 2 decades and has impacted to emergent economies since these constitute attractive markets that can offer, for example, a cheaper workforce or distinctive products (Sweeney & McFarlin, 2015; Truss, Mankin, & Kelliher, 2012). In turn, local markets are competitive and more volatile than ever, representing a fruitful scenario for international organizations. As a consequence of these processes, the workforce's demographics are more varied in terms of age, gender, religion, and culture, among other aspects (House, Hanges, Javidan, Dorfman, & Gupta, 2004; Kumra & Manfredi, 2012; Sweeney & McFarlin, 2015; Thomas & Peterson, 2015; Truss et al., 2012).

In this context, the presence of multinational organizations has grown worldwide, increasing the challenges related to actively managing an international and diverse workforce from different host countries. In addition, it is common to find cross-cultural teams, international trades, and subsidiary companies in different countries (Kumra & Manfredi, 2012; Stone, Stone-Romero, & Lukaszewski, 2007; Sweeney & McFarlin, 2015; Thomas & Peterson, 2015; Truss et al., 2012).

To address these challenges, there are two current perspectives on strategic human resource management that point to cross-cultural workforces. First, the *universalist* approach, which proposes that to manage organizational members, there is one best way that can be applied to all organizations. Second, the *contingency* approach suggests that the best way to manage people is designing local strategies that acknowledge the particular circumstances of the context (Bonache, Trullen, & Sanchez, 2012; Truss et al., 2012).

The present research is based on the second perspective (contingency) since the main argument of this study is related to highlighting the relevance of acknowledging particular cultural traits and how to understand them can contribute to achieving the competitive advantage and successful entrance of any organization (Bonache et al., 2012; Truss et al., 2012). Furthermore, in the field of international organizations, it has been argued that one essential characteristic of multinational corporations (MNCs) is that they learn from their host culture/country (Elvira & Davila, 2005; Thomas & Peterson, 2015).

The most relevant studies attempting to understand cultural differences are Hofstede's (1982) cultural dimensions, and later the global leadership and organizational behavior effectiveness (GLOBE) project report, published in 2004 (House et al., 2004). However, 15 years have passed since its publication, and so it would seem that we need for an updated knowledge about the topic. In addition, most of the literature and research on the subject has focused on Western and Asian societies, giving scarce attention to Latin American, which points to a gap in the literature (Coda et al., 2009; Griffin & Pustay, 2015; House et al., 2004; Scandura & Dorfman, 2004; Sweeney & McFarlin, 2015; Thomas & Peterson, 2015).

In this sense, the few studies that focus on Latin American tend to treat its countries as a homogeneous cluster (Pérez-Arrau, Eades, & Wilson, 2012; Rodríguez & Ríos, 2009). For this reason, it is argued that it becomes necessary to provide attention to its particularities in order to understand why some of the Latin American societies have achieved significant success in comparison to the others. For instance, Brazil and Chile represent globalized economies that are leaders in the region. Brazil owns one of the largest oil companies in the world, and Chile is the top exporter of copper and lithium in the world (Griffin & Pustay, 2015; Sweeney & McFarlin, 2015). Thus, the interest of MNCs in making business and establish their presence has grown in Chile and Brazil, which also represents challenges in terms of workforce management for these organizations (Elvira & Davila, 2005; Griffin & Pustay, 2015; Rodríguez & Ríos, 2007; Sweeney & McFarlin, 2015).

Considering the antecedents exposed, this research aims to explore, employing the GLOBE cultural dimensions, in some of the principal cultural characteristics of the Chilean and Brazilian workforce, and accordingly, to analyze the different human resource management (HRM) strategies that organizations implement in these countries.

LITERATURE REVIEW

Multinational Organizations

A multinational is an organization that operates in multiple countries (Elvira & Davila, 2005; Thomas & Peterson, 2015). An essential characteristic of these is that they adapt to local environments and exploit the local opportunities from the community where they are operating. Thus, these organizations are "decentralized and nationally self-sufficient" (Thomas & Peterson, 2015, p. 196), producing, managing, and retaining knowledge in their location.

In this sense, the cultural environment of the organization will impact on its practices and the subjectivity of the workers. Thus, in the case of multinational organizations, organizations should adapt their activities and strategies (such as recruitment, training, and reward system) with the characteristics, values, and legal systems of the host culture in order to have a positive impact on the motivation, performance, and organizational outcomes (Elvira & Davila, 2005; Griffin & Pustay, 2015; Sweeney & McFarlin, 2015; Truss et al., 2012). Indeed, Stone et al. (2007) in their study of the impact of cultural values in HRM found a positive relationship between the effectiveness of human resource (HR) practices and its congruence with the values of the incumbents and the culture.

The Paradigm of Culture

Culture can be understood as the particular interrelated set of values, assumptions, practices, beliefs, and attitudes that the members of a society share and transmit (Chartered Institute of Personnel and Development [CIPD], 2013; Elvira & Davila, 2005; Griffin & Pustay, 2015; House et al., 2004; Sweeney & McFarlin, 2015; Thomas & Peterson, 2015). Furthermore, Dickson, Den Hartog, and Mitchelson (2003) explain that culture is dynamic and evolves.

Following this definition, Stone et al. (2007), based on interpersonal attraction theory, explain that individuals tend to be attracted to people with similar attitudes, behaviors, and values. This argument supports the idea that organizations should understand the cultural characteristics of their members in order to propose strategies that align their behaviors and cosmo vision, with the organizational goals.

Consequently, it is plausible to consider that culture is a significant factor that influences the organizational functioning and, in consequence, their HRM. After all, individuals usually live an important part of their lives in a single culture, which shapes their subjectivities and perspectives. Furthermore, the current debate on the field suggests that, the congruence between organizational practices and the host culture can contribute to the organizational effectiveness and its competitive advantage. However, the lack of conciliation between the local culture and an organization could lead to disagreements and conflicts because of this convergence (Bonache et al., 2012; House et al., 2004; Sweeney & McFarlin, 2015). Interestingly, in their research related to the effects of culture in the organizations, McGregor and Doshi (2015) found that companies that provide the same services in different countries evidence different rates of customer satisfaction.

Research on Culture: The GLOBE Project

The GLOBE project proposes a framework inspired on Hofstede's (1982) cultural dimensions, Kluckhohn and Strodtbeck (1961), McClelland (1961), and Mulder's (1971) cross-cultural studies, and it has been considered one of the most relevant studies on the topic, since it offers an updated and representative exposition of cultural differences. The study was developed during 2004 in 62 societies by applying questionnaires to 17,000 managers in 951 organizations (Hartog, House, Hanges, & Ruiz-Quintanilla, 1999; House et al., 2004; Scandura & Dorfman, 2004; Sweeney & McFarlin, 2015; Thomas & Peterson, 2015). However, to develop the Latin American cluster,[1] the research did not include the participation of one of its stronger economies: Chile. Also, workers from the public sector were not considered, representing a gap in the knowledge that the study presents.

The GLOBE study identified leadership attributes and nine cultural dimensions reflected in social values and practices. An interesting finding is that, in many cases, the societal values did not correlate to the societal practices. This is exemplified in the results found for the case of Brazil (Dickson, Den Hartog, & Mitchelson, 2003; House et al., 2004; Scandura & Dorfman, 2004; Thomas & Peterson, 2015). The nine cultural dimensions are the following:

- *Power distance:* The extent to which power is distributed equally in an organization. The cultural values are related to the relevance of the position, power of the hierarchy, obedience, and inequality.
- *Uncertainty avoidance:* The extent to which the members of an organization or society rely on norms, rituals, or procedures to predict events from the future.
- *Humane orientation:* The degree to which society promotes and compensates individuals who are fair, kind, generous, and altruistic.
- *Collectivism I (Institutional collectivism):* The institutional encouragement and promotion of collective action and a grouped distribution

of resources. The cultural values identified are, participation and team orientation at the organizational level.

- *Collectivism II (In-group collectivism):* Expression of loyalty and cohesion of individuals to their organizations or reference groups. Cultural values identified are organizational loyalty and pride in ingroup members (reflected in team orientation and participation).
- *Assertiveness:* The extent to which individuals are encouraged to be "assertive, confrontational and aggressive in their relationship with others" (House et al., 2004, p. 30) or in opposition, nonaggressive, and tender in their relationships.
- *Gender egalitarianism:* The extent to which societies reduce inequality regarding gender. The cultural values are reflected in equal opportunities: men and women to be managers or/and to have equality in terms of possibilities of professional development.
- *Future orientation:* The degree to which people operate orienting their behaviors to the future. For societies that tend to be orientated to the future, planning is fundamental since individuals believe that current actions will influence their future.
- *Performance orientation:* The extent to which societies encourage the performance and improvement of individuals (Dickson et al., 2003; House et al., 2004; Sweeney & McFarlin, 2015; Thomas & Peterson, 2015).

The Latin American Context: A Shared Culture

Latin America has been traditionally analyzed as a homogeneous region that shares a common historical background explained by pre-Columbian cultures and the colonizing mission of the Spanish and Portuguese explorers (Davila & Elvira, 2012). The region has evidenced a significant economic improvement in the last years, in part for political, economic, and educational reforms. Also, for reducing entrance barriers for international organizations (Davila & Elvira, 2012; Elvira & Davila, 2005; Sweeney & McFarlin, 2015).

The key features that describe the Latin American cluster according to several studies are the collectivism, paternalism, personalism, compadrazgo, jeitinho, social distance, and inequality (Browaeys & Price, 2008; Davila & Elvira, 2012; Elvira & Davila, 2005; House et al., 2004; Martínez, 2005). However, the distinctive features of this cluster are still, to some extent, unknown. For this reason, this study explores these issues in two countries of the cluster.

Chile and Brazil: The Heterogeneity of Two Leading Economies

Chile and Brazil have made higher economic advances in the last 2 decades in comparison to other Latin American countries, becoming the most important economies in the region (Organization for Economic Cooperation and Development [OECD], 2020b; Sweeney & McFarlin, 2015). Thus, they should not be analyzed as part of a homogeneous cluster but for what is making them different and stronger economies.

Both countries, Chile[2] and Brazil, are also members of trade associations such as Andean Community and the Southern Common Market (Mercosur), which facilitate the export of assets to the European Union and other important markets. As it becomes evident, globalization is influencing and significantly shaping this region (Elvira & Davila, 2005; Griffin & Pustay, 2015; Mercosur, 2016; Sweeney & McFarlin, 2015).

METHODOLOGY

This research was developed through a qualitative methodology since one of its primary features is to explore, in some of the principal cultural characteristics of the Chilean and Brazilian workforce, and to analyze the different HRM strategies that organizations implement in these countries.

Considering this, the present study follows the method of integrative Literature Review (ILR), which has been characterized as an integral approach of review and critical analysis of existing literature about relevant issues. Moreover, ILR enables an analysis from different sources and methods, integrating diverse findings and understandings of a phenomenon (Hopia, Latvala & Liimatainen, 2016; Whittemore & Knafl, 2005). Accordingly, this method contributes to the creation of new and updated knowledge (Brock & Ryan, 2016; Hansen & Brooks, 1994; Hopia et al., 2016; Torraco, 2005).

The strategy included the phases that Brock and Ryan (2016), Hansen and Brooks (1994), and Hopia et al. (2016) propose to conduct ILR. First, the selection and search in relevant academic databases: Web of Science (WoS) and Scopus. WoS and Scopus are recognized for their exigent filters and parameters to publish influential peer-reviewed articles, ensuring high quality knowledge (Elsevier, 2016).

The keywords selected to conduct the search were "Chile," "Brazil," "Latin America," "Human Resource Management" (HRM), "culture," and "International human resource management" (IHRM).

The initial search showed a total of 869 documents where titles, keywords, and abstracts were examined to exclude studies that did not cover the topic. After the removal of duplicates and the application of the exclusion criteria, 199 studies were selected and fully analyzed, including reports, conference papers, articles, and book chapters.

The inclusion/exclusion criteria for retaining or discarding articles and books were:

- Language: Although the author did not exclude documents by language, at the moment of full assessment, most of the documents were written in either English, Portuguese, or Spanish.
- Year of publication: All the documents published up to and including 2018 were assessed.
- Documents analyzing contexts other than the Brazilian and the Chilean were excluded (i.e., Asia, North America, Nicaragua, Salvador, United States, etc.). At the same time, the studies centered on topics different than HRM or IHRM were assessed and excluded, for example, documents about religion, meteorological data, mining production, and urban management.

After the exclusion process, interestingly, only 19.1% ($n = 38$) of the documents were set in Chile, whilst the other 80.9% were set in Brazil ($n = 161$). Considering this unbalance, when needed, snowball sampling was used as an additional and complementary method that contributed in the allocation of other articles and books cited by the original retrieved articles (Blumberg, Cooper, & Schindler, 2014; Eriksson & Kovalainen, 2010). Figure 11.1 details the steps followed to conduct the strategy of this ILR, following a chronological order.

Finally, the data collected was analyzed through the content analysis technique, which was developed in two ways: to analyze the cultural dimensions, predetermined codes and categories inspired in the GLOBE project were set. Second, to analyze the HRM trends and practices in both countries, the analyzes was structured following a grounded theory perspective, which establishes codes from the information (bottom-up), and does not predetermine them (Cresswell, 2014; Hernández-Sampieri, Fernández-Collado, & Baptista-Lucio, 2006). The findings and analysis of this investigation are presented in the next section two sections, with respect to Chile and Brazil.

CHILE: FINDINGS AND ANALYSIS

Chile has been considered one of the most competitive economies in the world, and its success is accredited to the influence of the neoliberalism system that opened the country to international investors through its

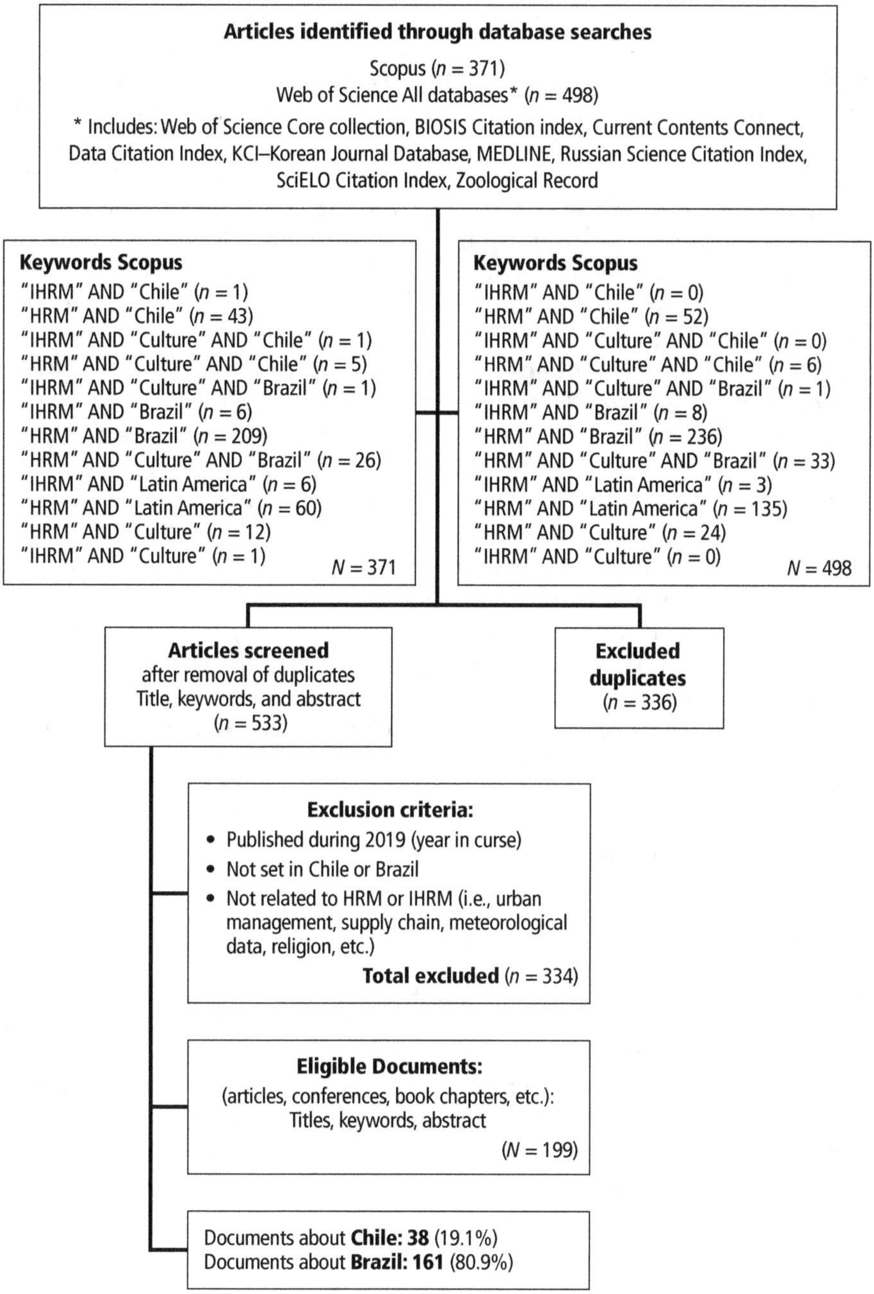

Figure 11.1 Strategy to select the literature.

free-market economic approach (Pérez-Arrau et al., 2012; Rodríguez, 2010; Sweeney & McFarlin, 2015).

The Chilean success began in the decade of the 1980s and has been reflected in the incomes per capita. For instance, the Gross Domestic Product (GDP) in 1960 was US$547,3 and in 2015 raised to US$13.383,9 locating Chile as a leader in GDP in Latin America, reducing poverty and implicating changes for people's life and working conditions of the Chilean workforce. In this sense, as it will be evidenced, in Chile, there is a hybrid workforce and management style, where the modernism coexists with the traditional cultural roots of the country (Pérez-Arrau et al., 2012; Rodríguez & Ríos, 2009; Wood, 2004; World Bank, 2016a). Some of the leading industries in Chile are mining, services, and agriculture (OECD, 2016a; Pablo, 2015; Rodríguez, 2010; Rodríguez & Gómez, 2009).

Additionally, it has been evidenced that in the last years, the top companies in the ranking created by "Great Place to Work" are foreign MNC (Great Place to Work, 2019). However, and despite the development that Chile has had in the last years, there are indicators of inequality and poverty that should be considered. For instance, the OECD (2016b, 2020b) reported that the wealthiest 10% of the population earns on average 26.5 times more than the poorest 10%. Thus, Chile is well-positioned in economic aspects than other Latin American countries, but among the members of the OECD is one of the countries with greater inequality and poverty. In consequence, the challenges for this country are substantial. The content analysis through the GLOBE cultural dimensions-follows.

Cultural Dimensions

Power Distance

In Chile, the influence of the *Hacienda* still survives.[3] Originally, the employers had power in their subordinates' lives, who were expected to be loyal to their boss (or *patrón*). The hacienda system did not allow mechanisms of social mobility since the aim was to perpetuate the established order and hierarchies. In other words, the poor and rich would remain the same. This system fostered paternalism, which still remains in hierarchical organizations. A reflection of this can be seen in the traditional pyramidal organization charts of public and private organizations and in the distrust of the ability of workers to make their own decisions (Martínez, 2005 Rodríguez & Gómez, 2009).

It has been suggested that a paternalistic relationship in hierarchical organizations undermines the proactivity, decision making, empowerment, and autonomy of the workers since the decisions and control rely on the figure of "the boss," the manager. Bureaucracy also plays a significant role by conditioning the organizational dynamics since there is no space for autonomy. In addition, the Chilean paternalism is distinguished for a perceived pressure, fear of possible repercussions, or sanctions to the workers if they question it. Furthermore, Chilean workers tend to not express their opinions and be passive instead of proactive in terms of decision making processes (Gómez & Rodríguez, 2006; Rodríguez, 2010; Rodríguez & Ríos, 2007, 2009; Rodríguez & Stewart, 2017).

Uncertainty Avoidance

The established bureaucratic system influences the dynamics and culture of organizations operating in this country. It has been explained that the establishment of formal procedures answers to a tendency to avoid and minimize uncertainty and risks, which has been shared for both workers and organizations. These rely on protocols to reduce ambiguity (Rodríguez, 2010; Rodríguez & Gómez, 2009).

Additionally, considering the geographical conditions of a country characterized for catastrophic phenomena of nature, this has influenced a tendency for fatalism where members of the society assume fatality as part of their fate. In the organizational context, this has been reflected in the perceptions of a pre-determined fate that cannot be changed or predicted; thus, what is given is accepted and not questioned (Gómez, 2001; Rodríguez, 2010).

Following this, the fear of uncertainty or for the "ridiculous" as Gómez (2001) highlights, is managed and silenced for a bureaucratic system that establishes formal procedures and determines the destiny and field of action of the organizational members. Indeed, it has been reported that leaders from societies with high uncertainty avoidance tend to be more controlling and less approachable with the workers (Dickson et al., 2003).

In consequence, this bureaucratic system traduces the psychological contract employee–employer into a utilitarian relationship by reducing anxiety and ambiguity for what is new (organizations) but also, limiting the spaces of innovation, creation and empowerment of the workers (Gómez, 2001; Gómez & Rodríguez, 2006; Pérez-Arrau et al., 2012; Rodríguez, 2010).

Collectivism I (Institutional Collectivism)

Organizations usually set policies and procedures without the participation of workers. Thus, decision making processes are hardly dialogued, fostering the organizational members' obedience and conformism (Gómez, 2001; Rodríguez, 2010).

Indeed, only 14.7% of Chilean workers belong to trade unions. This has been accredited to their association to be in "opposition" and hostile with the employer, and because they were abolished during the period of dictatorship (Dirección del Trabajo, 2014; Rodríguez, 2010; Rodríguez &

Gómez, 2009). In consequence, it is fostered a passive workforce who does not question the system established (Gómez & Rodríguez, 2006; Pérez-Arrau et al., 2012; Rodríguez & Gómez, 2009).

In practice, the research of Rodríguez (2010) and Rodríguez and Ríos (2009) evidence the cases of MNC that control significant features of the workers' lif—aspects where HR has a crucial role. Some examples are wages, vouchers for lunch instead of money for lunch, and the unilateral determination of benefits and sanctions.

Furthermore, with the impact of globalization, observations have been made of a new trend of young Chilean workers, who prefer to maintain impersonal relations with their employer. They are not passive or accept what is imposed, and they usually do not develop deep contractual relationships in order to find better opportunities regarding wages and professional development (Rodríguez & Ríos, 2007). In other words, new Chilean workers are more individualistic and tend to be more engaged with their own goals instead of the organization's (Dickson et al., 2003).

Collectivism II (In-Group Collectivism)

As aforementioned, the participation of Chilean workers in trade unions is low (Dirección del Trabajo, 2014; Rodríguez, 2010; Rodríguez & Gómez, 2009). In terms of in-group collectivism, the Chilean workforce tend to prefer uniformity, traduce in the establishment of reference groups, similar in needs and interests in order to be affiliated and recognized as part of them (sense of belonging; Gómez, 2001; Gómez & Rodríguez, 2006; Rodríguez, 2010). It has been suggested that this reflects the pursuit of homogenization since this workforce avoids uncertainty and what is new or different.

This logic is reinforced by the *compadrazgo* system[4] which emerges as convenient friendship networks (or social links) characterized by strong loyalty and that operates as a contract of reciprocity and favors. These networks operate connecting people in and outside the organization, for instance, by helping someone to gain a position or by giving promotions (Gómez, 2001; Gómez & Rodríguez, 2006; Rodríguez, 2010).

The compadrazgo also impacts on the trust/distrust of someone that does not belong to the network (House et al., 2004). A practical example can be found during the recruitment and selection of personnel, where usually the first call and preference will be directed to workers within the organization or to people with connections within the organization (Mendoza, 2010).

Finally, it has been suggested that new trends of Chilean workers (i.e., millennials) may be reshaping the dominant cultural values, by establishing impersonal, utilitarian, and competitive relationships in the workplace (Pérez-Arrau et al., 2012; Rodríguez & Gómez, 2009; Rodríguez & Ríos, 2007). However, Dickson et al. (2003) found that team performance and team efficacy are not related to individualistic characteristics of the members. In other words, employees who value collectivism tend to have a better performance when they have to work in groups.

Gender Egalitarianism

The equality of opportunities for men and women is still a critical issue in modern societies around the world. According to the BBC (2016) and the Dirección del Trabajo, Chile (2016), in Chile, an average women's salary, is one-third less than men's wages and only three in 10 senior managers or legislators are female. The literature advances to associate this to the *machismo,* culture,[5] where it is expected that men provide and women will develop a caring role in their families (Gómez & Rodríguez, 2006; Rodríguez, 2010; Rodríguez & Ríos, 2009).

Regarding organizations and HR practices, recruitment and selection processes have evidenced discriminatory practices: it is common to find job adverts specifying age, gender, and even specific physical characteristics. Also, have less opportunities of promotion and career development than men. Indeed, the literature suggests that female workers are "undesired" in Chile and have less opportunities since these are "vulnerable" to maternity leaves, which are associated with productivity reduction (Castro, 2001; Comunidad Mujer, 2016).

Future Orientation

The relationship of Chile with natural catastrophes has influenced the perception and relation with time. In organizational terms, Chilean workers tend to rely on an externalized management of their future and present, which gives them less responsibility about it. Organizations contribute to this by establishing bureaucratic mechanisms that control the present and future of the workers. Behind this, operates a logic where the unknown cannot be controlled (future). Thus, the primary orientation is to the past, the only "time" that provides certainty and works as a mechanism reduces the anxiety of the unpredictable (Gómez, 2001; Pérez-Arrau et al., 2012; Rodríguez, 2010; Rodríguez & Gómez, 2009).

In this context, at the organizational level, activities, practices, and systems that can provide predictability and stability are desired since these reduce anxiety, such as about the reward systems (Rodríguez, 2010; Rodríguez & Gómez, 2009).

Performance Orientation

In Chile, organizations have conducted training and development initiatives. However, it has been reported that these decisions are unilaterally determined by managers without the workers' participation or consideration to their professional needs and interests. Also, there is a perception that training opportunities is given to the managers' "friends" (compadrazgo system), highly productive workers or close "right-hand" employees (Rodríguez, 2010; Rodríguez & Gómez, 2009; Rodríguez & Ríos, 2009).

Furthermore, workers conceive performance appraisals as a "waste of time" or a non-valuable procedure, since these are perceived as biased practices. Thus, if performance appraisals are to be applied by organizations, they should be carefully managed and protocolized in order to reduce mistrust among the employees (Dickson et al., 2003). This demonstrates the challenges of HR areas in Chile in order to professionalize and offer accurate training, learning, and development practices not only centered in incentive systems for a few but as strategic tools that contribute to the development of organizations and their employees (Rodríguez, 2010; Rodríguez & Gómez, 2009).

Finally, Davila and Elvira (2012) and Rodríguez and Ríos (2007) analyze the case of a Dutch Bank operating in Chile that, through a contingent approach, adapted global policies to the local needs, for instance, providing benefits that met the expectations of the workers, encouraging equal opportunities, promotion, and career development.

Humane Orientation

It has been suggested that the rooted system of social stratification, the focus on maximization of profits, and the inequality in Chile promotes a perception of unfairness. Also, gender, disability, and ethnic discrimination contribute to this perception of injustice (Elvira & Davila, 2005; Pérez-Arrau et al., 2012; Rodríguez, 2010; Rodríguez & Gómez, 2009). Indeed, the lack of investment and participation in decision making processes impacts negatively on the workers' well-being. Additionally, the psychological contract will be impacted by the dependence (utilitarianism) and lack of mutual trust and loyalty from employee to employer (Rodríguez, 2010; Rodríguez & Gómez, 2009).

Despite this, Chile is advancing into the field of humane orientation by approving, for instance, the law of "labor inclusion for people with disabilities." This law attempts to establish a regulation that promotes access to fair opportunities for workers with disabilities (Gobierno de Chile, 2017). Indeed, to support employers in the field of inclusion, the Industrial Development Society (Sofofa, 2017) is creating initiatives such as the "inclusive enterprise" award, as well as reports and bulletins in the issue, to provide advice in diversity management and inclusion promotion.

Assertiveness

Considering the particular characteristics of the Chilean workforce (paternalism, dependence, and lack of initiative) and the continuous discouragement of unionization, it has been suggested that this workforce is passive and "loyal" towards their workplace. Workers are not encouraged to be confrontational and active in their work life. Indeed, the features of the society itself towards the homogenization of its members contribute to this non-confrontational trend (Davila & Elvira 2009; House et al., 2004; Rodríguez & Gómez, 2009).

Management Strategies in Chile

The present analysis is organized in four dimensions that emerged from the literature review: external factors, management strategies at the organizational level, corporate social responsibility, and management strategies at the human resource level.

External Factors

This category is organized analyzing two themes addressed by the literature and research that involves Chile. First, the legislation and/or public policies of the country, and second, the political and economic factors.

Regarding legislation and/or public policies of Chile, the research has argued that these are key determinants for the organizational functioning and the development of HRM practices and strategies (Elvira & Davila, 2005). Studies have centered in analyzing the normative framework about working time, wages (Poblete, 2018), and voucher programs from the State, that encourage training opportunities for workers. In this last aspect, the research of Novella, Rucci, Vázquez, and Kaplan (2018) found that these programs improve the possibilities and earnings of workers with low levels of education.

Following this, the literature suggests that factors such as the political stability, economic development, and even the geographical distance between the host and home nations, are fundamental for the organizational functioning in the host country (Amini & Dal Bianco, 2017; Baena, 2015). For instance, Fuenzalida and Ricucci (2018) suggests the relevance that the political environment has on the organization and HRM practices, arguing that the politicization of the analyzed institutions impacted their HRM processes.

Management Strategies at the Organizational Level

Concerning topics of management strategies at the organizational level, the main themes identified by the author are knowledge management and organizational change.

In regard to knowledge management (KM), the study of Pérez-Arrau (2015) explains that this is not common in the organizations of Chile, since the concept is still ambiguous in this context. Furthermore, the author proposes that the cultural characteristics of the Chilean workforce such as paternalism, lack of trust, and social inequalities could threaten strategies of

KM. For these reasons, organizations that wish to systematically coordinate their people, processes, and technologies (commonly understood as KM), need to incorporate as part of this, the cultural characteristics of the Chilean workforce; indeed, this is part of the knowledge that needs to be managed.

In relation to organizational change, the research conducted by Raineri (2011) showed that in the face of changes, the participant organizations developed more practices and were more prepared during the change preparation than during change implementation.

Corporate Social Responsibility

This dimension refers to the strategies and actions that attempt to manage organizations with an ethical and socially responsible perspective, which is known as corporate social responsibility (CSR). The literature identifies an internal (towards the own organizational practices and policies) and external (towards the community and environment) focus of action (Truss et al., 2012). The results are presented accordingly. In terms of internal actions, (a) diversity management and (b) life-quality and well being were identified as sub-categories. In terms of the external focus, the environmental management (EM) is revised.

Regarding the internal focus, first, diversity management is presented. Most of the literature studying the case of Chile, has focused on gender and aging. In this sense, gender barriers have been analyzed, such as discrimination, family demands, and the influence of a male-oriented culture (Salinas & Romaní, 2014). Moreover, there is an increasing interest in women' transitions to the labor market (Cronin, 2013), overcoming the pay gap, and promoting their career development (Meruane & Chau, 2016; Ugarte, 2017). Indeed, the research of Meruane and Chau (2016) suggest that to overcome these challenges, organizations should engage in actions such as facilitating women adaptation, promoting them to managerial positions, or assigning them more responsibilities in order to encourage symmetry between men and women.

Following this, the research has shown significant interest into analyzing differences between generations of workers (i.e., millennials and generation Y) (Zavala-Villalón & Castro, 2018). The study conducted by Vives, Gray, Gonzalez, and Molina (2018) analyzes the challenges for a growing older workforce, suggesting that Chile is not yet prepared for this. Indeed, the authors explain that the workers' health condition determines their likelihood to get and maintain a job.

In relation to life-quality and well-being, the research developed in Chile has reflected on initiatives that contribute to the work–life balance, such as flexi-time (Garuti & Sandoval, 2006; Yushimito, Holguín-Veras & Gellona, 2018). Indeed, the study conducted by Garavan, Idrovo, Leon, and Grau (2012) showed that when comparing organizations from Spain with organizations from Latin America (including Chile), the former were more supportive to work–family balance than the latter. However, in contrast to the Spanish, Latin American organizations had lesser formal policies and formal procedures in this issue. These findings clearly evidence that this is still a pending matter for these territories.

Regarding the external focus of CSR, the topic of environmental management has been relatively unexplored in the Chilean context; however, Elwell, Gelcich, Gaines, and López-Carr (2013) explain that EM can be an alternative to address community-company conflicts and improve the relationship with the societal sphere.

Finally, in general terms, it is relevant to highlight that the literature has emphasized the need for advancing CSR of organizations operating in Chile, explaining that it can contribute to achieving sustainable competitive advantage. For instance, Dávila and Troncoso (2018) showed that an internal focus of CSR, translated in practices such as health, safety, and professional development, showed a positive correlation with the organizational commitment.

Management Strategies at the Human Resource Level

This category aims to unveil the policies, procedures, and actions that directly concern the HR level, such as leadership and teamwork.

In terms of leadership, the literature relating to Chile, has studied the paternalistic relationships established between managers and workers (described earlier; Rodríguez & Stewart, 2017). In addition, the research of Meruane and Chau (2016) suggests the need to advance towards a transformational leadership with a gender perspective, where women have access to managerial positions.

In relation to teamwork, the research analyzes the importance of communication, clear goals, and sharing common goals for successful teams (Espinoza, Peduzzi, Agreli, & Sutherland, 2018; Silvestre, Ochoa, & Marques, 2016). Interestingly, virtual teams are starting to gain attention in the literature. Specifically, the analysis of conflict sources that affect teams' performance (Pazos & Canto, 2013; Pazos, Canto, & Magpili, 2012).

BRAZIL: FINDINGS AND ANALYSIS

Brazil has been recognized as the largest economy in Latin America, and it is part of the influential G20, attracting the attention of foreign investors (G20, 2020; Mustafa, 2016). Indeed, the Brazilian productive sector is predominantly composed by MNCs, the government, and large organizations that belong to Brazilian economic groups. These organizations contributed to the industrialization of the country. Many of these organizations have implemented programs of subcontract and consultancy that have shaped the relations with the Brazilian workforce. Thus, a certain hybridism is evident since modern styles of management interact with cultural customs and traditional styles of the Brazilian culture (Griffin & Pustay, 2015; Muritiba, Nunes, Campanario, & Albuquerque, 2010; Pérez-Arrau et al., 2012; Wood, 2004).

The first decade of 2000 was a time of prosperity for Brazil, for instance, the price of semi-manufactured exports rose 43%. Indeed, the Brazilian GDP in the last years has risen from US$209 in 1960 to US$13.000 in 2010. However, a decline followed this prosperity during 2015, as impact of both the global financial crisis and the internal crisis of the country. Consequently, the GDP decreased to US$8.540 (Cardoso & Teles; 2009; Tanure, 2005; World Bank, 2016b).

Additionally, Brazil has been impacted by scandals of corruption at all levels since essential members and high executives of Petrobras (a national company) were accused and judged for corruption. Also, former president Dilma Rousseff was destitute after several scandals related to the deviation of public funds and her participation in the scandal of Petrobras, and former president Lula Da Silva was imprisoned (BBC, 2016; Leahy, 2016; Petrobras Magazine Global Connections, 2016; Telesur, 2016).

Cultural Dimensions

Power Distance

This society has reported high power distance, reflected in a significant number of hierarchical organizations. In terms of values, Brazil scored low in power distance, but high in the societal practice (Cooke et al., 2013; House et al., 2004; Tanure, 2005; Thomas & Peterson, 2015; Wood, 2004).

To understand this contrast, it is relevant to analyze the figure of the *jeitinho* or "their way to do things" (Mello, 2012) which is a Brazilian cultural trait and mechanism to solve problems and to soften the rules and hierarchies. In this sense, although the Brazilian organizations are hierarchized, their relationship with the rules imposed is characterized for accepting them with certain sympathy, cordiality, empathy, and an easy-going behavior that allows them to get what is desired. Thus, in organizations, through the jeitinho trait, Brazilian workers make things happen in a more relaxed way because the relational bonds are more emotional, informal, and less impersonal, avoiding confrontations (Davila & Elvira, 2012; Pérez-Arrau et al., 2012; Wood, 2004).

Personal relations are relevant for the Brazilian workers, and the *jeitinho*[6] shapes hierarchical ties where trust and loyalty rely on the leader, evidencing another form of paternalism in comparison to the Chilean example. From this perspective, workers are willing to achieve the objectives established by their leaders if they feel a sense of belonging and trust him/her, but if the leadership is openly authoritarian—leaving little space to the jeitinho and trust—the fear and distrust can negatively impact on performances (Cooke et al., 2013; House et al., 2004; Tanure, 2005). As Mello (2012) mentions, a common Brazilian saying is "for my friends everything, for my enemies the law."

Uncertainty Avoidance

The Brazilian workers tend to follow rules and procedures defined by the leader, who is the central figure in the decision making process. Similar to the case of the Chilean workers, there is a vision of a passive intervention in the future since they cannot interfere with their destiny. Accordingly, they do not take unnecessary risks; instead, they adapt to whatever happens, but with flexibility to changes and less pessimism than the Chilean employees (Coda et al., 2009; House et al., 2004; Tanure, 2005; Wood, 2004). Indeed, Brazil was reported to be one of the countries with highest uncertainty avoidance according to the study of Hofstede (2001), and policies, procedures, practices, and laws tend to regulate the majority of aspects of the workers' lives.

Despite this, the research of House and colleagues (2004) identified contrasts, in terms of values, the Brazilian culture scored relatively high, but the practices' score was lower. These results could be ascribed to the jeitinho trait, which reduces tensions, avoids confrontations, and addresses rules and procedures with alternative informal methods. Another argument that explains this is great foreign investment in Brazil, which has promoted the impression that it is the land of opportunities (Coda et al., 2009; House et al., 2004; Tanure, 2005).

Collectivism I (Institutional Collectivism)

In the GLOBE project, Brazil evidenced high scores in terms of values but lower scores in practices, House et al. (2004) explain that societies tend to value collectivism more than practice it. In the case of Brazil, this could be influenced by two factors: the jeitinho and the increasing subcontract rates. Basically, jeitinho shapes relations centered on loyalty, sympathy, and trust towards their leaders' goals. Indeed, for them, these relationships are more important than the institutions. Indeed, Brazilian workers value the internal communication in their organizations (Coda et al., 2004; Davila & Elvira, 2012; House et al., 2004; Pérez-Arrau et al., 2012; Wood 2004).

Furthermore, the increasing number of subcontracted employees fosters the development of utilitarian impersonal relationships with the organization, reducing the belongingness, perhaps also because the benefits of this type of contract are limited (Griffin & Pustay, 2015; Pérez-Arrau et al., 2012; Wood, 2004).

Collectivism II (In-Group Collectivism)

It has been reported that the country possesses more than 15,000 trade unions but only 14% of the workers are affiliated to them, which is less than the proportion of Chilean workforce in trade unions and to the average of OECD countries (Dirección del Trabajo, 2014; Novais, 2012; OECD, 2020a). Additionally, in the GLOBE study, Brazil scored low in both practices and values, in comparison to the other societies analyzed (House et al., 2004).

These findings are different to the general importance of family and friend bonds to the Brazilian (Mello, 2012), but it can be ascribed to the *personalism,* which refers to the prioritization of their own interests and needs instead of the reference groups' (Tanure, 2005; Wood, 2004).

Although the sympathy in the relationships is transversal to the groups and it is a way to address people, the direct trust, and loyalty are directed to their leaders since workers rely on their decisions (Cooke et al., 2013; House et al., 2004; Tanure, 2005). From this perspective, the development of leaders is a fundamental aspect for organizations in Brazil.

Additionally, an alternative explanation for the low scores of in-group collectivism is related to the impact of the increase in subcontracts has had, as aforementioned. Subcontracts foster individualism since these encourage impersonal, competitive, and utilitarian relations (Cooke et al., 2013; Griffin & Pustay, 2015; Wood, 2004).

Gender Egalitarianism

The results evidenced in the GLOBE study indicate that Brazil is one of the societies with higher gender egalitarianism among the participants and in Latin America (House et al., 2004).

However, this is contrasted by research that indicates that Brazilian women work fewer hours in formal positions than men. Indeed, only 15% of them hold governmental positions, the unemployment among women is more than that among men, and that their wages are on average 15% less than men's wages (Agénor & Canuto, 2015; BBC, 2016).

Regardless, this demonstrates that if Brazil is compared to other countries, it is well positioned in terms of gender egalitarianism. However, if the analysis is centered only on internal factors without being compared to other societies, it is evident that there is still work to be done in terms of policies concerning gender equality (Agénor & Canuto, 2015).

Future Orientation

Despite the hierarchical system, in Brazil, the workforce is characterized by the loyalty and trust in the leaders' decision making when instead of holding an authoritarian relationship, friendly bonds are developed (in the case of Chile, hierarchies are openly authoritarian). This aspect influences flexibility, passiveness, and willingness to accept a destiny that is established by the leader. Thus, leadership style influences directly in the workers' perspectives of the future (Coda et al., 2009; House et al., 2004; Tanure, 2005; Wood, 2004).

Another factor that impacts on the orientation to the future is the entrepreneur mentality, in the case of Brazil related to the perception that it is the land of opportunities. This enhances a more flexible and optimistic view of the future (in contrast to Chile), a future that is already predetermined but is not necessarily dangerous or threatening because of that (Coda et al., 2009; Tanure, 2005).

This is also evident in the results of the GLOBE study, since according to House and his colleagues (2004), the country scored high in values and medium in practices.

Performance Orientation

In the GLOBE study, society values scored high in performance orientation, and medium in social practices (House et al., 2004). This can be attributed to the strong influence of modern HR strategies that MNC and large companies have implemented in Brazil. In general, training is one of the key aspects for these organizations, recognizing that this is an investment focused on the promotion of individual development (Coda et al., 2009; Jabbour, 2011; Wood, 2004).

However, the increase in the subcontracts and external workers has reduced the opportunities of transversal training and development, limiting this aspect to only a few employees and emerging as a gap and risk in terms of performance orientation (Tanure, 2005; Wood, 2004).

Humane Orientation

The GLOBE study results indicate that this society scored low in practices of humane orientation, but high in society values (House et al., 2004). This appreciation is sustained on the jeitinho values, which fosters an image related to a Brazilian who is loyal and protects harmony through the establishment of informal relationships. At the same time, personalism and high rates of subcontracts could explain the low practices of humane orientation (Pérez-Arrau et al., 2012; Tanure, 2005; Wood 2004).

As Muritiba et al. (2010), Pérez-Arrau et al. (2012), and Wood (2004) highlight, this phenomenon shows an evolving workforce influenced by the practices and policies that organizations develop (subcontracting, externalization of services, lack of practices to deal with the gender gap, etc.).

Assertiveness

The GLOBE evidence shows low values, but high society practices. In this regard, high values of humane orientation are related to high assertive practices as a response against injustice (House et al., 2004).

To understand the reason of why assertiveness scored low in social values, we can relate this once again to the jeitinho trait, since it is desirable to avoid conflicts with easy-going behavior. Thus, these values are socially promoted and shared (Davila & Elvira, 2012; Pérez-Arrau et al., 2012; Wood 2004).

Furthermore, the high number of trade unions can reflect the high scores in practices related to assertiveness, considering that these organizations represent the interests of the workers in order to avoid injustices and protect equality (Novais, 2012; Trade Unions Congress, 2016).

Management Strategies in Brazil

The structure of this section is organized according to the following categories: external factors, management strategies at the organizational level, CSR, and management strategies at the human-resource level.

External Factors

Similar to the case of Chile, the literature concerning Brazil also recognizes that the political stability, regulatory environment, and economic development are fundamental for the successful entrance of international organizations and MNCs (Baena, 2015; Clouse & Watkins, 2009; Elvira & Davila, 2005; Figueiredo & Piana, 2016; Muritiba et al., 2010).

In regard to the legislative framework of Brazil, the research has been focused on analyzing which labor laws exist for arbitrary dismissal (Roh, 2013) and unions (Friel & de Villechenon, 2018). The research conducted by da Silva et al. (2010); Friel and de Villechenon (2018); Mello e Silva (2014); and Siddique, Ansari, and Salman (2006) concluded that Brazil is a context where labor laws are predominantly neoliberal and have gaps in terms of protecting workers' social rights. Furthermore, due to a capitalist predominant nature, unions are weak and have been delegitimized, promoting turnover and unprotecting workers. In consequence, those MNC and companies that tried to empower workers and create teams, failed. In this line, also the research of Kim (2013) argued that the combination of cultural traits, summed with an inefficient, populist and bureaucratic law system, has an important impact on Brazilian HRM systems.

Management Strategies at the Organizational Level

In comparison to the case of Chile, where the research in these topics is only at the initial stage, the case of Brazil shows more development, revealing the following two main themes: knowledge management and organizational change.

Regarding knowledge management, compared to the scarce literature developed in Chile, the Brazilian research has advanced significantly on this issue. For instance, it has been highlighted the important contribution that cultural intelligence makes to KM and, in turn, to the organizational functioning, arguing that this is key for the cross-cultural adaptation of MNCs and other international organizations (Barakat, Lorenz, Ramsey, & Cretoiu, 2015; Krzywdzinski, 2017; Nunes, Felix, & Prates, 2017). Despite this, there still remain challenges for the organizational sector. For instance, the study conducted by Batista and Quandt (2016) showed that organizations that adopted a KM approach, were more concentrated in technologies, learning, and innovation aspects, than the knowledge processes or KM leadership, which are key issues to achieve a successful KM. In addition, the research of De Sá Freire, Dandolini, de Souza, Silva, and Couto (2017) investigated knowledge transfer in Brazilian organizations, and the study of Steffen and Oliveira (2015) explored interorganizational knowledge sharing.

In regard to organizational change, Fleury (1996) suggested that this aspect depends on the level of development that the sector or industry has in the country. Interestingly, in Brazil, a study found that managers showed resistance to change initiatives (Guimarães, Ribeiro, Renner, & De Oliveira 2014). Moreover, when organizations tried to set strategies to develop capabilities that were oriented towards the future, there were major difficulties (Trinidade, de Aluquerque, & Freire, 2017).

Corporate Social Responsibility

The results in this section are ordered following the internal and external focus of CSR actions (Truss et al., 2012). In terms of the internal focus, it was possible to identify the following sub-categories: diversity management, life-quality and well-being, and ethical management. Concerning the external focus, the sub-category of environmental management is presented.

This category acquires relevance since it has been identified that some organizations in Brazil commit to corporate sustainable management strategies with both an internal and external focus. This, in order to encourage workers to engage (Pintao, Chaves, & Branco, 2018) and to achieve a sustainable development (Duarte, 2017). However, authors have explained that there are still existent challenges in this issue. For instance, Duarte (2017) found that organizations lacked formal sustainability systems. Also, De Souza, Jabbour, Mangili, Filho, and De Oliveira (2012) studied communication systems that could contribute to bridging the gap between sustainable values and practices.

In regard to the *internal focus* of CSR, it has been highlighted that there is a need to align HR strategies with CSR (Angelo, Amui, Caldana, & Jabbour, 2012). For instance, in terms of diversity management, although the literature explains that this is still emergent in the Brazilian context (Jabbour, Gordono, Oliveira, Martinez, & Battistelle, 2011), the issue has been more developed in contrast to other countries of the region, such as Chile.

The literature analyzes disabilities, aging, gender, and ethnic minorities, centering on the need to overcome discriminatory practices and the role and responsibilities of organizations in including minorities (Jabbour et al., 2011). These are interesting suggestions considering that Santos and Garibaldi de Hilal (2018) explain that although the Brazilian national ethos promotes equality, issues such as gender roles in the workplace are still a challenge.

Following this, the studies conducted by Guimaraes, Barkokebas, and Martins (2018) and Guimaraes, Martins, and Barkokebas (2015) concluded that workers with disabilities showed lower levels of absenteeism in comparison to workers without disabilities.

Moreover, in terms of aging, differences between generations have been analyzed, in light of a population that is getting older. Interestingly, studies set in the Brazilian context found that managers discriminate against younger workers (Rego et al., 2018; Vasconcelos, 2016). In addition, the study of Silva, Dutra, Veloso, Fischer, and Trevisan (2015) analyzed the differences between Baby Boomers and Generation Y. The former valued more CSR in Brazil, whilst the latter showed more appreciation in learning, development, relations, and work–life balance.

Following this, ethnic groups are a relevant aspect for the Brazilian context, since an important number or inhabitants are identified as part of these groups. Moreover, the study of Nunes et al. (2017) highlighted that cultural intelligence related to Brazilian ethnic minorities, can contribute to a mutual understanding, reduce hostilities, tensions, as well as prejudices. However, in order to support diversity management, awareness, or cultural intelligence is not enough for diversity management. Indeed, as Vasconcelos (2015) explains, initiatives such as training programs are necessary to reduce discrimination, tackle stereotypes and biases, and to promote effective diversity and inclusion.

In terms of life quality and well-being, the research has analyzed several issues related to well-being, workplace commitment, engagement, reward systems, and ergonomic interventions. Renwick (2009) has proposed that the origins of employee well-being in Brazil can be attributed to historical factors, such as the relationship with native communities, and a history of slavery, protests, and lack of labor rights. Moreover, the research conducted by Van Dierendonck, Lankester, Zmyslona, and Rothweiler (2016) found that well-being practices have positive effects on reducing employee turnover.

Among the actions to support well-being, work–family balance has gained significant attention from studies that have analyzed the reconciliation of life and family in Brazilian organizations (Gaete Valderrama, Carmona, Elgueta, & Quiroz, 2009; Vasconcelos, 2016). For instance, Donato, Kubo, Pereira, and Oliva (2013) studied how actions that support it, were also set to promote a harmonious organizational climate. Furthermore, Jose, Las Heras, Russo, Rofcanin, and Grau (2018) associated family-supportive supervisor behavior with motivation. In addition, Gertsen and Søderberg (2012) add that work–life balance can facilitate and mediate both, a global company's culture and its insertion to different settings.

Another issue studied in the context of Brazil, has been related to job satisfaction and commitment. For instance, Wasti et al. (2016) highlight the importance of contextualizing workplace commitment. In addition, Abreu, Cunha, and Rebouças (2013) found that in Brazilian companies, the type of contractual relationship mediates commitment (hired by the company or by a contractor). In terms of job satisfaction, Steil, Dandolini, de Souza, de Cuffa, and Costa, (2018) negatively related it to the intention to leave and positively related it to the intention to stay in the organization. Moreover, it was observed in one study that in organizations where workers participated in decision making processes, there was more satisfaction at work (Kurganct, Melleiro, & Tronchin, 2008). Additionally, Barakat et al. (2015) showed that when global managers exhibit high cultural intelligence, there was also more job satisfaction.

Following this, another policy that supports life quality and well-being is related to reward systems, which have been identified as key for the entrance of MNCs and the management of a global workforce (Budhwar, Tung, Varma, & Do, 2017). The research of Posthuma (2011) analyzed the relationship of workplace rewards, with perceptions of distributive justice. In addition, Bloom, Genakos, Sadun, and Van Reenen (2012) suggested that labor markets with less regulations are associated with improved practices of incentive management.

Another aspect related to the life-quality and well-being that has been explored by research in Brazil, refers to ergonomic interventions in the workplace. In this sense, Guimarães, Ribeiro, Renner, and De Oliveira (2014) explained that participatory ergonomic interventions led to positive health and productive outcomes. Another study, conducted by Guimarães, Ribeiro, and Renner (2012), unveiled that organizations that implemented ergonomic interventions reduced HR costs, such as industrial accidents, musculoskeletal disorders, turnover, and absenteeism. In addition, the productivity improved.

Another aspect related to the internal focus of CSR, is concerned with ethical management. The literature focused on Brazil has unveiled the relevance of ethical reflection for organizations (Teodósio, 2001) and the need to advance into ethical business decisions and practices (Ardichvili, Jondle, & Kowske, 2010).

Finally, as an external focus of CSR, an issue that has received significant attention in the literature specializing in Brazil, has been environmental management. Authors argue the need to include environmental issues in organizational and HR functioning (Jabbour, 2011; Jabbour, De Sousa, Govindan, Teixeira, & De Souza, 2013). For instance, Jabbour, De Sousa et al. (2013) explain that there is a key relationship between HR and environmental management. This, through environmental or "green" training (Aragão & Jabbour, 2017; Dias-Angelo, Jabbour, & Calderaro, 2014; Jabbour, Teixeira, & Jabbour, 2013) that allows to apply "green" knowledge in daily activities (Teixeira, Jabbour, De Sousa, Latan, & De Oliveira, 2016). Jabbour (2015) and Teixeira, Chiappetta, and Lopes de Sousa (2012) explained that the actions that support this training are positively related to the environmental management maturity of the organization. Moreover, when these conditions are given, it has been suggested that environmental training positively influences eco-efficiency (Moraes et al., 2018). In addition, it has been suggested that if green teams are developed, these are expected to promote and implement actions that support environmental management (De Sousa, 2015; Jabbour, Santos, Fonseca, & Nagano, 2013).

Management Strategies at the Human Resource Level

As compared to the Chilean case, the policies, procedures, and strategies at the HR level in Brazil seem to be more developed, or at least, more issues have been explored by the research. In this section we review recruitment, leadership, teamwork, training and development, and labor relations.

The research about recruitment policies has centered in the relevance of adopting strategies to approach this issue, using their organizational learning and knowledge (Chiappetta, Mauricio, & Jabbour, 2017; Fernández, Ventura, Andrade, Lumbreras, & Cobo-Benita, 2017); to attract and recruit key talents (Moraes, 2007).

In regard to leadership, the research of Casado (2018) analyzed the relationship between leadership and CSR, and Chiappeta et al. (2017) suggested that managers are key in developing green HRM strategies. In addition, Park and Paiva (2018) explained that managers are fundamental for the organizational articulation and functional integration of organizational processes in different cultural settings.

In reference to teamwork, studies have analyzed the factors that can enhance them, such as decision making autonomy (Capra & Moreira, 2013), intellectual capital (Voichcoski & Miziara, 2018), and multi-skilling (Guimarães et al., 2014).

Regarding training and development, several topics have been researched. For instance, virtual training has been explored as a manner to develop knowledge and awareness (De Fátima, Torres, Do Carmo, Dos Santos, De Souza, & Alves, 2013; Moraes, 2007). In addition, training programs have emerged as an alternative to counterattack discrimination, gender bias, stereotypes, and advance towards diversity (Vasconcelos, 2016). Another training topic that is gaining attention is coherent with the aforementioned environmental trend of CSR. In this sense, environmental training is also gaining attention as it is a fundamental part of environmental management (Aragão & Jabbour, 2017; Dias-Angelo et al., 2014; Jabbour, 2015; Jabbour, Santos et al., 2013; Moraes et al., 2018).

Interestingly, considering the diverse population of Brazil, intercultural training has also been significantly analyzed, advising that this is a fundamental issue that needs to be addressed by MNCs and other organizations in order to have a successful entry and a positive relationship with the community (de Miranda & Braga, 2011; Zhang, 2011). In addition, Steil et al. (2018) found that organizations that provide training and development opportunities-negatively affected the intentions of the workers to leave.

Another relevant aspect for strategic HRM practices is related to providing elements for talent retention (Wood, Dibben, & Meira, 2016), career planning, and performance evaluation (Marx & Soares, 2008; Moraes, Coelho, & Gladis, 2012).

Finally, an interesting topic addressed pertains to labor relations. In this sense, the research of Friel and de Villechenon (2018) explains that in Brazil unions are weak due to labor laws. Furthermore, collective labor participation has been delegitimized in a capitalist state (Siddique et al., 2006). Moreover, Goncalves, Sarsur, Costa, Fischer, and Kassem (2017) suggest that employment relations are poorly integrated in Brazilian organizations. Indeed, Oliveira and Nogueira (2017) explored a case where managers and technicians from an organization in Brazil; were against union resistance in order to protect the company interests.

SUMMARIZING THE FINDINGS AND ANALYSES OF CHILE AND BRAZIL

Table 11.1 summarizes the findings and analyses of the data presented in the previous two sections as they relate to Chile and Brazil respectively, covering the GLOBE cultural dimensions. The table clearly illustrates noteworthy similarities and differences between the two societies. For instance, in both of them, the power distance is high, and the aversion of uncertainty is significant. However, among their differences, the way to face life is one of the most fundamental in their traits: whilst Brazilians have an easygoing, optimistic manner that permeates their cultural values, reflected in the jeitinho, Chileans show different characteristics. In this regard, the evidence shows that the cultural values of Chilean society are permeated by a pessimistic vision that is transversal to the different dimensions analyzed. Thus, these differences are key to understanding how these workforces will relate with their organizations.

TABLE 11.1 Summary of GLOBE Cultural Dimensions Applied to Chile and Brazil

Cultural Dimension	Chile	Brazil
Power Distance	High power distance. Paternalism, bureaucracy, and hierarchical organizational structures. Perceived pressure and fear of consequences among workers.	High power distance. Hierarchical organizational structures: Low scores in values, high in practices. Jeitinho as a trait that shapes non-confrontational, empathic, cordial and convenient relationships. Trust and loyalty to the leader (paternalism), not to the organization.
Uncertainty Avoidance	Bureaucracy and formal procedures as mechanisms to avoid uncertainty. A fatalistic vision of future, where the future cannot be predicted or changed but managed.	Aversion to uncertainty. Passive intervention in the future but more adaptability and flexibility. High values but low practices, related to the vision of Brazil as the land of opportunities and the jeitinho trait.
Collectivism I (Institutional collectivism)	Permeated by the hierarchical relationship with the organization. Imposed policies that are not agreed with the employees. New trend of workers who maintain impersonal relations with their employer.	High values, low practices. Jeitinho encourages loyalty and trust, but the increasing subcontract discourages it because there are no emotional links created.
Collectivism II (in-group collectivism)	Low participation in trade unions. Preference for homogenization by establishing reference groups. Compadrazgo system as a mechanism of friendship and social contact through mutual favors. New trends of workers establish individualism through utilitarian and competitive relationships.	Low in practices, high in values: High number of trade unions but scarce participation. Values of the jeitinho but practices inherited by the subcontract (individualism is promoted).
Gender Egalitarianism	Gender gap: salary, less participation of women in managerial roles. Machismo culture encourages gender roles.	High in comparison to other Latin American countries. Despite this, gender gaps remain.

(continued)

TABLE 11.1 Summary of GLOBE Cultural Dimensions Applied to Chile and Brazil (continued)

Cultural Dimension	Chile	Brazil
Future Orientation	Orientation to the past because it is the only time that can be controlled. A pessimistic vision of the future.	Willingness to accept the future but also, to adapt and be flexible towards it. Trust gives power and relies on the figure of the leader.
Performance Orientation	E-learning initiatives. Performance appraisals are not preferred. The perception that development opportunities are given for a few preferred employees.	High score in values, medium in practices. Training as a key aspect but subcontracts limit transversal opportunities of career development.
Humane Orientation	Sensation of unfairness. Weak mutual trust and loyalty worker-employee.	Low scores in social practices but high in values. Jeitinho protects the harmony among the relations. Increment in the externalization of services impacts on the practices.
Assertiveness	Passive and loyal to the organization, non-aggressive. However, new trends of workers are less passive.	Low society values but high practices. Jeitinho is a non-confrontational and easy-going behavior. Active role of trade unions that seek to reduce injustices and inequalities.

Note: Author elaboration.

In Table 11.2 we summarize the content related to strategic management research identified in regard to Chile and Brazil. It is clear from the table that there are similarities and differences between these two societies. For instance, the research on strategic management has developed a wider range of topics in Brazil than Chile, investigating issues of disabilities, ethnic groups, commitment, engagement, reward systems, recruitment, training, development, and labor relations. From this analysis, it becomes clear that strategic management has been scarcely addressed in Chile, if its neighbor country, Brazil, is contrasted. However, one of the common aspects identified in both societies, shows that cultural values as a key part of the organizational strategic management have been under-researched according to the evidence of the presented literature. Thus, it is possible to propose that in both societies, the understanding of cultural

TABLE 11.2 Summary of Categories, Subcategories, and Content of Strategic Management Research Identified in Chile and Brazil

	Chile	Brazil
Category	**Subcategory and Content**	**Subcategory and Content**
External Factors	Legislation and/or public policies	Legislation or public policies
	Political and economic factors	Political and economic factors
Management Strategies at the Organizational Level	Organizational change	Organizational change
	Knowledge management Organizational change	Knowledge management (cultural intelligence) Organizational change
Corporate Social Responsibility	Internal focus: Diversity management (gender and aging)	Internal focus: Diversity management (disabilities, aging, gender, and ethnic groups)
	Internal focus: Life quality and well-being (flexitime, work-family balance)	Internal focus: Life quality and well-being (workplace commitment, engagement, reward systems, and ergonomic)
		Internal focus: Ethical management (green or environmental training)
	External focus: Environmental management	External focus: Environmental management (green training)
Management Strategies at the HR Level		Recruitment
	Leadership (transformational)	Leadership
	Teamwork (virtual teams)	Teamwork (autonomy and intellectual capital)
		Training and development (virtual training, diversity management training, intercultural training, career planning, performance evaluation) Labor relations (trade unions)

Note: Author elaboration.

values has not yet been seen, or significantly acknowledged as a component that can contribute to providing a competitive advantage to organizations operating in Chile and Brazil. This supposes significant challenges for MNCs, transnationals, and other foreign organizations or leaders that aim to operate in the region.

DISCUSSION

The findings of this study highlight interesting cultural characteristics of Chilean and Brazilian workforces, as this research aimed to discuss why a homogeneous analysis of the Latin America cluster is superficial and why further cultural specificity is needed when devising strategies. The jeitinho and compadrazgo cultural traits are rooted in the Brazilian and Chilean cultures, and these shape relationships. Paternalism is another characteristic that has been associated with Latin American societies, but the cases of Chile and Brazil suggest particularities in this aspect. In Chile, paternalism is authoritarian and associated with fear, but in Brazil, paternalism is reflected in trust and loyalty to the leader. Despite this, in both cultures, paternalism is traduced in passiveness and lack of autonomy among workers (Cooke et al., 2013; Gómez & Rodríguez, 2006; Martínez, 2005; Pérez-Arrau et al., 2012; Rodríguez & Gómez, 2009; Rodríguez & Ríos, 2007; Wood, 2004).

In terms of the strategic management in both countries, the revised studies show major differences between both countries. For instance, the category of management strategies at the organizational level, the research in Brazil has been significantly developed in terms of knowledge management, analyzing how cultural intelligence impacts on this (Barakat et al., 2015; Krzywdzinski, 2017; Nunes et al., 2017). Whereas, in Chile, although it is not yet a common issue in organizational settings, there is an incipient interest on the topic (Pérez-Arrau, 2015).

Moreover, in terms of CSR, the diversity management in Chile has only focused on gender (Meruane & Chau, 2016; Ugarte, 2017) and ageing factors (Zavala-Villalón & Castro, 2018). Whereas, in addition to these topics, the Brazilian literature also explores disabled (Jabbour et al., 2011) and ethnic minorities (Nunes et al., 2017).

Issues of diversity management are particularly relevant in these cultures, since a hybrid diverse population inhabits both. For instance, these are societies where old and new trends of workers coexist (Generation Y, baby boomers, etc.), evidencing the complexity of constantly evolving cultures. This is also a global trend, and thus, it should not be ignored by organizations operating in these contexts (Davila & Elvira, 2012; Truss et al., 2012; Wood, 2004).

When analyzing the research regarding life quality and wellbeing in both countries, once again, the Chilean case shows incipient interest. Interestingly, both countries orient their efforts to different issues within this topic. For instance, in Chile flextime and work–family balance have been studied to explore their relationship with commitment and wellbeing in the workplace (Garuti & Sandoval, 2006; Yushimito et al., 2018). Whereas, the Brazilian literature analyzes commitment, engagement, reward systems, and ergonomic interventions as factors that improve life and well-being in the organizations (Guimarães et al., 2012; Guimarães et al., 2014). In this regard, issues of flextime and work–family balance were not present in the retrieved literature. In addition, an issue that was only present in the Brazilian literature, is the analysis of ethical management and its relevance to conduct ethical businesses, decisions, and practices (Ardichvili et al., 2010; Oliveira et al., 2017).

Following this, research in both countries explores environmental management as an external focus of CSR strategies. However, the literature in Chile only highlights its relevance (Dávila & Troncoso, 2018), whereas in Brazil, the issue has been significantly developed and explored, including green training, green HRM, and enhancement of relationships with indigenous communities (Aragão & Jabbour, 2017; Dias-Angelo et al., 2014; Jabbour, Teixeira et al., 2013).

Following this, the category with the most significant differences between Chile and Brazil is precisely the management strategies at the HR level. In this regard, in Chile studies have been narrowed to leadership (Meruane & Chau, 2010) and teamwork, exploring virtual teams (Pazos & Canto, 2013; Pazos et al., 2012). However, the studies set in Brazil explore recruitment and selection processes (Chiappetta et al, 2017; Fernández et al., 2017; Moraes, 2007), leadership (Casado, 2018; Chiappeta, Mauricio, & Jabbour, 2017; Park & Paiva, 2018), and teamwork factors such as autonomy (Capra & Moreira, 2013) and intellectual capital (Voichcoski & Miziara, 2018).

To study leadership in these contexts, acquires particular relevance in light of the cultural antecedents exposed. For instance, the dependence of workers on managers and leaders should be analyzed, explored and managed, since this can impact directly on the autonomy and creativity, which are fundamental abilities for the organizational functioning and achievement of competitive advantage. In this sense, to develop leaders through programs is an alternative for organizations in order to foster culturally aware leaders that workers can trust and rely on (Tanure, 2005; Truss et al., 2012).

Moreover, teamwork is another aspect that needs to be carefully explored and managed. This, in consideration to the rise of subcontracts in both societies, which is a factor that could be fostering individualism among workers, who in turn, are creating convenient utilitarian relationships with their employers and colleagues. In this sense, Dickson et al. (2005) proposes that teams are more successful and effective in collectivist societies. In other words, a possible alternative to inspire teamwork for organizations could be to discourage subcontracting, or to set strategies that attempt to reinforce relationships among employees or reduce leaving intentions.

Following this, in the category of management strategies at the HR level, studies conducted in Brazil explore training and development in topics such as diversity (Vasconcelos, 2016), e-learning (De Fátima et al., 2013;

Moraes, 2007), intercultural training (de Miranda & Braga, 2011; Zhang, 2011), career planning, and performance evaluation are analyzed (Marx & Soares, 2008; Moraes et al., 2012). Furthermore, the relation with trade unions also is gaining attention in a context where these are high in number but have been discouraged and delegitimized in a predominantly capitalist context (Siddique et al., 2006).

Finally, it is relevant to highlight that the research conducted in both countries highlights that the legislative, political, and economic environments of host countries are key to the insertion and functioning of both local and international organizations (Baena, 2015; Clouse & Watkins, 2009; Elvira & Davila, 2005; Figueiredo & Piana, 2016; Muritiba et al., 2010).

CONCLUSION

Cultural Characteristics of Chilean and Brazilian Workforces

In general terms, this research reflects certain similarities between Chilean and Brazilian workers. Both societies report high power distance, uncertainty avoidance, low assertiveness, and low future orientation. Regarding gender egalitarianism, the Chilean society tends to have a deeper gap, but Brazil still works towards reducing gender inequality (Cooke et al., 2013; Elvira & Davila, 2005; Gómez & Rodríguez, 2006; House et al., 2004; Tanure, 2005; Pérez-Arrau et al., 2012; Rodríguez, 2010; Rodríguez & Gómez, 2009; Rodríguez & Ríos, 2007; Thomas & Peterson, 2015; Wood, 2004).

Performance orientation in both societies is focused on training for a few privileged employees. In Brazil, those with a permanent contract and in Chile, those privileged by the compadrazgo and the contractual conditions (Rodríguez, 2010; Rodríguez & Gómez, 2009; Tanure, 2005; Wood, 2004).

Collectivism in Chile is negatively impacted by the hierarchical and authoritarian predominant model: workers tend to not feel identified with their organizations (sense of belonging) and consequently, relationships are impersonal. Differently, in Brazil, the jeitinho mechanism determines it because it operates promoting friendly, optimistic, and non-aggressive Brazilian relationships. However, the loyalty of Brazilian workers is directed towards their leaders, not to their institutions. Also, in both cases, new trends of workers tend to be more individualists than collectivists (Cooke et al., 2013; Gómez & Rodríguez, 2006; Rodríguez & Gómez, 2009; Wood, 2004).

Additionally, Chilean workers rely on a pessimistic/fatalist vision that apparently impacts transversally in the dimensions analyzed, especially in terms of future orientation and uncertainty avoidance. In this aspect, the jeitinho and the fatalist vision could be one of the most important differences when Chilean and Brazilian workforces are compared, since the latter are more optimistic and flexible towards their future (Davila & Elvira, 2012; Gómez, 2001; Pérez-Arrau et al., 2012; Rodríguez, 2010).

In terms of strategic management, the review presented here unveils an imbalance in the development of Chile and Brazil, where the latter has shown a significant advance in almost all the issues identified. For instance, in terms of HR, Chilean studies have unveiled aspects of leadership and teamwork, without giving significant attention to recruitment, training, career development, reward systems, and so on. In this regard, the challenges related to developing these issues are major for organizations entering to this particular country, as well as for current organizations.

Interestingly, in light of a diverse population, both nations evidence incipient research in terms of diversity management. In Chile, related to gender and aeing, whereas in Brazil, related to disabilities, aeing, gender, and ethnic groups. This unveils the need to advance in exploring other aspects of diversity management, such as religion, cult, socioeconomic level, race, immigrants and so on.

The sub-category life quality and well-being has shown relevant differences in terms of topics of CSR explored in both countries. On the one hand, Chile has centered its effort on analyzing work–family balance and flextime, whereas Brazilian research is centered in commitment, rewards and ergonomic interventions.

Furthermore, in regard to the external focus of CSR, Brazil is developing an interesting research centered in environmental management, exploring green training, green HRM policies and practices, and the relationship with the communities. This is a relevant and visionary contribution for other nations, in light of times where climate change has taken the daily schedule and sustainable development is needed more than ever.

Finally, in terms of HR strategies, the Brazilian research has advanced exploring a wide spectrum of issues, such as training, teamwork, leadership and talent retention among others. Whereas, Chile shows pending challenges in this issue, since most of the topics developed are only related to leadership and teamwork. In general terms, the imbalance of literature published in both countries (19.1% Chile, 80.9% Brazil) gives account of these pending issues and the need to expand research in terms of cultural characteristics and management strategies in the analyzed countries.

Recommendations and Limitations

Regarding HR strategies that should be managed and designed, it is plausible to relate the elements of culture recognized by authors such as Griffin and Pustay (2015), the CIPD (2013) and House and his colleagues (2004).

It has been reported that people tend to connect with other individuals that share the same values (Stone et al., 2007). This demonstrates that organizations need to adapt their practices to the visions and perspectives of the host culture in order to have a successful entry. Thus, studies such as those developed by House and his colleagues (2004) and other authors, are particularly relevant in providing a thorough comprehension in these topics.

Truss et al. (2012), Raines (2013), and Kumra and Manfredi (2012) describe the relevance of managing conflict, diversity, and performance appraisals, among other HR strategies. An alternative to managing this is through communication, a fundamental element of culture (Griffin & Pustay, 2015). For instance, in Brazil, it is essential to trust in their leaders and this can be enhanced by promoting open communication and reducing barriers between manager and worker.

Additionally, Truss et al. (2012) and Kumra and Manfredi (2012) explain that the autonomy and creativity of the workers is a desired aspect in a globalized world characterized for fast-paced environments, but to empower creative and autonomous workers it is not something that can be developed fast, especially in paternalistic cultures. Paternalism should not just be assumed as Brazilian or Chilean traits, but also be managed since it is one of the principal factors that affect the lack of autonomy and creativity of workers (Martínez, 2005; Rodríguez & Ríos, 2007). Furthermore, an alternative to manage autonomy and creativity and to overcome paternalism is to create programs of leadership that contribute to the establishment of positive trusty relationships employee–manager. Leaders are key in these relationships and need to receive support and tools to manage and foster an autonomous and creative workforce. Also, it is interesting to consider what type of leadership will be more successful in the two different societies: on the one hand, in Brazil a charismatic leader that suits the jeitinho it should be desirable (Davila & Elvira, 2012). On the other hand, instructional leadership might be a style that fits more with the Chilean culture.

Additionally, although these cultures are typically recognized as collectivist in terms of values, their practices are slightly different: there is evidence to consider that as the effect of new workers and subcontracts is the individualism (Rodríguez, 2010; Rodríguez & Gómez, 2009). Indeed, teams from collectivist cultures tend to work better and more successfully. Considering this, to foster this aspect of the worker's relationships it is also an option to strengthen teamwork.

Following this, organizations—especially MNCs—need to provide decent conditions, formal policies, and procedures to attract and retain the best workforce. This, especially in light of different generations of workers coexisting. For instance, if all the incumbents participate in the elaboration of benefits for the workers such as bonuses, promotions, training, and learning opportunities, the paternalistic dependence of workers could be tackled, as well as the belongingness and identification with the organization, trust, engagement, and loyalty (Truss et al., 2012). An interesting strategy to develop proactivity, belongingness, and a deep understanding of the business are the trainee and graduate programs (Hutchinson, 2013; Truss et al., 2012).

This research aims to contribute to the knowledge related to the cultural characteristics of Chilean and Brazilian workers, demonstrating that these cultures should not be treated only as part of a homogeneous zone. If organizations are conscious of the cultural particularities, they will be able to design and implement specific strategies designed for them. Finally, future research should attempt to validate the GLOBE project in Chile and also to include the public sector.

NOTES

1. Latin American cluster: Argentina, Bolivia, Brazil, Colombia, Costa Rica, Ecuador, El Salvador, Guatemala, México, and Venezuela.
2. Chile is also a member of the APEC, Asia-Pacific economic cooperation, a trade association where China, Australia, Brunei, Canada, Hong Kong, Indonesia, Japan, United States and other important economies are part (Griffin & Pustay, 2015).
3. Large farm owned by privates.
4. In English, it could be translated as "buddies" or "friends" although the direct translation is "co-parents" or "co-fathers" (*com-padre*, father), its roots derive from the Catholic ritual of christening (House et al., 2004).
5. *Machismo* derives from *macho*, male.
6. It can be understood as the way that Brazilians use to solve or reach something, despite contrary rules or options.

ACKNOWLEDGMENT

This work was funded by the National Agency for Research and Development (ANID)/DOCTORADO EN EL EXTRANJERO BECAS CHILE/2018 -72190192.

REFERENCES

Abreu, M., Cunha, M., & Rebouças, S. (2013). Effects of personal characteristics on organizational commitment: Evidence from Brazil's oil and gas industry. *International Journal of Human Resource Management, 24*(20), 3831–3852.

Ágenor, P., & Canuto, O. (2015). *Gender equality and economic growth in Brazil: A long-run analysis* (Working paper No. 6348). Washington, DC: World Bank.

Amini, C., & Dal Bianco, S. (2017). Corporate social responsibility and Latin American firm performance. *Corporate Governance: International Journal of Business in Society, 17*(3), 403–445.

Angelo F., Amui L., Caldana, A., & Jabbour, C. (2012). Towards a strategic CSR: A Brazilian case study. *Business Strategy Series, 13*(5), 224–238.

Aragão C., & Jabbour C. (2017). Green training for sustainable procurement? Insights from the Brazilian public sector. *Industrial and Commercial Training, 49*(1), 48–54.

Ardichvili, A., Jondle, D., & Kowske, B. (2010). Dimensions of ethical business cultures: Comparing data from 13 countries of Europe, Asia, and the Americas. *Human Resource Development International, 13*(3), 299–315.

Baena, V. (2015). European franchise expansion into Latin America: Evidence from the Spanish franchise system. *Management Research Review, 38*(2), 149–165.

Barakat, L., Lorenz, M., Ramsey, J., & Cretoiu, S. (2015). Global managers: An analysis of the impact of cultural intelligence on job satisfaction and performance. *International Journal of Emerging Markets, 10*(4), 781–800.

Batista, F., & Quandt, C. (2016). Job creation and job destruction in the presence of informal markets. *Journal of Development Economics, 98*(2), 270–286.

BBC. (2016). *Brazil's Dilma Rousseff to face impeachment trial.* Retrieved from http://www.bbc.co.uk/news/world-latin-america-36273916

Bloom, N., Genakos, C., & Van Reenen, J. (2012). Management practices across firms and countries. *Academy of Management Perspectives, 26*(1), 12–33.

Blumberg, B., Cooper, D., & Schindler, P. (2011). *Business research methods.* London, England: McGraw-Hill.

Bonache, J., Trullen, J., & Sanchez, J. (2012). Managing cross-cultural differences: Testing human resource models in Latin America. *Journal of Business Research, 65*(1), 1773–1781.

Brock, A., & Ryan, T. (2016). Exploring the gap between teacher certification and permanent employment in Ontario: An integrative literature review. *Canadian Journal of Educational Administration and Policy, 175,* 1–28.

Browaeys, M., & Price, R. (2008). *Understanding cross-cultural management.* Harlow, England: Financial Times/Prentice Hall.

Budhwar, P., Tung R. L., Varma, A., & Do, H. (2017). Developments in human resource management in MNCs from BRICS nations: A review and future research agenda. *Journal of International Management, 23*(2), 111–123.

Capra A., & Moreira M. (2013, August). *Investigation of internal and external design teams during the product development process in footwear companies.* Paper presentation at the International Conference on Engineering Design, ICED, Seoul, Korea.

Cardoso, E., & Teles, V. (2009). *A brief history of Brazil's growth.* Retrieved from https://www.oecd.org/eco/growth/43823436.pdf

Casado, R. (2018). The "hero-leader": A case of leadership in Brazil. *Leadership & Organization Development Journal, 39*(4), 495–506.

Castro, J. (2001). *Discriminación en las relaciones laborales: Algunos casos particulares. Boletín No. 146/2001* [Discrimination in labour relations: Some particular cases. Bullletin No. 146/2001]. Retrieved from https://www.dt.gob.cl/portal/1626/articles-65173_recurso_1.pdf

Chartered Institute of Personnel and Development. (2013). *International culture.* Retrieved from https://www.cipd.co.uk/knowledge/culture/working-environment/international-culture-factsheet

Chiappetta, C., Mauricio, A., & Jabbour, A. (2017). Critical success factors and green supply chain management proactivity: Shedding light on the human aspects of this relationship based on cases from the Brazilian industry. *Production Planning and Control, 28,* 671–683.

Clouse, M., & Watkins, M. (2009). Three keys to getting an overseas assignment right. *Harvard Business Review, 87*(10), 115–120.

Coda, R., Coelho, C., Bido, D., & Louffat, E. (2009). Strategic HR? A study of the perceived role of HRM departments in Brazil and Peru. *Brazilian Administration Review, 6*(1), 15–33.

Comunidad Mujer. (2016). *Género, educación y trabajo: La brecha persistente* [Gender, education and work: The gap persists]. Retrieved from http://www.informeget.cl/wp-content/uploads/2016/04/GET_Cmujer-RE-web-2604-1-1.pdf

Cooke, B., Macau, F., & Wood, T. (2013). Brazilian management gurus as reflexive soft-HRM practitioners: An empirical study. *International Journal of Human Resource Management, 24*(1), 110–129.

Cresswell, J. (2014). *Research design: Qualitative, quantitative and mixed methods approaches.* London, England: SAGE.

Cronin, S. (2013). Reflections on gender issues in work transitions in Chile. *Work: A Journal of Prevention Assessment & Rehabilitation, 44*(1), 89–91.

da Silva Junqueira, T., Cotta, R., Gomes, R., de Fátima, S., Siqueira-Batista, R., Pinheiro, T., & Sampaio, R. (2010). Labor relations under decentralized health management and dilemmas in the relationship between work expansion and casualization in the Brazilian unified national health system. *Cadernos de Saude Publica, 26*(5), 918–928.

Dávila, A., & Elvira, M. (2012). Humanistic leadership: Lessons from Latin America. *Journal of World Business, 47*(4), 548–554.

Dávila, M., & Troncoso, C. (2018). Labor practices and organizational commitment. *Ciencia & Trabajo, 20*(63), 145–150.

De Fátima Dos Santos, A., Torres, R., Do Carmo Barros, De Melo M., Dos Santos, S., De Souza C., & Alves, H. (2013, July). *The experience of the implementation of a telehealth resource management course in Brazil and in other countries of Latin America for training professionals in the telehealth area.* Paper presentation at the IADIS-International Association for Development of the Information Society, International Conference e-Health 2013 Prague, Czech Republic.

de Miranda, E., & Braga, B. (2011). Intercultural adjustment of Japanese expatriate executives in Brazil: An empirical study. *Revista de Administracao de Empresas, 53*(3), 243–255.

De Sá Freire, P., Dandolini, G., de Souza, J., Silva, T., & Couto, R. (2017). Knowledge governance (GovC): The state of the art about the term. *Biblios* [Libraries], *69,* 21–40.

De Sousa, A. (2015). Understanding the genesis of green supply chain management: Lessons from leading Brazilian companies. *Journal of Cleaner Production, 87*(1), 385–390.

De Souza, W., Jabbour, C., Mangili, L., Filho, W., &, De Oliveira, J. (2012). Building sustainable values in organizations with the support of human resource management: Evidence from one firm considered as the 'best place to work' in Brazil. *Journal of Human Values, 18*(2), 147–159

Dias-Angelo, F., Jabbour, C., & Calderaro, J. (2014). Greening the work force in Brazilian hotels: The role of environmental training. *Work, 49*(3), 347–356.

Dickson, M., Den Hartog, D., & Mitchelson, J. (2003). Research on leadership in a cross-cultural context: Making progress and raising new questions. *Leadership Quarterly, 14*(6), 14729–14768.

Dirección del trabajo, Chile. (2014). *Organizaciones sindicales* [Trade unions]. Retrieved from https://www.dt.gob.cl/portal/1626/w3-propertyvalue-26865.html

Dirección del trabajo, Chile. (2016). *El sueldo de una mujer es en promedio un tercio más bajo que el de un hombre* [A woman's wage is on average a third lower than a man's]. Retrieved from https://www.dt.gob.cl/portal/1627/w3-article-98691.html

Donato, J., Kubo, E., Pereira, R., & Oliva, E. (2013). Repensando a lógica de avaliação de desempenho individual: Um estudo empírico em um banco de desenvolvimento no nordeste do Brasil [Rethinking the logic of individual performance evaluation: An empirical study in a development bank in northeastern Brazil]. *Revista Portuguesa e Brasileira de Gestão, 12*(4), 50–62.

Duarte, F. (2017). Sustainability learning challenges in a Brazilian government organization. *International Journal of Organizational Analysis, 25*(4), 562–576.

Elsevier. (2016). *About Scopus.* Retrieved from https://www.elsevier.com/solutions/scopus

Elvira, M., & Dávila, A. (2005). *Managing human resources in Latin America: An agenda for international leaders.* London, England: Routledge.

Elwell, T., Gelcich, S., Gaines, S., & López-Carr, D. (2013). Using people's perceptions of ecosystem services to guide modelling and management efforts. *Science of the Total Environment, 637,* 1014–1025.

Eriksson, P., & Kovalainen, A. (2008). *Qualitative methods in business research.* London, England: SAGE.

Espinoza, P., Peduzzi, M., Agreli, H., & Sutherland, M. (2018). State capitalism and clusters: The case of Brazilian shipbuilding. *International Journal of Emerging Markets, 11*(2), 214–231.

Fernández, L., Ventura, A., Andrade, J., Lumbreras, J., & Cobo-Benita, J. (2017). The effect of clean development mechanism projects on human resource management practices in Brazil. *International Journal of Operations and Production Management, 37*(10), 1348–1365.

Figueiredo, P., & Piana, J. (2016). When "one thing (almost) leads to another": A micro-level exploration of learning linkages in Brazil's mining industry. *Resources Policy, 49,* 405–414.

Fleury, M. (1996). Managing human resources for learning and innovation: A comparative study of Brazilian, Japanese and Korean firms. *International Journal of Human Resource Management,* 7(4), 812.

Friel, D., & de Villechenon, F. (2018). Adapting a lean production program to national institutions in Latin America: Danone in Argentina and Brazil. *Journal of International Management, 24*(3), 284–299.

Fuenzalida, J., & Riccucci, N. (2018). The effects of politicization on performance: The mediating role of HRM practices. *Review of Public Personnel Administration, 39*(4), 544–569.

G20. (2020). *What is the G20?* Retrieved from https://g20.org/en/about/Pages/whatis.aspx

Gaete, R., Valderrama, C., Carmona, G., Elgueta, A., & Quiroz, J. (2009). Diagnóstico de la función de gestión de recursos humanos de los servicios públicos de la ciudad de Antofagasta en Chile desde la perspectiva de la responsabilidad social corporativa interna [Diagnosis of the human resources management function of the public services of the city of Antofagasta in Chile from the perspective of internal corporate social responsibility]. *Documentos y Aportes en Administración Pública y Gestión Estatal, 9*(13), 39–71.

Garavan, T., Idrovo-Carlier, S., Leon-Llorente, C., & Grau, G. (2012). Comparing work–life balance in Spanish and Latin-American countries. *European Journal of Training and Development, 36*(2/3), 286–307.

Garuti, C., & Sandoval, M. (2006). The AHP: A multicriteria decision making methodology for shift work prioritizing. *Journal of Systems Science and Systems Engineering, 15*(2), 189–200.

Gertsen, M., & Søderberg, A. (2012). Inpatriation in a globalising MNC: Knowledge exchange and translation of corporate culture. *European Journal of International Management, 6*(1), 29–44.

Gobierno de Chile. (2017). *Conoce las novedades de la ley de inclusión laboral para personas con discapacidad* [Know all the news about the new law in labour inclusion for people with disabilities]. Retrieved from https://www.gob.cl/noticias/conoce-las-novedades-de-la-ley-de-inclusion-laboral-para-personas-con-discapacidad/

Gómez, C. (2001). Chilean culture: Entrepreneurs and workers. *Asian Journal of Latin American Studies, 14*(2), 113–160.

Gómez, C., & Rodríguez, J. (2006). Four approximations to Chilean culture: Authoritarianism, legalism, fatalism and compadrazgo. *Asian Journal of Latin American Studies, 19*(3), 43–65.

Goncalves, M., Sarsur, A., Costa, W., Fischer, A., & Kassem, M. (2017). The complex interaction between human resources management, the labor market and employment relations in Brazil. *Tourism & Management Studies, 13*(4), 65–72.

Great Place to Work. (2019). *Best workplaces in Latin America 2019.* Retrieved from http://www.greatplacetowork.cl/mejores-empresas/las-mejores-empresas-para-trabajar-en-america-latina

Griffin, R., & Pustay, M. (2015). *International business: A managerial perspective.* London, England: Pearson.

Guimaraes, B., Barkokebas, B., & Martins, L. (2018). Absenteeism of people with disabilities in the construction industry in Brazil. *Work: A Journal of Prevention Assessment & Rehabilitation, 60*(3), 411–419.

Guimaraes, B., Martins, L., & Barkokebas, B. (2015). Workplace adaptation of people with disabilities in the construction industry. *Procedia Manufacturing, 3*, 1832–1837.

Guimaraes, L., Ribeiro, J., & Renner, J. (2012). Cost-benefit analysis of a socio-technical intervention in a Brazilian footwear company. *Applied Ergonomics, 43*(5), 948–957.

Guimarães L., Ribeiro J., Renner J., & De Oliveira P. (2014). Worker evaluation of a macroergonomic intervention in a Brazilian footwear company. *Applied Ergonomics, 45*(4), 923–935.

Hansen, C., & Brooks, A. (1994). A review of cross-cultural research on human resource development. *Human Resource Development Quarterly, 5*(1), 55–74.

Hartog, D., House, R., Hanges, P., & Ruiz-Quintanilla, A. (1999). Culture specific and cross-culturally generalizable implicit leadership theories: Are attributes of charismatic/transformational leadership universally endorsed? *Leadership Quarterly, 10*(2), 219–256.

Hernández-Sampieri, R., Fernández-Collado, C., & Baptista-Lucio, P. (2006). *Análisis de los datos cuantitativos. Metodología de la investigación* [Quantitative data analysis. Research methodology]. Mexico City, Mexico: McGraw Hill.

Hofstede, G. (1982). *Culture's consequences. International differences in work-related values.* Newbury Park, CA: SAGE.

Hopia, H., Latvala, E., & Liimatainen, L. (2016). Reviewing the methodology of an integrative review. *Scandinavian Journal of Caring Sciences, 30*(4), 662–669.

House, R., Hanges, P., Javidan, M., Dorfman, P., & Gupta, V. (2004). *Culture, leadership and organizations: The GLOBE study of 62 societies.* London, England: SAGE.

Hutchinson, S. (2013). *Performance management.* Retrieved from https://www.cipd.co.uk/knowledge/fundamentals/people/performance/factsheet

Jabbour, C. (2011). How green are HRM practices, organizational culture, learning and teamwork? A Brazilian study. *Industrial and Commercial Training, 43*(2), 98–105.

Jabbour, C. (2015). Environmental training and environmental management maturity of Brazilian companies with ISO14001: Empirical evidence. *Journal of Cleaner Production, 96*, 331–338.

Jabbour, C., De Sousa, A., Govindan, K., Teixeira, A., & De Souza, W. (2013). Environmental management and operational performance in automotive companies in Brazil: The role of human resource management and lean manufacturing. *Journal of Cleaner Production, 47*, 129–140.

Jabbour, C., Gordono, F., Oliveira, J., Martinez, J., & Battistelle, R. (2011). Diversity management: Challenges, benefits, and the role of human resource management in Brazilian organizations. *Equality, Diversity and Inclusion, 30*(1), 58–74.

Jabbour, C., Santos, F. C., Fonseca, S., Nagano, M. (2013). Green teams: Understanding their roles in the environmental management of companies located in Brazil. *Journal of Cleaner Production, 46*, 58–66.

Jabbour, C., Teixeira, A., & Jabbour, A. (2013). Environmental training in organizations with ISO 14001 certification: A multiple case study and identification of co-evolution with environmental management. *Producao, 23*(41), 80–84.

Jose, M., Las Heras, M., Russo, M., Rofcanin, Y., & Grau, M. (2018). How context matters: The relationship between family supportive supervisor behaviours and motivation to work moderated by gender inequality. *Journal of Business Research, 82*(1), 46–55.

Kim, D. (2013). Brazilian human resource management dilemma: The interplay between national culture and labor institutions. *Journal of Organization and Management, 37*(2), 105–153.

Kluckhohn, F., & Strodtbeck, F. (1961). *Variations in value orientations.* New York, NY: Harper Collins.

Krzywdzinski, M. (2017). Accounting for cross-country differences in employee involvement practices: Comparative case studies in Germany, Brazil and China. *British Journal of Industrial Relations, 55*(2), 321–346.

Kumra, S., & Manfredi, S. (2012). *Managing equality and diversity, theory and practice.* Oxford, England: Oxford University Press.

Kurganct, P., Melleiro, M., & Tronchin, D. (2008). Evaluation of quality indicators for human resources management in nursing. *Revista Brasileira de Enfermagem, 61*(5), 539–544.

Leahy, J. (2016). *What is the Petrobras scandal that is engulfing Brazil?* Retrieved from http://www.ft.com/cms/s/2/6e8b0e28-f728-11e5-803c-d27c7117d132.html #axzz48HOqaQiq

Martínez, P. (2005). Paternalism as a positive form of leadership in the Latin American context: leader benevolence, decision-making control and human resource management practices. In M. Elvira & A. Dávila (Eds.), *Managing human resources in Latin America: An agenda for international leaders* (pp. 75–92). London, England: Routledge.

Marx, R., & Soares, J. (2008). Organizational context variables to be considered in the reward system design oriented to product innovation. *Revista Brasileira de Gestao de Negocios, 18*(60), 267–289

McClelland, D. (1961). *The achieving society.* Princeton, NJ: Van Nostrand.

McGregor, L., & Doshi, N. (2015). *How company culture shapes employee motivation.* Retrieved from https://hbsp.harvard.edu/product/H02I48-PDF-ENG

Mello e Silva, L. (2014). The state, unions, and work reorganization lessons from today's Brazil. *Latin American Perspectives, 41*(5), 22–41.

Mello, J. (2012). *The Brazilian way of doing things.* Retrieved from https://thebrazil business.com/article/the-brazilian-way-of-doing-things

Mendoza, M. (2010). El compadrazgo desde la perspectiva antropológica [The compadrazgo from an antropologic perspective]. *Alteridades, 20*(40), 141–147.

Mercosur. (2016). *Países del Mercosur* [Countries from the Mercosur]. Retrieved from http://www.mercosur.int/innovaportal/v/7823/4/innova.front/paises -del-mercosur

Meruane, P., & Chau, C. (2016). Transformación de los liderazgos en la minería: Gestión estratégica para incorporar mujeres a la industria [Transformation of leaders in mining: Strategic management to incorporate women into the industry]. *Innovar, 26*(61), 119–130.

Moraes, P., Coelho, G., & Gladis, C. (2012). Maslow's theory of motivation, hierarchy of needs: Results from construction operational workers in São Paulo city, Brazil. *Applied Mechanics and Materials, 174-177,* 2339–2342.

Moraes, R. (2007). The human side of technology. *O Papel Brazil, 68*(1), 18–19.

Moraes, S., Chiappetta, C., Battistelle, R., Rodrigues, J., Renwick, D., Foropon, C., & Roubaud, D. (2018). When knowledge management matters: Interplay between green human resources and eco-efficiency in the financial service industry. *Journal of Knowledge Management, 23*(9), 1691–1707.

Mulder, M. (1971). Power equalization through participation. *Administrative Science Quarterly, 16*(1), 31–38.

Muritiba, P., Nunes, S., Campanario, M., & Albuquerque, L. (2010). International HR strategy in Brazilian technology multinationals. *BAR Curitiba, 7*(4), 325–344.

Mustafa, J. (2016). *What is the G20 and how does it work?* Retrieved from https://www.dw.com/en/g20-what-is-it-and-how-does-it-work/a-46505067

Novais, A. (2012). *Labor unions in Brazil.* Retrieved from https://thebrazilbusiness.com/article/labor-unions-in-brazil

Novella, R., Rucci, G., Vazquez, C., & Kaplan, D. (2018). Training vouchers and labour market outcomes in Chile. *Labour-England, 32*(2), 243–260.

Nunes, I., Felix, B., & Prates, L. (2017). Cultural intelligence, cross-cultural adaptation and expatriate performance: A study with expatriates living in Brazil. *Revista de Administração, 52*(3), 219–232.

Oliveira, É., Silva, J., Santos, C., & Miranda, R. (2017). Ética e ensino de administração: Um referencial protestante no ensino de administração. *Revista de Administração Contemporânea [Contemporary Administration Journal], 21*(5), 730–742.

Oliveira, M., & Nogueira, A. (2017). Resistance and organized counter-resistance in conflict areas: An ethnography with Embraer's workers. *Revista de Administração, 52*(4), 392–402.

OECD. (2016a). *Economic survey of Chile.* Retrieved from http://www.oecd.org/eco/surveys/economic-survey-chile.htm

OECD. (2016b). *Active with Brazil.* Retrieved from http://www.oecd.org/brazil/Brazil%20brochureWEB.pdf

OECD. (2020a). *Trade union density.* Retrieved from https://stats.oecd.org/Index.aspx?DataSetCode=TUD

OECD. (2020b). *Chile.* Retrieved from https://www.oecd.org/chile/

Pablo, T. (2015). *Chile lidera el PIB per cápita de América Latina* [Chile leads the GDW per capita in Latin America]. Retrieved from http://www.eleconomistaamerica.cl/empresas-eAm-chile/noticias/7067999/10/15/Chile-lidera-el-PIB-per-capita-de-America-Latina.html

Park, C., & Paiva, E. (2018). How do national cultures impact the operations strategy process? *International Journal of Operations & Production Management, 38*(10), 1937–1963.

Pazos, P., & Canto, A. (2013, May). *The role of team preparation processes and task conflict on virtual team performance.* Paper presentation at the 2013 Industrial and Systems Engineering Research Conference San Juan, Puerto Rico.

Pazos, P., Canto, A., & Magpili, N. (2012, May). *Case study of key factors driving global virtual team effectiveness.* Paper presentation at the 2012 Industrial and Systems Engineering Research Conference, Orlando, FL.

Pérez-Arrau, G. (2015, September). *Knowledge management in the context of developing countries: The case of Chile.* Paper presentation at the European Conference on Knowledge Management, Udine, Italy.

Pérez-Arrau, G., Eades, E., & Wilson, J. (2012). Managing human resources in the Latin American context: The case of Chile. *International Journal of Human Resource Management, 23*(15), 3133–3150.

Petrobras Magazine Global Connections. (2016). *CEO Aldemir Bendine talks about our challenges and achievements.* Retrieved from https://petrobras.com.br/en/news/ceo-aldemir-bendine-talks-about-our-challenges-and-achievements.htm

Pintao, S., Chaves, C., & Branco, M. (2018). Employees' recognition of corporate sustainability: A case study. *Corporate Governance: The International Journal of Business in Society, 18*(1), 104–118.

Poblete, L. (2018). The ILO domestic workers convention and regulatory reforms in Argentina, Chile and Paraguay. A comparative study of working time and remuneration regulations. *International Labour Review, 157*(3), 435–459.

Posthuma, R. (2011). Conflict management and performance outcomes. *International Journal of Conflict Management, 22*(2), 108–110.

Raineri, A. (2011). Change management practices: Impact on perceived change results. *Journal of Business Research, 64*(3), 266–272.

Raines, S. (2013). *Conflict management for managers: Resolving workplace, client and policy disputes.* San Francisco, CA: Jossey-Bass.

Rego, A., Vitoria, A., Tupinamba, A., Reis, D., Reis, D., Pina e Cunha, M., & Lourenco-Gil, R. (2018). Brazilian managers' ageism: A multiplex perspective. *International Journal of Manpower, 39*(3), 414–433.

Renwick, D. (2009). The origins of employee wellbeing in Brazil: An exploratory analysis. *Employee Relations, 31*(3), 312–321.

Rodríguez, D., & Ríos, R. (2007). Latent premises of labor contracts, paternalism and productivity: Two cases from the banking industry in Chile. *International Journal of Manpower, 28*(5), 354–368.

Rodríguez, J. (2010). Employment relations in Chile: Evidence of HRM practices. *Industrial Relations, 65*(3), 424–446.

Rodríguez, J., & Gomez, C. (2009). HRM in Chile: The impact of organizational culture. *Employee Relations, 31*(3), 276–294.

Rodríguez, M., & Ríos, R. (2009). Paternalism at a crossroads: Labor relations in Chile in transition. *Employee Relations, 31*(3), 322–333.

Rodríguez, M., & Stewart, P. (2017). HRM and work practices in Chile: The regulatory power of organisational culture. *Human Resources for Health, 39*(3), 378–390.

Roh, H. (2013). A study on the dismissal system of Brazil. *Labor Law Review, 35,* 89–147.

Salinas, P., & Romaní, G. (2014). Gender barriers in Chilean mining: A strategic management. *Academia Revista Latinoamericana de Administracion, 27*(1), 92–107.

Santos, C., & Garibaldi, A. (2018). Same, same but different? Women's experiences with gender inequality in Brazil. *Employee Relations, 40*(3), 486–499.

Scandura, T., & Dorfman, P. (2004). Leadership research in an international and cross-cultural context. *Leadership Quarterly, 15*, 277–307.

Siddique, M., Ansari, J., & Salma, Q. (2006). Governing the labour market: The impossibility of corporatist reforms. *Pakistan Development Review, 45*(4), 981–1000.

Silva, R., Dutra, J., Veloso E., Fischer A., & Trevisan L. (2015). Generational perceptions and their influences on organizational commitment. *Management Research, 13*(1), 5–30.

Silvestre, L., Ochoa, S., & Marques, M. (2016, November). *Understanding the design of software development teams for academic scenarios.* Paper presentation at the 34th International Conference of the Chilean Computer Science Society, Santiago, Chile.

Sofofa. (2017). *Empresa inclusiva: Herramientas de apoyo para la inclusión laboral* [Inclusive enterprise: Tools to support labor inclusion]. Retrieved from https://web.sofofa.cl/centros-sofofa/centro-discapacidad/cil/

Steffen, M., & Oliveira, M. (2015, September). *Inter-organizational knowledge sharing in incubated companies: Reality or myth?* Paper presentation at the European Conference on Knowledge Management, Udine, Italy.

Steil, A., Dandolini, G., de Souza, J., de Cuffa, D., & Costa, R. (2018). Behavioral intentions and retention of technical and scientific staff in research and development organizations. *International Journal of Human Capital and Information Technology Professionals, 9*(2), 16–31.

Stone, D., Stone-Romero, E., & Lukaszewski, K. (2007). The impact of cultural values on the acceptance and effectiveness of human resource management policies and practices. *Human Resource Management Review, 17*, 152–165.

Sweeney, P., & McFarlin, D. (2015). *International management: Strategic opportunities and cultural challenges.* New York, NY: Routledge.

Tanure, B. (2005). Human resource management in Brazil. In M. Elvira & A. Dávila (Eds.), *Managing human resources in Latin America: An agenda for international leaders* (pp. 111–127). London, England: Routledge.

Teixeira, A., Chiappetta, C., & Lopes de Sousa, A. (2012). Relationship between green management and environmental training in companies located in Brazil: A theoretical framework and case studies. *International Journal of Production Economics, 140*(1), 318–329.

Teixeira, A., Jabbour, C., De Sousa, A., Latan, H., & De Oliveira, J. (2016). Green training and green supply chain management: Evidence from Brazilian firms. *Journal of Cleaner Production, 116*, 170–176

Telesur. (2016). *What you need to know about Brazil's Petrobras scandal.* Retrieved from http://www.telesurtv.net/english/analysis/What-You-Need-to-Know-About-Brazils-Petrobras-Scandal-20160313-0012.html

Teodósio, A. (2001). "Moral infrastructure" and virtual enterprises: Ethics as a competitive factor for the internet commerce in Brazil. *IFIP Advances in Information and Communication Technology, 56*, 425–432.

Thomas, D., & Peterson, M. (2015). *Cross-cultural management: Essential concepts.* London, England: SAGE.

Torraco, R. (2005). Writing integrative literature reviews: Guidelines and examples. *Human Resource Development Review, 4*(3), 356–367.

Trinidade, L., de Aluquerque, L., & Freire, C. (2017). Organizational capabilities: A study on the Brazilian northeast hotel sector. *Revista de Gestao, 24*(2), 170–180.

Truss, C., Mankin, D., & Kelliher, C. (2012). *Strategic human resource management.* Oxford, England: Oxford University Press.

Trade Unions Congress. (2016). *About unions.* Retrieved from https://www.tuc.org.uk/about-unions

Ugarte, S. (2017). The gender pay implications of institutional and organisational wage-setting practices in banking: A case study of Argentina and Chile. *International Journal of Human Resource Management, 28*(18), 2594–2621.

Van Dierendonck, D., Lankester, A., Zmyslona, M., & Rothweiler, H. (2016). Linking HRM practices and institutional setting to collective turnover: An empirical exploration. *Administrative Sciences, 6*(4), 1–17.

Vasconcelos, A. (2015). The contemporary experience of work: Older workers' perceptions. *Management Research Review, 38*(4), 381–403.

Vasconcelos, A. (2016). Organizations workforce demographic age preferences: Multiple case studies from Brazil. *Journal of Management Development, 35*(3), 406–427.

Vives, A., Gray, N., Gonzalez, F., & Molina, A. (2018). Gender and ageing at work in Chile: Employment, working conditions, work–life balance and health of men and women in an ageing workforce. *Annals of Work Exposures and Health, 62*(4), 475–489.

Voichcoski, B., & Miziara, A. (2018, November). *Intellectual capital: Tangible measures of intangible learning.* Paper presentation at the International Conference on Intellectual Capital, Knowledge Management and Organisational Learning, ICICKM, Cape Town, South Africa.

Wasti, A., Peterson, M., Breitsohl, H., Cohen, A., Jorgensen, F., Rodrigues, A., . . . Xu, X. (2016). Location, location, location: Contextualizing workplace commitment. *Journal of Organizational Behaviour, 37*(4), 613–632.

Whittemore, R., & Knafl, K. (2005). The integrative review: Updated methodology. *Journal of Advanced Nursing, 52*(5), 546–553.

Wood, G., Dibben, P., & Meira, J. (2016). Colonização e neocolonização da gestão de recursos humanos no Brasil (1950–2010) [Colonization and neocolonization of human resource management in Brazil (1950–2010)]. *Revista de Administração de Empresas, 51*(3), 232–243.

Wood, T. (2004). Gestión de recursos humanos en Brasil: Tensiones e hibridismo [Human Resource management in Brazil: Tensions and hybridism]. *Academia: Revista Latinoamericana de Administración, 33,* 68–80.

World Bank. (2016a). *GDP per capita (current US$) – Chile.* Retrieved from http://data.worldbank.org/indicator/NY.GDP.PCAP.CD?locations=CL

World Bank. (2016b). *GDP per capita (current US$) – Brazil.* Retrieved from http://data.worldbank.org/indicator/NY.GDP.PCAP.CD?locations=BR

Yushimito, W., Holguín-Veras, J., & Gellona, T. (2018). Firm's efficiency and the feasibility of incentives for flexitime adoption: A preliminary analysis of Chilean employer's response. *Transportation Letters, 10*(4), 202–214.

Zavala-Villalón, G., & Castro, P. (2018). Millennial discourse and challenges in human resources management in Chile. *Psicoperspectivas, 17*(3), 52–63.

Zhang, X. (2011). Intercultural HRM study on "Culture Clash" from Chinese enterprises investment in Brazil. *Australian Journal of Business and Management Research, 2*(5), 47–51.

ABOUT THE CONTRIBUTORS

Francisca Álvarez-Figueroa is a doctoral candidate at the Global Development Institute, University of Manchester, Manchester, England. She obtained her master's degree in human resource management from the University of Liverpool, Liverpool, England, and her bachelor's degree in psychology from the Pontifical Catholic University of Valparaíso, Valparaíso, Chile. Her research focuses on educational leadership, diversity management, citizenship, and inclusion.

Email: francisca.alvarezfigueroa@manchester.ac.uk

David Arditi is professor of civil and architectural engineering, and the founder and director of the construction engineering and management program at Illinois Institute of Technology, Chicago, IL. His area of expertise covers all aspects of construction management, engineering, and support. He conducted several funded research projects sponsored by federal and state agencies. He and his research associates have published over 350 research papers in refereed national and international journals and in peer-reviewed conference proceedings. He is currently serving on the editorial boards of 11 journals. He was elected to the College of Fellows of CMAA in 2013.

Email: arditi@iit.edu

Erica Wen Chen is an assistant professor of the School of Labor and Human Resources at Renmin University of China, Beijing, China. She received her PhD in management from Nanyang Technological University, Singapore.

Cultural Values in Strategy and Organization, pages 327–334

Her research interests lie in exploring cognitive and emotional mechanisms underlying organizational paradoxes in entrepreneurial contexts. Her work has appeared in journals such as *Cross-Cultural & Strategic Management.*

Email: ericachenwen@ruc.edu.cn

Mantiaba Coulibaly-Ballet is an associate professor at IAE Graduate School of Management, Université Côte d'Azur, Nice, France, and co-director of the Master of Business Administration. Her research and publications are based on interorganizational relationships in alliances. She also works on corporate social responsibilities principles in SMEs and is the general secretary of the association Fairness (a research network on fair trade).

Email: mantiaba.coulibaly@univ-cotedazur.fr

Atilla Damci is an associate professor in the Department of Civil Engineering, Istanbul Technical University, Istanbul, Turkey. His research interests include motivation, culture, scheduling, resource management, and most aspects of construction management. He has been involved in research projects funded by Istanbul Technical University (ITU) and the Scientific and Technological Research Council of Turkey (TUBITAK). His research work over the years has resulted in over 50 technical papers in refereed international journals and in peer-reviewed conference proceedings. He regularly reviews papers for several publications.

Email: damcia@itu.edu.tr

T. K. Das is professor emeritus of strategic management at the City University of New York, New York, NY, where he taught for over three decades and served concurrently as a member of the University's doctoral faculty. Prior to entering the academic life, Professor Das had extensive experience as a senior business executive. Professor Das received his PhD in organization and strategic studies from the Anderson Graduate School of Management, University of California at Los Angeles, Los Angeles, CA (UCLA). He has a bachelor's degree in physics, two master's degrees in mathematics and management, and a professional certification in banking. His research interests are in strategic alliances, strategy making, organization studies, temporal studies, and executive development. Professor Das is the author or editor of 28 academic research books, mainly on strategy, organization, and management, and also 6 booklets on bank management for practicing executives. His research articles have appeared in over 45 journals, of which some of the later ones include *Academy of Management Executive, Academy of Management Review, Accounting, Organizations and Society, British Journal of Management, Cross Cultural Management: An International Journal, Entrepreneurship Theory and Practice, International Journal of Entrepreneurial Behaviour & Research, International Journal of Organizational Analysis, International Jour-*

nal of Strategic Business Alliances, International Journal of Strategic Change Management, Journal of Business and Psychology, Journal of Business Ethics, Journal of General Management, Journal of International Management, Journal of Management, Journal of Management Development, Journal of Management Studies, Journal of Managerial Psychology, Long Range Planning, Management Decision, Management International Review, Organization Science, Organization Studies, Scandinavian Journal of Management, Strategic Management Journal, and *Time & Society.* Also, by invitation, he has contributed book reviews in *Administrative Science Quarterly, Contemporary Psychology,* and *Journal of Management,* and authored the entry on "Strategic Alliances" in *Oxford Bibliographies in Management.* His work has been cited in over 1,500 journals in a wide variety of disciplines. For a number of years now he has been consistently ranked in the top 2 percent of scholars in his field of Business & Management in terms of research impact. Most recently, a Stanford University professor led a comprehensive study of the career-long research impact of more than 8 million researchers across 174 fields during the 60-year period 1960–2019, based on the article citations included in the well-known multidisciplinary citation database SCOPUS, and this study has ranked Professor Das among the top 50,000 scholars (complete list published in the journal *PLOS Biology*). Professor Das is a former senior editor of Organization Studies and has previously served, or is serving, on the editorial boards of a number of other academic journals, and has been an ad hoc editorial reviewer for over 70 journals. He is the founding (and current) series editor of the three book series, *Research in Strategy Science, Research in Strategic Alliances,* and *Research in Behavioral Strategy* (all published by Information Age Publishing).

Email: TK.Das@baruch.cuny.edu

Ard-Pieter de Man is an independent boardroom consultant and professor of knowledge networks and innovation at the Vrije Universiteit Amsterdam, Amsterdam, Netherlands. Both his academic work and his consulting assignments focus on alliances, ecosystems, and new organizational forms. Key themes he addresses are designing alliance governance structures, building up alliance capabilities, alliance evaluation, ecosystem management, self-organization, and open innovation. He is a prize-winning author and is the co-author of nearly a hundred articles and 15 books, mainly on alliances, networks, ecosystems, and innovation. His latest books, *Alliances: An Executive Guide to Designing Successful Strategic Partnerships* (Wiley, 2013) and *How to Survive the Organizational Revolution* (BIS Publishers, 2019), are widely used by practitioners.

Email: a.p.de.man@vu.nl

Angela Dettori is a research fellow at the Department of Economics and Business, University of Cagliari, Cagliari, Italy. She received her PhD in management and holds a master's degree in economics from the same university, and has been teaching corporate social responsibility there for several years. She has published articles in various journals, including *Journal of Management and Sustainability* and *International Journal of Marketing Studies*. Her research focuses on sustainable development and sustainability-oriented behavior, especially in family businesses.

Email: angela.dettori@unica.it

Jingjing Du is an associate professor at the School of Management, Anhui University of Finance and Economics, Bengbu, China. She has a PhD degree from the University of Science and Technology of China, Hefei, China. Her research interests center on international strategy and entrepreneurship.

Email: phoenix@aufe.edu.cn

Djamila Elidrissi is an associate professor at IAE Graduate School of Management, Université Côte d'Azur, Nice, France, and head of the master's program in management and business administration as well as a member of the Research Group in Management (GRM). She has the degree of a habilitated doctor in management sciences. She has research interests in interorganizational relations and strategic alliances, as well as dynamics of innovation, international entrepreneurship, and corporate social responsibility in SMEs. She has published in journals such as *Journal of Entrepreneurship, International SME Review*, and *International Business Review*.

Email: djamila.elidrissi@univ-cotedazur.fr

Michela Floris is an associate professor of management in the Department of Economics and Business, University of Cagliari, Cagliari, Italy. She received her PhD in management and holds a master's degree in economics from the same university, and has been teaching family business management for several years. She has published articles in journals such as *Family Business Review* and *Journal of Small Business and Enterprise Development*, and received conference awards such as Academy of Management Best Paper (2009 and 2015) and Carolyn Dexter Award (2015), and IFERA & STEP Best Paper on conference theme (2019). Her research focuses on strategy, organizational goals, and goal-driven behaviors in family firms, including entrepreneurship, marketing, innovation, and growth.

Email: micfloris@unica.it

Joseph W. Harder is principal, Spirit of the New Workplace LLC, and adjunct associate professor of business administration at the Darden Business School, University of Virginia, Charlottesville, VA, where he has taught since 1998. Earlier, he was Anheuser-Busch term assistant professor of management and associate director of the leadership program at the Wharton

School of Business, University of Pennsylvania, Philadelphia, PA, following his PhD in organizational behavior from the Stanford University Graduate School of Business, Stanford, CA, in 1989. His research interests center around justice, culture, and performance, and the ways in which leaders can create environments where people thrive. His work on distributive justice and performance, drawn from his dissertation on pay and performance in professional sports, was published in *Journal of Applied Psychology* and *Administrative Science Quarterly* (and also mentioned in *Sports Illustrated*), and featured in other academic journals and news outlets as well. In 1999, in collaboration with Peter J. Robertson, he developed and began teaching the transformational leadership development program "Spirit of the New Workplace," a mind, body, heart, and soul experience, and have developed several cases in conjunction with the course (e.g., W. L. Gore and Associates, Phil Jackson and the Chicago Bulls, Lou Gerstner and Lotus Development Corporation, and the multi-media case Play, which won Darden's Wachovia Award for Most Innovative Case). This collaboration continues with writing related to the course on leading a living organization, holistic human asset practices, and creating and sustaining collaborative community.

Email: HarderJ@virginia.edu

Zorana Jerinic is a PhD in management sciences, a member of the research unit Research Group in Management (GRM) at IAE Nice, and a teaching assistant at the Université Côte d'Azur at IUT Nice, France. Her research focuses on intercultural competence, cultural diversity, and expertise in services.

Email: zorana.jerinic@univ-cotedazur.fr

Joshua Keller is an assistant professor of strategy, management, and organizations at Nanyang Technological University, Singapore. He received his PhD in management from the University of Texas at Austin, TX. His research, which applies cognitive approaches to paradoxes, has been published in journals such as *Organization Science, Organization Studies,* and *Management and Organization Review.*

Email: jwkeller@ntu.edu.sg

Rajesh Kumar is a strategy consultant who specializes in cross-cultural management and international negotiations. Earlier, he was professor of international management at Menlo College, Atherton, CA. He has a PhD degree from New York University, New York, NY. He has published in leading international journals such as *Journal of Management, Journal of Management Studies, Organization Science, Journal of World Business, Industrial Marketing Management, Journal of Applied Behavioral Science, International Marketing Review,* and *International Journal of Conflict Management.*

Email: rjk499@yahoo.com

Dave Luvison is an executive in residence at the Sellinger School of Business and Management, Loyola University Maryland, Baltimore, MD. His research focuses on collaborative behaviors, teamwork, and interorganizational alliances. His academic research has been published in *Group and Organization Management, Business Horizons, International Journal of Strategic Business Alliances, Management Decision,* and *Journal of Applied Management and Entrepreneurship,* as well as in various edited books. Prior to his academic career, he spent 25 years creating and directing partner and alliance programs in industry. He holds a Certified Strategic Alliance Professional credential from the Association of Strategic Alliance Professionals (ASAP), and is a member of the United States Technical Advisory Group for the development of the ISO 44000 standards for collaboration.

Email: dluvison@loyola.edu

Eva-María Mora-Valentín holds a PhD and is associate professor of management at Rey Juan Carlos University, Madrid, Spain. Her research interests include strategic alliances, cooperative agreements, mergers and acquisitions, university-firm relationships, science and technology parks, open innovation, and open data. Her research has been published in *Journal of Technology Transfer, Research Policy, International Journal of Technology Management, Journal of Knowledge Management, International Business Review, Science and Public Policy, International Journal of Manpower, Government Information Quarterly,* and *Journal of Organizational Change Management,* among others.

Email: evamaria.mora@urjc.es

Arash Najmaei earned his PhD in strategy and entrepreneurship in 2014 from the Macquarie Graduate School of Management, Sydney, Australia. He also has an MBA and an undergraduate degree in civil engineering. He is currently working as a marketing consultant in Australia. He is also the head of the Centre for Applied Management Research and an adjunct lecturer at the Peter Faber Business School at Australian Catholic University, Sydney, Australia, as well as the International College of Management Sydney.

Email: arash.najmaei@acu.edu.au

Kyle Neabel is a lecturer and research associate at the Faculty of Business Administration, Lakehead University, Thunder Bay, Canada. He is an entrepreneur, with interests in understanding the creation of value and its implications for strategy and organization in different contexts.

Email: kdneabel@lakeheadu.ca

Marta Ortiz-de-Urbina-Criado holds a PhD and is associate professor of management at Rey Juan Carlos University, Madrid, Spain. Her research interests include strategic alliances, mergers and acquisitions, human resources, innovation, and open data. Her research has been published in the *Government Information Quarterly, Journal of the Association for Information Science and Technology, Journal of Technology Transfer, Cities, International Business Review, International Journal of Manpower, Journal of Knowledge Management,* and *Journal of Organizational Change Management,* among others.

Email: marta.ortizdeurbina@urjc.es

Jack Pearson retired from Quintiles (now IQVIA) as the global vice president of alliance management and market development, where he managed a team of senior level executives who composed Quintiles's award-winning Global Alliance Management Group. This role was created to manage comprehensive structural and financial partnerships, thus ensuring that all of Quintiles's business alliances functioned effectively. While at Quintiles, he sat on numerous executive advisory boards and boards of directors serving to guide Quintiles's global partnerships in the area of establishing and facilitating strategic partnership arrangements. He served as board vice chairman/interim CEO at the Association of Strategic Alliance Professionals (ASAP) organization and participated on its executive committee. Currently, as chief alliance officer at Alliance Development International, he is engaged in supporting organizations as they strive to optimize their potential through strategic partnership planning and execution. He also enjoys serving as a mentor with various local business development organizations.

Email: jackp3927@gmail.com

Gul Polat is professor of civil engineering at Istanbul Technical University, Ankara, Turkey. She conducted her PhD studies at Istanbul Technical University and Illinois Institute of Technology, Chicago, IL. Her research interests include decision support techniques, bidding strategies, resource management, marketing management, risk management, precast concrete systems, and most aspects of construction management. She has been involved in several research projects funded by different agencies. Her research work over the years has resulted in over 100 technical papers in refereed journals and proceedings.

Email: gulpola@itu.edu.tr

Peter J. Robertson received his PhD in organizational behavior from the Stanford University Graduate School of Business, Stanford, CA, and is an associate professor at the University of Southern California Price School of Public Policy, Los Angeles, CA. His research and teaching interests focus on the development and implementation of collaborative organizational systems that enhance the quality of life for human beings, their communities, and the natural environment. The foci of his latest publications include conceptual papers proposing a set of organizing principles for collaborative organizational and governance systems, investigations into real-world efforts to create interorganizational collaboration, and the results of agent-based computer simulations exploring the dynamics of collaborative decision-making mechanisms. Other research has addressed issues pertaining to interorganizational networks, employee attitudes and behavior, the process and outcomes of organizational change, and school-based management as a mechanism for public school reform. His research has been published in a number of journals and books, including *Academy of Management Journal, Journal of Public Administration Research and Theory, Public Management Review, Public Administration Review, Nonprofit and Voluntary Sector Quarterly, Educational Administration Quarterly*, and *Research in Organizational Change and Development.* He has provided consulting and training for a variety of organizations, and is a member of the Academy of Management, the Public Management Research Association, and the Institute of Noetic Sciences.

Email: robertso@usc.edu

José-Luis Rodríguez-Sánchez holds a PhD and is associate professor of management at Rey Juan Carlos University, Madrid, Spain. His research interests include mergers and acquisitions and human resources management. He has published in *International Journal of Manpower, Journal of Organizational Change Management, Sustainability*, and *Información Tecnológica*, among others.

Email: joseluis.rodriguez.sanchez@urjc.es

Harun Turkoglu is a research assistant in the Department of Civil Engineering, Istanbul Technical University Istanbul, Turkey. His research interests include decision support techniques, scheduling, and resource management. He has published 27 technical papers in refereed international journals and in peer-reviewed conference proceedings.

Email: hturkoglu@itu.edu.tr

W. G. (Will) Zhao is an assistant professor in management at Lakehead University, Thunder Bay, Canada, and a former postdoctoral SCANCOR scholar at Stanford University, Stanford, CA. He earned his PhD in management from EM Lyon Business School, Lyon, France. His research interests include organizational and institutional change, (social) innovation and entrepreneurship, and multimodal data analysis.

Email: will.zhao@lakeheadu.ca

INDEX

Cultural Values in Strategy and Organization, pages 335–362

B

C

D

E

G

H

I

J

K

L

M

N

O

P

Q

R

S

T

U

V

W

X

Y

Z

www.ingramcontent.com/pod-product-compliance
Lightning Source LLC
LaVergne TN
LVHW052226200926
848481LV00001B/225
9781648025129